HIS EXCELLENCY

HIS EXCELLENCY

George Washington

JOSEPH J. ELLIS

R A N D O M   H O U S E
LARGE PRINT

**The Library of Congress has established a
Cataloging-in-Publication record for this title.**

0-375-43190-X

www.randomlargeprint.com

FIRST LARGE PRINT EDITION

10 9 8 7 6 5 4 3 2 1

This Large Print edition published in accord with
the standards of the N.A.V.H.

For W. W. Abbot

CONTENTS

PREFACE: THE MAN IN THE MOON   xi

CHAPTER ONE: *Interior Regions*   3

CHAPTER TWO: *The Strenuous Squire*   68

CHAPTER THREE: *First in War*   125

CHAPTER FOUR: *Destiny's Child*   190

CHAPTER FIVE: *Introspective Interlude*   255

CHAPTER SIX: *First in Peace*   327

CHAPTER SEVEN: *Testament*   418

ACKNOWLEDGMENTS   481

NOTES   485

INDEX   555

PREFACE
THE MAN IN THE MOON

My own relationship with George Washington began early. I grew up in Alexandria, Virginia, and attended St. Mary's grade school, about eight miles down Mount Vernon Boulevard from the estate where the great man once walked the earth. Because my school was so proximate to Mount Vernon, my teachers—all nuns—forced us to make frequent pilgrimages to the historic site where the spirit of America's greatest secular saint resided. Back then the tour was less historically informed than it is now. I don't recall slavery being mentioned at all. I do recall being told that the story of Washington's wooden teeth was a myth—my first encounter with the notion that you could not always trust what you read in history books. I remember this clearly because the high point of the tour was Washington's dentures, which were encased in glass and looked to me like a really gross instrument of torture made of metal and bone. The only other thing I remember is the majestic view of the Potomac from the piazza on the east side of the mansion.*

In the early 1950s, when I was about ten years old, I was lying on top of a one-story, tar-paper garage with my buddies to watch the annual parade down Washington Street to celebrate the great man's birthday. We loved the occasion because it got us out of school and allowed us to view the bands from the aptly named George Washington and Washington and Lee High Schools. My mother also gave me a dollar bill— big money then—to spend in those local stores promoting "dollar-day sales" in honor of Washington, whose picture adorned each bill. All this was happening in the shadow of the city across the river that bore his name, where my father went to work each day, and where the dominating feature of the landscape was a massive monument to one man's memory.

My point is that Washington was ubiquitous for me as I was growing up, an inescapable presence that hovered all around. But apart from the

---

*Apparently I am one of several visitors to Mount Vernon in the 1950s who remembers Washington's dentures on display, despite the fact that, according to official records, they were never exhibited for the general public until the 1980s. The staff at Mount Vernon cannot explain the discrepancy, nor can I.

dentures and the piazza at Mount Vernon, Washington remained a mysterious abstraction. He was like one of those Jeffersonian truths, self-evident and simply there. And the beauty of all self-evident truths was that no one needed to talk about them. They were so familiar that no one felt obliged to explain why they merited an annual parade.

Washington was more omnipresent for me than Thomas Jefferson or Abraham Lincoln, but also more distant. If you went to the Tidal Basin or the Mall you could read the magic words on the Jefferson or Lincoln Memorial ("We hold these truths to be self-evident . . ."; "With malice toward none, with charity toward all . . ."). But there were no words on the Washington Monument, just graffiti scrawled on the walls along the staircase to the top. Jefferson, it seemed, was like Jesus, who had come to earth and spoken directly to us. Washington was like God Himself, levitating above it all. Or, as I eventually came to describe him, Jefferson was like one of those dirigibles at the Super Bowl, flashing inspirational messages to both sides. Washington was aloof and silent, like the man in the moon.

You might wish to regard the pages that follow, then, as my attempt at a lunar landing. The technology to reach the moon was not available when I was lying atop that garage on Washington Street.

Nor was there a fully annotated modern edition of Washington's correspondence, providing access to every letter he sent and received, along with extensive editorial notes on all the major players, moments, and controversies. Now there is. To be sure, a perfectly serviceable edition has been available since the 1930s, and anyone wishing to pursue Washington's life and times has never been wanting for historical evidence. But the modern edition of the **Washington Papers** is the mother lode, all the scattered pieces of paper in the family attic gathered together, catalogued, and classified. This massive project is complete except for the final three years of the War for Independence and the final term of the presidency, though the crowded character of those years will keep the editors fully occupied for longer than one might guess. Nevertheless, it seems fair to say that we now have at our disposal every surviving remnant of evidence that biographers and historians can ever expect to see. The great American patriarch sits squarely in front of us: vulnerable, exposed, even talkative at last.

Are we ready to listen? This is not just a rhetorical question. For reasons best explained by Shakespeare and Freud, all children have considerable difficulty approaching their fathers with an open mind. Washington poses what we might call the Patriarchal Problem in its most virulent form:

on Mount Rushmore, the Mall, the dollar bill and the quarter, but always an icon—distant, cold, intimidating. As Richard Brookhiser has so nicely put it, he is in our wallets but not in our hearts. And speaking of our hearts, a volatile psychological chemistry bubbles away inside all children in simmering pools of dependency and rebellion, love and fear, intimacy and distance. As every parent can testify, initially our children believe we can do no wrong; later on they believe we can do no right—indeed, in Oedipal terms they actually want to kill us. For most of American history our response to Washington in particular and the Founding Fathers in general has been trapped within the emotional pattern dictated by these primal urges, oscillating in a swoonish swing between idolization and evisceration. In Washington's case the arc moves from Parson Weems's fabrications about a saintly lad who could not tell a lie to dismissive verdicts about the deadest, whitest male in American history.

This hero/villain image is, in fact, the same portrait, which has a front and back side that we rotate regularly. It is really a cartoon, which tells us less about Washington than about ourselves. The currently hegemonic narrative within the groves of academe cuts in the Oedipal direction, making Washington complicitous in creating a nation that was imperialistic, racist, elitist, and patriarchal. While there are some important exceptions to the rule, the reigning orthodoxy in the academy regards Washington as either a taboo or an inappropriate subject, and any aspiring doctoral candidate who declares an interest in, say, Washington's career as commander in chief, or president, has inadvertently confessed intellectual bankruptcy. (A study of the ordinary soldiers in the Continental army or the slaves at Mount Vernon would be more fashionable.) When not studiously ignored, Washington is noticed primarily as an inviting target for all the glaring failures of the revolutionary generation to meet our own superior standards of political and racial justice. This approach is thoroughly ahistorical and presentistic; but so, for that matter, is its opposite, the heroic-icon tradition. We are back again to the rotating cartoon character. Or perhaps we ought to think of that alluring dockside light in **The Great Gatsby,** flickering on and off like some synchronized signal of our fondest illusions.

How can we avoid this hyperbolic syndrome? To put it differently, once we land on the moon in the vehicle provided by the modern edition of the **Washington Papers,** how can we accurately map the terrain without imposing the impossible expectations we carried with us on the trip? Well, if we find ourselves being merely celebratory, or its judgmental twin, dismissive, we should rub our eyes and look again. On the one hand, we should begin our quest looking for a man rather than a statue, and any statues we do encounter should be quickly knocked off their pedestals. On the other hand, we should presume that we are engaged in a search rather than a hunt, thereby avoiding the temptation to cast Washington into the ideological abyss where his modern-day detractors—the Oedipal contingent—would like to consign him and his legacy. Ralph Waldo Emerson, who was preaching rebellion to the next generation, once observed that the founders were so intimidating because their propitious placement in American history had allowed them to see God face-to-face, while all who came after them could only see Him secondhand. Our goal should be to see Washington face-to-face—or, if you will, as grown-ups rather than children.

I began my own exploration with two convictions and one question. The first conviction was that I wanted to write a modest-sized book about a massive historical subject. Two of my most distinguished predecessors—Douglas Southall Freeman and James Thomas Flexner—had produced prodigious, multivolume biographies. The monumental size of these projects, so it seemed to me, implicitly endorsed the larger-than-life approach toward Washington and recalled the wicked comment by Lytton Strachey about Victorian biography: namely, that the interminable tomes had become an endless row of verbal coffins. This is not quite fair to either Freeman or Flexner, especially the latter, who never felt obliged to round off the sharp edges of Washington's personality or to make his biography into an encyclopedia. Let me salute both of them as venerable pioneers on the Washington Trail. In my judgment, and in part because of what they have already achieved, we do not need another epic painting, but rather a fresh portrait focused tightly on Washington's character. In that sense, the predecessor who taught me the most was Marcus Cunliffe, whose **Washington: Man and Monument,** though nearly fifty years old, has aged remarkably well. Cunliffe deserves a separate and special salute.

My second conviction concerned the historical scholarship on the revolutionary era that has altered the landscape around Washington since Cunliffe wrote. We now have a keener sense of the intellectual and even emotional ingredients that came together to create a revolutionary ideology in colonial America, a more robust understanding of the social and economic forces that drove Virginia's planter class toward rebellion, a more intriguingly complicated appreciation of the strategic options facing both sides in the War of Independence, a more paradoxical recognition of the incompatible version of "the spirit of '76" that exploded into partisan political warfare in the 1790s. Washington's life was lived, and his career congealed, within these tangled historical threads and themes, which taken together comprise a new context for assessing his evolution and achievement. Most significantly, the burgeoning scholarship on slavery and the fate of Native Americans have moved topics that were formerly in the background into the foreground. These themes can no longer be treated as peripheral matters. Coming to terms with Washington means making them, especially slavery, central concerns.

I also began my odyssey with a question that had formed in my mind on the basis of earlier research in the papers of the revolutionary generation. It seemed to me that Benjamin Franklin was wiser than Washington; Alexander Hamilton was more brilliant; John Adams was better read; Thomas Jefferson was more intellectually sophisticated; James Madison was more politically astute. Yet each and all of these prominent figures acknowledged that Washington was their unquestioned superior. Within the gallery of greats so often mythologized and capitalized as Founding Fathers, Washington was recognized as **primus inter pares**, the Foundingest Father of them all. Why was that? In the pages that follow I have looked for an answer, which lies buried within the folds of the most ambitious, determined, and potent personality of an age not lacking for worthy rivals. How he became that way, and what he then did with it, is the story I try to tell.

Joseph J. Ellis
Plymouth, Vermont

HIS EXCELLENCY

CHAPTER ONE

Interior Regions

HISTORY FIRST noticed George Washington in 1753, as a daring and resourceful twenty-one-year-old messenger sent on a dangerous mission into the American wilderness. He carried a letter from the governor of Virginia, Robert Dinwiddie, addressed to the commander of French troops in that vast region west of the Blue Ridge Mountains and south of the Great Lakes that Virginians called the Ohio Country. He was ordered to lead a small party over the Blue Ridge, then across the Allegheny Mountains, there to rendezvous with an influential Indian chief called the Half-King. He was then to proceed to the French outpost at Presque Isle (present-day Erie, Pennsylvania), where he would deliver his message "in the Name of His Britanic Majesty." The key passage in the letter he was carrying, so it turned out, represented the opening verbal shot in what

American colonists would call the French and Indian War: "The Lands upon the river Ohio, in the Western Parts of the Colony of Virginia, are so notoriously known to be the Property of the Crown of Great Britain, that it is a Matter of equal Concern & Surprize to me, to hear that a Body of French Forces are erecting Fortresses, & making Settlements upon that River within his Majesty's Dominions."[1]

The world first became aware of young Washington at this moment, and we get our first extended look at him, because, at Dinwiddie's urging, he published an account of his adventures, **The Journal of Major George Washington,** which appeared in several colonial newspapers and was then reprinted by magazines in England and Scotland. Though he was only an emissary— the kind of valiant and agile youth sent forward against difficult odds to perform a hazardous mission—Washington's **Journal** provided readers with a firsthand report on the mountain ranges, wild rivers, and exotic indigenous peoples within the interior regions that appeared on most European maps as dark and vacant spaces. His report foreshadowed the more magisterial account of the American West provided by Lewis and Clark more than fifty years later. It also, if inadvertently, exposed the somewhat ludicrous character of any claim by "His Britanic Majesty," or any European power, for that matter, to control such an expansive frontier that simply swallowed up and spit out European presumptions of civilization.[2]

Although Washington is both the narrator and the central character in the story he tells, he says little about himself and nothing about what he thinks. "I have been particularly cautious," he notes in the preface, "not to augment." The focus, instead, is on the knee-deep snow in the passes through the Alleghenies, and the icy and often impassably swollen rivers, where he and his companions are forced to wade alongside their canoes while their coats freeze stiff as boards. Their horses collapse from exhaustion and have to be abandoned. He and fellow adventurer Christopher Gist come upon a lone warrior outside an Indian village ominously named Murdering Town. The Indian appears to befriend them, then suddenly wheels around at nearly point-blank range and fires his musket, but inexplicably misses. "Are you shot?" Washington asks Gist, who responds that he is not. Gist rushes the Indian and wants to kill him, but Washington will not permit it, preferring to let him escape. They come upon an isolated farmhouse on the banks of the Monongahela where two adults and five children have been killed and scalped. The decaying corpses are being eaten by hogs.[3]

In stark contrast to the brutal conditions and casual savagery of the frontier environment, the

French officers whom Washington encounters at Fort Le Boeuf and Presque Isle resemble pieces of polite Parisian furniture plopped down in an alien landscape. "They received us with a great deal of complaisance," Washington observes, the French offering flattering pleasantries about the difficult trek Washington's party had endured over the mountains. But they also explained that the claims of the English king to the Ohio Country were demonstrably inferior to those of the French king, which were based on Lasalle's exploration of the American interior nearly a century earlier. To solidify their claim of sovereignty, a French expedition had recently sailed down the Ohio River, burying a series of lead plates inscribed with their sovereign's seal that obviously clinched the question forever.[4]

The French listened politely to Washington's rebuttal, which derived its authority from the original charter of the Virginia Company in 1606. It had set the western boundary of that colony either at the Mississippi River or, even more expansively, at the Pacific Ocean. In either case, it included the Ohio Country and predated Lasalle's claim by sixty years. However persuasive this rather sweeping argument might sound in Williamsburg or London, it made little impression on the French officers. "They told me," Washington wrote in his **Journal**, "it was their absolute Design to take Possession of the Ohio, & by G____ they wou'd do it." The French commander at Fort Le Boeuf, Jacques Le Gardner, sieur de Saint Pierre, concluded the negotiations by drafting a cordial letter for Washington to carry back to Governor Dinwiddie that sustained the diplomatic affectations: "I have made it a particular duty to receive Mr. Washington with the distinction owing to your dignity, his position, and his own great merit. I trust that he will do me justice in that regard to you, and that he will make known to you the profound respect with which I am, Sir, your most humble and most obedient servant."[5]

But the person whom Washington quotes more than any other in his **Journal** represented yet a third imperial power with its own exclusive claim of sovereignty over the Ohio Country. That was the Half-King, the Seneca chief whose Indian name was Tanacharison. In addition to being a local tribal leader, the Half-King had received his quasi-regal English name because he was the diplomatic representative of the Iroquois Confederation, also called the Six Nations, with its headquarters in Onondaga, New York. When they had first met at the Indian village called Logstown, Tanacharison had declared that Washington's Indian name was Conotocarius, which meant "town taker" or "devourer of villages," because this was the name originally given to Washington's great-grandfather, John Washington, nearly a century earlier. The persistence of that memory in Indian oral history was a dramatic reminder of the long-standing domination of the Iroquois Confederation over the region. They had planted no lead plates, knew nothing of some English king's presumptive claims to own a continent. But they had been ruling over this land for about three hundred years.[6]

In the present circumstance, Tanacharison regarded the French as a greater threat to Indian sovereignty. "If you had come in a peaceable Manner like our Brethren the English," he told the French commander at Presque Isle, "We shou'd not have been against your trading with us as they do, but to come, Fathers, & build great houses upon our Land, & to take it by Force, is what we cannot submit to." On the other hand, Tanacharison also made it clear that all Indian alliances with European powers and their colonial kinfolk were temporary expediencies: "Both you & the English are White. We live in a Country between, therefore the Land does not belong either to one or the other; but the GREAT BEING above allow'd it to be a Place of Residence for us."[7]

Washington dutifully recorded Tanacharison's words, fully aware that they exposed the competing, indeed contradictory, imperatives that defined his diplomatic mission into the American wilderness. For on the one hand he represented a British ministry and a colonial government that fully intended to occupy the Ohio Country with Anglo-American settlers whose presence was ultimately incompatible with the Indian version of divine providence. But on the other hand, given the sheer size of the Indian population in the region, plus their indisputable mastery of the kind of forest-fighting tactics demanded by wilderness conditions, the balance of power in the looming conflict between France and England for European domination of the American interior belonged to the very people whom Washington's superiors intended to displace.

For several reasons, this story of young Washington's first American adventure is a good place to begin our quest for the famously elusive personality of the mature man-who-became-a-monument. First, the story reveals how early his personal life became caught up in larger public causes, in this case nothing less grand than the global struggle between the contending world powers for supremacy over half a continent. Second, it forces us to notice the most obvious chronological fact, namely that Washington was one of the few prominent members of America's founding generation—Benjamin Franklin was another—who were born early enough to develop their basic convictions about America's role in the British Empire within the context of the French and Indian War. Third, it offers the first example of the interpretive dilemma posed by a man of action who seems determined to tell us what he did, but equally determined not to tell us what he thought about it. Finally, and most importantly, it establishes a connection between Washington's character in the most formative stage of its development and the raw, often savage, conditions in that expansive area called the Ohio Country. The interior regions of Washington's personality began to take shape within the interior regions of the colonial frontier. Neither of these places, it turned out, was as vacant as it first appeared. And both of them put a premium on achieving mastery over elemental forces that often defied the most cherished civilized expectations.

GLIMPSES

BEFORE 1753 we have only glimpses of Washington as a boy and young man. These sparsely documented early years have subsequently been littered with legends and lore, all designed to align Washington's childhood with either the dramatic achievements of his later career or the mythological imperatives of America's preeminent national hero. John Marshall, his first serious biographer, even entitled the chapter on Washington's arrival in the world "The Birth of Mr. Washington," suggesting that he was born fully clothed and ready to assume the presidency. The most celebrated story about Washington's childhood—the Parson Weems tale about chopping down the cherry tree ("Father, I cannot tell a lie")—is a complete fabrication. The truth is, we know virtually nothing about Washington's relationship with his father, Augustine Washington, except that it ended early, when Washington was eleven years old. In all his voluminous correspondence, Washington mentioned his father on only three occasions, and then only cryptically. As for his mother, Mary Ball Washington, we know that she was a quite tall and physically strong woman who lived long enough to see him elected president but never extolled or even acknowledged his public triumphs. Their relationship, estranged in those later years, remains a mystery during his childhood and adolescence. Given this frustrating combination of misinformation and ignorance, we can only establish the irrefutable facts about Washington's earliest years, then sketch as best we can the murkier patterns of influence on his early development.[8]

We know beyond any doubt that George Washington was born in Westmoreland County, Virginia, near the banks of the Potomac River, on February 22, 1732 (New Style). He was a fourth-generation Virginian. The patriarch of the family, John Washington, had come over from England in 1657 and established the Washingtons as respectable, if not quite prominent, members of Virginia society. The Indians had named him "town taker," not because of his military prowess, but because he had manipulated the law to swindle them out of their land.

The bloodline that John Washington bequeathed to his descendants exhibited three distinctive tendencies: first, a passion for acreage, the more of it the better; second, tall and physically strong males; and third, despite the physical strength, a male line that died relatively young, all before reaching fifty. A quick scan of the genealogy on both sides of young George's ancestry suggested another ominous pattern. The founder of the Washington line had three wives, the last of whom had been widowed three times. Washington's father had lost his first wife in 1729, and Mary Ball Washington, his second wife, was herself an orphan whose own mother had been widowed twice. The Virginian world into which George Washington was born was a decidedly precarious place where neither domestic stability nor life itself could be taken for granted. This harsh reality was driven home in April 1743, when Augustine Washington died, leaving his widow and seven children an estate that included ten thousand acres divided into several disparate parcels and forty-nine slaves.[9]

Washington spent his early adolescence living with his mother at Ferry Farm in a six-room farmhouse across the Rappahannock from Fredericksburg. He received the modern equivalent of a grade-school education, but was never exposed to the classical curriculum or encouraged to attend college at William and Mary, a deficiency that haunted him throughout his subsequent career among American statesmen with more robust educational credentials. Several biographers have called attention to his hand-copied list of 110 precepts from **The Rules of Civility and Decent Behaviour in Company and Conversation,** which was based on rules of etiquette originally composed by Jesuit scholars in 1595. Several of the rules are hilarious (#9, "Spit not into the fire . . . especially if there be meat before it"; #13, "Kill no vermin, or fleas, lice, ticks, etc. in the sight of others"); but the first rule also seems to have had resonance for Washington's later obsession with deportment: "Every action done in company ought to be done with some sign of respect to those that are present." As a reminder of an earlier era's conviction that character was not just who you were but also what others thought you were, this is a useful point that foreshadows Washington's flair for disappearing within his public persona. But the more prosaic truth is that **Rules of Civility** has attracted so much attention from biographers because it is one of the few documents of Washington's youth that has survived. It is quite possible that he copied out the list as a mere exercise in penmanship.[10]

The two major influences on Washington's youthful development were his half brother, Lawrence, fourteen years his senior, and the Fairfax family. Lawrence became a surrogate father, responsible for managing the career options of his young protégé, who as a younger son had little hope of inheriting enough land to permit easy entrance into the planter class of Chesapeake society. In 1746, Lawrence proposed that young George enlist as a midshipman in the British navy. His mother opposed the suggestion, as did his uncle in England, who clinched the negative verdict by observing that the navy would "cut him and staple him and use him like a Negro, or rather, like a dog."[11]

Lawrence's two other contributions to Washington's future career were richly ironic. In 1751 he traveled to Barbados, seeking a tropical cure for his tuberculosis, and took Washington along as a companion. This turned out to be Washington's one and only trip abroad and the occasion for his contraction of smallpox. He carried barely discernible pockmarks on his face for the rest of his life, but also immunity against the most feared and fatal disease of the era. Then, in 1752, Lawrence lost his bout with tuberculosis, thereby sustaining the family tradition of short-lived males. His 2,500-acre plantation, now named Mount Vernon, became part of the estate that Washington eventually inherited. Lawrence's premature death made possible his greatest legacy.[12]

The Fairfax influence also had its ironies. At about the age of fifteen Washington began to spend much of his time at Mount Vernon with Lawrence, who had married Ann Fairfax of the Fairfax dynasty at nearby Belvoir. The patriarch of the clan was Lord Thomas Fairfax, an eccentric member of the English peerage whose disdain for women and love for horses and hounds soon carried him across the Blue Ridge to pursue his passion for foxhunting undisturbed by the nettlesome duties of managing his estates. His cousin William Fairfax assumed that responsibility, which was a truly daunting task. The much-disputed Fairfax claim, only recently validated by the Privy Council in London, gave Lord Fairfax proprietary rights to more than five million acres, including the huge Northern Neck region between the Potomac and Rappahannock. The Fairfaxes, in short, were a living remnant of European feudalism and English-style aristocracy, firmly imbedded within Virginia's more provincial version of country gentlemen. As such, they were the supreme example of privileged bloodlines, royal patronage, and what one Washington biographer has called "the assiduous courting of the great." Though Washington was destined to lead a revolution that eventually toppled this whole constellation of aristocratic beliefs and presumptions, he was initially a beneficiary of its powers of patronage.[13]

In 1748, William Fairfax gave sixteen-year-old Washington his first job. He accompanied William's son, George William Fairfax, on a surveying expedition of the Fairfax holdings in the Shenandoah Valley. Washington's first diary entries date from this time, so we get our initial glimpse of his handwriting and prose, as well his impression of the primitive conditions on the far side of the Blue Ridge: "Went into the Bed as they call'd it when to my Surprize I found it to be nothing but a Little Straw—Matted together without Sheets or any thing else but only one Thread Bare blanket with double its Weight of Vermin such as Lice Fleas & c." The few settlers in this frontier region struck him as strange creatures, who wore tattered clothes and tended to speak German rather than English. He also saw an Indian war party, returning from a skirmish with one scalp and celebrating their victory by dancing around their campfire to the music of a kettledrum.[14]

If the Fairfax family represented the epitome of English civilization, the area west of the Blue Ridge represented the far edge of civilization's progress. Beyond that edge lay the Ohio Country, where anything that Europeans called civilization ceased to exist altogether. The previous year, in 1747, Lawrence had joined a group of investors to form the Ohio Company, which obtained a royal grant of half a million acres to bring Virginia's version of civilization to that distant place west of the Alleghenies, where Washington would soon test his manhood against the elements in the name of the British king. For now, however, and for the next three years, he remained on the eastern edge of Virginia's frontier, surveying the Fairfax holdings in the Northern Neck and Shenandoah Valley, mastering his new trade by conducting more than 190 surveys, usually camping under the stars, doing well enough financially to permit his first purchase of land, a 1,459-acre plot on Bullskin Creek in the lower Shenandoah.[15]

Again, the historical record affords only glimpses of the emerging young man. There are pieces of adolescent doggerel about his "Poor Resistless Heart" pierced by "cupid's feather'd Dart," perhaps a reference to an unknown "Low land Beauty" that stirred his passions, perhaps a reference to his futile pursuit of Betsy Fauntleroy, a sixteen-year-old coquette who found him unacceptable. His name appears as plaintiff in a Fredericksburg court case, filing charges against one Mary McDaniel for rifling through his clothes while he was bathing in the local river. (She received fifteen lashes.) Later on women would swoon at his appearance, but at this early stage he struck them as awkward, even oafish, and paralyzingly shy.[16]

No full physical description exists for this period, but accounts from a few years later allow us to project backward to envision a very tall young man, at least six feet two inches, which made him a head higher than the average male of the time. He had an athlete's body, well proportioned and trim at about 175 pounds with very strong thighs and legs, which allowed him to grip a horse's flanks tightly and hold his seat in the saddle with uncommon ease. His eyes were grayish blue and widely set. His hair was hazel brown, destined to darken over the years, and usually tied in a cue in the back. He had disproportionately large hands and feet, which contributed to his awkward appearance when stationary, but once in motion on the dance floor or in a foxhunt the natural grace of his movements overwhelmed the initial impression. Well-muscled and coordinated, he never threw a silver dollar across the Potomac (to do so at the Mount Vernon shore would have been physically impossible), but he did throw a rock over the Natural Bridge in the Shenandoah Valley, which was 215 feet high. He was the epitome of the man's man: physically strong, mentally enigmatic, emotionally restrained.[17]

In June 1752, while Lawrence lay dying at Mount Vernon, Washington petitioned Governor Dinwiddie for one of the adjutant-general posts in the Virginia militia. He had no military experience whatsoever, and, apart from being an impressive physical specimen, no qualifications for the job. Here the two major influences on his early years converged in their customary ways. Lawrence's death created an opening in the adjutancy corps, and William Fairfax used his influence to assure Dinwiddie that the young man was up to the task. As Washington himself put it: "I am sensible my best endeavors will not be wanting." Dinwiddie concurred, made himself Washington's new mentor and patron, then dispatched Major Washington into the western wilderness the following year.[18]

ASSASSINATION AND NECESSITY

OVER THE COURSE of the next five years, from 1754 to 1759, Washington spent the bulk of his time west of the Blue Ridge, leading a series of expeditions into the Ohio Country that served as crash courses in the art of soldiering. They also provided him with a truly searing set of personal experiences that shaped his basic outlook on the world. Instead of going to college, Washington went to war. And the kind of education he received, like the smallpox he had contracted in Barbados, left scars that never went away, as well as immunities against any and all forms of youthful idealism.

The first adventure began in the spring of 1754, when the Virginia House of Burgesses voted funds to raise a regiment of three hundred men to protect settlers in the Ohio Country from the mounting French threat. Washington was made second in command with the rank of lieutenant colonel. In April he left Alexandria at the head of 160 troops charged with the mission of securing the strategic location at the juncture of the Allegheny and Monongahela, where the Ohio Company had already begun to construct a fort. Soon after he completed the difficult trek over the Alleghenies, Washington learned that a French force of more than a thousand had seized the half-built fort, renamed it Fort Duquesne, and were proceeding to radiate French influence over the several Indian tribes in the region. The best intelligence came from his former companion and major Indian ally, Tanacharison, who apprised Washington that the situation was truly desperate: "If you do not come to our Assistance now," he wrote, "we are entirely undone, and imagine we shall never meet again." Faced with a vastly superior enemy force, Washington decided to build a makeshift fort near Tanacharison's camp, rally whatever Indian allies he could find, and wait for reinforcements. Tanacharison promised his support, but also warned that the odds were stacked against them.[19]

On May 27, Tanacharison reported the appearance of French troops in the vicinity and brought a delegation of warriors to join Washington's garrison at Great Meadows about forty miles from Fort Duquesne. On the morning of May 28, Washington found a French patrol of thirty-two soldiers encamped in a forest glen that Tanacharison described as "a low obscure place." His detachment of forty, plus the Indian allies under Tanacharison, encircled the French camp. Washington's report on the action that ensued, sent to Dinwiddie the next day, was succinct: "I there upon in conjunction with the Half-King . . . formed a disposition to attack them on all sides, which we accordingly did and after an Engagement of abt 15 minutes we killed 10, wounded one and took 21 Prisoners, amongst those that were killed was Monsieur De Jumonville, the Commander." His diary account, even more succinct, was also more revealing: "we killed Mr. de Jumonville—as also nine others . . . the Indians scalped the Dead."[20]

What actually happened at what came to be called Jumonville Glen soon became an international controversy about who fired the first shot in the French and Indian War. It has remained a scholarly debate ever since, in part because it was Washington's first combat experience, in part because there is good reason to believe that he found himself overseeing a massacre. Though the eyewitness accounts do not agree—as they seldom do—the most plausible version of the evidence suggests that the French troops, surprised and outgunned, threw down their weapons after the initial exchange and attempted to surrender. The French commander, Joseph Coulon de Villiers, sieur de Jumonville, though wounded in the exchange, tried to explain that he had come on a peace mission on behalf of his monarch, Louis XV, exactly the same diplomatic mission that Washington had performed the previous year on behalf of the British monarch, claiming sovereignty over the disputed Ohio Country.

As Washington sought to understand the translation of this diplomatic message, Tanacharison, who apparently spoke fluent French and therefore grasped Jumonville's point before Washington did, decided to take matters into his own hands.

He stepped up to where Jumonville lay, in French declared, "Thou art not yet dead, my father," then sank his hatchet into Jumonville's head, split his skull in half, pulled out his brain, and washed his hands in the mixture of blood and tissue. His warriors then fell upon the wounded French soldiers, scalped them all, and decapitated one and put his head on a stake. All this happened under the eyes of the shocked and hapless commanding officer, Lieutenant Colonel Washington.[21]

While he did not tell an outright lie to Dinwiddie, neither did Washington speak the whole truth about the episode. In his diary he attempted to convince himself that Jumonville's claim to be on a diplomatic mission was "a pure Pretence; that they never intended to come to us but as Enemies." In effect, he was rationalizing the massacre to himself. In a letter home to his brother, he glossed over the killings by focusing on his own personal response to the sense of danger: "I heard Bullets whistle and believe me there was something charming in the Sound." This self-promoting statement made it into the Virginia newspapers, prompting a flurry of stories depicting Washington as America's first war hero. The bravado remark even made the rounds in London, where no less than George II reportedly dismissed it as youthful bragging: "He would not say so, if he had been used to hear many."[22]

Whether he was a hero, a braggart, or an accomplice in murder, the skirmish at Jumonville Glen had convinced Washington that his detachment, though outnumbered by the French forces in the area, could hold its own until reinforcements arrived. "We have just finish'd a small palisaded Fort," he wrote Dinwiddie, "in which with my small Numbers I shall not fear the attack of 500 Men." He named the crude circular stockade where he intended to make his stand Fort Necessity, a glancing recognition of his precarious situation. In early June, Dinwiddie endorsed the decision to defend the fort, while also sending word that the commander of the Virginia Regiment, Joshua Fry, had recently died after falling off his horse, making Washington the new man in charge, with the rank of colonel. (Yet again, another's death led to his own advancement.) A militia detachment of about two hundred was also on the way to reinforce him.[23]

To his credit, Washington realized that his fate depended less on the British reinforcements than on the support of local Indians, who continued to control the balance of power in the region. On June 18, Tanacharison arranged a Council of Indians at which Washington responded to questions about English intentions toward the Ohio Country. He apprised the several chiefs that the sole purpose of the English military effort was "to maintain your Rights . . . to make that whole Country sure to you." He claimed that the English had no other goal than to recover for the various Indian tribes "those Lands which the French had taken from them." This was a bald-faced lie, rendered necessary by Washington's recognition, as he put it, "that we can do nothing without them." Apparently the chiefs found the argument unpersuasive, or perhaps they simply knew that the size of the advancing French force made any alliance with Washington's embattled troops a bad gamble. At any rate, Tanacharison led all the Indians into the woods, leaving Fort Necessity to its fate. Captain James McKay arrived with his reinforcements shortly thereafter, whereupon Washington and McKay began to debate command authority, McKay claiming that his commission as a captain in the British army trumped Washington's colonial rank as a colonel.[24]

They could not argue for long, because by early July they learned what Tanacharison had probably known earlier, namely that a force of about eleven hundred French and Indians led by Louis Coulon de Villiers, who happened to be Jumonville's aggrieved brother, was about to descend upon them. On the morning of July 3 the first French soldiers appeared on the horizon about six hundred yards from the fort. Accounts disagree as to who fired the first shots. Because Washington had only cleared the trees and brush sixty yards around Fort Necessity, the entire French and Indian force closed to the edge of the perimeter, took refuge behind trees and stumps, and began to pour a murderous fire down upon the beleaguered defenders. The result was a slow-paced slaughter lasting for nine hours. A driving downpour filled up the trenches inside and outside Fort Necessity, rendering much of the gunpowder useless. By dark nearly a third of Washington's force had been killed or wounded, and the survivors, sensing imminent catastrophe, broke into the rum supply to bolster their courage. Rumors spread within the garrison that four hundred Indian warriors were marching to join the French, anticipating a massacre laden with trophies and scalps. The defenders faced not just humiliating defeat, but total annihilation.[25]

Washington's version of what happened next, reiterated and revised throughout his life, does not fit the bulk of the evidence. He claimed that the defenders of Fort Necessity were inflicting heavy casualties on the enemy—more than three hundred dead or wounded by the end of the day—so the French commander, Captain de Villiers, decided to call a truce and propose generous terms of surrender. In return for promising to remove themselves from the Ohio Country for one year, the defenders were permitted to evacuate the fort carrying their arms, their colors, and their honor. In Washington's version, the battle at Fort Necessity was not a defeat so much as a stalemate, in which the Virginians and British conducted themselves with gallantry and composure despite the superior French force arrayed against them.[26]

The more unattractive truth was that Washington had placed his troops in a hopelessly vulnerable position at Fort Necessity. He had suffered one hundred casualties compared with only five deaths on the enemy side. The relentless musket fire and horrible weather conditions had caused the defenders to panic, and the panic only intensified when news of imminent Indian reinforcements created the prospect of a wholesale massacre of the garrison. (In the Articles of Capitulation the French promised to "restrain, as much as shall be in our power, the Indians that are with us.") Most awkwardly, the Articles of Capitulation referred to "the Assassination of M. de Jumonville," meaning that Washington's signature on the surrender document endorsed the conclusion that the British in general and he in particular were responsible for murdering a diplomatic emissary of the French crown, which in turn meant that the British were responsible for the hostile action that launched the French and Indian War.[27]

Washington went to his grave claiming that he never realized that the word "assassination" was included in the Articles of Capitulation, and blamed the misunderstanding on a poor translation from the French original and the rain-soaked character of the document. He claimed that he would never have agreed to such terms if he had known their full meaning. Given the utterly desperate situation he faced, however, it is difficult to imagine what choice he had, which is probably one reason why he felt obliged to deny any sense of desperation.

He led the beleaguered remnant of his regiment out of Fort Necessity on July 4—a day he surely never thought he would celebrate—with his reputation up for grabs. Horatio Sharpe, the governor of Maryland, published a critical account of Washington's conduct at Fort Necessity, describing the battle as a debacle and Washington himself as a dangerous mixture of inexperience and impetuosity. The French, for their part, found him a convenient symbol of Anglo-American treachery for his role in the Jumonville massacre. They had confiscated his journal at Fort Necessity and cited the misleading section on the Jumonville incident as evidence of his duplicity. The French commander in North America, General Duquesne, identified Washington as the epitome of dishonor: "He lies very much to justify the assassination of sieur de Jumonville, which has turned on him, and which he had the stupid-ity to confess in his capitulation. . . . There is nothing more unworthy and lower and even blacker, than the sentiments and the way of thinking of this Washington. It would have been a pleasure to read his outrageous journal under his very nose." For French propaganda purposes Washington became the ideal villain, and he was featured as such in an epic poem published in France designed to demonstrate the evil character of the enemy.[28]

Back in Williamsburg, on the other hand, William Fairfax was using his influence to depict Fort Necessity as a noble, if futile, effort to block the French invasion of Virginia's western lands. After all, if the French regarded Washington as a diabolical character, did that not constitute a recommendation of sorts? Responding to pressure from Fairfax and Dinwiddie, in September the House of Burgesses issued an order recognizing Washington and several of his officers at Fort Necessity "for their late gallant and brave Behavior in the Defense of their Country." Whatever happened at Jumonville Glen, however ill-advised the futile stand at Fort Necessity, the young man was unquestionably brave, and with the outbreak of war on the frontier, Virginia needed a hero who also happened to look the part.[29]

Though vindicated, Washington himself felt frustrated: "What did I get by this?" he asked his brother. "Why, after putting myself to a considerable expense in equipment and providing Necessarys for the Campaigne—I went out, was soundly beaten, lost them all—came in, and had my Commission taken from me." The latter lament referred to the decision by the burgesses not to vote new taxes for a major expedition against the French, which meant that the Virginia Regiment was disbanded into several independent companies, leaving Washington to serve at a lower rank. This struck him as a gross insult. He was touchy about his rank; lacking aristocratic credentials like Fairfax, or London connections like Dinwiddie, his military position was his primary indication of social standing in the Virginia hierarchy. Rather than accept the demotion, he preferred to resign. He did so in November 1754, all the while convinced that he had found his proper calling as a soldier. "My inclinations," he acknowledged, "are strongly bent to arms." Events were about to demonstrate that he was in the ideal location to exercise those inclinations.[30]

MASSACRE AT THE MONONGAHELA

THE CATALYST for these events arrived in Virginia in February 1755 with two regiments of British regulars, a sweeping mandate to assume supreme authority over British military policy for all of North America, and specific orders to launch the campaign against the French menace by capturing Fort Duquesne. His name was General Edward Braddock, a thirty-five-year veteran who knew all there was to know about drilling troops in garrison, something about waging war in the arenas of Europe, and nothing whatsoever about the kind of savage conditions and equally savage battlefields he would encounter in the American interior.

His superiors, hunched over maps in London, had described his mission as a triumphal procession through the Ohio Country, the capture of Fort Duquesne, and then a campaign to roll up the string of French forts on the Great Lakes and the eventual seizure of all of French Canada. No one even remotely familiar with the mountains, rivers, and Indian tribes within this terrain would have drawn up such orders. Braddock's mission, in effect, was inherently impossible. He made it even more so by proceeding to issue imperious commands to the respective governors and legislatures of Virginia, Maryland, and Pennsylvania for additional funds, thereby alienating all the colonial governments. He sealed his fate completely at a meeting with a delegation of Indian chiefs by telling them that their historic claims to land in the Ohio Valley were worthless and that British troops had no need for aid from savages, prompting most of the tribes in the region to go over to the French. As Braddock saw it, he commanded the largest and best equipped military force ever assembled on the North American continent, making victory inevitable. In fact, the campaign was doomed from the start.[31]

In the spring of 1755, Washington had no inkling of these larger intractables. He was living at Mount Vernon, which he was leasing from Lawrence's widow, trying to decide what to do with his life. His letterbook for this phase is a somewhat contaminated document, because he went back to revise his language on two later occasions, 1786–87 and 1797–98, in order to improve his spelling and syntax and conceal his youthful ambivalence. By restoring his original language alongside the revisions, the modern editors of his papers allow us to recover his confusion at this moment, along with his solicitous and awkwardly deferential attitude toward British authority as embodied in Braddock.

In March he wrote Robert Orme, Braddock's chief of staff, in somewhat stilted fashion: "I must be ingenuous enough to confess that . . . I wish earnestly to attain some knowledge of the Military Profession and, believing a more favourable oppertunity cannot offer than to serve under a Gentleman of General Braddock's abilities and experience." More than the educational experience of serving under a veteran British officer, Washington wanted the patronage that Braddock's stature could provide. "I have now a good oppertunity," he wrote his brother, "and shall not neglect it, of forming an acquaintance which may be serviceable hereafter, if I shall find it worth while to push my Fortune in the Military line." His sensitivity about rank—once a colonel, he would now be only a captain—was resolved when Orme assured him that Braddock "will be very glad of your Company in his Family"—meaning as aide-de-camp on his staff—"by which all inconveniences of that kind [rank] will be obviated." He joined Braddock's swelling entourage of horses, wagons, and men at Frederick, Maryland, in early May 1755.[32]

Braddock recognized that he faced a massive logistical problem. In order to mount a proper siege of Fort Duquesne according to orthodox European-style standards for success, he required overwhelming superiority in both manpower and artillery. His main force of more than two thousand men needed to be fed along the route, his heavy cannon needed to be pulled by horses, and all the food for them needed to be carried on wagons, which required more horses—about 2,500 in all—plus the wagon masters and ubiquitous camp women following in the rear. This cumbersome cavalcade, stretching out over six miles, had to carve its own road through more than one hundred miles of wilderness terrain that Washington knew to be almost impassable and that even Braddock acknowledged "would occasion great Trouble and retard me considerably." All of Braddock's extensive military experience worked against him: he knew in considerable detail how to conduct a conventional campaign in Europe, but in the Ohio Country everything he knew proved either irrelevant or wrong.[33]

After stepping off at a brisk pace in mid-May, Braddock's column ground to a near halt once it hit the Alleghenies in June. Washington began to sense disaster at this time, writing his brother that "this prospect was soon clouded & all my hopes brought very low indeed when I found . . . they were halting to Level every Mole Hill, & to erect Bridges over every brook; by which means we were 4 Days gttg 12 Miles." Stragglers were also being killed and scalped routinely, a sign that the Indian intelligence network was fully aware of their location and destination. Washington apprised Braddock that the ponderous pace of the baggage train virtually assured that they would be marooned in Indian country once the snows in the mountains began to make any advance at all impossible. He recommended that a "flying column" of twelve hundred lightly equipped troops be disengaged from the main body and proceed at full speed toward Fort Duquesne. Braddock accepted this advice, probably one of the reasons why Washington never engaged in the widespread Braddock bashing that haunted subsequent accounts of the eventual debacle. Just as the flying column went forward, Washington came down with dysentery and had to remain with the wagons in the rear. He extracted a promise from Braddock that, once they approached striking distance of their objective, he would be brought forward to participate in the attack. On July 8, as the advance party prepared to cross the Monongahela, though he was still feverish and afflicted with a painful case of hemorrhoids that required him to place cushions on his saddle, Washington rode forward to join Braddock.[34]

The disaster occurred the following day. Subsequent accounts of the battle, blaming Braddock for a tactical blunder in maneuvering his troops carelessly across several streams, have been discredited. Braddock's mistake was not tactical but strategic—not understanding that European rules of war could not be imposed on America without translation. The engagement began as an accident of war rather than a planned ambush. A large reconnaissance detachment from Duquesne of nearly nine hundred men, two-thirds of them Indians, stumbled upon Braddock's vanguard at the edge of a clearing in the forest, immediately spread out in a semicircle around the clearing, then started firing.

The Virginia troops rushed into the woods to engage the enemy at close quarters. The British regulars, obedient to their training, formed themselves into concentrated rows in the open field. Within the first ten minutes their ranks were decimated and panic set in. Despite heroic efforts by their officers to rally them, the regulars broke. The Virginia troops ended up being caught in the crossfire between the Indians and the British. Entire companies were wiped out by "friendly fire" from British muskets. As Washington described it later, "they behavd like Men, and died like Soldiers," while the regulars "broke & run as sheep before Hounds." Braddock himself, as fearless as he was obstinate, rode into the center of the killing zone and was quickly cut down with wounds in his shoulder and chest.[35]

With Braddock down and the other aides-de-camp casualties, it fell to Washington to rally the remnants. Riding back and forth amidst the chaos, two horses were shot out beneath him and four musket balls pierced his coat, but he miraculously escaped without a scratch, while, as he put it, "death was levelling my companions on every side of me." Irony as well as destiny made its appearance on the battlefield that day. One of the few British officers to survive unhurt was Captain Thomas Gage, whom Washington would encounter as commander of the British army outside Boston twenty years later. In the rear, supervising the horses for the baggage train, was Daniel Boone, who also survived to become an American legend.[36]

It was a complete debacle. Out of a total force of thirteen hundred men, the British and Americans suffered over nine hundred casualties while the French and Indians reported twenty-three killed and sixteen wounded. For the rest of his life, Washington remembered the scenes of the dead and the screams of the wounded as they were being scalped. Braddock died three days into the retreat, and Washington buried him in the middle of the road, then ran wagons over the grave in order to prevent his body from being desecrated and his scalp claimed as a trophy. After reaching safety, Washington wrote his mother and brother to assure them he was alive: "As I have heard . . . a circumstantial acct of my death and dying Speech, I take this first opportunity of contradicting the first and assuring you that I have not, as Yet, composed the latter."[37]

This piece of understated bravado masked Washington's dominant reaction to the defeat, which initially was disbelief that a force so large and well equipped could be so thoroughly routed. Dinwiddie concurred, confessing that "it appears to me as a dream, wn I consider the Forces & the train of artillery he had with him." But the more Washington thought about it, the more he realized that the very size of Braddock's force, plus his cumbersome artillery train, which eventually proved useless, actually contributed to the fiasco. Braddock himself was not personally to blame, but rather the entire way of waging war he carried in his head, which simply did not work in that foreign country "over the Mountains," where the forest-fighting tactics of the Indians reigned supreme. The relationship between officers and troops had to change in the frontier environment because "in this kind of Fighting, where being dispersd, each and every of them . . . has greater liberty to misbehave than if they were regularly, and compactly drawn up under the Eyes of their superior Officers." For now, given the obvious fact that most of the Indian tribes were allied with the French, any conventional campaign on the Braddock model into the Ohio Country would meet the same fate. The massacre at the Monongahela was a costly and painful way to learn this hard lesson, but Washington learned it deep down, which was becoming his preferred way to absorb all the essential lessons.[38]

As for his reputation, for the second time he emerged from a disastrous defeat with enhanced status. No one blamed him for the tragedy—

Braddock was the obvious and easy target—and he came to be called "the hero of the Monongahela" for rallying the survivors in an orderly retreat. His specialty seemed to be exhibiting courage in lost causes, or, as one newspaper account put it, he had earned "a high Reputation for Military Skill, Integrity, and Valor; tho' Success has not always attended his Undertakings." There was even talk—it was the first occasion—that his remarkable capacity to endure marked him as a man of destiny. "I may point out to the Public," wrote Reverend Samuel Davies, "that heroic youth Col. Washington, who I cannot but hope Providence has hitherto preserved in so signal a Manner for some important Service to his Country." This proved prescient later on, but for now it underlined the young man's chief characteristic, which was a knack for sheer survival.[39]

THE REGIMENT

IN AUGUST 1755, though he was only twenty-three, Washington's ascending reputation made him the obvious choice to command the newly created Virginia Regiment. In the next three and a half years he recruited, trained, and led what became an elite unit of, at times, over a thousand men which combined the spit-and-polish discipline of

British regulars with the tactical agility and proficiency of Indian warriors. During this time the main theater of the French and Indian War, now officially declared, moved north to the Great Lakes, New England, and Canada, making the Virginia frontier a mere sideshow and Washington himself what one biographer has called "the forgotten man on a forgotten front."[40]

But if he languished in obscurity from some larger strategic and historical perspective, the experience as commander in chief of Virginia's army provided his most direct and intensive schooling in military leadership prior to his command of the Continental army twenty years later. Moreover, in part because the historical record begins to thicken during this phase, and in part because the young man was growing up, the mere glimpses we had before become fuller pictures, though still fuzzy at the edges. Finally, the Virginia Regiment itself was very much his own creation, the first institution over which he exercised executive authority, and in that sense was a projection of his own developing convictions as both an officer and an aspiring gentleman.

From start to finish, he complained, as he would throughout the War for Independence, he had been given responsibilities without the resources to meet them. "I have been posted . . . upon our cold and Barren Frontiers," he lamented, "to perform I think I may say impossibilitys, that is, to protect from the Cruel Incursions of a Crafty Savage Enemy a line of Inhabitants of more than 350 Miles extent with a force inadequate to the taske." What he meant was that the dominant Indian tribes of the Ohio Country, chiefly the Shawnee and Delaware, had interpreted Braddock's defeat as a mandate to maraud and plunder all the English settlements west of the Blue Ridge. The initiative, the numbers, and the tactical advantage were on the enemy's side: "No troops in the universe can guard against the cunning and wiles of Indians," he explained. "No one can tell where they will fall, 'till the mischief is done, and then 'tis vain to pursue. The inhabitants see, and are convinced of this; which Makes each family afraid of standing in the gap of danger." There were no set-piece battles, just savage skirmishes that often ended in massacres. As he saw it, he was responsible for providing security over a region that was inherently indefensible, the epitome of mission impossible.[41]

His effort to change this fatal chemistry began with a plea to Dinwiddie for more Indian allies. "Indians," he claimed, "are the only match for Indians." This was less a statement of racial or ethnic enlightenment than a practical assessment that ten Indians were worth more than one hundred

Virginia soldiers in a forest fight. He strongly supported the attempt to recruit Catawba and then Cherokee warriors from the Carolinas and gave orders to his troops "to be cautious what they speak before them: as all of them understand english, and ought not to be affronted." Despite his best efforts, the Indian populations of the region remained resolutely pro-French and the decisive factor in making his mission a wholly defensive holding action, which eventually took the shape of multiple forts or stockades strung out on the west side of the Blue Ridge and garrisoned by detachments of his Virginia "blues."[42]

They were called that because of their distinctive uniforms, which Washington designed himself: "Every officer of the Virginia Regiment is, as soon as possible, to provide himself with uniform Dress, which is to be of fine Broad Cloath: The Coat Blue, faced and cuffed with Scarlet, and Trimmed with Silver: The Waistcoat Scarlet, with a plain Silver Lace, if to be had—the Breeches to be Blue, and every one to provide himself with a silver-laced Hat, of a Fashionable size." The officers' uniforms were but the outward manifestation of Washington's larger goal, which was to make the Virginia Regiment a truly special unit, "the first in Arms, of any Troops on the Continent, in the present War." They were to look sharper and drill with greater precision than any group of British regulars, and they were to master the mobile tactics of "bushfighting" with Indian-like proficiency. Within a year Washington believed he had created just such an elite force, which, because it was constantly engaged in combat operations patrolling the Virginia frontier, had a battle-tested edge no other colonial or British troops could match.[43]

His pride in them was both professional and personal. "If it shou'd be said," he wrote Dinwiddie, "that the Troops of Virginia are Irregulars, and cannot expect more notice than other Provincials, I must beg leave to differ, and observe in turn, that we want nothing but Commissions from His Majesty to make us as regular a Corps as any upon the Continent." He had come to regard himself as superior to anyone, British or American, in conducting this kind of guerrilla war, and it rankled him that neither he nor his troops were paid at the same rate as British regulars. "We cannot conceive," he complained to Dinwiddie in what turned out to be prophetic language, "that because we are Americans, we shou'd therefore be deprived of the Benefits Common to British Subjects." His protest on this score was more personal than ideological; that is, it derived less from any political convictions about colonial rights than from his own disappointment that neither he nor his regiment were sufficiently appreciated. In the spring of 1756 he traveled all the way to Boston, his first trip to the northern colonies, to plead his case for equal pay and higher rank as a British officer to William Shirley, then acting commander for North America, who listened attentively but did nothing. He was a serious young man who took himself and his Virginia Regiment seriously, and expected others to do the same.[44]

He also managed to combine a broad-gauged grasp of his mission, in all its inherent frustrations, with a meticulous attention to detail. He drafted literally thousands of orders that all began "You are hereby ordered to . . ." and then proceeded, in language more incisive and grammatically cogent than his earlier writing, to focus tightly on a specific assignment: If you come upon a massacred settlement, harvest the corn crop before moving on; when constructing stockades, clear the surrounding trees and brush beyond musket range (a lesson he had learned from Fort Necessity); when a ranger in the regiment is killed in action, continue his salary for twenty-eight days to pay for his coffin; if ambushed in a clearing, rush toward the tree line from which the shots came while the enemy is reloading. Officers were held to a higher standard of deportment, to include controlling their wives: "There are continual complaints to me of the misbehavior of your wife," he apprised one captain. "If she is not immediately sent from the camp . . . I shall take care to drive her out myself, and suspend you." The old adage applied: if God were in the details, Colonel Washington would have been there to greet Him upon arrival.[45]

The raw material from which Washington recruited his regiment was raw indeed. He kept several rosters of the enlisted men, that reveal that most of his recruits were recently arrived immigrants, primarily from England, Ireland, or Scotland, or second-generation carpenters, bricklayers, and tanners from the Pennsylvania or Virginia backcountry. Washington duly recorded their names, age at enlistment, height, trade, place of origin, then a brief physical description: "Dark Complexion & Hair, lame in his right thigh by a wound"; "Fair Complexion, sandy Hair, well made"; "Red face, pitted with the small pox, Red Hair." Though he maintained a proper social distance from the enlisted men, he knew most of them personally. And though most of them were older than he was, he cultivated the image of a caring but strict father toward his children.[46]

Discipline was harsh. Those found guilty of drunkenness or lewd behavior sometimes received up to a thousand lashes. Deserters, even those who returned voluntarily, faced death by hanging. A surge in desertions in the summer of 1757 produced a string of public executions. "I have a

Gallows near 40 feet high erected," Washington boasted to a British officer, "and I am determined . . . to hang two or three on it, as an example to others." He suffered no sleepless nights after endorsing the executions, even when a condemned man made a special plea based on previous bravery in combat. There were clear lines in his mind, and if you crossed them, there was no forgiveness.[47]

He routinely contrasted the discipline of his own regiment with the undependable militia, whom he described as "those hooping, hallowing, Gentleman-Soldiers!" The ranks of most militia units were actually filled with yeomen farmers a notch above his own troops in the pecking order of Chesapeake society. But their short terms of enlistment and inveterate independence made them virtually worthless, as he saw it, in a war that put a premium on staying power. They were the wind. His Virginia Regiment was the wall. He described one scene in which a thirty-man militia unit refused to assist in the construction of a fort unless paid forty pounds of tobacco for each day of labor, this despite the fact that the fort was designed to protect their own families from annihilation. On another occasion, when reports of a large Canadian and Indian patrol arrived at his headquarters at Winchester, most of the militia assigned to his command declared their enlistments up and simply walked out. Washington resented that his Virginia Regiment was frequently mistaken for a mere militia unit. He did not believe you could trust in the principle of voluntarism, or the spontaneous expression of public virtue, to meet a wartime crisis. This was one youthful conviction that he never saw fit to abandon; indeed, it foreshadowed his low estimate of militia throughout the Revolutionary War.[48]

His abiding respect for civilian authority, most especially his insistence on strict obedience to the principle of civilian control over the military, eventually became one of his greatest legacies. But when he commanded the Virginia Regiment he violated the principle on several occasions, beginning with the whispering campaign he instigated against Dinwiddie when his requests for higher pay, more troops, and greater discretion in choosing the location of forts were routinely rejected. He opened a separate channel of communication with John Robinson, Speaker of the House of Representatives, blaming Dinwiddie for decisions that left the entire Shenandoah Valley, "the best land in Virginia," vulnerable to Indian domination.[49]

Washington understood the open secret of Virginia politics, which was that the governor's sovereign authority was more theoretical than real, because the legislature had managed to use its constitutional control over money bills as a weapon to limit gubernatorial power. So there were really two power sources to appease, and Washington's covert communications with Robinson represented his realistic response to the bifurcated character of Virginia politics. For over a year he demonstrated considerable dexterity in negotiating a two-track approach without Dinwiddie's knowledge.[50]

By 1757, however, the relationship with Dinwiddie had deteriorated badly, and the official correspondence became loaded with mutual accusations of deceit. Washington charged Dinwiddie with encouraging hostile gossip among the burgesses about his conduct of the war, which was precisely what he was doing to Dinwiddie. In fact, Dinwiddie had resolutely supported Washington in the backrooms of Williamsburg, despite gossipy criticisms from some burgesses that he was submitting inflated estimates of Indian strength in order to promote greater tax levies. Through it all, Washington maintained a posture of absolute probity: "But this know," he wrote Dinwiddie, "that no man that ever was employed in a public capacity has endeavored to discharge the trust reposed in him with greater honesty, and more zeal for the country's interest, than I have done." There was truth in this claim, but not the whole truth, which would have included the behind-the-scenes machinations. Two features of the emerging Washington personality come into focus here: first, a thin-skinned aversion to criticism, especially when the criticism questioned his personal motives, which he insisted were beyond reproach; second, a capacity to play politics effectively while claiming total disinterest in the game.[51]

There was yet another political game he found himself playing, which operated by a wholly different set of rules and at a higher level in the imperial hierarchy. This was the aristocratic game of deference and patronage that he had played successfully with the Fairfax family and had hoped to play with Braddock. The eventual successor to Braddock as the commander of His Majesty's forces in North America was John Campbell, the Earl of Loudoun, who turned out to be another ill-fated and short-lived emissary from London, brimming over with that wicked combination of confidence in his abilities and ignorance of his theater of operations. Upon his arrival in 1756, Washington wrote him in the properly deferential style: "We the officers of the Virginia Regiment beg leave to congratulate your Lordship on your safe arrival in America: And to express the deep Sense We have of his Majesty's Wisdom and paternal Care for his Colonies in Sending your Lordship to their Protection at this critical Juncture."

He concluded his letter with a special plea based on the loyalty to Britain's goals embodied in the Virginia Regiment, "as it in a more especial Manner entitles Us to Your Lordship's Patronage."[52]

Lord Loudoun represented the privileged and presumptive aristocratic culture that beckoned to Washington as the epitome of influence. In the Virginia Regiment, on the other hand, officers and rangers were promoted on the basis of their performance, and Washington often resisted efforts by Fairfax to have unqualified friends given commissions. But Britain, and to a great extent Virginia as well, still operated within a social matrix where power flowed within bloodlines and where coats-of-arms trumped merit. Loudoun would have been hard-pressed to distinguish the Alleghenies from the Alps, but by a combination of royal whim and family fortune he controlled British policy and therefore the fate of the Virginia Regiment and its commander. Washington's attempt to solicit his attention and support for a regular commission was almost comical in its fumbling effort to affect the proper deferential style:

> Although I have not the Honour to be known to Your Lordship: Yet your Lordship's Name was familiar to my Ear, on account of the Important Services performed to His Majesty in other parts

of the World—don't think My Lord I am going to flatter. I have exalted Sentiments of your Lordship's Character, and revere your Rank; yet, mean not this (could I believe it acceptable). My nature is honest, and Free from Guile.[53]

Loudoun not only ignored the request, but even decided temporarily to disband the Virginia Regiment in order to send several companies to fight in South Carolina. Still determined to make an impression, Washington named one of his forts after Loudoun, which then proved a lingering embarrassment when Loudoun's failure to mount a successful campaign against Cape Breton caused London to recall and replace him. It seems safe to conclude that Washington understood the rules of the aristocratic game, felt obliged to play by its rules to further his career, but often came off as the provincial American incapable of mastering the deferential vocabulary.

For the truth was that he had come to feel superior to his superiors, just as he had come to regard his Virginia Regiment as perhaps the finest fighting unit in North America. He and his "blues" had learned the hard way how to fight this kind of war and what it would take to win it. Ultimately, the strategic key remained that fountainhead of French power at the forks of the Ohio. But another Braddock-style campaign would surely end up in the same heap of blood and sorrow. Washington believed that he, more than anyone else, knew how to mount a successful campaign against Fort Duquesne, and he expressed only disdain for the various schemes British officers proposed. When he received one such proposal in March 1758, he apprised his purported superior that the plan was "absurd," and "A Romantick whim that may subsist in Theory, but must fail in practice." He ended on a sarcastic note, speculating that perhaps the tactical genius who dreamed up the plan "intended to provide them first with Wings, to facilitate their Passage over so Mountainous & extensive a Country; else whence comes this flight?"[54]

Nevertheless, something big was obviously brewing, something designed to move the Virginia frontier off the back burner of British strategy and make the Ohio Country a major theater of operations once again. In April 1758, Washington learned that General John Forbes, a Scotsman with more than thirty years of experience in the British army, had been given the mission of capturing Fort Duquesne with a force over twice the size Braddock had commanded three years earlier. Washington immediately wrote Thomas Gage, a fellow survivor of the Monongahela massacre, requesting an introduction to Forbes. This time he dispensed with the awkwardly obsequious tone of the Loudoun letter and suggested he was not asking a favor so much as offering one himself:

> I mean not, Sir, as one who has favors to ask of him—on the contrary, having entirely laid aside all hopes of preferment in the military line (and being induced at present to serve this campaign from abstract motives, purely laudable), I only wish to be distinguished in some measure from the general run of provincial Officers, as I understand there will be a motley herd of us. This, I flatter myself, can hardly be deemed an unreasonable request, when it is considered, that I have been much longer in the Service than any provincial officer in America.[55]

Forbes and his extremely capable second in command, Henry Bouquet, welcomed Washington's advice, in part because they found it compelling, in part because the entire expedition moved beneath the shadow of the Braddock tragedy and needed to avoid his mistakes. First, they agreed to retain a large detachment of Cherokees as scouts, which Washington insisted were "the only Troops fit to Cope with Indians on such Ground." Second, they adopted the ranger uniforms of enlisted men in the Virginia Regiment instead of the traditional redcoats of the British army. Forbes called it "Indian dress," adding that "wee must comply and learn the Art of Warr, from Enemy Indians, or anything else who have seen the Country and Warr carried on in it." In effect, Forbes was acknowledging that the Virginia Regiment was the professional model and the British regulars the rank amateurs in this kind of campaign. Third, Forbes and Bouquet agreed to train their lead units in the forest-fighting tactics Washington had developed. If ambushed, the troops should "in an Instant, be thrown into an Order of Battle in the Woods," meaning they should advance in two groups to the tree line and flank the enemy on the left and right while the Indian scouts circled to the rear. Finally, the Virginia Regiment would be included in the vanguard, since, as Washington put it, "from long Intimacy, and scouting in these Woods, my Men are as well acquainted with all the Passes and difficulties as any Troops that will be employed."[56]

In all respects save one, Washington got his way, but the one exception drove a wedge between him and Forbes that eventually caused him to display his bottled-up contempt for British superiors in a form that verged on gross insubordination. The contentious issue was the proper route to Fort Duquesne. Washington presumed the expedition would follow Braddock's course across northern Virginia and southern Maryland, then northwest across Pennsylvania to the forks of the Ohio.

Braddock's Road seemed the obvious choice to Washington because it had already been cut. And it was vastly preferable to all Virginians because it linked the prospective bounty of the Ohio Country to the Old Dominion. The clinching argument, as Washington saw it, was that Braddock's Road followed an old Indian path, so that the people who knew the region better than anyone else had identified it as the preferred route.[57]

The trouble was that Forbes's main force was based at Carlisle, Pennsylvania, and British engineers had proposed cutting a new road straight across that colony which would be about thirty miles shorter than Braddock's Road and did not require an initial detour south to the Shenandoah Valley. (It follows much the same course as the modern-day Pennsylvania Turnpike.) Washington proposed a special meeting with Bouquet to protest this decision, which he believed had been unduly influenced by Pennsylvanians eager to make their colony the permanent gateway to the American interior. Bouquet agreed, presuming that, whatever the resolution, Washington would accept it as final. "I See with utmost Satisfaction," wrote Bouquet, "that you are above all the influences of Prejudices and ready to go heartily where Reason and judgment Shall direct." Bouquet listened to Washington's case for Braddock's Road, describing it as sensible and "deliverd with that openness and candor that becomes a Gentleman and a Soldier." Four days later, after consulting with Forbes, Bouquet apprised Washington that his advice had been heard and rejected: "I cannot therefore entertain the least doubt that we shall all now go on hand in hand and that some zeal for the service that has hitherto been so distinguishing a part of your character will carry you . . . over the Alligeny Mountains to Fort Du Quesne."[58]

Bouquet could not have been more wrong. Washington immediately wrote Francis Fauquier, who had recently replaced Dinwiddie as governor of Virginia, to register his vehement opposition to the Pennsylvania route and his "moral certainty" that the entire campaign was now doomed. He used much the same language with Speaker of the House Robinson, describing the decision as a corrupt bargain designed to swindle Virginia out of its rightful role as the archway to the west, calling Forbes an "evil genius" in cahoots with the Pennsylvanians, even threatening to go all the way to London in order to expose and discredit him. Throughout the fall of 1758, as Forbes's army hacked its way across the Alleghenies, Washington kept up a steady stream of criticism: Forbes and Bouquet were both incompetent idiots; the pace of the march, slowed by the need to cut the new road, virtually assured that the campaign would stall in the mountains when the snows came and never reach Fort Duquesne; no one should blame him when this inevitable failure happened and all the world witnessed a repeat of the Braddock fiasco.[59]

The truth of the matter was that both Forbes and Bouquet were excellent and honorable officers, had very much acknowledged Washington's expertise, and made the decision about the route for logistical rather than political reasons. (Forbes, it turns out, was dying, probably of cancer, and made the difficult trek in a blanket stretched between two horses.) If anyone were guilty of allowing political considerations to color his judgment, it was Washington, whose Virginia prejudices were blatantly exposed in his letters to Williamsburg. Moreover, his prediction that the expedition would never reach its objective proved wrong. The lead elements of Forbes's column, including Washington's Virginia Regiment, reached the outskirts of Fort Duquesne in early November. What happened next might serve as a classic illustration of the unpredictable fortunes of war.

Forbes called a council of war to solicit the advice of his officers about how to proceed. The ghost of Braddock had hung over the campaign from the start, and the officers urged caution. Washington himself argued that an assault would be "a little Imprudent" because no one knew the size of the garrison inside Fort Duquesne. Forbes reluctantly agreed. Matters were now at a stalemate, and Washington expressed personal satisfaction that his intimations of futility were coming true, even though he had a hand in the apparent outcome.[60]

But on the next day, November 12, the Virginia Regiment encountered a reconnaissance patrol out from the fort. In the skirmish that ensued, Washington stepped between two groups of his own troops that were mistakenly firing at each other, using his sword to knock up their muskets. (Many years later, in 1786, he claimed that his life was in greater danger at this moment than at the Monongahela or at any time during the American Revolution.) The regiment suffered heavy casualties, most the result of "friendly fire," but captured three prisoners who reported that Fort Duquesne was undermanned and vulnerable. Forbes ordered an immediate assault with Washington and his troops part of the vanguard. (Washington was so concerned about surprise that he ordered all the dogs in the regiment killed before the attack.) But when they reached Fort Duquesne, it was deserted and burning. There was no battle because the French troops, recognizing they were outnumbered, had fled down the Ohio the previous day. It was an empty, anticlimactic victory-of-sorts. Critical of Forbes to the end, Washington complained to Fauquier that not enough troops were left behind to rebuild and garrison the fort, which would probably be recaptured and lead to a repeat of the whole bloody business on the Virginia frontier the following year.[61]

How to explain Washington's insubordinate behavior during the Forbes campaign, which proved to be an atypical chapter in his long career as a soldier and statesman? Three overlapping explanations suggest themselves, each perhaps containing a portion of the answer. First, he was still very young, only twenty-six, headstrong about his own prowess as the founder of the Virginia Regiment, and overeager to ingratiate himself with the planter elite in Virginia, which had vested interests in making Braddock's Road the preferred route into the Ohio Country. Second, he mistakenly regarded Bouquet and Forbes as updated versions of Braddock and Loudoun, imperious symbols of British privilege who thought of American colonists in much the same way colonists thought of Indians, namely as a semicivilized inferior people. He was factually wrong on this score, but his experience of British authority still smoldered, and his own sense of pride gave that experience a special edge of resentment. Third, and finally, he was in emotional turmoil at this moment, because he had fallen in love with one woman and was about to marry another.

LOVE AND MARRIAGE

THE WOMAN he was planning to marry was Martha Dandridge Custis, probably the wealthiest widow in Virginia, with an inherited estate of eighteen thousand acres valued at £30,000, making her the prize catch of Chesapeake society. (All the other eligible women Washington had previously pursued were also wealthier than he was, extending the male tradition in his line of marrying up.) Washington had begun courting her in the spring of 1758. The preceding year he had launched major renovations at Mount Vernon in anticipation of creating a more suitably lavish household, a risky wager on his future prospects made before he knew of Martha's availability, but a sign that he was confident that an appropriate consort would turn up soon. He probably proposed in June. The following month he stood successfully for election to the House of Burgesses in Frederick County. On one previous occasion he had permitted his name to be put forward, but had made no concerted effort to win. This time he mobilized his friends to campaign for him and opened accounts with four taverns in Winchester to provide impressive quantities of rum, wine, and beer at the polls. Even as the Forbes campaign was getting underway, he had already decided to surrender command of the Virginia Regiment for a more settled life on the banks of the Potomac with an attractive and much-coveted partner. His thoughts were on the new chapter he planned to open up in his life, east rather than west of the Blue Ridge.[62]

His emotions, on the other hand, were swirling around another subject altogether. Her name was Sally Fairfax, wife of George William. The evidence is scanty, but convincing beyond any reasonable doubt, that Washington had fallen in love with his best friend's wife several years earlier. Just when the infatuation began, and whether it ever crossed the sexual threshold, has resisted surveillance by generations of historians and biographers. What we do know is based primarily on two letters Washington wrote to Sally in September 1758 while serving in the Forbes campaign, and one letter he wrote near the end of his life in an uncharacteristically sentimental mood. In the latter he confessed to an elderly Sally that she had been the passion of his youth, that he had never been able to forget her, "nor been able to eradicate from my mind those happy moments, the happiest in my life, which I have enjoyed in your company."[63]

The earlier letters of 1758 are convoluted documents, in part because the act of writing them threw Washington into such emotional disarray that his grammar and syntax lost their customary coherence, in part because he deliberately used imprecise and elliptical language to prevent any prying eyes from knowing his secret. Here are the most salient passages:

> 'Tis true, I profess myself a Votary to Love—I acknowledge that a Lady is in the Case—and further I confess that this Lady is known to you.—Yes Madam, as well as she is to one, who is too sensible of her Charms to deny the Power, whose Influence he feels and must ever Submit to. I feel the force of her amiable beauties in the recollection of a thousand tender passages that I coud wish to obliterate, till I am bid to revive them.—but experience alas! Sadly reminds me how Impossible this is.—and evinces an opinion which I have long entertained, that there is a Destiny, which has the Sovereign Controul of our Actions—not to be resisted by the Strongest efforts of Human Nature.
>
> The World has no business to know the object of my Love, declard in this manner to you—you

when I want to conceal it—One thing, above all things in this World I wish to know, and only one person of your Acquaintance can solve me that, or guess my meaning.—but adieu to this, till happier times, if I shall ever see them. . . .

Do we still misunderstand the true meaning of each others Letters? I think it must appear so, tho I would feign hope the contrary as I cannot speak plainer without—but I'll say no more, and leave you to guess the rest. . . . I should think my time more agreable spent believe me, in playing a part in Cato with the Company you mention, & myself doubly happy in being the Juba to such a Marcia as you must make.[64]

In Joseph Addison's **Cato** (1713), Marcia is the daughter of Cato, and Juba is the Prince of Numidia, who is required to conceal his secret love for her. Only someone dedicated to denying the full import of this evidence could reject the conclusion that Washington was passionately in love with Sally Fairfax.

The titillating "consummation" question is almost as irrelevant as it is unanswerable. The more important and less ambiguous fact is that Washington possessed a deep-seated capacity to feel powerful emotions. Some models of self-control are able to achieve their serenity easily, because the soul-fires never burned brightly to begin with. Washington became the most notorious model of self-control in all of American history, the original marble man, but he achieved this posture—and sometimes it **was** a posture—the same hard-earned way he learned soldiering, by direct experience with difficulty. Unlike Thomas Jefferson, he wrote no lyrical tribute to the interior struggle entitled "Dialogue Between the Head and Heart," but he lived that dialogue in a primal place deep within himself. Appearances aside, he was an intensely passionate man, whose powers of self-control eventually became massive because of the interior urges they were required to master.

Nothing was more inherently chaotic or placed a higher premium on self-control than a battle. He had played a leading role in four of them: one a massacre that he oversaw; the other a massacre that he survived; one an embarrassing defeat; the other a hollow victory. Whether it was a miracle, destiny, or sheer luck, he had emerged from these traumatic experiences unscathed and with his reputation, each time, higher than before. He had shown himself to be physically brave, impetuously so at Fort Necessity, and personally proud, irrationally so in the Forbes campaign. His courage, his composure, and his self-control were all of a piece, having developed within that highly lethal environment that was the Ohio Country, where internal shields provided the only defense against dangers that came at you from multiple angles.

One of the reasons he proved clumsy and ineffectual at playing the patronage game with British officials was that deference did not come naturally to him, since it meant surrendering control to a purported superior, trusting his fate and future to someone else. Though capable of obeying orders, he was much better at giving them. Though fully aware of the layered aristocratic matrix ruled by privileged superiors in Williamsburg and London, he was instinctively disposed to regard himself as better than his betters. The refusal of the British army to grant him a regular commission did not strike him as a statement of his own unworthiness, but rather a confession of their ignorance. His only experience of complete control was the Virginia Regiment and—no surprise to him—it was his only unqualified success.

If we are looking for emergent patterns of behavior, then the combination of bottomless ambition and the near obsession with self-control leaps out. What will in later years be regarded as an arrogant aloofness began in his young manhood as a wholly protective urge to establish space around himself that bullets, insults, and criticism could never penetrate. Because he lacked both the presumptive superiority of a British aristocrat and the economic resources of a Tidewater grandee, Washington could only rely on the hard core of his own merit, his only real asset, which had to be protected by posting multiple sentries at all the vulnerable points. Because he could not afford to fail, he could not afford to trust. For the rest of his life, all arguments based on the principle of mutual trust devoid of mutual interest struck him as sentimental nonsense.

A few other abiding features were also already locked in place. He combined personal probity with a demonstrable flair for dramatic action whenever opportunity—be it a war or a wealthy widow—presented itself. He took what history offered, and was always poised to ride the available wave in destiny's direction. Speaking of direction, he looked west to the land beyond the Alleghenies as the great prize worth fighting for. And although he did not know it at the time, the rewards he received for his soldiering in the form of land grants in the Ohio Country would become the lifetime foundation of his personal wealth. Though he was still developing—the sharp edges of his ambitions were inadequately concealed, his sense of honor was too anxious to declare its purity—the outline of Washington's mature personality was already assuming a discernible shape.

When he resigned his commission in December 1758, the officers of the regiment composed a touching tribute, lamenting "the loss of such an excellent Commander, such a sincere Friend, and so affable a Companion." Washington responded in kind, observing that their final salute "will constitute the greatest happiness of my life, and afford in my latest hour the most pleasing reflections." The regiment had been his extended family for more than three years, but now he was moving on to Mount Vernon to establish a more proper family, over which he intended to exercise equivalent control. Whatever he felt toward Sally Fairfax, she was a forbidden temptation who could not be made to fit into the domestic picture he had formed in his head; memories of her had to therefore be safely buried deep in his heart, where they could not interfere with his careful management of his ascending prospects. Whatever he felt toward Martha Dandridge Custis, she did fit, indeed fit perfectly. They were married on January 6, 1759. Writing from Mount Vernon later that spring, he described his new vision: "I have quit a Military Life; and shortly shall be fix'd at this place with an agreable Partner, and then shall be able to conduct my own business with more punctuality than heretofore as it will pass under my own immediate supervision."[65]

CHAPTER TWO

The Strenuous Squire

OVER THE COURSE of his long public career, Washington made several decisions that shaped the basic contours of American history, but nothing he ever did had a greater influence on the shape of his own life than the decision to marry Martha Dandridge Custis. Her huge dowry immediately catapulted Washington into the top tier of Virginia's planter class and established the economic foundation for his second career as the master of Mount Vernon. His first career as a professional soldier still hovered about his reputation in the form of the title "Colonel Washington." And it apparently still hovered about in his own head as well, since in 1759 he ordered four large busts of military heroes—Alexander the Great, Julius Caesar, Charles XII of Sweden, and Frederick the Great—to decorate the mansion he was already in the process of enlarging. The invoice to his London agent requesting the busts included requests for kid gloves, negligee, a velvet cape, and several purgatives for intestinal disorders. The agent was able to find all the other items, but not the military busts. This was prophetic, because for the next sixteen years Washington devoted his energies to perfecting the elegant lifestyle of a Virginia aristocrat, making his military experiences into memories, but eventually worrying himself sick that he and his fellow Virginia grandees were trapped in an imperial network designed to reduce them all to bankruptcy and ruin.[1]

DOMESTICITIES

HE WAS ENTERING what turned out to be the most settled period of his life. The physical centerpiece for his newfound stability was, of course, Mount Vernon, both the mansion itself and the lands surrounding it. Renovations in the mansion had proceeded apace during his absence in the Forbes campaign, effectively adding a full story to the home he had inherited from Lawrence—or, more accurately, from Lawrence's widow, who died in 1761. Though not in the same league with brick mansions like the Fairfaxes's Belvoir or Thomas Jefferson's Monticello, the enlarged and embellished interiors of the new Mount Vernon were designed to make a statement. The home now visited by more than a million tourists a year looks different than the home that the newly married couple inhabited in 1759—the distinctive cupola, piazza, and several of the grandest rooms were not added until later—but Mount Vernon still effectively announced the arrival of an impressive new member of Virginia's elite. Passing through in the summer of 1760, the inveterate English traveler Andrew Burnaby was suitably impressed: "This place is the property of Colonel Washington, and truly deserving of its owner. The house is most beautifully situated upon a very high hill on the banks of the Potowmac, and commands a noble prospect of water, of cliffs, of woods and plantations."[2]

Burnaby spoke of plantations in the plural because Mount Vernon, like most Virginia estates in the revolutionary era, was not a centralized agrarian factory like the cotton plantations of the antebellum South, but a series of loosely connected farms, each with its own distinctive name, slave workforce, and overseer. Between the time he moved in with Martha and the time he departed for the war against Great Britain in 1775, Washington more than doubled the size of Mount Vernon, from about 3,000 to 6,500 acres, chiefly by buying up adjoining parcels of land when they became available. He more than doubled the size of the slave population, from fewer than fifty to well over a hundred, much of the increase coming from the forty-six new slaves he purchased during this time. Although appearances turned out to be deceptive, the newly ensconced master of Mount Vernon appeared to hold sway over a burgeoning and flourishing enterprise.[3]

The emotional centerpiece of Washington's new world was Martha, who came complete with two young children, Jackie (four) and Patsy (two). If the main source of Martha's appeal was initially more economic than romantic, there is reason to believe that the relationship soon developed into an intimate and mutually affectionate bond of considerable affinity. We cannot know for sure—matters of this sort can seldom be known for sure—because Martha destroyed their private correspondence soon after her husband's death. (Only three letters between them survive, compared to over a thousand between John and Abigail Adams, the most fully revealed marriage of the age.) But later efforts to suggest that Washington's marriage lacked passion, and that the slogan "George Washington slept here" had promiscuous implications, have all been discredited by most scholars.

The fact that they had no children of their own is almost certainly not a sign that they were sexually incompatible, but rather that Washington himself was most probably sterile. Although these are not the kind of questions we can answer conclusively, and it is possible that Martha lost the capacity to conceive after delivering her last child, it is more likely that the man who would become known as the "Father of his Country" was biologically incapable of producing children of his own. As for the suppressed feelings for Sally Fairfax, all the evidence indicates that everyone behaved themselves. Sally and George William Fairfax were the closest neighbors and became good friends of George and Martha, the most frequent guests at Mount Vernon, intimate accomplices in the hurly-burly of the ambitiously genteel social life within the Northern Neck. It seems likely that both Martha and George William realized that their respective partners had a past, but the longer no one mentioned it, the more it became history.[4]

As a stepfather, Washington was dutiful and engaged, especially when it came to Jackie, whom he wanted to receive the kind of classical education that he had missed. In fact, the boy was raised with all the advantages and privileges that Washington himself had been denied: his own personal servant; a private tutor who resided at Mount Vernon; the newest toys and finest clothes, all ordered from London; his own horses and hounds for fox-hunting. The only item Jackie was denied was adversity, and the predictable result began to surface soon after he went to study Latin and Greek with Jonathan Boucher, first at Fredericksburg and then Annapolis. "His mind is a good deal relaxed from Study," Washington admitted to Boucher, "& more than ever turned to Dogs, Horses & Guns." Boucher wrote back to apprise Washington that it was worse than he knew: "I must confess to You I never did in my Life know a Youth so exceedingly indolent or so surprisingly voluptuous: one wd suppose Nature had intended Him for some Asiatic Prince."[5]

If Jackie had been his own son, perhaps Washington would have raised him differently. But he consistently deferred to Martha on all final decisions concerning the children. He was their guardian; she was their parent. He was to provide, but not to decide. So off Jackie went to King's College (now Columbia) in New York— the College of William and Mary was not good enough for him—where he lasted only a few months. In 1773, at age nineteen, he announced his decision to marry Eleanor Calvert, the daughter of Benedict Calvert, a descendant of Maryland's founding family. Under prodding from Martha, Washington acquiesced, then did everything he could to establish Jackie and Nelly in proper style on one of the inherited Custis estates. Poor Jackie predictably failed at managing his plantation and died young, in 1781, just when Washington was sealing American victory in the American Revolution at nearby Yorktown.[6]

Patsy's story was even sadder than Jackie's. Even as a little girl she began to experience seizures that only worsened with time and eventually took the form of almost weekly epileptic fits. The latest London dolls and toys were ordered for her every year, along with medicinal potions, to include—a clear sign of parental desperation—a medieval iron ring with allegedly magical curative power. Even with these efforts, and despite several trips to different doctors and health spas that Washington personally supervised, nothing worked. She died suddenly after one of her seizures in 1773 at the age of seventeen. Washington ordered a black cape for Martha to wear in mourning for the following year.[7]

THE SQUIRE

BEYOND THE DOMESTIC centerpieces of Washington's world at Mount Vernon there lay a broad spectrum of different roles and responsibilities that, taken together, allow us to conjure up several different mental pictures of the mature man in his pre-icon phase. Perhaps the most jarring picture, because it clashes so dramatically with his subsequent reputation as the epitome of public virtue, is that of the indulged Virginia gentleman for whom the phrase "pursuit of happiness" meant galloping to hounds.

And the foxhunt is not just a metaphor. According to his diary, Washington spent between two and five hours a day for forty-nine days in 1768 on horseback pursuing the elusive fox. He also devoted considerable energy to breeding his hounds, who frequently confounded him with their ingenuity at linking up—what he called "lining"—with partners of their own choosing. Especially after 1765, when Lund Washington, a distant relative, assumed many of the managerial responsibilities at Mount Vernon, Washington enjoyed a great deal of leisure time. He traveled to Alexandria, Annapolis, and Williamsburg to take in the horse races. After 1768 his trips were often made in an expensive chariot, custom-made in London, with leather interiors and his personal crest emblazoned on the side. His record of card-playing expenses from 1772 to 1774 reveals that he played twenty-five times a year and just about broke even in his wagers. He purchased his wine, usually Madeira, by the butt (150 gallons) and the pipe (110 gallons). On any given day he enjoyed the attention of two manservants, Thomas

Bishop, a white servant who had been with him since the Braddock campaign, and Billy Lee, a mulatto slave, who came on the scene in 1768.[8]

This picture of the provincial aristocrat at play would not be complete without noticing his clothing. His coats, shirts, pants, and shoes were all ordered from a London tailor, but they invariably did not fit. He complained that "my Cloaths have never fitted me well," but the reason for the persistent problem was that the instructions he customarily gave his tailor were misleading. For example, when ordering an overcoat he directed the tailor to "make it to fit a person Six feet high and proportionally made, & you cannot go much amiss." But Washington was at least two inches taller than six feet and disproportionately made, with very broad shoulders and huge hips. When Charles Willson Peale came down from Philadelphia to paint his portrait in 1772, Washington chose to wear his old military uniform from the Virginia Regiment days. Biographers have speculated that his decision to be depicted as a soldier might have been a premonition of his looming role in the American Revolution. It is also possible that he wore the only suit of clothes that fit him.[9]

The clothing scene is comical, but so is any one-dimensional picture of Washington as a laconic embodiment of Virginia's leisure class. (The Peale portrait, by the way, which is generally regarded as a poor likeness, reinforces the laid-back image, paunch and all.) Most of the time Washington was on horseback he was not fox-hunting but riding out to his farms, in effect overseeing his own overseers, offering meticulous instructions about when to harvest his tobacco crop, what fields to plant with corn and peas, how many hogs to slaughter. Or he was riding over to Truro Parish to perform his duties as a vestryman. (A lukewarm Episcopalian, he never took Communion, tended to talk about "Providence" or "Destiny" rather than God, and—was this a statement?—preferred to stand rather than kneel when praying.) Or he was traveling down to a session of the House of Burgesses in Williamsburg, where he served on two standing committees and handled most of the veterans' claims. Though his diary entries are usually devoted to the weather—when he describes which way the wind is blowing, he is not being metaphorical—they also record the busy, fully engaged life of a typical Virginia planter with multiple responsibilities to his family, neighbors, and workers.[10]

Most of those workers were African slaves, at least some recently arrived in Virginia, with distinctive tribal markings and little command of English. Later in his career, especially after his experience in the American Revolution exposed him to a broader set of opinions on the matter,

Washington developed a more critical perspective on the institution of slavery. At this stage of his life, however, there is no evidence of any moral anxiety about owning other human beings. Like most Chesapeake planters, Washington talked and thought about his slaves as "a Species of Property," very much as he described his dogs and horses. When they ran away, he posted notices for their recapture, included descriptions (which is how we know about the African markings), and if they ran away again, he sold them off. One recalcitrant slave named Tom, for example, was shipped off to the Caribbean. Washington's instructions to the ship captain described Tom as "a Rogue & Runaway," but also a hard worker who should fetch a decent price "if kept clean & trim'd up a little when offered to Sale." Washington estimated that Tom was worth one hogshead of molasses, one of rum, a barrel of limes, a pot of tamarinds, ten pounds of sweetmeats, and a few bottles of "good old spirits."[11]

His one concession to the humanity of his slave workers, an attitude shared by Jefferson and many of the wealthier Virginia planters, was that he would not sell them without their consent if it broke up families. He was also solicitous about their health, warning overseers not to overwork them in bad weather and taking personal charge if disease broke out in the slave quarters. But even here his motives were mixed, for if his slaves were incapacitated for an extended period, or died, it hurt the productivity of his plantation. There were trusted slaves who enjoyed considerable freedom of movement and personal discretion, like his servant Billy Lee, and a favorite messenger empowered to make minor business transactions named Mulatto Jack. But these were the exceptions. Most of the slaves who worked his farms he treated as cattle and referred to only by their first names. His instructions concerning the criteria for purchasing new slaves expressed his detached attitude with unintended candor: "Let there be two thirds of them Males, the other third Females. . . . All of them to be straight Limb'd & in every respect strong and likely, with good teeth & good Countenances—to be sufficiently provided with cloathes."[12]

If his views on slavery were typical of his time and his class, there was one area in which he proved an exception to the pattern of behavior expected of a prominent Virginia gentleman: he was excessively and conspicuously assiduous in the defense of his own interests, especially when he suspected he was being cheated out of money or land. He took out an indictment against the local iron maker for fraud when he concluded, wrongly as it turned out, that the iron had been improperly weighed. He disputed the terms of a contract to purchase Clifton's Neck, one of the parcels adjoining Mount Vernon, generating a tangled legal conflict that stayed in the courts for thirty years. He accused his wine dealer of thievery for not filling one cask of Madeira to the top. Ship captains delivering his wheat and flour for sale in the Caribbean never got the price he thought he deserved. When he hired a friend, Valentine Crawford, to assist in the management of his western lands, he drafted the following instructions:

> as you are now receiving my Money, your time is not your own; and that every day or hour misapplied, is a loss to me, do not therefore under a belief that, as a friendship has long subsisted between us, many things may be overlooked in you. . . . I shall consider you in no other light than as a Man who has engaged his time and Service to conduct and manage my Interest . . . and shall seek redress if you do not, just as soon from you as an entire stranger.[13]

Neither Jefferson nor most other members of Virginia's planter elite could have written such words, for they convey an obsessive concern with his own economic interests that no proper gentleman was supposed to feel, much less express so directly. (Perhaps this is the underlying reason why Jefferson and so many other Virginia planters would die in debt, and Washington would die a very wealthy man.) The picture one conjures up on the basis of this kind of evidence contrasts completely with the Peale portrait of a serenely nonchalant Virginia squire, about to discard his old uniform for his riding clothes, then go off with his horses and hounds. This is not a man "to the manor born," but a recently arrived aristocrat who, before he married a fortune, was accustomed to scrambling, literally dodging bullets; a man unwilling, indeed unable, to take anything for granted. It is not that he was insecure, quite the opposite; but the security he enjoyed had a sharp edge designed to clear the ground around it of any and all threats to its survival. He is the kind of man who will impose impossibly meticulous expectations on his overseers, even on his hounds, and always come away disappointed in their performance. Finally, this is the kind of man who will regard any failure to meet his exacting standards as a personal affront, and persistent failure as evidence of a conspiracy to deprive him of what is rightfully his. Pity the London merchant who has to deal with him.[14]

THE EMPIRE'S FACE

WASHINGTON'S MAN in London was Robert Cary, head of Cary & Company, one of the city's largest and most successful mercantile houses. The Cary connection was another legacy of the Custis estate, since the firm had handled the business of Martha's first husband, as well as her own business during her brief time as a widow. One of Washington's earliest letters to Cary set the tone and defined the subsequent direction of the relationship. He complained about the price his first tobacco shipment received and about the multiple charges for shipping, insurance, and freight, plus Cary's own commission. This was not the kind of arrangement that Washington had expected, and from the very start he threatened to take his business elsewhere. "I shall be candid in telling you," he warned, "that duty to the Charge with which I am entrusted as well as self Interest will incline me to abide by those who gives the greatest proof of their Abilities."[15]

His reference to "the Charge with which I am entrusted" did not just mean his patriarchal responsibility for Martha, Jackie, and Patsy. It also meant the Custis estate, three plantations totaling eighteen thousand acres spread out along the York River in the Tidewater region of Virginia, lands that were worked by more than two hundred, eventually nearly three hundred, slaves. His marriage to Martha made Washington the legal owner of one-third of these "dower plantations," and his status as legal guardian of her children made him responsible for managing the other two-thirds. Mount Vernon may have been his signature statement as a new member of the planter elite, but the Custis plantations in the Tidewater, devoted almost entirely to tobacco, produced the bulk of his cash crop.[16]

And it was the size of his annual tobacco production that made him eligible for the services of Cary & Company. Smaller growers, and by the middle of the eighteenth century the majority of Virginia planters, sold their crops to domestic buyers and purchased most of their consumer goods locally. But the planters with the largest estates, those at the very top of the social pyramid, preferred the consignment system, whereby they consigned or entrusted sale of their crop to mercantile houses in England. At least theoretically, this arrangement assured the highest price for one's crop. But the greatest advantage of the consignment system was the access it offered to London's shops and stores.

A consumer revolution was brewing in England, producing newly affordable commodities like Wedgwood china for a burgeoning middle-class market. By consigning his tobacco crop to

Robert Cary, Washington was joining the elite within the Virginia elite, who could wear the latest English fashions and, in their own provincial world, consume just as conspicuously as members of polite society back at the metropolitan center of the empire in London. A letter from Washington to Cary conveys the flavor of the enterprise: "Mrs. Washington would take it as a favor, if you would direct Mrs. Shelby to send her a fashionable Summer Cloak & Hatt, a black silk apron . . . and a pair of French bead Earings and Necklace—and I should be obliged to you for sending me a dozen and a half Water Plates (Pewter) with my Crest engraved."[17]

Even more eloquent as testimonials to the spending frenzy going on at Mount Vernon were the invoices of goods that were boxed, crated, and shipped by Cary & Company during the early 1760s, when Washington was furnishing and embellishing the house. A veritable cascade of essentials and fineries came pouring in: dessert glasses by the dozen, a hogskin hunting saddle, a custom-made mahogany case filled with sixteen decanters, a 124-pound cheese, sterling silver knives and forks with ivory handles, satin bonnets, custard cups, snuff, felt hats, engraved stationery, wineglasses by the score, prints of foxhunts in the English countryside, even six bottles of Greenough's Tincture with accompanying sponge brushes to clean Washington's notoriously bad teeth. In an average year Washington ordered more than £300 worth of goods from Cary & Company. And this did not include his expenses for new slaves and adjoining land. Modern dollar equivalencies are impossible to calculate with any precision, but a rough estimate would place his spending during five years in the early 1760s in the range of two to three million dollars.[18]

Gradually, it began to dawn on Washington that he was running through his entire Custis inheritance. In 1763 he rejected a request for a loan from an old army friend, explaining that his Mount Vernon expenses had "swallowed up before I knew where I was, all the money I got by marriage nay more." But he was truly stunned the following year when Cary apprised him that his account was more than £1,800 in arrears, a debt that was only going to increase once Cary began charging 5 percent interest annually on the principal. Washington was caught in the trap that was snaring so many other Virginia planters and that Thomas Jefferson, another victim, described as the chronic condition of indebtedness, which then became "hereditary from father to son for many generations, so that the planters were a species of property annexed to certain mercantile houses in London." In Jefferson's version of the sad syndrome, once a planter crossed the line, it was virtually impossible to recover: "If a debt is once contracted by a farmer, it is never paid but by a sale," meaning bankruptcy proceedings.[19]

Washington's initial reaction to Cary's horrible news was the farmer's perennial lament: bad luck and bad weather. Then he began to question Cary about the tobacco market. He understood that markets fluctuated, almost by definition. But why was it that swings in the market always seemed to go against his interest? And why was it that the price he received for his tobacco stayed low while the prices he paid for Cary's shipments kept going up? He had been complaining about both the quality and the cost of the imported goods from the beginning—the linens wore out in a few months, the nails were brittle, the shoes fell apart after a few wearings, the clothes never fit—but now he accused Cary of deliberately selling him inferior goods and hiking the price by 20 percent because he was a mere American colonist, who presumably was too ignorant to know the difference. He also claimed that Cary and his kind sold him outdated items "that could only be used by our forefathers in the days of yore" instead of the fashionable styles requested. The goods shipped to him, in short, were inferior because Cary regarded him as inferior, a provincial rube, a soft touch, another one of those vapid and vacant Virginia grandees.[20]

The more Washington thought about it, the more he concluded that no amount of diligence on his part, no spell of excellent weather, no favorable fluctuations in the tobacco market, could combine to pull him out of debt, because the mercantile system itself was a conspiracy designed to assure his dependency on the likes of Cary. When Washington thought of that abstract thing called the "British Empire," he did not think politically, envisioning the Hanoverian kings and the members of Parliament. He thought economically. The face he saw was Robert Cary's. And he did not trust him.

Was Washington's diagnosis of his predicament correct? As far as Robert Cary is concerned, all the evidence suggests that he was an honest merchant who provided his Virginia clients with fair market value for their tobacco, charged them appropriately for their purchases, and did not smuggle excessive charges into his invoices. What's more, historians of the planter class in Virginia have documented the inherent difficulties of growing tobacco as a cash crop. From the very origins of the colony, skeptical observers were troubled by an economy built on smoke and a plant that seemed to possess a unique capacity to deplete the fertility of the soil. More recently, economic historians have called attention to the vagaries of the tobacco market in Europe, chiefly because of

Spanish production of cheap tobacco which drove down prices. And most recently, social historians have targeted the lavish lifestyles of the Virginia planters, which combined a blissful obliviousness to the proverbial bottom line with an apparently irresistible urge to imitate the styles and consumption levels of the English gentry.[21]

On the other hand, the consignment system, by its very definition, **did** place Washington's economic fate entirely in Cary's hands, providing him with total control over the price Washington got for his tobacco, the cost and quality of all the goods he received in return, and the debits and credits to Washington's account, as well as the separate accounts kept for Jackie and Patsy based on their Custis inheritance. All the risks of weather, spoilage, market fluctuations, and shipping mishaps fell on Washington's side of the ledger. All the leverage lay with Cary. Every time one of the invoices from Cary & Company arrived at Mount Vernon, it served as a stark statement of Washington's dependence on invisible men in faraway places for virtually his entire way of life. If the core economic problem was tobacco, the core psychological problem was control, the highest emotional priority for Washington, which, once threatened, set off internal alarms that never stopped ringing.

By sheer coincidence, in the fall of 1765, just as
Washington was grappling with the bad news
from Cary and his own response to it, the much-
despised Stamp Act was scheduled to go into
effect in Virginia. This provocative piece of legislation, Parliament's first effort to impose a direct
tax on the colonies in order to help defray the
costs of managing its expanding empire, generated widespread opposition throughout Virginia
and all the American colonies. Washington was
not an active participant in the debate, but he was
a strongly supportive witness for the opposition.
"The Stamp Act Imposed on the Colonies by the
Parliament of Great Britain engrosses the conversation of the Speculative part of the Colonists," he
observed, "who look upon this unconstitutional
method of Taxation as a doleful Attack upon their
Liberties & loudly exclaim against the Violation."
But while most outspoken opponents of the
Stamp Act, those whom Washington called "the
Speculative part," emphasized the constitutional
argument, his response more directly reflected his
personal experience with Cary & Company. Such
"ill judged Measures" as the Stamp Act, he suggested, were likely to have the ironic but salutary
effect of reducing American dependence on
British imports: "And the Eyes of our People—
already beginning to open—will perceive that

many Luxuries which we lavish our substance to Great Britain for, can well be dispens'd with while the necessaries of Life are mostly to be had within ourselves." Others could make the legal arguments about taxation and representation. Washington's thinking, conditioned by his personal experience with the practical operation of the British Empire, moved instinctively to the much more palpable issue of economic independence.[22]

He also chose to act in a direct and personal fashion to recover his own independence from Cary & Company. Starting in 1766, he abandoned tobacco as his cash crop at Mount Vernon, one of the first of the major Virginia planters to make the change. From now on he would grow wheat, construct his own mill to grind it into flour, and sell the flour in Alexandria and Norfolk. Nor was that all. He built his own schooner—or, rather, had slaves build it for him—to harvest the herring and shad of the Potomac and sell the fish locally or in the Caribbean. He eventually purchased a ship, which he christened **The Farmer,** to carry his flour, fish, and corn to such distant markets as Lisbon. Along the way, he developed a full-scale spinning and weaving operation at Mount Vernon to produce linen and wool fabric for workers' clothing. He was not completely free of tobacco, since it remained the chief crop in his Custis plantations. Nor was he completely free of

Cary & Company, which continued to fill annual orders for Washington until 1774, though usually for smaller shipments. Despite these lingering London dependencies, his preferred course after 1765 made it quite clear that this was a man determined to defy the pattern of indebtedness that swallowed up so much of the Virginia planter class, and hell-bent on freeing himself from the clutches of Robert Cary. If only in retrospect, he was already in personal rebellion against the slavish seductions of the British Empire.[23]

FACING WEST

IN THE FIRST renovation of Mount Vernon, completed in 1759, the main entrance was switched from the east to the west side of the mansion. There were architectural and landscaping reasons for the change, to be sure, but the symbolism of the switch, from an eastward to a westward facing, accurately expressed one of Washington's deepest convictions; namely, that the future lay in those wild and wooded lands of the Ohio Country that he had explored and fought over as a young man. Gaining control of the vast American interior, after all, had been the central achievement of the French and Indian War, at least as Washington understood it. When John Posey, one of his foxhunting companions, complained about the impoverished condition of his own debt-ridden plantation, Washington urged him to abandon his eastern prejudices and make a fresh start: "there is a large Field before you," he explained, "an opening prospect in the back Country for Adventurers . . . where an enterprising Man with very little Money may lay the foundation of a Noble Estate in the New Settlements upon Monongahela for himself and posterity." Even while ensconced on the eastern edge of the continent at Mount Vernon, Washington spent a good deal of his time and energy dreaming and scheming about virgin land over the western horizon.[24]

The dreaming received considerable inspiration when Washington looked out his back door at the majestic view Mount Vernon afforded of the Potomac. Though it might seem bizarre to modern students of American geography, Washington shared the eighteenth-century version of "Potomac fever" that was especially virulent among Virginians, believing that the very river that flowed past his mansion provided the most direct access to the interior waterways of North America. The illusion probably derived its credibility from the long-standing claim that the western borders of the Old Dominion extended to the Mississippi, or even to the Pacific, producing a habit of mind that regarded Virginia as the gateway to the West. Washington embraced this illusion with passionate intensity—so did Jefferson—and starting in 1762 began joining and leading several organizations for improving navigation on the upstream sections of the river. The Potomac mythology stayed with him all his life. (It even played a significant role in the decision to locate the national capital on the Potomac in 1790.) His strenuous efforts yielded no practical results—the natural water route to the interior did not exist, and the man-made version, the Erie Canal, turned out to be in New York—but they did reveal where his thoughts were flowing.[25]

In 1763 he briefly turned his attention south to an undeveloped plot of ground rather ominously called the Dismal Swamp, which was a geological anomaly, a kind of Louisiana bayou mistakenly plopped down on the border of Virginia and North Carolina. He joined a group of ten investors, most members of the Virginia Council or House of Burgesses, who used their influence as insiders to purchase forty thousand acres of swampland that they proposed to drain and develop. Each investor also agreed to provide five slaves to do the draining and dredging. As with his Potomac improvements, nothing much came of this venture, though Washington held on to his four thousand acres until 1795. An aberration within his more enduring obsession with western land, the story of the Dismal Swamp Company does expose his voracious appetite for acreage of any and all sorts, along with his willingness to use political connections in Williamsburg to get what he wanted.[26]

But the big prize lay over the mountains. Washington's several initiatives to acquire tracts in the Ohio Country crisscrossed in dizzying patterns of speculation, and the jurisdictional problem created by border disputes between Virginia and Pennsylvania, the overlapping claims of different Indian tribes, and the shifting policies of the British government all enhanced the confusion. But at bottom lurked a basic conflict about the future of the Ohio Country: Washington believed it was open to settlement; the British government believed it was closed; and the Indians believed it was theirs.[27]

In 1763, George III issued a proclamation, in effect making the enormous region from the Great Lakes to the Gulf of Mexico and the Mississippi to the western slope of the Appalachians an Indian reservation, closed to Anglo-American settlers. From the beginning, Washington regarded the proclamation as a preposterous joke. "I can never look upon that Proclamation in any other light," he acknowledged, "than as a temporary expedient to quiet the minds of the Indians." He regarded the Indian tribes of the region as a series of holding companies destined to be displaced as the growing wave of white settlers flowed over the Alleghenies. There was nothing right or wrong about this development, as he saw it. It was simply and obviously inevitable. The Indians, under-standably and even justifiably, would resist. After all, they had dominated the region for several cen-turies. But they would lose, not because they were wrong, but because they were, or soon would be, outnumbered. (Later on, during his presidency, he would attempt to guarantee tribal control over Indian enclaves, his effort to make a moral state-ment amidst a relentlessly realistic diagnosis of the demographic facts.) And if the strategists in Lon-don chose to block this manifest destiny, they were either stupid, not understanding what the French and Indian War had won, or sinister, plot-ting to reserve the bounty of the American inte-rior for themselves, all the while confining the colonists to the Atlantic coastline.[28]

Washington's most grandiose western venture, called the Mississippi Land Company, was launched in 1763, the very year of George III's proclamation. Fifty investors requested propri-etary control over 2.5 million acres on both sides of the Ohio River. In 1765 the company retained a London agent to lobby the Privy Council and Parliament on behalf of their proposal, which envisioned nothing less than the creation of a

feudal kingdom in the Ohio Valley with the settlers as serfs and the owners as lords. The British
ministry not only rejected the proposal, claiming
such a grant would violate treaties recently signed
with the Iroquois and Cherokee, but then, in
1770, approved a similar request for 2.5 million
acres by a group of English investors to create a
whole new colony called Vandalia in the same
region. Washington wrote off his investment as a
loss in 1772, eventually describing the experience
as clear evidence of the British government's
"malignant disposition towards Americans."[29]

His singular triumph, in fact the result of multiple efforts over thirteen years of complex negotiations, was largely a product of his status as a
veteran of the French and Indian War. In 1754,
during the darkest days of the war, Governor Dinwiddie had issued a proclamation making available 200,000 acres of "bounty land" on the east
side of the Ohio River to Virginians who
answered the call. Moreover, the infamous Proclamation of 1763 had included one vaguely worded
provision, granting 5,000 acres apiece to former
officers who had served the cause. (The location
of the land was never made clear.) Washington
was relentless in pressing his claims according to
these two proclamations. He organized the veterans of the Virginia Regiment and led the political
fight in Williamsburg for patents on plots of land

bordering the Ohio and Great Kanawha Rivers in what are now southwestern Pennsylvania, southeastern Ohio, and northwestern West Virginia. In the fall of 1770 he personally led an exploratory surveying expedition to the Ohio and Great Kanawha, and the following year commissioned William Crawford, another veteran of the regiment, to complete the survey. He devised a scheme, eventually abandoned, to transport immigrants from Germany as indentured servants who would settle his own plots and thereby deter poachers. When that idea fizzled, he gave orders to purchase ten white servants, four of them convicts in the Baltimore jail, to occupy his land on the Great Kanawha. The total domain he claimed for himself, all choice bottomland, exceeded twenty thousand acres.[30]

There were two sour notes. The first came from several veterans, who believed that Washington's land was too choice, meaning that he had reserved the most fertile acreage bordering the rivers for himself and relegated the other claimants to less valuable plots. Washington effectively admitted the accusation was true, later acknowledging that he had taken "the cream of the country." But when one disgruntled veteran confronted him with the charge, it provoked a thunderous rebuke: "As I am not accustomed to receive such from any Man, nor would have taken the same language from you personally. . . . All my concerns is that I ever engag'd in behalf of so ungrateful & dirty a fellow as you are." As Washington saw it, he was the senior officer of the regiment who had almost single-handedly managed the entire operation to acquire the land. In effect, he deserved what he took. And everyone who questioned his integrity on any matter involving his own self-interest triggered internal explosions of seismic proportions.[31]

The other sour note came from Washington himself. As different governors in Virginia and different ministries in London came and went, different interpretations of British policy toward the American interior also came and went. The core issue was the Proclamation of 1763, which in one version rendered all of Washington's western claims null and void, all his time and energy wasted, because London had declared that the entire Ohio Country was off-limits to settlement. Washington, of course, regarded this version of British policy as a massive delusion that was also wholly unenforceable. The British monarch could proclaim whatever he wished, but the practical reality was that thousands of colonial settlers were swarming across the Alleghenies every year, establishing their claims, not by any legal appeal to colonial or British authority, but by the physical act of occupying and cultivating the land: "What

Inducements have Men to explore uninhabited Wilds but the prospect of getting good Lands?" he asked. "Would any Man waste his time, expose his Fortune, nay life, in search of this if he was to share the good and the bad with those that came after him. Surely no!" Washington believed there was a race going on for the bounty of half a continent. If he were to play by British rules, which refused to recognize the race was even occurring, others who ignored the rules would claim the bounty. His solution, elegantly simple, was to regard the restrictive British policies as superfluous and to act on the assumption that, in the end, no one could stop him.[32]

Several biographers have looked upon this extended episode of land acquisitions as an unseemly and perhaps uncharacteristic display of personal avarice, mostly because they are judging Washington against his later and legendary reputation for self-denial, or against some modern, guilt-driven standard for treatment of Native Americans. In fact, Washington's avid pursuit of acreage, like his attitude toward slavery, was rather typical of Virginia's planter class. He was simply more diligent in his quest than most. And his resolutely realistic assessment of the Indians' eventual fate was part and parcel of his instinctive aversion to sentimentalism and all moralistic brands of idealism, an instinct that deservedly won plaudits in later contexts, as disappointing as it was in this one.

Two more telling and less judgmental points have greater resonance for our understanding of the different ingredients that would shape Washington's character. The first is that he retained his youthful conviction that careers, fortunes, and the decisive developments in America's future lay in the West, on a continental stage so large and unexplored that no one fully fathomed its potential. This was a prize worth fighting for. The second is that the interest of the American colonies and the interest of the British Empire, so long presumed to be overlapping, were in fact mutually exclusive on this seminal issue. Constitutional niceties did not concern him. The more elemental reality was that the colonies needed to expand and grow, and the British government was determined to block that expansion and stifle that growth.

Once again there was a personal edge to that conviction. In 1774, Washington learned that Earl Hillsborough, secretary of state for the American colonies, had ruled that land grants to veterans of the French and Indian War promised in the Proclamation of 1763 would be restricted to British regulars. Washington greeted the news with contempt: "I conceive the services of a Provincial officer as worthy of reward as a regular one," he observed, "and can only be witheld from him with injustice." And since Hillsborough's decision was, as he put it, "founded equally in Malice, absurdity, & error," Washington felt no obligation to obey it. As far as the American West was concerned, he was already declaring his independence.[33]

A LAST RESORT

IF ONE were searching for early glimmerings of a broader belief in American independence, Washington's remarks about the Stamp Act—a clear and unequivocal denial of Parliament's authority to tax the colonies without their consent—might be offered up as evidence of his prescient premonitions as early as 1765. Such selective readings distort the larger pattern, however, which suggests that neither Washington nor any other colonist was thinking seriously about seceding from the British Empire at this early stage. Washington expressed his relief that the British government had come to its senses, in part because of pressure from merchants like Robert Cary, and repealed the Stamp Act in 1766. He seemed unconcerned about the lingering constitutional question of Parliament's authority, presumably believing that as long as it remained theoretical it could and would be completely ignored. "All therefore who were instrumental in procuring the repeal," he wrote Cary, "are entitled to the Thanks of every British Subject." He still considered himself such a creature. The wave, it seemed, had passed safely under the ship.[34]

For the next three years, from 1766 to 1769, Washington's mind remained focused on more proximate and pressing problems: cultivating his new wheat crop; worrying about Patsy's health; lobbying in Williamsburg for the "bounty lands" in the Ohio Country. He was not even present at the session of the House of Burgesses in April 1768 when the delegates protested the Townshend Act, a clever (ultimately too clever) measure imposing new duties on colonial imports which the British ministry claimed were not, strictly speaking, taxes. Over the next year, he did not participate in the public debate that raged in Virginia and that produced non-importation schemes in Massachusetts and New York.[35]

Then, in April 1769, he entered the debate in a major and quite distinctive way. In a letter to George Mason, his neighbor down the road at Gunston Hall, Washington began to use the language of a prospective revolutionary: "At a time when our Lordly Masters in Great Britain will be satisfied with nothing less than the deprevation of American freedom," he wrote, "it seems highly

necessary that something shou'd be done to avert
the stroke and maintain the liberty which we have
derived from our Ancestors." Petitions and
remonstrances to the king or Parliament, he
believed, were ineffectual. They had been tried
before without success. And their plaintive character irritated Washington, because it seemed to
reinforce the sense of subordination and sub-
servience the colonists were protesting against and
that he found so personally offensive. The only
sensible course, he argued, was a comprehensive
program of non-importation that, "by starving
their Trade & manufacturers," would exert pressure on the British government to alter its course,
as it had done after the Stamp Act. But if the
"Lordly masters in Great Britain" persisted in
their imperious policies—and here, for the first
time, Washington did glimpse the future—then
the two sides were on a collision course that could
only end in war, which he called "a dernier
resort."

Then he added a revealing corollary, very much
rooted in his own experience with Cary & Company:

That many families are reduced almost, if not
quite, to penury & want, from the low ebb of
their fortunes, and Estates selling for the discharge of Debts, the public papers furnish but

too many melancholy proofs of. And that a scheme of this sort [i.e., non-importation] will contribute more effectually than any other I can devise to immerge [remove?] the Country from the distress it at present labours under, I do most firmly believe, it can be generally adopted.

In other words, a collective decision to stop purchasing British commodities would enforce a level of discipline and austerity on the Virginia planter elite that most of its members—and, truth be known, he himself—had shown themselves unable to enforce voluntarily. While such a scheme risked a collision course with the British Empire, it reduced the risk that so many Virginia planters were running of remaining on a collision course with bankruptcy. Washington was not just drawing on his own deep contempt toward English presumptions of superiority; he was also urging Virginians to embrace the same economic self-sufficiency he had decided to implement at Mount Vernon. This was the moment when Washington first began to link the hard-earned lessons that shaped his own personality to the larger cause of American independence.[36]

It was also the occasion when Washington first played a leadership role in the House of Burgesses on an issue that transcended local election disputes or veterans' claims. On May 18, 1769, he presented the proposal calling for a colony-wide boycott of enumerated English manufactured goods, to include a cessation of the slave trade. George Mason had actually drafted the proposal, but he could not present it himself because his long-standing reluctance to leave the secure confines of Gunston Hall meant that he refused to stand for election to the House of Burgesses. This was an important moment in Washington's public career, for he now became an acknowledged leader in the resistance movement within Virginia's planter class. Back at Mount Vernon in July he wrote to Cary, ordering only a few new items, saying that he intended to observe the terms of the boycott "religiously," but giving Cary final approval, oddly enough, of what to include or exclude.[37]

There was then, in the strange way that history happens, a five-year hiatus. Though Washington himself observed the terms of the boycott "religiously," as he put it again to Cary, the Virginia Association proved as difficult to enforce as Great Britain had found the mercantile empire to regulate. Most importantly, Parliament had repeated its backpedaling pattern after the Stamp Act, this time disavowing all the Townshend duties except the one on tea, it being intended to remain as the principled symbol of British authority. Most observers, Washington included, believed that the wave had once again passed under the ship.

The next surge began in the summer of 1774, in response to parliamentary legislation the colonists called the Intolerable Acts, which closed Boston's port and imposed martial law on Massachusetts as punishment for the orchestrated riot that came to be called the Boston Tea Party. Writing to George William Fairfax, who had moved back to England with Sally the previous year, Washington vowed that "the cause of Boston . . . ever will be considered as the cause of America (not that we approve their conduct in destroying the Tea.)" The escalation of British repression produced an equally dramatic escalation in Washington's thinking, or at least in the language he used to characterize British policy. In addition to his familiar themes—petitions were worse than worthless, abstract arguments must be accompanied by economic pressures—now he detected a full-blooded conspiracy against American liberty. "Does it not appear," he asked rhetorically, "as clear as the sun in its meridian brightness, that there is a regular, systematic plan formed to fix the right and practice of taxation upon us?" In a long letter to Bryan Fairfax, George William's half brother, he repeated the conspiracy charge, then added the provocative argument that, unless the colonies stood together against this challenge, Great Britain would "make us as tame, & abject Slaves, as the Blacks we rule over with such arbitrary Sway."[38]

The slavery analogy is startling, both because of its stark depiction of the power emanating from London, and because its potency and credibility grew directly out of Washington's personal familiarity with the exercise of just such power over his own slaves. During the American Revolution several English commentators called attention to the hypocrisy of slave owners wrapping their cause in the rhetoric of liberty. In Washington's case, the rhetoric was heartfelt precisely because he understood firsthand the limitless opportunity for abuse once control was vested in another. He did not see himself as a hypocrite so much as a man determined to prevent the cruel ways of history from happening to him.

His belief that a British conspiracy was afoot serves as an almost textbook example of the radical Whig ideology that historians have made the central feature of scholarship on the American Revolution for the past forty years. These historians have discovered a cluster of ideas about the irreconcilable tension between liberty and power that English dissenters, called "the Country Party," hurled at the Hanoverian court and the inordinately long-standing ministry of Robert

Walpole in the middle third of the eighteenth century. There is now a well-established consensus that many prominent American revolutionary thinkers, including John Adams, Thomas Jefferson, and George Mason, were familiar with the writings of such English Whigs as John Trenchard, Thomas Gordon, and Viscount Bolingbroke, and that their response to Parliament's legislative initiative in the 1760s was at least partially shaped by what they read about the inherently corrupt and conniving character of British government as depicted by the Country Party.[39]

There is some reason to believe that Washington's political vocabulary grew in this more radical direction because of increased interaction with Mason in the summer of 1774. Mason was generally regarded as Virginia's most learned student of political theory, well versed in all the Whig writers. He and Washington conferred several times in July as Mason was drafting the Fairfax Resolves, which also warned of a concerted British plan to make all colonists into slaves and imposed the dramatic dichotomy of English corruption and American virtue over all its recommendations. Washington actually chaired the meeting in Alexandria where the Fairfax Resolves were adopted. (The most important recommendation was for convening a Continental Congress to approve a comprehensive boycott of British imports.) Washington's escalating rhetoric, in short, probably reflected the intensive collaboration with Mason, who provided him with instruction on the language of radical Whig ideology.[40]

Interestingly, Washington himself acknowledged that he was an unsophisticated student of history and English politics, and that "much abler heads than my own, hath fully convinced me that it [current British policy] is not only repugnant to natural right, but Subversive of the Laws & Constitution of Great Britain itself." But he placed the emphasis for his radical evolution elsewhere, indeed inside himself: "an Innate Spirit of freedom first told me," he explained, "that the Measures which [the] Administration hath for sometime been, and now are, most violently pursuing, are repugnant to every principle of natural justice."[41]

While we cannot know, at least in the fullest and deepest sense, where that voice inside himself originated, it does seem to echo the resentful voice of the young colonel in the Virginia Regiment, bristling at the condescending ignorance of Lord Loudoun and the casual rejection of his request for a regular commission in the British army. It harks back to the voice of the master of Mount Vernon, lured by Cary & Company (and, truth be told, his own urge to replicate the lifestyle of an English country gentleman) into a mercantile system apparently designed to entrap him in a spiraling network of debt. (Indeed, less than a year earlier, in November 1773, when he had instructed Cary to pay off the remainder of his debt with funds from Patsy's inheritance, Cary had refused, correctly claiming that the two accounts were not transferable.) The voice also resonates with the same outraged frustration he felt whenever some distant and faceless British official, the most recent version of the vile breed being Earl Hillsborough, blocked his claim for western lands, allegedly to protect Indian rights but more probably, he believed, to reserve the land for London cronies.

All of which is to suggest that Washington did not need to read books by radical Whig writers or receive an education in political theory from George Mason in order to regard the British military occupation of Massachusetts in 1774 as the latest installment in a long-standing pattern. His own ideological origins did not derive primarily from books but from his own experience with what he had come to regard as the imperiousness of the British Empire. Mason probably helped him to develop a more expansive vocabulary to express his thoughts and feelings, but the thoughts, and even more so the feelings, had been brewing inside him for more than twenty years. At the psychological nub of it all lay an utter loathing for any form of dependency, a sense of his own significance, and a deep distrust of any authority beyond his direct control.

He spent the first week of August in Williamsburg at the Virginia Convention, called to select seven delegates to the Continental Congress. When all the votes were counted, he came in third, just behind Richard Henry Lee and comfortably ahead of Patrick Henry. The vote was a measure of his growing stature as a stalwart, coolheaded leader of the protest movement in Virginia. (As one of his ablest biographers put it, his fellow burgesses knew that Henry could be counted on to say the magnificent thing, whereas Washington could be counted on to say little, but do the right thing.) Off he then went to Philadelphia, where he performed according to form: silent during the debates but thoroughly dedicated to opposing the Intolerable Acts and supporting a rigorous Continental Association against British imports.[42]

While in Philadelphia he received a letter from Robert McKenzie, a veteran of the Virginia Regiment who had subsequently obtained a commission in the British army, warning him that the colonial cause was hopeless, that "all the best characters" were on the other side. Since Washington regarded himself as a charter member of that exclusive club, he diplomatically questioned

McKenzie's assessment, then offered his own best guess at where history was headed: "more blood will be spilt on this occasion (if the Ministry are determined to push matters to an extremity) than history has ever yet furnished instances of in the annals of North America." Before he left town he purchased a new sash and epaulets for his military uniform, inquired about the price of muskets, and ordered a book by Thomas Webb entitled **A Military Treatise on the Appointments of the Army.** Though he still hoped it could be avoided, he was preparing for the last resort.[43]

THE SELF-EVIDENT EXCEPTION

ONCE BACK at Mount Vernon his mind moved along two separate tracks. While a political crisis of enormous magnitude was obviously in the air, there had been crises before, and each time the British government had stepped back from the precipice. Although newspaper reports were hardly encouraging, with some suggesting that George III had ordered his European ambassadors to regard the American colonies as already in a state of rebellion, Washington remained cautiously optimistic that cooler heads in London would again prevail. "There is reason to believe," he explained in February 1775, that "the Ministry would willingly change their ground, from a conviction the forcible measures will be inadequate to the end designed." Now at any rate was not the time for rash or provocative decisions. "A little time must now unfold the mystery," he cautioned, "as matters are drawing to a point."[44]

Washington chose to use that time to recover familiar rhythms. He chaired meetings of the Potomac Company, where fifty "Negro Men" were hired to dredge the upper reaches of the river. He worked extensively on settling business associated with the now empty Fairfax estate at Belvoir. He outfitted a new expedition to occupy and develop his large tract of land on the Great Kanawha, this despite the fact that Lord Dunmore, the new governor of Virginia, apprised him that all his surveys of the land in the Ohio Country had been voided. Even more defiantly, he decided to go forward with another major renovation of Mount Vernon, the one that gave the mansion the size and style we recognize today. The decisions to pursue his land claims and renovate Mount Vernon on the cusp of an imperial crisis seem to suggest more than a guarded hope that the crisis would pass. They constitute a personal statement that his own agenda would not be dictated by men he had contemptuously described as those "Lordly Masters in Great Britain."[45]

The other track, just the opposite of his defiant recovery of routine, led toward war and what turned out to be destiny. During the winter and spring of 1775, county militia units, calling themselves "independent companies," were being organized throughout the colony. As Virginia's most famous war hero, Washington was the obvious choice as commander, and by March five independent companies had invited him to lead them. Also in March, a second Virginia Convention was called, this time in Richmond, and ordered that the colony "be immediately put into a posture of Defence." This was the occasion when Patrick Henry gave his famous "liberty or death" speech, but it also marked the moment when military preparation replaced political argumentation in Virginia as the highest priority. With that change, Washington succeeded orators like Henry as the most crucial figure. In the balloting to select delegates to the Second Continental Congress he received 106 of the 108 votes cast.[46]

Throughout April and May, Mount Vernon became the unofficial headquarters for planning Virginia's response to the burgeoning crisis and Washington became the acknowledged central player. One small event captured the headiness of the times, as well as Washington's emerging role as the singular, soon to become transcendent, leader.

Mason had drafted a proposal for the Fairfax Independent Company, recommending that all officers be elected annually and rotate between officer and enlisted status on a regular basis. The notion that an army should be organized democratically was a truly radical suggestion, and one that Washington himself regarded as ridiculous, but Mason coupled his proposal with a corollary designed to disarm critics who doubted that such an arrangement could ever work: namely, that Washington would be the exception to the rotation principle, thereby providing the enduring stability required. As Mason put it, "the exception made in favor of the gentleman who by the unanimous vote of the company now commands it, is a very proper one, justly due to his public merit and experience . . . , peculiarly suited to our circumstances, as was dictated, not by compliment, but conviction." It was a prophetic premonition of Washington's abiding role throughout his subsequent career as the elite exception that proved the egalitarian rule.[47]

The late spring of 1775 was an intense time for both American independence and the public career of George Washington, a crowded moment when a great deal of history happened quickly, when events dictated decisions that in turn determined the direction of an emerging nation and the character of its preeminent hero. For all those reasons, this is an extended moment worth lingering over, searching through the dizzying details of the story for at least the outline of answers to the three most salient questions: First, when did Washington conclude that war with Great Britain was inevitable? Second, how and why was Washington singled out to lead what soon became known as the Continental army? And third, what was Washington's response, not just publicly, but personally, to this assignment?

The answer to the first question is reasonably if not perfectly clear. When the British troops occupied Boston in 1774, Washington believed an important line had been crossed. After that date, war became a distinct possibility that could only be avoided if the British ministry altered its course. Over the course of the following year, as the evidence mounted that George III and his ministers fully intended to make Massachusetts an object lesson of where sovereign power resided within the British Empire, Washington believed that war had become a probability. When he departed Mount Vernon for Philadelphia on May 4, 1775, he took along his military uniform, both a sign and a statement of his aggressive intentions.

But the truly clinching evidence came in mid-May, when reliable news of the actions at Lexington and Concord reached Philadelphia, along with reports from London that a major British force was on the way to support General Thomas Gage's beleaguered garrison in Boston. As he wrote to George William Fairfax in London, Washington's mind was made up: "Unhappy it is though to reflect, that a Brother's Sword has been sheathed in a Brother's breast, and that, the once happy and peaceful plains of America are either to be drenched with Blood, or Inhabited by Slaves. Sad alternative! But can a virtuous Man hesitate in this choice?" His cash accounts for early June show purchases of a tomahawk, several cartouch boxes, new coverings for his holsters, and five books on the military art. He was preparing to go to war.[48]

But how was he selected to lead the entire American army? That question has provoked a lively debate across several generations of biographers and historians. In his autobiographical recollection of the decision, John Adams claimed the lion's share of credit for choosing Washington, suggesting that he overruled the New England delegation in the Continental Congress, which had presumed that one of their own would be chosen because the current battle was raging around Boston. Adams's claim is almost surely a self-serving piece of mischief designed to exaggerate his own influence; it obscures the more elemental fact that, once the members of the Congress realized that they were facing a military as well as political crisis, the selection of Washington as the military commander was a foregone conclusion. In fact, at that confused and highly improvisational moment within the Congress, more delegates could agree that Washington should lead the American army than that there should be an American army at all. His unanimous elevation to the position as commander in chief actually preceded the creation of a national military force that he could command.[49]

Why did the choice seem so obvious? The short answer is that the appointment of a Virginian was politically essential in order to assure the allegiance of the most populous and wealthiest colony to the cause, and Washington was unquestionably the most eligible and qualified Virginian. Another short answer, subsequently offered by Adams as a joke, was that Washington was always selected by deliberative bodies to lead, whatever the cause, because he was always the tallest man in the room. Even as a joke, however, Adams was making a serious point that a veritable legion of his contemporaries made, especially upon first meeting Washington; namely, that he was physically majestic. As Benjamin Rush, the Philadelphia physician and staunch revolutionary, put it: "He has so much martial dignity in his deportment that you would distinguish him to be a general and a soldier from among ten thousand people." First impressions and appearances are often described as misleading, but in Washington's case they established the favorable initial context for all subsequent judgments. In the highly charged atmosphere of the Continental Congress, where nervous men—all prominent figures in their own respective colonies—tended to talk too much, Washington's sheer physicality made his reserve and customary silence into a sign of strength and sagacity.[50]

Looking backward from June 1775, with all the advantage of hindsight, one can see it coming. During the sessions of the Congress in May, Washington was the only delegate to attend in military uniform and was asked to chair four committees charged with military readiness. (In the First Continental Congress he had been given no committee assignments at all.) When he approached Philadelphia in his custom-built chariot in early May, a throng of five hundred riders escorted him into the city, a tribute accorded no other delegate. Nearly a year earlier, at the First Continental Congress, he had been the beneficiary of a widely circulated rumor that Adams recorded in his diary: "Coll Washington made the most eloquent Speech at the Virginia Convention that ever was made. Says he, 'I will raise 1000 Men, Subsist them at my own Expence, and march myself at their Head for the Relief of

Boston.' " This was a complete fabrication. Washington had made no such speech, in fact had made no speech at all. But the mythology was already starting to build. As the need intensified for a symbol of inter-colonial unity who could consolidate the disparate and even chaotic response of thirteen different colonies to the British military threat, he satisfied the requirements visually and politically more completely than anyone else.[51]

Finally, what was going on inside Washington's own mind and heart? His diary entries for June 15 and June 16, respectively the day he was appointed and the day he delivered his brief acceptance speech to Congress, are characteristically unhelpful, telling us only where he dined and spent his evenings. The speech itself makes two distinctive points: that he did not feel qualified for the position, and that he would serve without pay. Here is the most revealing passage: "But lest some unlucky event should happen unfavourable to my reputation, I beg it may be remembered by every Gentn in the room, that I this day declare with the utmost sincerity, I do not think myself equal to the Command I (am) honoured with."[52]

One is tempted to read this kind of public modesty with a skeptical eye, as a ritualized statement of humility designed to demonstrate gentlemanly etiquette, rather than as a candid expression of what he truly felt. After all, Washington had been talked about as the leading candidate for the job of military commander for several weeks, had done nothing to discourage such talk, and had been wearing his uniform as a rather conspicuous statement of his candidacy. But in his private correspondence to his wife and brother Washington also described his appointment as "a trust too great for my capacity" and even claimed that he had done everything in his power to avoid it. He said much the same thing to his brother-in-law, Burwell Bassett:

> I am now Imbarked on a tempestuous Ocean from whence, perhaps, no friendly harbour is to be found. . . . It is an honour I wished to avoid. . . . I can answer but for three things, a firm belief of the justice of our Cause—close attention to the prosecution of it—and the strictest Integrity—If these cannot supply the places of Ability & Experience, the cause will suffer & more than probably my character along with it, as reputation derives its principal support from success.[53]

What, then, is going on here? It helps to recognize that Washington engaged in the same pattern of postured reticence on two subsequent occasions: when he agreed to chair the Constitutional Convention; and when he accepted the office of the presidency. In all three instances he denied any interest in the appointment, demeaned his own qualifications, and insisted that only a unanimous vote left him no choice but to accept the call. The pattern suggests he had considerable trouble acknowledging his own ambitions. His claim that he had no interest in the commander-in-chief post was not so much a lie as an essential fabrication that shielded him from the recognition that, within a Continental Congress filled with ambitious delegates, he was the most ambitious—not just the tallest—man in the room. He needed to convince himself that the summons came from outside rather than inside his own soul.

If Washington was playing hide-and-seek within himself on the question of his own ambition, he was being honest and realistic about his qualifications to lead the American army to victory. Though a battle-tested veteran, he had never commanded any unit larger than a regiment. He had no experience deploying artillery or maneuvering cavalry and no background whatsoever in the engineering skills required to construct defensive positions or conduct sieges. Compared to the British officers he was sure to face on the battlefield, he was a rank amateur. We do not know the specific titles of the military books he purchased before departing Philadelphia, but they repre-sented his effort to teach himself how to organize an army. The misgivings he expressed in the wake of his appointment, then, were not affectations of false humility, but rather rigorously realistic assessments during an intense moment of self-evaluation in which he was mercilessly honest about his prospects for success. While everyone around him was caught up in patriotic declara-tions about the moral supremacy of the American cause, Washington remained immune to the inflated rhetoric, keenly aware that a fervent belief in the worthiness of a crusade was no guarantee of its ultimate triumph.

And he was right. For the larger truth was that no one was qualified to lead an American army to victory, because the odds against such an outcome appeared overwhelming. No matter how glorious the cause, the prospects of thirteen disparate and contentious colonies defeating the most powerful army and navy in the world were remote in the extreme. It would take almost exactly a year before Thomas Jefferson would draft the document in which the delegates in the Continental Congress pledged "our lives, our fortunes, and our sacred honor" on behalf of American independence. Washington fully recognized that by accepting the appointment as commander in chief he was making a personal pledge before anyone else. And if he failed in the high-stakes gamble, his Mount Vernon estate would be confiscated, his name would become a slur throughout the land, and his own neck would almost surely be stretched.[54]

If the decision to marry Martha Custis most shaped his own life, the decision to take command of the Continental army most shaped his place in history. He made it with his eyes open, with a realistic sense of how much was at stake and with a keen appreciation of what he was up against. In late June, as he was preparing to leave Philadelphia, his thoughts turned momentarily to those lands on the Great Kanawha which royal officials were attempting to deny him. If the military campaign floundered at the start, and he was able to avoid capture, that was the place to which he would flee, taking with him as many troops as he could salvage, holding out as a guerrilla band in wilderness terrain he knew so well and that no British army could conquer. If he was looking for omens, the first one was not encouraging. He assumed command of sixteen thousand militia outside Boston on July 3, 1775, the twenty-first anniversary of his ignominious defeat at Fort Necessity. This time he could not afford to lose.[55]

CHAPTER THREE

First in War

ALTHOUGH THERE WAS no way he could have known it at the time, Washington was assuming command of the army in the longest declared war in American history. He was forty-three years old when he rode out of Mount Vernon toward Philadelphia. He was fifty-one when he arrived back at Mount Vernon on Christmas Eve, 1783, the most famous man in the world. He started his odyssey with the presumption that he was fighting a war for American independence, nothing more and nothing less. He ended it with the realization that the war for independence had become the American Revolution. Which is to say that the cause he headed had not only smashed two British armies and destroyed the first British Empire, it had also set in motion a political movement committed to principles that were destined to topple the monarchical and aristocratic dynasties of the Old World.

The American Revolution was the central event in Washington's life, the crucible for his development as a mature man, a prominent statesman, and a national hero. And while zealous students of the Civil War might contest the claim, the movement that Washington found himself heading was also the most consequential event in American history, the crucible within which the political personality of the United States took shape. In effect, the character of the man and the character of the nation congealed and grew together during an extended moment of eight years. Washington was not clairvoyant about history's next destination. But he did realize from the start that, wherever history was headed, he and America were going there together.

With only a few exceptions—his conferences with the Continental Congress, and his stopover at Mount Vernon on the way to Yorktown in the fall of 1781—Washington spent the entire war in the field with the Continental army. He was not, by any standard, a military genius. He lost more battles than he won; indeed, he lost more battles than any victorious general in modern history. Moreover, his defeats were frequently a function of his own overconfident and aggressive personality, especially during the early stages of the war, when he escaped to fight another day only because the British generals opposing him seemed choked with the kind of caution that, given his resources, Washington should have adopted as his own strategy. But in addition to being fortunate in his adversaries, he was blessed with personal qualities that counted most in a protracted war. He was composed, indefatigable, and able to learn from his mistakes. He was convinced that he was on the side of destiny—or, in more arrogant moments, sure that destiny was on his side. Even his critics acknowledged that he could not be bribed, corrupted, or compromised. Based on his bravery during several battles, he apparently believed he could not be killed. Despite all his mistakes, events seemed to align themselves with his own instincts. He began the war at the siege of Boston determined to deliver a decisive blow against more disciplined and battle-tested British regulars. He ended it at the siege of Yorktown doing precisely that.

One incident near the end of the war provides a clue to the transformation in his character wrought by the intense experience of serving so long as the singular embodiment of commitment to the cause. In 1781, Lund Washington reported that a British warship had anchored in the Potomac near Mount Vernon, presumably with orders to ravage Washington's estate. When the

British captain offered assurances that he harbored no hostile intentions, Lund sent out a boatload of provisions to express his gratitude for the captain's admirable restraint. When Washington learned of this incident he berated Lund: "It would have been a less painful circumstance to me, to have heard, that in consequence of your non-compliance with their request, they had burnt my House, and laid the Plantation in ruins." The estate he had spent so long building now paled in comparison to the reputation earned as the primal symbol of American independence. Lund Washington was protecting the interest of the foxhunting Virginia squire who had gone off to war. But that man, Washington was at pains to explain, had grown into something else.[1]

CAMBRIDGE PREVIEWS

THE STORY of the siege of Boston can be told in one sentence: Washington's makeshift army kept more than ten thousand British troops bottled up in the city for over nine months, at which point the British sailed away to Halifax. Less a battle than a marathon staring match, the conflict exposed the anomalous political circumstance created by the Continental Congress, which was prepared to initiate a war a full year before it was ready to declare American independence. Although Washington subsequently claimed that he knew by the early fall of 1775 that George III was determined to pursue a military rather than political solution to the imperial crisis, he went along with prevalent fiction that the British garrison in Boston contained "Ministerial Troops," meaning that they did not represent the king's wishes so much as the policy of his evil and misguided ministers. And although he eventually expressed his frustration with the moderate faction in the Continental Congress, who were "still feeding themselves upon the dainty food of reconciliation," Washington also recognized that the radical faction, led by John Adams, needed to exhaust all the diplomatic alternatives and patiently wait for public opinion outside New England to mobilize around the novel notion of American independence.[2]

But if the siege of Boston was more an anomalous preliminary than the main event, it was also Washington's debut as commander in chief. Here, for the first time, he encountered the logistical challenges he would face during the ensuing years of the war. He met many of the men who would comprise his general staff for the duration. And here he demonstrated both the strategic instincts and the leadership skills that would sustain him, and sometimes lead him astray, until the glorious end. The Cambridge encampment, then, was a preview of some tumultuous coming attractions.

Events of enduring significance occurred before Washington arrived at Cambridge. On June 17, 1775, about 2,200 British troops made three frontal assaults on New England militia units entrenched on Breed's Hill. Later misnamed the Battle of Bunker Hill, the fight was a tactical victory for the British, but at the frightful cost of more than one thousand casualties, nearly half the attacking force. When word of the battle reached London, several British officers observed caustically that a few more such victories and the entire British army would be annihilated. On the American side, Bunker Hill was regarded as a great moral triumph that reinforced the lesson of Lexington and Concord; namely, that militia volunteers fighting for a cause they freely embraced could defeat disciplined British mercenaries. Several newspaper stories made the connection between Braddock's defeat at the Monongahela and Bunker Hill, which seemed to suggest that the very man who had once rescued the redcoats could now lead inspired American amateurs to a quick and easy victory by mobilizing their superior virtue against plodding professionals.[3]

Two seductive illusions were converging here. The first was the perennial belief harbored by both sides at the start of most wars that the conflict would be short. The second, which became the central myth of American military history, was that militia volunteers fighting for principle made better soldiers than trained professionals. Washington was not completely immune to the first illusion, though his version of a quick American victory depended on the willingness of Commander Gage's replacement, General William Howe, to commit his force in a decisive battle outside Boston, in a repeat of the Bunker Hill scenario, which would then prompt the king's ministers to propose acceptable terms for peace. Neither Howe nor the British ministry was prepared to cooperate along these lines, and since the only acceptable peace terms on the American side—independence of Parliament's authority—was at this stage non-negotiable on the British side, even Washington's narrow hope had no realistic prospects.[4]

Washington was thoroughly immune to the second illusion about the innate superiority of militia. Based on his earlier experience as commander of the Virginia Regiment, reinforced by what he witnessed on a day-to-day basis at his Cambridge encampment, he became convinced that an army of short-term volunteers, no matter how dedicated to the cause, could not win the war. "To expect then the same service from Raw, and undisciplined Recruits as from Veteran

Soldiers," he explained, "is to expect what never did, and perhaps never will happen." His convictions on this score only deepened and hardened over the years, but from the start he believed that militia were only peripheral supplements to the hard core, which needed to be a professional army of disciplined troops who, like him, signed on for the duration. His model, in effect, was the British army. This, of course, was richly ironic, since opposition to a standing army had been a major source of colonial protest during the prewar years. To those who insisted that a militia army was more compatible with revolutionary principles, Washington was brutally frank: those principles can only flourish, he insisted, if we win the war, and that can only happen with an army of regulars.[5]

Another significant development occurred on his way to Cambridge, an event less conspicuous than the Battle of Bunker Hill but with even more far-reaching implications. Both the New York and the Massachusetts legislatures wrote congratulatory letters addressed to "His Excellency," which soon became his official designation for the remainder of the war. To be sure, "His Excellency" is not quite the same thing as "His Majesty," but throughout the summer and fall of 1775, even as delegates to the Continental Congress struggled to sustain the fiction that George III remained a friend to American liberty, poets and balladeers were already replacing the British George with an American version of the same name.[6]

In October 1775, the African-born slave and poet Phillis Wheatley sent Washington her lyrical tribute, which concluded: "A crown, a mansion, and a throne that shine / With gold unfading, Washington! Be thine." (Washington wrote Wheatley to express his thanks, the only occasion in his correspondence when he directly addressed a slave.) The public disavowal of George III that Tom Paine launched with **Common Sense** in January 1776, and that Thomas Jefferson then made official in the Declaration of Independence the following July, destroyed George III as the singular symbol of authority for American subjects in the British Empire. The obvious, indeed the only personal replacement as the new symbol of authority for American citizens in the nascent yet-to-be-named nation, was Washington. Unlike European monarchs, the source of his authority was neither biological nor spiritual (i.e., divine right), but rather the purity of his revolutionary credentials. He was not an accident of blood; he had chosen and had been chosen. When General Gage questioned the legitimacy of his rank, Washington responded in a letter that was widely circulated in the American press: "You affect, Sir, to despise all Rank not derived from the same Source with your own. I cannot conceive any more honourable, than that which flows from that uncorrupted Choice of a brave and free People—the purest Source & original Fountain of all Power."[7]

This new semi-royal status fit in the grooves of his own personality and proved an enduring asset as important politically as the Custis inheritance had been economically. The man who was obsessed with control was now the designated sovereign of the American Revolution. The man who could not bear to have his motives or personal integrity questioned was assured that he enjoyed more trust than any American alive. The British would change commanding general four times; Washington was forever. Certain deficiencies in his character—aloofness, a formality that virtually precluded intimacy—were now regarded as essential by-products of his special status, indeed expressions of his inherent dignity. And the man who had bristled at the presumptive condescension of British officers and officials was now in charge of the military instrument designed to obliterate the British army and all vestiges of British power in North America. In sum, his new status as "His Excellency" gave him the starring role in a historical drama that seemed tailor-made for him.

On the other hand, the political and even psychological ramifications of his public role did require some personal adjustments. In August

1775 he made several critical comments about the lack of discipline in the New England militia units under his command and described New Englanders in general as "an exceedingly dirty & nasty people." As a mere Virginia planter such expressions of regional prejudice would have been unexceptional. But as the symbolic spokesman for what were still being called "the United Colonies," the comments created political firestorms in both the Massachusetts legislature and the Continental Congress. When Joseph Reed, a Philadelphia lawyer who served briefly as Washington's most trusted aide-de-camp, apprised him of the hostile reaction, Washington expressed his regrets for the indiscretion: "I will endeavor at a reformation, as I can assure you my dear Reed that I wish to walk in such a Line as will give most general Satisfaction." By nature a reserved and self-contained personality, Washington was discovering that his new public obligation to be all things to all men required him to suppress even the smallest residue of private opinion that might otherwise leak out. Several months later, when Reed reported that the gossip machines in the Continental Congress continued to produce whisperings about regional prejudice against New England, Washington again vowed "to make my conduct coincide with the wishes of Mankind as far as I can consistently." But it was not easy, even for him, to extinguish completely his personal thoughts and feelings. "I have often thought," he complained to Reed, "how much happier I should have been, if, instead of accepting of a command under such Circumstances I had taken my Musket upon my Shoulder & enterd the Ranks, or . . . had retir'd to the back Country, and livd in a Wig-wam."[8]

Even within what he called "my family," Washington needed to remain circumspect, because his family meant the staff and aides-de-camp at his headquarters. We know that Billy Lee, his mulatto servant, accompanied him on foot and on horseback at all times, brushed his hair and tied it in a queue every morning, but no record of their conversations has survived. We know that Martha joined him at Cambridge in January 1776, as she would at winter quarters during all subsequent campaigns, but their correspondence, which almost surely contained the fullest expression of personal opinion Washington allowed himself, for that very reason were destroyed after he died. The bulk of his correspondence during the war years, so vast in volume and officious in tone that modern-day readers risk mental paralysis, was written by his aides-de-camp. It is therefore the expression of an official, composite personality, usually speaking a platitudinous version of revolutionary rhetoric. For example, here are the General Orders for February 27, 1776, when Washington was contemplating a surprise attack on the British defenses: "it is a noble Cause we are engaged in, it is the Cause of virtue and mankind, every temporal advantage and comfort to us, and our posterity, depends upon the Vigour of our exertions; in short, Freedom or Slavery must be the result of our conduct, there can therefore be no greater Inducement to men to behave well." The inflated rhetoric concluded with the more candid warning that anyone attempting to retreat or desert "will be **instantly shot down.**"[9]

Aware of his own limited formal education, Washington selected college graduates who were "Pen-men" as aides, whose facility with language assured that the grammar and syntax of his correspondence was worthy of "His Excellency." His most trusted aides—Joseph Reed was the first, followed by Alexander Hamilton and John Laurens later in the war—became surrogate sons who enjoyed direct access to the general in after-dinner sessions, when Washington liked to encourage conversation as he ate nuts and drank a glass of Madeira. Part extended family and part court, these favored aides traded influence for total loyalty. "It is absolutely necessary therefore, for me to have persons that can think for me," Washington explained, "as well as execute Orders." The price for what he called his "unbounded confidence" was their equally unbounded service to his reputation. It was understood as a matter of honor that they would write no revealing memoirs after the war, and none of them did.

His other "family" was the cast of senior officers that assembled around him during the siege of Boston. Twenty-eight generals eventually served under Washington in the Continental army over the course of the war. Almost half of them were present at Cambridge in 1775–76. A full accounting of even that smaller group, interesting though it may be, would carry us down twisting side roads and astray of our proper objective, which is Washington himself. Four of Washington's chief lieutenants—Charles Lee, Horatio Gates, Nathanael Greene, and Henry Knox—provide the outline of the prevalent patterns that would shape his treatment of high-ranking subordinates.

Lee and Gates were both former officers in the British army with greater professional experience than Washington. Charles Lee was a colorful eccentric. The Mohawks had named him "Boiling Water" for his fiery temperament, which at Cambridge took the form of threats to place all deserters on a hill as targets within musket-shot of British pickets. Lee presumed a greater familiarity with Washington than other generals, addressing him as "My Dear General" rather than "His Excellency." He also questioned Washington's preferred strategy of engaging British regulars on their own terms in a European-style war, preferring guerrilla tactics and a greater reliance on militia. Lee also liked to make conspicuous displays of his irreverence toward military etiquette, was forever disheveled in his appearance, and was often seen conversing with his ever-present pack of dogs, again the exact opposite of Washington's dignified formality.

Horatio Gates was called "Granny Gates" because of his advanced age (he was fifty) and the wire-rimmed spectacles dangling from his nose. He cultivated a greater familiarity with his troops than Washington thought appropriate and, like Lee, favored a greater reliance on militia. Gates thought that Washington's plan for an assault on the British garrison in Boston was pure madness and, given his experience, felt free to speak out for a more defensive strategy in several councils of war. Both Lee and Gates ended up colliding with Washington later in the war and becoming early exhibits of the primal principle of revolutionary era politics: Cross Washington and you risk ruination.

Greene and Knox were both inexperienced amateurs drawn to military service by their zeal for American independence. Nathanael Greene was a Rhode Island Quaker, eventually called "the fighting Quaker," who was cast out of the Society of Friends because of his support for the war. He volunteered to serve in a local militia company, the Kentish Guards, at the rank of private, but ascended to brigadier general within a year on the basis of his obvious intelligence and disciplined dedication. By the end of the war, especially during the Carolina campaigns, he demonstrated strategic and tactical brilliance; he was Washington's choice as successor if the great man went down in battle. At Cambridge, however, Greene was described as "the rawest, the most untutored being" and placed himself squarely beneath Washington's authority as an aspiring general officer.

Henry Knox was also a gifted amateur, a Boston bookseller well read in engineering whom Washington plucked from the ranks to head an artillery regiment. He demonstrated his resourcefulness in December 1775 by transporting the British cannon captured at Ticonderoga over the ice and snow on forty sleds driven by eighty yoke of oxen to the Cambridge encampment. Like Greene, he worshipped the ground Washington walked on. Both Greene and Knox were subsequently showered with glory, Knox living on to become Washington's secretary of war in the 1790s.[10]

The pattern is reasonably clear. Washington recruited military talent wherever he could find it, and he had a knack for discovering ability in unlikely places and then allowing it to ride the

The earliest known portrait of Washington, wearing his old
uniform from the French and Indian War, painted by
Charles Willson Peale in 1772

A later portrait by Charles Willson Peale, done in Philadelphia in 1787 while Washington attended the Constitutional Convention

Two presidential portraits, both from life but each strikingly different in its depiction of the elder statesman.
ABOVE: by Rembrandt Peale, 1795;
OPPOSITE PAGE: by Gilbert Stuart, 1796

Realistic and romantic images of Washington.
ABOVE: the bust by Jean Antoine Houdon, based on the
life mask of 1785; BELOW: the Sears, Roebuck catalogue
cover by Norman Rockwell, 1932

The highly staged depiction of Washington crossing the
Delaware by Emanuel Leutze, wrong in most details, right in
its mood of heroic desperation, painted in 1851

The ill-fated attack on Chew House during the battle of
Germantown, as rendered by Howard Pyle in 1898

The case and decanters Washington purchased from Robert
Cary and found so outrageously expensive

An 1804 engraving of the piazza on the Potomac side of the mansion, where Washington liked to socialize with guests after dinner

Two final Washington projects. ABOVE: plans for the city of Washington, 1792; BELOW: the census of slaves at Mount Vernon in 1799, compiled while Washington drafted his will

same historical wave he was riding into the American pantheon. But he was extremely protective of his own authority. While he did not encourage sycophants, if dissenters ever broached their criticism out-of-doors, as both Lee and Gates ended up doing, he was usually unforgiving. One could make a plausible case, and several scholars have done so, that Washington's insistence on personal loyalty was rooted in his insecurity in the face of Lee's and Gates's superior military credentials. But the more compelling explanation is that he understood instinctively how power worked, and that his own quasi-monarchical status was indispensable to galvanize an extremely precarious cause. Moreover, as it turned out, his chief liability as a military strategist was not his sense of inferiority, but just the opposite. His special status as "His Excellency" fit him better than any of his old suits, and he was determined to protect it from tearing and shredding. Just as the standing army he sought to create contradicted the political principles it claimed to be fighting for, Washington's king-like status contradicted the potent anti-monarchical ethos in revolutionary ideology. In both cases, Washington acknowledged the incongruity but preferred victory to consistency.[11]

From the very start, however, he made a point of insisting that his expansive mandate was dependent upon, and subordinate to, the will of the American citizenry as represented in the Continental Congress. His letters to John Hancock, the first president of the Congress, always took the form of requests rather than demands. And he established the same posture of official deference toward the New England governors and provincial governments that supplied troops for his army. Washington did not use the term "civilian control," but he was scrupulous about acknowledging that his own authority derived from the elected representatives in the Congress. If there were two institutions that embodied the emerging nation to be called the United States—the Continental army and the Continental Congress—he insisted that the former was subordinate to the latter.[12]

In truth, important precedents were being established on the fly during this first year of the war, as both Washington and the leadership in the Congress improvised on the edge of the imperial crisis. What, for example, should one call the army? Before the term "Continental army" gained acceptance, the preferred term was the "Army of the United Colonies of North America." (The colonies had yet to become states, and the term "American," which had been used as an epithet by Englishmen to describe the provincial creatures on the western periphery of the British Empire, still retained its negative connotation.) When

Washington approved the design for a "union flag," it looked eerily similar to the Union Jack, so when first hoisted over Cambridge in January 1776 the British troops inside Boston cheered, thinking it signaled surrender. The first official manifestation of civilian control occurred in October 1775, when a delegation from the Continental Congress that included Benjamin Franklin met with Washington and his staff in Cambridge to approve troop requests for an army of 20,372 men.[13]

Strictly speaking, the Continental army did not exist until the start of the new year; until then, Washington was commanding a collection of provincial militia units whose enlistments ran out in December 1775. Politically speaking, the endorsement of Washington's troop requests by the Continental Congress was deceptively encouraging, since compliance depended upon approval by the respective state governments, which insisted that all recruits be volunteers and serve limited terms of no more than one year. And logistically speaking, the vaunted principles of state sovereignty, volunteerism, and limited enlistments—all expressions of revolutionary conviction—produced a military turnstile that bedeviled Washington throughout the war. Instead of a hard core of experienced veterans, the Continental army became a constantly fluctuating stream of amateurs, coming and going like tourists. "It is not in the pages of History, perhaps, to furnish a case like ours," Washington complained to Hancock, "to maintain a post within Musket Shot of the Enemy for Six Months together . . . and at the same time to disband one Army and recruit another, within that distance of twenty odd British regiments." The very term "Continental army," then, implied a level of coherence and stability that was permanently at odds with the transitory collective he was commanding.[14]

In this first year of the war, when the revolutionary fires burned their brightest, Washington presumed that he would enjoy a surplus of recruits. In October 1775 a council of war voted unanimously "to reject all slaves & by a great Majority to reject Negroes altogether." The following month Washington ordered that "Neither Negroes, Boys unable to bear arms, nor old men unfit to endure the fatigues of the campaign, are to be enlisted." But within a few months, as it became clear that there would not be enough new recruits to fill the ranks as the militia units disbanded, he was forced to change his mind: "It has been represented to me," he wrote Hancock, "that the free negroes who have Served in this Army, are very much dissatisfied at being discarded—and it is to be apprehended that they may Seek employ in the ministerial Army—I have presumed to depart from the Resolution respecting them, & have given licence for them being enlisted; if this is disapproved of by Congress, I will put a stop to it." In this backhanded fashion Washington established the precedent for a racially integrated Continental army, except for a few isolated incidents the only occasion in American military history when blacks and whites served alongside one another in integrated units until the Korean War.[15]

Finally, the siege of Boston afforded the first extended glimpse at Washington's cast of mind as a military strategist. His motives for supporting American independence were always more elemental than refined. Essentially, he saw the conflict as a struggle for power in which the colonists, if victorious, destroyed British presumptions of superiority and won control over half a continent for themselves. While it would be somewhat excessive to say that his central military goal was an equally elemental urge to smash the British army in one decisive battle, there was a discernible **mano a mano** dimension to his thinking, a tendency to regard each engagement as a personal challenge to his own honor and reputation. At Cambridge it took the form of several risky offensive schemes to dislodge the British regulars, once it became clear that Howe was unwilling to come out from behind his Boston redoubts and face him in open battle. On three occasions, in September 1775, then again in January and February 1776, Washington proposed frontal assaults against the British defenses, arguing that "a Stroke, well aim'd at this critical juncture, might put a final end to the War." (In one of the plans he envisioned a night attack across the ice with advanced units wearing ice skates.) His staff rejected each proposal on the grounds that the Continental army lacked both the size and the discipline to conduct such an attack with sufficient prospects for success. Eventually Washington accepted a more limited tactical scheme to occupy Dorchester Heights, which placed Howe's garrison within range of American artillery, thereby forcing Howe's decision to evacuate or see his army slowly destroyed. But throughout the siege Washington kept looking for a more direct and conclusive battle, suggesting that he himself was ready for a major engagement even if his army was not.[16]

His most aggressive proposal, which **was** adopted, called for a separate campaign against Quebec. Once it was clear that Howe did not intend to oblige him by coming out of Boston, Washington decided to detach twelve hundred troops from his Cambridge camp and send them up the Kennebec River into Canada under the command of a young colonel named Benedict Arnold. Washington's thinking about the importance of the Canadian theater reflected his memories of the French and Indian War, in which Canadian forts had been the strategic keys to victory, as well as his belief that the stakes in the current war included the entire eastern half of North America. As he put it to Arnold, "I need not mention to you the great importance of this place & the consequent possession of all Canada in the Scale of American affairs—to whomsoever It belongs, in there favour probably, will the Balance turn." By capturing Quebec, Arnold would "restore the only link wanting in the great chain of Continental union."[17]

However conventional his thinking about Quebec's strategic significance, Washington's commitment to a Canadian campaign was recklessly bold. Arnold's force had to traverse 350 miles of the most difficult terrain in New England during the outset of the winter snows. Within a month the troops were eating their horses, dogs, and moccasins, dying by the scores from exposure and disease. It is difficult to imagine such a campaign ever being contemplated later in the war, but at this early stage Washington shared the prevalent belief that patriotic fervor, combined with sheer courage, could defeat the elements and the odds.

Despite truly heroic efforts by Arnold and his troops, the Canadian campaign exposed the illusory character of Washington's convictions. After linking up with a force commanded by General Richard Montgomery as planned, Arnold's depleted army made a desperate night assault on Quebec in a blinding snowstorm on December 31, 1775. The result was a catastrophic defeat, both Arnold and Montgomery falling in the first minutes of the battle. (Arnold suffered a serious leg wound but survived, while Montgomery had his face shot off and died on the spot.) If Canada was the key, the British now held it more firmly than before. The Quebec debacle was a decisive blow, but not the kind Washington had intended.[18]

Finally, the Cambridge chapter revealed another Washington trait that has not received sufficient attention in the existent scholarship because it is only indirectly connected to military strategy. Historians have long known that more than two-thirds of the American casualties in the war were the result of disease. But only recently—and this is rather remarkable—have they recognized that the American Revolution occurred within a virulent smallpox epidemic of continental scope that claimed about 100,000 lives. Washington first encountered the epidemic outside Boston, where he learned that between ten and thirty funerals were occurring each day because of the disease. British troops, though hardly impervious to the smallpox virus, tended to possess greater immunity because they came from English, Scottish, and Irish regions, where the disease had existed for generations, allowing resistance to build up within families over time. The soldiers in the Continental army, on the other hand, tended to come from previously unexposed farms and villages, so they were extremely vulnerable. At any point in time, between one-fourth and one-fifth of Washington's army at Cambridge was unfit for duty, the majority down with smallpox. Quite probably Arnold's force at Quebec was also decimated by the disease in the weeks before the fatal attack.[19]

Washington, of course, was immune to smallpox because of his youthful exposure in Barbados. (Subsequent admirers claimed that he was immune to everything.) Equally important, he understood the ravaging implications of a smallpox epidemic within the congested conditions of his encampment, and he quarantined the patients in a hospital at Roxbury. When the British began their evacuation of Boston in March 1776, he ordered that only troops with pockmarked faces be allowed into the city. And although many educated Americans opposed inoculation, believing that it actually spread the disease, Washington strongly supported it. It would take two years before inoculation became mandatory for all troops serving in the Continental army, but the policy began to be implemented in the first year of the war. When historians debate Washington's most consequential decisions as commander in chief, they are almost always arguing about specific battles. A compelling case can be made that his swift response to the smallpox epidemic and to a policy of inoculation was the most important strategic decision of his military career.

After lingering in the Boston harbor for over a week, the British fleet sailed away on March 17, 1776. The American press reported the retreat as a crushing blow to the British army. The Continental Congress ordered a gold medallion cast in Washington's honor. Harvard College awarded him an honorary degree. And John Hancock predicted that he had earned "a conspicuous Place in the Temple of Fame, which Shall inform Posterity, that under your Directions, an undisciplined Band of Husbandmen, in the Course of a few Months became Soldiers," defeating "an Army of Veterans, commanded by the most experienced Generals." While uplifting, subsequent events would soon show that this was an overly optimistic appraisal.[20]

PANORAMA

AS WASHINGTON took his army south from Boston to New York in the spring of 1776, the Continental Congress moved closer to declaring American independence, and a British fleet carrying 33,000 soldiers and sailors—the largest expeditionary force yet to cross the Atlantic—moved closer to the American coastline. The conjunction of these two dramatic developments virtually assured that the formerly remote prospects for a peaceful reconciliation were now gone altogether. One of the great ironies imbedded in that propitious moment, available to us only in retrospect, was that widespread support for what Washington described as the "American Cause" was in fact cresting, and would never again reach the height it achieved during the Boston siege. "The spirit of '76" should more accurately (if less lyrically) be called "the spirit of late '75 and early '76," because patriotic fervor began to erode just as the war became politically official and militarily threatening.[21]

Though Washington himself never wavered—in the end, steadfastness was his most valuable attribute, along with the stamina that accompanied it—popular enthusiasm for the war faded alongside the illusion that it would be a brief affair. The mythological rendition of dedicated citizen-soldiers united for eight years in the fight for American liberty was, in fact, a romantic fiction designed by later generations to conceal the deep divisions and widespread apathy within the patriot camp. The fundamental strategic challenge facing Washington was to fight a conventional war against the British army in the midst of a civil war for the hearts and minds of the American people. And the very term "American people" suggests a national collective that was still in the process of being born. If we are to properly assess his achievement, we need to fully understand his predicament after the Boston phase. That means moving to a higher elevation from which to scan the historical terrain more panoramically than anyone on the ground could manage at the time.[22]

Why was that huge British fleet sailing toward the American coast? The obvious answer is that George III and his chief ministers, Lord North and Lord George Germain, had decided to crush the rebellion with one massive projection of British military power. But since, at least in retrospect, this decision has gone down as one of the biggest blunders in the history of British statecraft, and since, again in retrospect, the ingredients for a viable political solution to the imperial crisis were clearly present from 1774 onward, why did the ministry regard war as its only option? The political solution had been offered by the Continental Congress in 1774 and again in 1775. Three years later, after the disastrous defeat at Saratoga, Lord North proposed essentially the same solution: freedom from Parliament's authority over colonial domestic affairs in return for continued economic membership in the British Empire. But by then it was too late. This principle of shared or overlapping sovereignty between the home government and peripheral states eventually became the political framework for the British Commonwealth, and before that the federal idea at the core of the American Constitution. By embracing it in 1775 the British government would have prolonged American membership in the British Empire until well into the next century and avoided the American Revolution, and American history would have flowed forward in a direction that took little if any account of George Washington.

More recent American history should allow us to comprehend more empathetically the reasons for the fatal British miscalculation. In the late eighteenth century Great Britain was a newly arrived world power still learning how to manage its recently acquired empire. A version of the "domino theory" haunted all the ministry's deliberations: if the American colonies were granted political autonomy over their domestic affairs, then Canada, Ireland, and the British Caribbean possessions would surely demand equivalent status and the entire empire, India included, would gradually unravel. Military advisors tended to view the looming conflict through the prism of the French and Indian War, where the British army captured French forts at the strategic strong-points (such as Louisbourg, Quebec, and Pittsburgh) and won a decisive victory, all the while developing only contempt for the fighting prowess of American militia. (The Earl of Sandwich informed the ministry that, based on his experience, 1,000 British regulars could defeat 100,000 provincial troops.) Dissenting voices warned that the lessons of the French and Indian War were irrelevant, since there were no strategic strong-points that, once captured, produced a decisive conclusion. Lord Camden, for example, cautioned his colleagues in Parliament that the British army would find itself adrift in a boundless sea of troubles: "To conquer a great continent of 1,800 miles, containing three millions of people . . . seems an undertaking not to be rashly engaged in." But such dissenters were ignored. The best and brightest minds in the government were confident that the bulk of the American population were loyal to the king and that, regardless of colonial loyalty, the British army was invincible.[23]

In short, the arrogance of British power should strike a chord that is eerily and painfully familiar to students of the American empire in its own formative phase, most especially its twentieth-century commitment in Southeast Asia. For our present purposes the most salient point is that the British commitment represented the ministry's misguided but deeply felt conviction that the very future of the British Empire was at stake. This conviction would continue to animate the highest echelons of the government long after British popular opinion had grown weary of the war and even after a succession of battlefield setbacks had demonstrated that the war was unwinnable in any traditional sense of the term. Conventional wisdom is that space and time were on the American side. But no one in 1776 fully appreciated how long the British ministry was prepared to stay the course, or how quickly the revolutionary fires would subside and in several regions of America nearly die out completely. It was a recipe for a protracted war of attrition.[24]

What were the major military advantages and disadvantages facing the British army? On the positive side, it possessed two enormous assets. First, it enjoyed nearly total naval supremacy, which meant that all the major American cities— Boston, Newport, New York, Philadelphia, Baltimore, and Charleston—were vulnerable to destruction and occupation. It also meant that in any engagements along the coast or on coastal rivers the British army possessed superior mobility. Second, although the Earl of Sandwich's estimate of British military prowess was wildly exaggerated, the discipline and combat experience of British regulars gave them a decisive advantage on any battlefield where they were not greatly outnumbered, especially in any open-field battle conducted along the orthodox lines of European warfare.

On the negative side, the British army was an ocean away from its logistical base of operations, which not only created problems of resupply but also meant that it could ill afford to suffer heavy casualties, since replacements could not be produced easily or quickly. But the major problem was suggested by the Earl of Camden's warning about the sheer vastness of the American theater. Rather than dissipate its force in a futile attempt at occupying terrain, the British commanders needed to identify and then destroy the strategic center of the rebellion. Veterans of the French and Indian War first thought that the proper target was that corridor along the Hudson River from Montreal to New York City which, once captured and controlled, would effectively cut off New England from the middle and southern colonies. We can never know if this assessment was correct, because the campaign to achieve that goal failed spectacularly at Saratoga, the pivotal battle in the war. The other option, which turned out to be the only strategic target certain to produce a decisive outcome, was not a piece of ground. It was the Continental army itself.[25]

What were Washington's chief options? The British expeditionary force cruising toward New York meant that all presumptions of a quick resolution based on London's willingness to meet the American peace terms were now gone forever. This left Washington to choose among three courses of action. First, he could take the Continental army over the Alleghenies and avoid any full-scale engagements in favor of hit-and-run guerrilla tactics, thereby forcing the British army to pursue him in the wilderness or wander up and down the coast conducting marauding operations against local militia. Second, he could fight what was called "a War of Posts," meaning a series of tactical engagements and withdrawals designed to inflict casualties on the British army but not risk his own troops in one all-or-nothing battle. Third, he could confront the British directly with his entire force and risk the consequences of a major battle, preferably on terrain favorable to a strong defensive position that forced the British to make frontal attacks in the Bunker Hill mode.

Washington never gave the first option any serious consideration. He regarded flight to the western frontier as a desperate last resort only after his army had experienced a major setback. One of his generals, Charles Lee, favored this option, but Washington opposed it for two reasons: first, moving to the west was, as he saw it, flight, and he wanted to fight; second, granting the British army a free hand throughout the most densely populated coastal region meant trusting in the fighting prowess of the militia, and Washington had no faith in militia as independent fighting units. The second option also struck him as a more diluted form of cowardice, a decision to avoid the British challenge that verged on dishonorable behavior. It also, in effect, meant sacrificing New York, and then Philadelphia and wherever else the British army chose to march, to enduring occupation, which would give additional courage to the Loyalists and push the neutrals toward at least a temporary British affiliation. He also worried about the political reaction in the Continental Congress and, more generally, in the populace-at-large to a defensive strategy that seemed to acknowledge the superiority of British arms.[26]

That left the third option, at once the most dangerous strategically and the most appealing personally. Washington, in fact, never hesitated. In June 1776, while Jefferson was drafting the words that declared American independence and the principles on which it claimed to be based, Washington was moving his fifteen thousand troops into positions on Long Island and Manhattan in preparation for a major engagement with the larger British force commanded by General William Howe and his older brother, Admiral Richard Howe. This bold decision flowed directly out of his own personality, which welcomed the opportunity to demonstrate its contempt for British pretensions of supremacy. If there was an excellent fit between his quasi-monarchical powers as commander in chief and his psychic chemistry, there was an equally poor fit between the strategic options in 1776 and the impulses of his character. Washington's decision in fact presented the British commanders with a golden opportunity to destroy the Continental army at the start of the war. Enamored throughout the Boston siege with the prospects for a quick American victory, Washington had placed the Continental army in the most vulnerable position possible and created the conditions for dramatic defeat.[27]

TRYING MEN'S SOULS

IT WOULD HAVE been difficult to imagine a more perfect place for the British army to confront and crush the Continental army than New York City. Strategically, it was the southern entrance to the

Hudson corridor, which, once occupied, sealed off New England from the other rebellious colonies. Topographically, it was tailor-made for the kind of amphibious operations that British naval supremacy made possible and that Washington's force could only contemplate in its dreams. Politically, both Long Island and Manhattan were hotbeds for Loyalists prepared to greet the Howe brothers as conquering heroes. Small wonder, then, that on July 2–3, 1776, the very days the Continental Congress voted to approve American independence and revised the language of Jefferson's draft declaring this revolutionary act, the advance elements of Lord Howe's fleet of thirty warships and four hundred transport vessels began pouring troops onto Staten Island. It was the largest military force ever assembled on the North American continent and the largest army the British would ever gather in one place during the entire war.

In late May, Washington had traveled down to Philadelphia to consult with the Continental Congress about strategy. (Martha went along and, under prodding from her husband, underwent smallpox inoculation in Jefferson's old quarters.) The consultation produced two decisions: first, Washington would make a maximum effort to defend New York; and second, a Board of War and Ordnance would be created with John Adams as its chairman to facilitate coordination between the congress and the army. Though outnumbered, and with nearly a quarter of his soldiers ill with smallpox despite his best efforts to contain the epidemic, Washington was confident he could produce a victory, or at the least inflict sufficient casualties to repeat the Bunker Hill experience for Howe. "If our Troops will behave well," he apprised John Hancock, "having everything to contend for that Freemen hold dear, they [Howe's troops] will have to wade through much blood & Slaughter before they can carry any part of our Works, If they carry 'em at all." As the British buildup on Staten Island continued, Washington's orders reflected the revolutionary conviction that the purity of the cause, combined with sheer courage under fire, would more than compensate for inferior numbers and inexperience: "Remember officers and Soldiers, that you are Freemen, fighting for the blessings of Liberty—that slavery will be your portion, and that of posterity, if you do not acquit yourself like men." How much of this rhetoric Washington himself believed is unclear. His letters to Hancock are more circumspect, predicting that the enemy "will not succeed in their views without considerable loss." What is clear is that Washington believed that his own personal honor, bound tightly to the course of independence now officially declared, left him no choice but to fight.[28]

Sighting: July 20, 1776

An aide to General Howe, Lieutenant Colonel James Patterson, has been admitted behind American lines to confer with Washington. Patterson carries a document from Howe purporting to offer peace terms that will avoid further bloodshed. The document is addressed to "George Washington Esq. & c.& c.& c." Washington's staff had already apprised Patterson that no such document could be delivered because no such person existed to receive it, the only Washington in camp being "His Excellency General Washington." Patterson regrets that General Howe cannot recognize that title without endorsing the legitimacy of the rebellion. But he is eventually admitted to an hour-long interview with the American commander-in-chief in which he relates the content of the document. Washington explains that the document is addressed to a private person, which is no longer who he is, and that the designation "&c.&c.&c. implied every thing & also implied anything." Furthermore, General Howe appeared empowered only to grant pardons, and "those who had committed no Fault wanted no Pardon." Patterson is then escorted back to his barge, disappointed but "Sociable and Chatty all the way." [29]

As the British prepared for an assault on Long Island, Washington issued orders describing "our Glorious Cause" and contrasting the motivation of dedicated patriots to mere mercenaries. Smallpox continued to ravage his regiments, leaving several units without field grade officers. He probably sensed the coming disaster but felt obliged to maintain a public posture of confidence. On the eve of the battle he wrote a long letter to Lund Washington, searching for relief from his apprehensions by issuing orders about where to plant cherry and locust trees at Mount Vernon and which horses to sell. Back in Philadelphia, John Adams wrote to his beloved Abigail: "The Eyes of the World are upon Washington and How, and their armies." [30]

What the world witnessed was a humiliating American defeat. Long Island was lost in a day, along with three hundred casualties and a thousand prisoners. By dividing his force between Manhattan and Long Island, Washington had presented Howe with the opportunity to destroy the Continental army in pieces. (Asked to explain the defeat, Adams put it succinctly: "In general, our Generals were out generalled.") Washington's only redeeming action was the rescue of surviving units from Brooklyn Heights under the cover of fog and rain on the night of August 29. But that was only the half of it. The remainder of his army on Manhattan was now vulnerable to entrapment once Howe transported troops up the East River and cut off his escape route on the peninsula. The ever-realistic General Greene urged a quick evacuation: "I give it as my Oppinion that a General and speedy Retreat is absolutely necessary and that the honour and Interest of America requires it. I would burn the City & its suburbs." Topography, British mobility, and Washington's own inexperience had combined to place the entire Continental army at risk of annihilation. Upon hearing from her husband that Howe was poised to close the trap that would destroy Washington's beleaguered force, Abigail Adams remained defiant; even if all America's brave men were killed or captured, she declared, the British army would find itself opposed by "a race of Amazons in America."[31]

Then a very strange thing happened. Washington called a council of war in which its generals voted ten to three in favor of Greene's recommendation for an evacuation of Manhattan as soon as possible. But Washington rejected the advice. As he reported to Hancock, his officers had urged him to adopt a defensive strategy, to fight what they called "a War of Posts." But despite the recent setbacks and losses, he remained committed to the offense and victory. New York remained "the Key to the Northern Country," and a wholesale retreat would reflect badly on him as well as on what he called "the Common cause." All these negative consequences would be offset "if a brilliant stroke could be made with any probability of Success, especially after our Loss upon Long Island." He would, then, maintain his army on the northern edge of Manhattan at Harlem Heights, wait for the chance to pounce, and if eventually forced to withdraw, inflict heavy casualties as he retreated. It was as if a mouse, cornered by a bevy of cats, had declared itself a lion.[32]

As several generations of historians have noted, Washington's decision to linger on Manhattan was militarily inexplicable and tactically suicidal. A letter back home to Lund suggests that Washington was aware of the risks he was running and preferred to go down fighting rather than acknowledge defeat. Again, he saw the war in highly personal terms: "I see the impossibility of serving with Reputation," he wrote to Lund, "and yet I am told that if I quit the command inevitable ruin will follow. . . . If I fall, it may not be amiss that these circumstances be known. . . . And if the men stand by me (which by the by I despair of), I am resolved not to be forced from this ground while I have life."

Ultimately, Washington's army and life were spared, because General Howe also behaved inexplicably. Perhaps because he saw himself primarily as a peace negotiator instead of a general, or perhaps for reasons only fathomable by psychiatrists, Howe did not close the trap around the Continental army. He dallied, and then focused his efforts on capturing Fort Washington, near the present-day George Washington Bridge. Washington had ordered its evacuation, but then acceded to Greene's bizarre decision to defend it at all costs, which contradicted the prudent advice Greene had been urging earlier. It fell on November 16, 1776, all of its nearly three thousand defenders killed or captured. With Howe preoccupied at Fort Washington, the remnant of Washington's army escaped across the Hudson at Peekskill and assumed full flight across New Jersey.[33]

There was not much of an army left. When Hancock wrote him to inquire about his military intentions, Washington responded politely: "Give me leave to say Sir . . . that our Affairs are in a more unpromising way than you seem to apprehend. . . . Your Army . . . is upon the eve of its political dissolution." The heady era of "rage militaire," the belief that patriotic conviction would

trump British military superiority, was dead forever. More New York and New Jersey colonists
were now signing up with the British than the
American army. Washington himself, whose fervor for the cause had made him temporarily vulnerable to the belief that virtuous amateurs could
defeat mercenary veterans, now abandoned his
own hopes for a quick end to the conflict. A short
war meant a British victory, which was in fact
imminent. The only hope was a long war, fought
by the kind of seasoned troops who would have
stood their ground in New York. The old Continental army was now effectively defunct. Unless a
new army could be raised "with all possible Expedition," Washington warned, "I think the game is
pretty near up."[34]

One of the quaint customs of eighteenth-
century warfare was the belief that armies should
not fight during the winter. Having botched his
chance to trap Washington's decimated force on
Manhattan, Howe now proceeded to miss another
opportunity—it would turn out to be his last—to
hunt down the crippled residue of the Continental
army as it limped across New Jersey in November
1776. He chose instead to place his troops in winter quarters around Trenton while he himself
returned to New York and the arms of his mistress.
Washington, on the other hand, who by all rights
should have welcomed the opportunity to hiber-

nate and lick his wounds, was still thinking offen-
sively. "As nothing but necessity obliged me to
retire before the Enemy," he wrote to Hancock, "I
conceive it my duty, and it corresponds with my
Inclination, to make head against them so long as
there shall be the least probability of doing it with
propriety." Apart from his own inclinations,
which probably referred to his personal urge to
redeem his somewhat tattered reputation after the
New York debacle, Washington recognized that
the entire movement for American independence
was on the verge of extinction and might very well
expire on its own over the winter. He needed to
"strike some Stroke."[35]

The result took the form of a surprise attack, on
Christmas night, across the ice-choked Delaware
River, subsequently immortalized in Emanuel
Leutze's famous painting. Recent scholarship has
corrected certain long-standing misconceptions
about this pivotal battle, which is generally
regarded as Washington's most tactically brilliant
operation of the war and the moment when the
Continental army went on the offensive for the
first time.

First, art historians have argued that Washington could not possibly have been standing in the
prow of the boat, as the Leutze painting claims,
for he would have been hurled headlong into the
ice. But the boats used for the crossing were not as

Leutze described. They were high-walled barges akin to the landing craft used for amphibious assaults in World War II, and everyone stood up in them. The Leutze painting is at least symbolically correct in the sense that Washington personally led the assault across the river in a driving sleet storm and was in the vanguard of the attack on the garrison of Hessian mercenaries at Trenton.

Second, the legend that the Hessian soldiers were drunk, sleeping off their Christmas cheer, is a myth. The Hessians were exhausted because they had been on round-the-clock alert for over a week expecting an attack. When Washington's 2,400 troops descended upon them, they fought bravely, but were outgunned by the eighteen artillery pieces Henry Knox had somehow managed to transport across the river. They suffered about a hundred casualties, and nine hundred were captured. American casualties were minimal, though among the handful of wounded was a future president, Lieutenant James Monroe.

Third, Washington's plan for the attack on Trenton, like most of his tactical schemes, was excessively intricate, calling for a carefully timed four-pronged assault. Three of the four American units never made it across the river, confronting Washington with the decision to proceed with questionable resources or abandon the attack. He chose to run the risk, figuring that the American cause was so desperate that boldness ran fewer risks than caution. It was an all-or-nothing wager, and he won it.[36]

A week later he did it again at Princeton. Embarrassed at the unexpected defeat at Trenton, the British sent General Charles Cornwallis with a superior force to attack Washington's army encamped at Trenton. But Washington learned of the planned attack and quietly slipped away in the night, marching his six thousand troops toward Princeton, where Cornwallis's rear guard was stationed. Again the British were surprised, this time in a more conventional battle with several artillery exchanges and bayonet charges.

Sighting: January 3, 1777

The Pennsylvania militia have just broken in the face of heavy musket fire and grape shot. Suddenly, Washington appears among them, urging them to rally and form a line behind him. A detachment of New England Continentals joins the line, which first holds and then begins to move forward with Washington front-and-center astride his white English charger. The British troops are placed behind a fence at the crest of a hill. Within fifty yards bullets begin to whistle and men in the front of the American line begin to drop. At thirty

yards Washington orders a halt and both sides
exchange volleys simultaneously. An aide,
Colonel Edward Fitzgerald, covers his face
with his hat, certain that his commander, so
conspicuous a target, was cut down. But
while men on both sides of him have fallen,
Washington remains atop his horse,
untouched. He turns toward Fitzgerald, takes
his hand, and says: "Away my dear Colonel,
and bring up the troops. The day is ours."
And it was.[37]

The Trenton-Princeton combination did not
inflict serious military damage on the British, but
it did force Howe to rethink his troop deployments in New Jersey, and, most importantly, it had
a massive psychological effect on American public
opinion. What had appeared to be a lost cause now
enjoyed a new lease on life. The two actions also
served as defiant gestures by Washington himself
that fight was still in him. Having made that point,
though his aggressive instincts would remain a
dangerous liability, he never again felt it necessary
to risk his entire army in one battle. It was as if he
had successfully answered the challenge to duel,
and now could afford to adopt a more defensive
strategy without worrying about his personal
honor and reputation. He also began to realize that
the way to win the war was not to lose it.

THE FABIAN CHOICE

EVEN BEFORE HE entered his winter quarters at Morristown, Washington apprised Hancock that his only non-negotiable request, verging on a demand, was for "a permanent standing army" which he would have total power to shape into the kind of hard and sharp instrument necessary to persevere in a long war. "It may be said, that this is an application for powers, that are too dangerous to be intrusted," he acknowledged. "I can only add, that desperate diseases require desperate remedies, and with truth declare, that I have no lust for power but wish with as much fervency as any man upon this wide extended Continent for an Opportunity of turning the Sword into a ploughshare." The Continental Congress granted his request for a temporary delegation of dictatorial power—the situation truly was desperate, and they had no alternative—but its own limited power over the states to fill the manpower quotas meant that Hancock's strong expressions of support, plus the bounties offered for volunteers who served three-year enlistments, remained hopeful wishes that never quite came true. "It is certainly astonishing and will hardly be credited hereafter," wrote one of Washington's in-laws, "that the most deserving, the most favorite General of the 13 united American States, should be left by them, with only about 2500 men, to support the most important Cause that mankind ever engaged in agst the whole Power of British Tyranny." Actually, as enlistments expired in January 1777, Washington's army probably numbered about three thousand, though he felt obliged to conceal the real number, lest the British realize that a winter campaign would surely end the war, almost by default. Washington spent much of the winter waiting to see if enough new recruits would show up to form an army capable of a spring campaign.[38]

He made two important decisions at Morristown. First, he recognized that the smallpox problem required a more comprehensive solution. "If the Hospitals are in no better condition," he told Hancock, "our Regiments will be reduced to Companies by the end of the Campaign, and those poor Wretches who escape with life, will either be scattered up and down the Country and not to be found, or if found, totally enervated and unfit for further duty." Given his manpower difficulty, he could ill afford to see a quarter of his troops incapacitated, as had occurred in New York; or else, he warned, "we must look for Reinforcements to some other places than our own States," presumably referring to the Kingdom of

Heaven. In March 1777 he made inoculation mandatory and set up special hospitals in Philadelphia to implement the new policy.[39]

Second, less out of conviction than a realistic recognition of his limited resources, Washington came to accept the fact that he must adopt a more defensive strategy and fight a "War of Posts." Also called a "Fabian strategy" after the Roman general Fabius Cunctator, who defeated the Carthaginians by withdrawing whenever his army's fate was at risk, it was a shift in thinking that did not come naturally to Washington. A Fabian strategy, like guerrilla and terrorist strategies of the twentieth century, was the preferred approach of the weak. Washington did not believe that he was weak, and he thought of the Continental army as a projection of himself. He regarded battle as a summons to display one's strength and courage; avoiding battle was akin to dishonorable behavior, like refusing to move forward in the face of musket and cannon fire. Nevertheless, he was now forced to face what he called "the melancholy Truths." New York had demonstrated that the Continental army could not compete on equal terms with British regulars on the conventional battlefield; and given the reduced size of his current force, "it is impossible, at least very unlikely, that any effectual opposition can be given to the British Army with the Troops we have." The most bitter and melancholy truth of all was that popular support for the war, the essential engine for producing new recruits, continued to sputter despite the Trenton and Princeton victories. (One French partisan of the cause claimed that "there is a hundred times more enthusiasm for the Revolution in any Paris café than in all the colonies together.") In effect, he had no choice but to become an American Fabius, or else simply surrender.[40]

In late March 1777 he dispatched Nathanael Greene to brief the Continental Congress on his revised strategy. "I explained to the House your Excellency's Ideas of the next Campaign," Greene reported; "it appeared to be new to them." The Congress was apparently taken aback, because a Fabian strategy meant that Washington did not intend to defend Philadelphia at all costs if Howe chose to make it his target. His highest priority was not to occupy or protect ground, but rather to harass Howe while preserving his army. Adams, writing from Philadelphia, assured Abigail that he was safe: "We are under no more apprehensions here than if the British Army was in the Crimea. Our Fabius will be slow, but sure." Richard Henry Lee, another delegate in the Congress, informed Washington not to worry about defending Philadelphia: "Your Army Sir, feeble as it is, and the North river, are more tempting objects."[41]

What Lee called the North River was another name for the Hudson. Lee's assessment, in retrospect, was strategically correct: Howe should either have attempted to destroy Washington's army, or he should have occupied the Hudson corridor, probably by joining up with General John Burgoyne's army coming down from Lake Champlain. Each of these goals had decisive strategic implications. Instead, Howe decided to capture Philadelphia, which had symbolic but no strategic value, and he chose to launch his campaign in the most roundabout manner imaginable. Rather than march overland across New Jersey, he loaded his army onto ships at Staten Island, sailed out into the Atlantic, and eventually circled back toward Philadelphia through the Chesapeake Bay. Befuddled by Howe's summer cruise, Adams joked that he "might as well imagine them gone round Cape horn into the South Seas to land at California." If nothing else, Howe's odd tactics thoroughly confused Washington, who needed to keep his troops ready to move quickly either toward the Hudson or toward Philadelphia, contingent on where the winds carried Howe. By August 1777, once it was clear that Howe's army was coming up from the south toward Philadelphia, Washington entered his Fabian phase.[42]

The orders issued from headquarters continued to reflect the old patriotic rhetoric and the old Washington preference for decisive and aggressive action: "Now is the time for our most strenuous exertions—One bold stroke will free the land from rapine devastations and burnings, and female innocence from brutal lust and violence. . . . The eyes of all America, and of Europe are turned upon us, as on those on whom the event of the war is to be determined." His personal correspondence also exhibited his reflexive urge to throw caution to the winds and engage Howe without fear and without constraints: "I shall take every measure in my power to defend it [Philadelphia]," he wrote to one worried city official, "and hope you will agree with me that the only effectual Method will be to oppose Gen. Howe with our whole united Force." But in all the councils of war his generals, especially Greene and Knox, kept reminding him—and one senses that they **had** to keep reminding him—that preserving the Continental army was a higher priority than protecting Philadelphia. The lion had to become the fox.[43]

The first battle occurred at Brandywine Creek on September 11, 1777. Washington was outmaneuvered by Howe's quite simple flanking tactic, which split the American defenders and created a complete rout. Howe subsequently claimed that the entire Continental army could have been destroyed but for the cover of darkness at the end, but that extravagant assessment failed to recognize that Washington had left himself an escape route once the battle went badly. (It also failed to recognize the upside of the American troops' failure to stand and fight; namely, they ran away very well.) British casualties totaled about six hundred, American nearly double that number. In the aftermath of what was clearly another British victory, Washington attributed the defeat to bad luck and claimed, in an eighteenth-century version of spin control, that American casualties were fewer than the enemy's, a falsehood that he probably justified as a public service to the wavering cause. Brandywine reinforced two unattractive facts: first, that the superior discipline of British regulars made them masters of the battlefield unless vastly outnumbered; and second, that Washington's inexperience at managing his force on a large battlefield beyond his visual control virtually guaranteed that he would be outgeneralled by Howe.[44]

The second battle occurred at Germantown on October 4. A textbook illustration of the phrase "the fog of war," Germantown was a near victory for Washington that was transformed into a defeat when, at a crucial moment in the battle, American troops fired on each other amidst dense fog and smoke, thereby permitting the British to regroup. Washington's original attack plan was an excessively intricate four-pronged scheme that proved impossible to coordinate, especially during the night march toward the British lines. The attack was intended to be a complete surprise, but Howe was alerted to Washington's plan at the last moment by Loyalists.

Sighting: October 4, 1777

With the battle in the balance, Washington has ridden forward with his staff to the sound of heavy musket fire. The American advance has stalled at a stone house, a sturdy two-and-a-half-story dwelling owned by Benjamin Chew, now occupied by over 100 British troops pouring a murderous fire from the windows. Washington asks his staff whether this formidable fortress should be by-passed or attacked. Henry Knox insists on the latter course ("we must not leave a castle in the rear") and Washington defers to his judgment. Knox then directs four light cannons to fire on the house, but the cannon balls bounce off the stone walls. The heavy fog thickens, limiting visibility to a few yards and causing confused American troops to fire on one another. An officer volunteers to go forward under a white

flag to propose terms of surrender to the defenders, but they shoot him down in the foggy confusion. Washington supervises several assaults on the house, all futile. The Chew house is never taken, the American advance is stalled, perhaps fatally. After-action reports agree on two points: the fortress should have been by-passed; and seventy-five American bodies lay bayoneted in the doorways and windowsills, while the interior walls, splattered with blood, resembled a slaughter house.[45]

At the end of the battle the British still held the field, and American casualties, about one thousand, doubled those on the British side. Nevertheless, Washington insisted that the battle could easily have gone the other way. The troops had fought valiantly, exposing the British army as "not that Invincible Body of Men which many suppose them to be." In his correspondence afterward, he again distorted the casualty lists to exaggerate the American achievement and, in effect, claimed victory. He even adopted the posture of the victorious commander toward Howe, making a point of returning Howe's dog, which had been found wandering the battlefield searching for his master. A grimmer version of Germantown as an example of strategic victory came from Thomas McKean, a prominent Pennsylvania lawyer and ardent patriot: "If your Excellency attacks & disables a thousand of the Enemy a week, and are constantly reinforced equal to the numbers you lose, as I trust you will, You must soon prove triumphantly victorious, and get the game, tho' you should not throw sixes," presumably meaning risk and lose your entire army in the process.[46]

As Washington was learning to play his new role as a somewhat aggressive fox, the pivotal battle of the war—actually a series of battles—was being waged north of Albany. Throughout the summer of 1777, Washington received regular reports about the steady progress of General John Burgoyne's army as it moved down from Canada, presumably for a rendezvous with Howe somewhere along the Hudson corridor. Howe's inexplicable decision to sail south toward the Chesapeake takes on truly bizarre status in the larger strategic context, since it left Burgoyne's force of eight thousand troops marooned in a sea of hostile militia from western New England, which rallied by the thousands to reinforce the contingent of Continentals commanded by Horatio Gates. Washington sent Benedict Arnold, his most daring and battle-tested general, along with Daniel Morgan's brigade of sharpshooters, his elite infantry unit, to assist Gates, but the Battle of Saratoga became a textbook example of the decisive role that swarming militia could play when teamed effectively with regulars. (It was also one of the few occasions in the war when militia functioned according to the Minuteman ideal, prompting Washington to observe that he could have obliterated Howe's army outside Philadelphia if New Jersey and Pennsylvania militia had rallied with equivalent zeal.) The outcome was devastating to British presumptions of inevitable victory. On October 17, Burgoyne surrendered the surviving remnant of his battered army, nearly six thousand men.[47]

Saratoga radiated shock waves as far as London and Paris, causing the British ministry to consider getting out of the war and the French government to consider getting in. Tremors were also felt within the Continental Congress, where the stupendous success at Saratoga cast Gates's star in ascendance and invited behind-the-scenes comparisons with Washington's failure to prevent Howe's capture of America's capital city. The discrepancy was not lost on Washington, who found it difficult to acknowledge that he had played only a minor role in America's greatest victory of the war. His congratulatory letter to Gates ended on a sour note: "I cannot but regret," he wrote Gates, "that a matter of such magnitude and so interesting to our General Operations, should have reached me by report only," meaning that Gates should have sent a letter under his own signature.

Gates was also informed that Washington was sending one of his most trusted aides, Alexander Hamilton, to Albany in order to detach the bulk of Gates's force and bring it down to Pennsylvania to join "the Main Army" under his direct command. Saratoga, in short, was a splendid victory, but it must not encourage anyone, including Gates himself, to forget who was the commander in chief.[48]

The truth was that Saratoga unleashed a whispering campaign against Washington that had been simmering beneath the surface ever since the debacle at Fort Washington. The larger truth was that criticism of Washington could only take the form of whispers, since his transcendent status as "His Excellency" levitated above all political squabbles, making direct criticism almost sacrilegious. Nevertheless, there were audible murmurings in the corridors of the Continental Congress, asking how such a supposedly brilliant general could lose so many battles, the last one permitting capture of America's capital city. Benjamin Rush, who had once championed Washington's distinctive status as quasi-king, now wondered out loud whether such power was compatible with republican principles. Most of the criticism was more muted. John Adams offered the shrewdest assessment: "Now we can allow a certain Citizen to be wise, virtuous, and good, without thinking him a Deity or a saviour."[49]

Within the army anti-Washington sentiment was especially virulent among the small but politically influential group of French officers who had been promised high rank by members of the Congress anxious to encourage a Franco-American alliance. As a general rule, these French claimants were unqualified in all areas except their own exhaggerated sense of superiority. And it was invariably Washington who was forced to inform them that neither the promises made nor their inflated military credentials would suffice to qualify them as generals. One of the most arrogant and irritating of the group, Philippe Du Condray, ended his protests dramatically by spurring his horse onto a ferry on the Schuylkill River, then drowning when the horse, which could swim much better than Du Condray, kept going out the other end of the ferry. But the most troublesome protester was Thomas Conway, an Irishman by birth who had risen to the rank of colonel in the French army. Washington had described Conway's proposed promotion to general as "as unfortunate a measure as ever was adopted," and Conway himself as a man whose "importance in the Army, exists more in his imagination than in reality."[50]

Conway did not take kindly to such assessments. What came to be called the "Conway Cabal" was more a gossip network involving a handful of disgruntled players within the Congress and the army that questioned Washington's judgment than it was a full-fledged conspiracy to have him replaced, presumably with Gates. Once Washington let it be known that his own network of informants kept him fully apprised of the loose talk behind the scenes, both Conway and Gates fell all over themselves disclaiming any malevolent intentions and insisting on their total loyalty to him and to the cause. If Conway's gossip campaign had the possibility to grow into a more serious challenge to Washington's authority, or to the assumption that "His Excellency" and the cause were synonymous, this quickly evaporated with Washington's deft exposure of the not-so-secret conversations. For their part, Conway and Gates had learned that questioning Washington's judgment, and implicitly his unique authority, was akin to purchasing a one-way ticket to the sidelines, which, in the end, is where both of them landed.[51]

But the episode did generate more revealing reverberations within Washington's own mind. Because the Fabian role had never rested comfortably alongside his own more aggressive instincts, the accusation that he should have been able to prevent the capture of Philadelphia reinforced his own sense of failure at Brandywine and Germantown. The whisperings in the corridors, in other words, echoed the whispering in his own head and his honor-driven belief that the refusal to engage Howe's army in one all-or-nothing battle was somehow a betrayal of his personal reputation. He kept asking his staff to formulate plans for one more engagement, presumably victorious, that would then permit him to take his depleted and frazzled army, a third of whom did not have shoes, into winter quarters. The strategic decision to make the survival of the Continental army the highest priority, the realization that he must fight a protracted defensive war, remained at odds with his own more decisive temperament. Greene tried to remind him that he really had no choice: "your Excellency has the choice of but two things," Greene advised, "to fight the Enemy without the least Prospect of Success . . . or remain inactive, & be the subject of Censure of an ignorant & impatient populace." Knox chimed in with the same opinion: "But I believe there is not a single maxim in War that will justify a number of undisciplined troops attacking an equal number of disciplined troops strongly posed in redoubts and having a strong city in their rear such as Philadelphia."[52]

The clear lesson of Brandywine and Germantown, Greene argued, was that the Continental army was no match for Howe's regulars. Let the gossipmongers in the Congress, all blissfully ignorant of this unattractive truth, persist in their naive chatter and their veiled preference for another Gates-like victory. Washington's greatest responsibility was to ignore such critics. He must also ignore those voices in his head that regarded the presence of Howe's army in Philadelphia as a standing challenge to his reputation: "I wish that it was in our power to give that Army some capital wound—the reputation of the Army and the happiness of the country loudly calls for it—but in consulting our wishes rather than our reason, we may be hurried by an impatience to attempt something splendid into inextricable difficulties." Washington's highest duty was not to answer his critics or satisfy his sense of personal honor, but rather to win the war.[53]

He knew that Greene was right, but he could not resist the memory of the Trenton-Princeton successes of the previous winter and kept searching for the opportunity to repeat that moment of glory in order to end the current campaign on a triumphant note. Once again, Greene warned him against entangling his personal agenda with the strategic imperatives or his public responsibilities as commander in chief. "The successes of last winter," Greene observed, "were brilliant and attended with the most happy consequences in changing the complexion of the times," but they were really only psychological victories, and "if the bills of mortality were to be consulted, I

fancy . . . we were no great gainers by those operations." He concluded with another lecture:

> Let us consider the consequences that will result
> from a disappointment in a measure of this
> nature—In the first place it will be attended
> with a vast expence and the loss of many lives to
> no valuable purpose—it will prove a great
> obstruction to the recruiting service and a defeat
> will give a general alarm and spread universal
> discontent throughout the continent—It will
> expose the weakness of the militia to the enemy
> and not only them but to all europe who now
> consider them much more formidable than they
> really are.[54]

It took every ounce of Washington's legendary
self-control to hear and accept Greene's counsel,
which ran against his grain, as well as his
wounded pride at being the butt of unofficial criticism. But eventually he embraced Greene's realistic appraisal as his own. This is one of several
moments in Washington's career when his decision **not** to act merits special recognition, since
another major engagement with Howe outside
Philadelphia risked the existence of the Continental army. It also marks the moment when Washington, who had been struggling with the
unpalatable idea for over a year, finally and fully

accepted his Fabian role, emotionally as well as rationally, along with the recognition that it would be a protracted war in which the preservation of the Continental army was the priority. These decisions, in turn, completed his transformation into a public figure whose personal convictions must be suppressed and rendered subordinate to his higher calling as an agent of history, which in this case meant that winning the war was more important than being himself. On December 17, the General Orders announced the end of the campaign and the decision to move the army into winter quarters near a previously obscure location in Pennsylvania called Valley Forge. The orders declared that "He himself," meaning Washington, "will share in the hardship and partake in every inconvenience." This, it turned out, was not really true. It was true, however, that the man and the cause were now completely synonymous, not just in the public mind, but in Washington's as well.[55]

CHAPTER FOUR

Destiny's Child

L ooking back from the privileged perspective
of the present, American victory in the War of
Independence became inevitable after William
Howe missed his chance to destroy Washington's
army in 1776, and then the disastrous British
defeat at Saratoga the following year prompted
France to enter the conflict on the American side.
Space and time, so the story goes, then became
the inexorable allies of independence, both swallowing up and wearing down British military
pretensions. The decision by the British ministry
to adopt a southern strategy in 1778–79 proved
a futile effort, which bogged down in the Carolina swamps after a series of tactical British victories that, thanks to the inspired leadership of
Nathanael Greene, added up to strategic defeat in
a savage war of attrition. Eventually, Lord Cornwallis found his battered army marooned in the

Yorktown peninsula, where Washington, with the invaluable assistance of the French fleet, delivered the decisive blow he had been dreaming about for six long years.

While this version of the Revolutionary War possesses all the seductive charm of a great adventure story with a happy ending, at least for the American side, it is not one that Washington himself would have recognized or endorsed. The problem is not simply that what we might call "hindsight history" glides smoothly toward preordained conclusions, whereas Washington was traveling a bumpy road toward an uncertain destination; the major problem is the presumption that time was an unalloyed American asset. In fact, to the extent that waging war was about raising money and men, time was on the British side, because the London government had developed, during the course of the eighteenth century, the most powerful and efficient machine for waging war in the world, fully capable of projecting and sustaining its power almost indefinitely.[1]

When Washington took his army into winter quarters at Valley Forge, on the other hand, the Continental Congress lacked the authority to supply either money or men, popular support for the war continued to decline, and few of the state governments were prepared to impose taxes on their residents or meet their enlistment quotas. "I am now convinced beyond a doubt," Washington wrote to Henry Laurens, president of the Continental Congress, "that unless some great and capital change suddenly takes place in that line, this Army must inevitably be reduced to one or other of these three things. Starve—dissolve—or disperse." The unpalatable and ironic truth was that the institutions that had alienated American colonists from the empire—Parliament's taxing power and a well-equipped standing army—gave the British a significant advantage in a protracted war.[2]

How, then, did the improbable become the inevitable? Washington's fullest answer, composed soon after victory was assured, suggested that historians would have a difficult time explaining the triumph.

> If Historiographers should be hardy enough to fill the page of History with the advantages that have been gained with unequal numbers (on the part of America) in the cause of this contest, and attempt to relate the distressing circumstances under which they have been obtained, it is more than probable that Posterity will bestow on their labors the epithet and marks of fiction; for it will not be believed that such a force as Great Britain has employed for eight years in Country could be baffled . . . by numbers infinitely less, com-

posed of Men oftentimes half starved; always in Rags, without pay, and experiencing, at times, every species of distress which human nature is capable of undergoing.[3]

More succinctly, Washington also observed that the war was won "by a concatenation of causes" which had never occurred before in human history, and which "in all probability at no time, or under any Circumstance, will combine again." In the midst of the bedeviling concatenations, he called attention to one abiding core of perseverance, the officers and soldiers of the Continental army, whose sacrifices would never be fully understood or appreciated. He did not mention the other abiding presence—modesty forbade it.[4]

The crucial event, where the abiding pattern first emerged, was not Saratoga but Valley Forge. The heroes were not the mass of ordinary citizens, but rather a pathetically small collection of marginal men, the common soldiers of the Continental army. The main theme was not romantic but paradoxical; namely, the unattractive but irrefutable fact that the War of Independence had only been won by defying many of the values the American Revolution claimed to stand for. And the lesson Washington drew from that experience, learned not from books but from struggling on a day-by-day basis with its implications, was that the meaning of the American Revolution, at least as he understood it, had been transformed during the course of the war into a shape that neither he nor anyone else had foreseen at the start. It was a war not just for independence, but also for nationhood.

BLOOD ON THE SNOW

THE MOST GRAPHIC piece of visual evidence about the legendary winter at Valley Forge happens to be true. No less a source than Washington himself described the shoeless soldiers tracking blood on the snow. "To see Men without Cloathes to cover their nakedness, without Blankets to lay on, without Shoes, by which their Marches might be traced by the Blood from their feet," he recalled, "is a mark of Patience and obedience which in my opinion can scarce be parallel'd." Most of the horses died from starvation or exposure, and their decaying carcasses filled the air with a stench that joined with the blood in the snow to create sensory scenes that Washington never forgot. When other leading members of the revolutionary generation subsequently spoke or wrote about the importance of virtue during the American Revolution, they invariably described a classical ideal enshrined in political treatises by prominent philosophers like Montesquieu. Washington's understanding of virtue was more palpable and primal, shaped by direct exposure to scenes of mass suffering that, as he put it, "will not be credited but by those who have been spectators." Nearly a century later, when Abraham Lincoln referred in his first inaugural to those "mystic chords of memory" that linked his Civil War generation with those predecessors who had created the American republic, the haunting imagery suggested a shared political idea. Washington's memory was less mystic but equally haunting; it was men shedding blood.[5]

The men shedding most of the blood at Valley Forge, and throughout the remaining years of the war, came from the lowest rung of American society. "When men are irritated, and the Passions inflamed," Washington observed somewhat caustically, "they fly hastily and chearfully to Arms." Those exuberant days of popular enthusiasm for the war were now gone forever, as were the enlistments by yeoman farmers and men of "the middling sort" who had manned the barricades during the Boston siege. Their places in the ranks of the Continental army were now filled by indentured servants, former slaves, landless sons, and recent immigrants from Ireland and England. These were the young men, usually between fifteen and twenty-five years of age, who lived in the makeshift log huts at Valley Forge and signed on "for the duration" of the war because, in most cases, they had no brighter prospects.[6]

Washington harbored no romantic illusions about these ordinary soldiers, claiming that "to expect, among such People, as comprise the bulk of an Army, that they are influenced by any other principles than those of Interest, is to look for what never did, and I fear never will happen." He was prepared to string them up if they attempted to desert or fell asleep on sentinel duty, and order one hundred lashes to their bare backs for minor infractions. For their part, the soldiery (as he called them) routinely defied regulations about hair length and decorated their uniforms with ribbons, feathers, and fur in order to make the very term "uniform" a standing joke. Despite the distance between them, which Washington regarded as an accurate reflection of the social hierarchy that God intended and all his experience as a Virginia planter-aristocrat confirmed, the general and his troops enjoyed a mutual sense of admiration. The soldiers were known to chant the singsongy tune "War and Washington" so endlessly that visiting civilians complained of mental paralysis. And Washington not only saluted their silent suffering at Valley Forge but also recognized their staying power as the decisive factor in the eventual American victory.[7]

Given the potent (if latent) egalitarian convictions of the American Revolution, the camp culture at Valley Forge was richly ironic: a near-perfect embodiment of the Aristotelian hierarchy—the one, the few, and the many. The enlisted men were obviously the many, a faceless multitude of castoffs that one soldier described, on the march, as "a cavalcade of wild beasts." Washington was obviously the one, the singular figure whose birthday was about to be celebrated as a national holiday, like European monarchs, and who was first described in a Pennsylvania almanac for 1778 (albeit in German) as "The Father of His Country." That left the officers as the designated few.[8]

During the Valley Forge encampment the officers of the Continental army began to assume the manners and trappings of a self-conscious American aristocracy. Their claim to elite status was not inherited bloodlines, though a few officers (i.e., Lord Stirling, Baron de Kalb) did affect full-fledged European titles. Their presumed superiority was based on their revolutionary credentials as the ultimate repository of commitment to the cause of American independence. They had come to see themselves—and Washington encouraged this perception—as the chosen few who preserved and protected the original ethos of 1775–76 after it had died out among the bulk of the American citizenry; they were the "band of brothers" that sustained the virtuous ideal amidst an increasingly corrupt and disinterested civilian society.

Whereas English aristocrats could rest comfortably in their privileged role—it was, after all, a socially sanctioned birthright—the officers at Valley Forge were constantly trying to prove they deserved their elite status. Washington spent countless hours overseeing questions of rank between officers who refused to serve under anyone they considered junior. Officers frequently demanded court-martials to answer hearsay accusations of negligence or cowardice bandied about at the campfires. General officers vied with each other for status by employing multiple servants to handle their horses and baggage. And in this honor-driven world of fragile egos, the ultimate recourse when one's reputation was impugned was the duel. Although dueling was officially illegal in the Continental army, it became commonplace at Valley Forge. (John Laurens felt the obligation to defend Washington's honor against the libels of Thomas Conway, challenged him, and gained satisfaction by shooting Conway in the mouth.) As the soldiers shivered and starved in silence, their officers, who enjoyed more comfortable quarters and warmer clothing, made Valley Forge into a noisy arena for their personal pretensions.[9]

And if we think of Valley Forge as a stage, three men destined to have a significant impact on Washington's career made their appearance on it at this time. The first was a young lieutenant attached to Daniel Morgan's elite corps of Virginia sharpshooters named John Marshall. Even though he was recovering from a wound in the hand received at Brandywine, Marshall's athletic prowess in footraces and jumping contests—he could supposedly leap over obstacles six feet high—caught the attention of the troops and earned him the nickname "Silverheels." Though there is no record that Washington noticed him, Marshall certainly noticed Washington, and at Valley Forge began his lifelong role as the champion of Washington's legacy in American history. Marshall wrote the definitive Washington biography of his time and subsequently imposed, for all time, Washington's version of America's original intentions in his landmark decisions as the nation's preeminent jurist and most influential interpreter of the Constitution.[10]

Then there was the Marquis de Lafayette, a nineteen-year-old French nobleman who was also recovering from a wound suffered at Brandywine. Lafayette came by his title the old-fashioned European way: he inherited it. Initially Washington looked upon Lafayette as another of those imperious and unqualified French volunteers who kept showing up in camp and demanding to be made a general. But his personal courage in battle ("The Marquis is determined to be in the way of danger") and willingness to serve at any rank endeared him to Washington, making Lafayette the French exception and eventually the chief symbol of the gloriously effective Franco-American alliance.[11]

More than his military contribution, which proved crucial in the early stages of the Yorktown campaign, Lafayette's importance to Washington was deeply personal. The bond of cordial affection established at Valley Forge grew into a mutual affinity and emotional attachment that made Lafayette, even more than aides like Hamilton and Laurens, Washington's surrogate son. In the presence of Lafayette the famous Washington aloofness melted into pools of candor and intimacy, and the letters addressed to "My Dear Marquis" are the most expressive, playful, and unprotective in the entire Washington correspondence. (Presumably, the letters to Martha were equivalently revealing, all the more reason to decry their destruction.) Washington liked to tease Lafayette, for example, with the accusation that his failure to bring his young wife to America was rooted in a silent fear that she would fall in love with an older man, namely Washington himself. Lafayette was the major outlet for Washington's human side, and their letters provide the clearest evidence that he had one.[12]

Finally, there was Friedrich Wilhelm August Heinrich Ferdinand, Baron von Steuben. Steuben's title was a complete fabrication, as was his claim of intimacy with Frederick the Great and his rank of general in the Prussian army. But in addition to being a lovable fraud, Steuben possessed a thorough knowledge of Prussian and French military procedures and an infectious enthusiasm for drilling troops on the parade ground. Soon after turning up as an unannounced volunteer at Valley Forge, Steuben was briskly, if rather incoherently—his English was studded with German profanities—shouting marching orders to platoons, then companies, then whole regiments.

Steuben's impact on the discipline of the Continental army only becomes comprehensible when one realizes that, prior to his arrival, there had been no uniform standards of march and maneuver at all. And whereas modern-day soldiers complain that daily drilling is a tiresome and mostly useless exercise designed to occupy time, on eighteenth-century battlefields the ability to move precisely from column to line formations, and vice versa, made a crucial difference in delivering maximum firepower at the point of attack or maintaining military order during a strategic retreat. (This is not to mention that standing calmly at attention while the man abreast of you is disemboweled by a cannon ball is an acquired skill and not a natural act.) In May 1778, Steuben became inspector general of the Continental army, and soon thereafter his **Regulations,** popularly known as "The Blue Book," became the standard source of disciplinary standards for all units. More than anyone else, Steuben was responsible for injecting a professional standard of performance into the Continental army, blending a European code of obedience to authority onto an American army of inveterate individualists, shaping the raw material huddled in the huts of Valley Forge into the hard instrument Washington needed but, until 1778, had not commanded. The last official letter Washington wrote as commander in chief was sent to Steuben, acknowledging that his contribution to American victory ranked near the top because it permitted the Continental army to compete on equal terms with British regulars.[13]

What did not happen at Valley Forge is probably more important than what did. Throughout the winter of 1777–78 the murmurings against Washington in the Continental Congress continued, and it gradually became clear that the Conway Cabal should have been called (to preserve the alliteration) the "Mifflin Maneuver." The chief conspirator was actually Thomas Mifflin, who had once served as Washington's aide outside Boston, where apparently Washington had offended Mifflin's bottomless but fragile ego by not giving him a combat command. Scholars do not agree about Mifflin's scheming—some think the purported conspiracy was merely loose talk in the corridors of the Congress—but Mifflin was clearly engaged in some kind of political campaign to undermine Washington's sovereign control over the army. Despite Mifflin's adroit leaks and political machinations—to include a list of Washington's forty-five greatest military blunders deposited by an anonymous "Freeman" on the steps of the Congress—Washington remained calm and collected. The plot, to the extent there ever was one, dissolved when Washington leaked his own story to the press: "Whenever the public gets dissatisfied with my services, or a person is found better qualified to answer her expectations, I shall quit the helm . . . and retire to private life with as much content, as ever the wearied pilgrim felt upon his safe arrival in the Holy-Land." The publication of Washington's readiness—or was it a threat?—to resign was more than sufficient to expose and therefore destroy Mifflin's scheme. It was the last occasion during the war when Washington's authority was seriously challenged.[14]

But the most important event that did not happen was the dissolution of the Continental army. It is not clear how many men died of disease and exposure at Valley Forge, but new recruits and, even more important, reenlistments "for the duration," bolstered the size of the army to twelve thousand in March 1778, with a core of about five thousand battle-tested veterans. And more were on the way. One of the dominant themes in Washington's early life had been the elemental fact that success followed survival. His military reputation after the Braddock debacle, his inheritance of Mount Vernon, his marriage to Martha Custis, all had occurred when others fell by the wayside and he was left standing. If Washington regarded the Continental army as the institutional projection of his own personality, then the troops marching out of winter quarters at Valley Forge in May 1778 represented a new chapter in that same elemental story.

The month of May, in fact, seemed to brim over with evidence that the war itself was entering a new and perhaps climactic phase. Congress ratified the treaty with France, which promised to alter the strategic chemistry of the conflict, and shortly thereafter passed legislation offering financial incentives (i.e., half pay for seven years for officers, an eighty-dollar bonus for enlisted men) to all serving until the end of the war. Down in

Philadelphia, the British army was preparing to evacuate, thereby confirming Washington's assessment that "the possession of our Towns, while we have an Army in the field, will avail them little," even when the town happened to be the American capital. General Howe, forced to face his failure at locating the strategic center of the rebellion, had resigned and was replaced by Sir Henry Clinton. And the British ministry, revealing its increasing sense of frustration, had released forged documents purporting to disclose that Washington was really a secret agent who had sold out the American cause for money. As laughable as it was ludicrous, the effort to undermine Washington's authority only prompted newspaper editorials joking that Howe's record of failure suggested that he must be an American spy.[15]

When Clinton began to move his ten thousand troops out of Philadelphia toward New York, Washington was torn between his urge to test his better-trained army in battle and his Fabian resolution to avoid any full-scale engagement. After much brooding and several councils of war, he eventually chose a middle course designed to harass Clinton's rear without provoking a major fight. During the debate among his general staff about how to proceed, Charles Lee had argued most vociferously against any action, claiming that it was folly to risk casualties now that the

French, like the proverbial cavalry, were speeding across the Atlantic to the rescue. What became the Battle at Monmouth Court House was neither foreseen nor intended but became unavoidable when Lafayette, whom Washington had unwisely trusted with command of the advance wing of the American army, blundered into Clinton's main force.[16]

Sighting: June 28, 1778

It is very hot, nearly 100 degrees, and Billy Lee has assumed unofficial command of the servants and valets for all the general officers, leading them on horseback to the top of a hill beneath a large sycamore tree where they can more easily observe the looming action and catch the cooling breeze. As Billy Lee takes out his telescope to survey the battlefield, Washington looks up at the group and is heard to observe: "See those fellows collecting on yonder height; the enemy will fire on them to a certainty." And just as Washington speaks a six-pound artillery ball lands in the sycamore tree, scattering but not injuring Billy Lee and his fellow servants, whom the British had apparently mistaken for Washington and his staff.[17]

Washington supposedly smiled at this incident. He surely also smiled if he witnessed a more famous scene—there is no evidence that he did— during the height of the battle, when a woman known in the lore as Molly Pitcher (real name, Mary Ludwig Hayes) replaced her fallen husband loading the muzzle of a cannon and showed no concern when a British ball passed between her legs. (A few inches higher, one soldier heard her say, and she would have lost her occupation.) Though witnesses disagree about another famous scene at Monmouth Court House, all agree that Washington was not smiling, some say was trembling with outrage, others claim was cursing a proverbial blue streak.[18]

He had come upon Lee leading a headlong retreat. Whether the retreat was justified, as Lee and his subsequent scholarly defenders have insisted, is beyond knowing. What is clear beyond any doubt is that Washington considered Lee's conduct as either cowardly or an insubordinate effort to sabotage an attack he had earlier opposed. Washington relieved Lee on the spot, then rallied the American troops on more favorable terrain— which is what Lee's supporters argue he was trying to do—while calmly sitting astride his horse in the midst of a blistering British artillery barrage. Under Washington's direct command, and moving now with a professional polish that Steuben's drilling made second nature, the troops of the Continental army held the field at the end of the sweltering day and inflicted almost twice their casualties on Clinton's regulars. As Washington saw it, two conclusions were clear: the Continental army was now a match for British professionals and could hold its own in a conventional, open-field engagement; and Charles Lee was finished as an army officer. What Washington could not know was that Monmouth Court House was the last major action he would command until York-town.[19]

A central lesson of his life—survive and you shall succeed—seemed to be holding true in the months after Valley Forge. Once Clinton barricaded his army in New York, and as Washington took up defensive positions around the city, he recalled being in the same location two years earlier in much less favorable circumstances: "It is not a little pleasing, nor less wonderful to contemplate, that after two years of Maneuvering and undergoing the strangest vicissitudes that perhaps ever attended any one contest since the creation, that both Armies are brought back to the very point they set out from." Only this time it was the British who were "now reduced to the use of the spade and pick axe for defense." Victory seemed imminent.[20]

FRENCH CONNECTIONS AND
SOUTHERN STRATEGIES

As IT turned out, victory in the full and final sense that Washington came to define the term was actually five years away. In one sense the War of Independence might best be described as a marathon, and Washington's distinguishing virtue thus becomes his sheer stamina. But in another sense the marathon metaphor misses the peaks and valleys that made his experience as commander in chief less like a long-distance race and more like a roller-coaster ride. While stamina— the capacity to hold on until the end of the ride— remains an important virtue in this undulating version of the story, Washington's experience of the trip on the downward dips forced him to develop another set of virtues, indeed to revise his previous understanding of virtue itself. The thirty months between the fall of 1778 and the spring of 1781 felt to Washington like one long, downward dip, the most frustrating and difficult period of his life, the true testing time for both himself and what he believed he was fighting for.

One source of his frustration was the French fleet. Naval supremacy had proved to be Britain's chief strategic asset in the war, permitting Howe and then Clinton to move troops quickly and with impunity, as well as to threaten every major

American city. From the moment the French alliance became official, Washington began dreaming of the day when the presence of a French fleet would offset this British advantage and afford him the same mobility. And the dramatic culmination of his dream was a joint Franco-American operation in which the French fleet bottled up a large British army while the Continental army encircled it along the lines of the Boston siege. But Washington's dream kept receding into the middle distance, primarily because France insisted on basing its main fleet in the Caribbean in order to protect its interests in the West Indies. Early on, in August 1778, Washington attempted a small-scale version of his larger dream, an amphibious assault on the British garrison of five thousand troops in Rhode Island. When it failed because the smaller French fleet felt obliged to withdraw, Washington himself felt obliged, as he put it, "to put the best face upon the matter," meaning conceal the fact that, despite French entry into the war, the British navy remained supreme on the Atlantic coast.[21]

The dream, however, refused to die, in part because it represented the only plausible scenario that permitted Washington to remove his Fabian mask and resume his more natural role as the aggressor, and in part because he did not believe that the British government would ever abandon its American empire without suffering another decisive defeat at the same level as Saratoga. By 1779 the fuzzier features of the dream had formed into a sharper image with New York at its center. New York was the great British enclave in North America, the nest from which ships and troops radiated British power and, not so incidentally, the scene of Washington's most humiliating defeat three years earlier. Washington therefore came to regard its capture as "the first and capital object, upon which every other is dependent." Amidst confused reports about the location of the main French fleet—one report had it in the English Channel supporting an invasion that was about to capture London—Washington kept coming back to that mental picture of French ships blocking New York Harbor and the Continental army marching into the captured city with him at the lead, redeeming his own honor and ending the war in one dramatic stroke.[22]

Although that hope kept colliding with the reality of British naval supremacy and French priorities in Europe and the Caribbean, it remained the centerpiece of Washington's strategic thinking for nearly three years. During that time Washington deployed the main elements of the Continental army in a giant arc that extended from northern New Jersey into the Hudson Highlands near West Point and then eastward into the hill country of western Connecticut. This deployment served multiple purposes: it permitted a quick retreat to the west if the British managed to assemble a superior force in the region; it protected the Hudson corridor if the British tried again to sever New England from the Middle Atlantic states; and it established a dominant American military presence in a populous region where the allegiance of the civilian inhabitants tended to require reminders of who was in charge. But mostly it left the Continental army poised to strike the decisive blow at New York whenever the winds and the gods delivered the French fleet of Washington's dream.[23]

His fixation on New York also meant that Washington adamantly opposed arguments for another Canadian campaign. Once an ardent advocate of a Canadian invasion, he now saw it as a mere sideshow to the main event which would divert troops and treasure needed elsewhere. When pressure from the Congress mounted for a prospective Franco-American expedition into Quebec, Washington objected on the grounds that, once the French planted their flag in a country "attached to them by all the ties of blood, habits, manner, religion and former connexion of government," they were unlikely ever to leave. He concluded with his unsentimental assessment of the French connection, and with what turned out to be one of the earliest and most forceful statements of the realistic tradition in American foreign policy: "Men are very apt to run into extremes; hatred to England may carry some into excessive Confidence in France . . . ; I am heartily disposed to entertain the most favourable sentiments of our new ally and to cherish them in others to a reasonable degree; but it is a maxim founded on the universal experience of mankind, that no nation is to be trusted farther than it is bound by its interest; and no prudent statesman or politician will venture to depart from it."[24]

For more than two years the singular exception to Washington's New York rule was the western frontier, the Ohio Country he knew so well. The Iroquois Confederation or Six Nations had made the wholly sensible but spectacularly misguided decision that America was destined to lose the war. And so, alongside British troops from Canada, they had staged raids on settlers in western New York and Pennsylvania designed to annihilate the American presence forever. Reports of the typically savage fighting on the frontier included stories of British officers collecting scalps (definitely true) and joining their Indian allies in cannibalistic victory orgies (probably untrue). In the spring of 1779, Washington ordered a substantial detachment of four thousand troops under John Sullivan to retaliate against the Six

Nations with equivalently savage intentions. "Your immediate objects," he wrote Sullivan, "are the total destruction and devastation of their settlements and the capture of as many prisoners of every age and sex as possible." Washington, who knew the contested terrain as well or better than anyone else, offered detailed instructions to Sullivan, who during the summer of 1779 conducted a merciless campaign that wholly destroyed about twenty Indian towns and villages. Only the Oneida tribe, which had come over to the American side, was spared. The Six Nations, which had once dominated the Ohio Country and then had vied on equal terms for imperial supremacy with France and Great Britain, never recovered from this blow. While Washington did not believe that Sullivan's campaign contributed significantly to the immediate cause of defeating Great Britain, it did help establish American control of the trans-Allegheny treasure after the war.[25]

While Washington was sending a detachment of his army to the west, the British were sending a much larger force to the south. Eventually he realized that the New York garrison, which he regarded as the nucleus of British power on the continent, was becoming a launching site for a full-scale campaign in the Carolinas; as he put it, "the operations in the Southern States do not resemble a transient incursion, but a serious conquest." Many Americans had presumed that the triumph at Saratoga marked the beginning of the end, but the British ministry had decided that it was merely the end of the beginning. Instead of withdrawing, the British had redoubled their efforts, replacing the troops lost at Saratoga and then adding another army of equivalent size in order to mount an invasion of the highly vulnerable American South.[26]

THE NADIR

IF BRITAIN's southern strategy surprised Washington, the resourcefulness of its war machine terrified him. "While we have been either slumbering and sleeping or disputing upon trifles," he lamented, the British had mobilized "the whole strength and resources of the Kingdom . . . against us." His dream of a Franco-American conquest of New York now had to compete with a nightmare in which the war did not end in one climactic battle, but in a grinding competition between warmaking institutions in which his side was outgunned, outspent, and outlasted. "In modern wars the longest purse may chiefly determine the event," he lamented, and "their system of public credit is such that it is capable of greater exertions than any other nation." Up until now, when

Washington thought about the importance of virtue as a source for patriotic commitment, he thought in personal terms: the courage of soldiers advancing against a British artillery position; the silent sacrifices of half-naked troops trudging through the snow at Valley Forge; his own decision to risk everything to serve a cause he believed in. Another more impersonal version of virtue now began to circulate in his thinking, a version not dependent on sheer willpower but rather on institutions capable of delivering resources. If the essence of personal virtue was bravery, the essence of institutional virtue was fiscal responsibility. And if the latter version of virtue determined the current contest, Washington acknowledged that "my feelings upon the subject are painful," for he was saddled with a fiscal system that seemed designed to produce, as he put it, only "false hopes and temporary expedients."[27]

His initial understanding of the political liabilities afflicting the Continental Congress, like his initial understanding of virtue, emphasized personal failures of will. The best men, he told Benjamin Harrison of Virginia, preferred to serve in the state governments, where they could "slumber or sleep at home . . . while the common interests of America are mouldering and sinking into irretrievable . . . ruin." While the second-tier delegates in the Continental Congress dithered over trifling issues, where were the first-tier leaders from Virginia?: "Where is Mason, Wythe, Jefferson, Nicholas, Pendleton, Nelson and another [i.e., Harrison] I could name?" Why was the Congress failing to prosecute profiteers and "forestallers" (hoarders who jacked up the prices of supplies needed by the army), who were obviously "pests of society," all of whom ought to be "hung in Gibbets upon a gallows five times as high as the one prepared by Haman?" How could a responsible group of legislators allow the currency to become a standing joke—not worth a Continental—and the inflation to spiral to such heights that "a rat, in the shape of a Horse, is not to be bought at this time for less than £200?" Given any semblance of equivalent resources, he was prepared to take on the British army and promise victory. But the failure of political leadership at the national level, which had permitted inflation, corruption, and broken promises to become "an epidemical disease," meant that sheer indifference had become a more formidable enemy "infinitely more to be dreaded than the whole force of G. Britain." It was beyond belief, he confided to an old Virginia friend, to watch America's best prospects become "over cast and clouded by a host of infamous harpies, who to acquire a little pelf, would involve this great Continent in inextricable ruin."[28]

The real problem, which Washington came to recognize only gradually, was less personal than structural, not so much a lack of will as a deep-rooted suspicion of government power that severely limited the authority of the Continental Congress. Parliament and the British ministry could impose taxes and raise armies because they possessed the sovereign power to speak for the British nation. During the early months of the war the Continental Congress had assumed emergency powers of equivalent authority, which rendered possible the creation of the Continental army and Washington's appointment to head it. But by behaving as a national legislature, an American version of Parliament, the Congress made itself vulnerable to the same criticism that the colonies had directed at Parliament itself. The central impulse of the American Revolution had been a deep aversion to legislation, especially taxes, emanating from any consolidated government in a faraway place beyond the direct control and supervision of the citizens affected. From the perspective of Virginia and Massachusetts, the delegates gathered in Philadelphia were distant creatures who could not tax them any more than could the House of Commons in London. And since voting in the Continental Congress had always been by state—one state, one vote—it could not plausibly claim to represent fairly or fully accurately the American population as a whole. The Articles of Confederation, officially adopted in 1781, accurately embodied the same one-vote principle and did not create, or intend to create, a unified American nation but rather a confederation of sovereign states.

Washington had given little thought to these political questions before the war. His revolutionary convictions, to be sure, included a staunch rejection of Parliament's power over the colonies. But the core of his hostility to British power had been rooted in questions of control rather than an aversion to political power per se, in the fact that it was **British** more than it was power. Personally, he despised the British presumptions of superiority that rendered him a mere subject. Politically, he believed that only an independent America could wrest control of the untapped riches west of the Alleghenies from London nabobs. He had left more finely tuned arguments about the proper configuration and character of an indigenous American government to others.

In 1780 he decided that he could no longer afford to remain silent. Although there were a few glimmerings before that date, he had been reluctant to express his opinions, lest in so doing he violate the near-sacred principle of civilian control. In 1777 he began the practice of sending routine Circulars to the States requesting money, supplies, and fresh recruits, his implicit recognition that ultimate power over these essentials lay with the state governments. By 1780 his growing sense of desperation pushed him over the edge as he became an outspoken advocate for expanded powers at the national level. "Certain I am," he informed one Virginia delegate in the Congress, "that unless Congress speaks in a more decisive tone; unless they are vested with powers by the several States competent to the great purposes of War, or assume them as a matter of right . . . that our Cause is lost. We can no longer drudge on in the old way. I see one head gradually changing into thirteen." The Congress needed to do more than recommend; it needed to dictate. "In a word," he complained, "our measures are not under the influence and direction of one council, but thirteen, each of which is actuated by local views and politics." If the Congress failed to expand its mandate and become a true national government, he warned, "it will be madness in us, to think of prosecuting the War."[29]

These were controversial conclusions about what the American Revolution must come to mean if it were to succeed. They were not destined to receive a full hearing until later, after the war had been won. Washington had reached them earlier than most precisely because he did not believe the war could be won unless they were immediately implemented. And in typical fashion, his thinking was not driven by theoretical arguments about republican government but by the harsh realities of war he faced as commander in chief, which by 1780 had come to resemble a more painful and protracted version of Valley Forge.

In January, for example, as two fully equipped British regiments prepared to embark from New York for South Carolina, sixty troops in the Massachusetts line had not been paid for a year and had not eaten in four days. Half the men had no shoes, but were intending to walk home because they had long since eaten their horses. Down in New Jersey, where the countryside had been picked clean after four years of foraging, Washington was forced to order a general confiscation of cattle and grain from the local farmers, noting that the choice was between stealing or starving: "We must assume the odious character of plunderers instead of the protectors of the people." No one could be sure about the current size of the Continental army—the best guess was around ten thousand—because many enlistments ended with the new year, creating what Washington described as a forever fluctuating force "constantly sliding from under us as a pedestal of Ice would do from a Statue in a Summers day." And no matter what the official rolls claimed, the number of starved, sick, and shoeless soldiers was so large that, as

Washington put it, "there is greater disproportion between the total number, and the men fit for duty . . . than in any army in the world." Even if the long-awaited French fleet magically appeared off Long Island, Washington estimated that he had only about half the troops necessary under his direct command to conduct a successful siege of New York.[30]

Over the ensuing months, what was already a dangerous situation became truly desperate. The winter encampment at Morristown in 1780 was more deplorably difficult than Valley Forge, with deaths and desertions reducing Washington's army to about eight thousand, of which fully one-third were not fit for duty. In the summer Washington learned of two major British victories in the South. Despite heroic efforts by its defenders, Charleston fell victim to British naval supremacy, the entire American garrison of over five thousand taken prisoner. Then Gates's army, recently sent south by the Congress with Washington's grudging endorsement of Gates's choice, was wholly routed at Camden. Washington tried to put the best face on these catastrophes, claiming that British naval supremacy had probably made Charleston indefensible, and that Gates's futile attempt to repeat his Saratoga triumph by relying heavily on militia only demonstrated the folly of that celebrated but misguided tactic. In October,

Washington recommended sending Greene, his most trusted general, to take charge of the surviving remnants of the army in the south. He confessed to Greene that it was probably an impossible mission, like sending one of the "forlorn hope" squads into battle and near-certain death.[31]

The fall brought more bad news, this time from a direction Washington least expected it. In August he had sent Benedict Arnold to command the garrison at West Point, which Washington regarded as the linchpin of the Hudson corridor and therefore the most strategic location in the entire northern theater. On September 25 he wrote Greene that "Transactions of a most interesting nature and such as will astonish you have just been discovered." Arnold, it turned out, had for several months been negotiating with the British for a substantial bribe in return for delivering West Point into their hands. The plot was exposed at the last moment and almost by chance when Arnold's British contact, Major John André, was stopped and searched by local militia. Arnold himself got word of his exposure in the nick of time and escaped down the river to New York, where he was instantly welcomed into the British army. André was tried and convicted as a spy. Despite pleas from several of his aides, including Hamilton, that André be executed by firing squad as befits a soldier, Washington ordered that he be hanged as a spy. He was not in a sentimental or generous mood.

In addition to creating the most notorious traitor in American history, the incident intensified Washington's fears that the sacrifices made by his officers' corps over the past three years, and the virtuous code they embodied, had both reached the breaking point. After all, if Arnold could sell out, the prospects were dim indeed. Though modern biographers have concluded that Arnold's treachery was more predictable and prosaic (that is, a matter of money), at the time Arnold seemed to symbolize the crumbling of an ideal and the collapsing of the cause.[32]

Events in January 1781 seemed to confirm this end-of-the-road reading. A large delegation of one thousand troops from the Pennsylvania line, who had not been paid in over a year and had no winter clothes, decided to march on the Continental Congress brandishing several artillery pieces. Two officers who attempted to stop them were shot down. The mutineers made a point of declaring that they were not traitors ("We are not Arnolds"), but rather dedicated soldiers fed up with broken promises. A second mutiny occurred three weeks later in the New Jersey line, this time the mutineers threatening to march on the state capital at Trenton with similar grievances. The first group was persuaded to turn back without further incident. But Washington ordered his officers to make an example of the second group, who were surrounded by six hundred loyal troops, then required to watch as the two leaders of the mutiny were executed on the spot.[33]

It was the lowest point of the dip. The British army was victorious in the south, and the Continental army was on the verge of dissolution in the north. And, rather incredibly it seemed to Washington, the Continental Congress claimed to be powerless to reverse the course by providing revenue. (To complete this depressing picture, the main French fleet was still cruising in the West Indies.) Whether one thought that the British were winning the war or the Americans were losing it, the end result was the same for Washington. Having pledged his life, his fortune, and his honor, he was about to lose them all. He told John Laurens that "our present force (which is but the remnant of an Army) cannot be kept together this Campaign" and the once glorious cause was now "suspended in the Balle; not from choice but from hard and absolute necessity."[34]

STRANGE VICTORY

WHEN WASHINGTON SPOKE of "a concatenation of causes," he was referring to the jagged course of the war as he experienced it. But it was a characterization that applied with special intensity to the last seven months of the conflict, which began in April 1781 with the American army and economy in disarray, and ended in October at Yorktown with a devastating British defeat that struck the British ministry "like a ball in the breast," as one witness reported, ending both the ministry itself and the bulk of the British Empire in North America. It was as if a spirited but overmatched boxer, reeling and about to collapse from exhaustion, stepped forward in the final round to deliver a knockout punch.[35]

How did it happen? The story begins with a series of double-edged developments that seemed to offer hope and then snatch it away, all in one motion. On the political front, after five years of haggling, the states finally managed to ratify the Articles of Confederation, thereby providing a constitutional foundation for that new entity called the United States of America. But the operative term remained "confederation," because sovereignty resided in the states rather than their union. The establishment of a new frame of government did permit long-overdue administrative reform, primarily a quasi-cabinet system creating secretaries of finance, war, and foreign affairs that presumably would provide greater coherence in managing the war effort. But as Robert Morris, the new secretary of finance, told Washington, the coffers of the government remained an empty cavern, or more accurately a large bottle of red ink, because the state delegations refused to approve new taxes. If one looked for financial relief to rescue the army from dissolution, Philadelphia was less promising than Paris, where Benjamin Franklin was attempting to arrange a French loan.

A French army of six thousand troops commanded by Count Rochambeau, a battle-scarred veteran of the European theater, had landed in Rhode Island the previous summer. But the force remained encamped at Newport throughout the following year as Washington and Rochambeau corresponded and met in three conferences to negotiate its deployment. Washington remained convinced that the only worthwhile target was the British garrison at New York. But that target required naval supremacy for any chance of success and—the problem of the missing French fleet again—Rochambeau refused to commit his troops as long as British ships controlled the Atlantic. Finally, in May 1781, at a conference in Wethersfield, Connecticut, the deadlock was broken when Rochambeau agreed to move his troops overland to link up with Washington outside New York. While the union of the French and American armies buoyed Washington's hopes for fulfillment of his New York dream, the failure of the states to meet their troop levies left his own army pitifully small—he expressed embarrassment when Rochambeau arrived and saw how under-manned and poorly equipped they were—so until fresh troops arrived in sufficient numbers, New York remained impregnable.[36]

Finally, news from the southern theater took a turn for both the better and the worse. On the better side, Washington learned in February 1781 that Daniel Morgan's riflemen had combined with local militia to inflict a stunning defeat on Cornwallis's troops at Cowpens. Then word arrived that Greene, though vastly outnumbered, was working his customary magic as the ultimate American Fabius, inflicting heavy losses with hit-and-run tactics that historians would eventually describe as the most brilliantly conducted campaign of the war. In one of the few full-scale battles, at Guilford Court House in March, Greene's army abandoned the field only after leaving it littered with a quarter of Cornwallis's troops dead or wounded.[37]

But the rays of light in the Carolinas were over-shadowed by ominous clouds in Virginia, where none other than Benedict Arnold, now a British general, was running amok over an almost defenseless countryside. In retrospect, it seems strange that the British army had steered clear of Virginia for so long, since it was a major cradle of revolutionary fervor that was also topographically tailor-made for amphibious operations along its long rivers and Chesapeake coastline. Washington had sent two thousand troops under Lafayette to counter the British campaign in Virginia, but by April 1781 it had become clear that this meager force could only harass the larger and more mobile British army, which was about to be rendered even more formidable by the imminent arrival of Cornwallis's troops moving up from North Carolina. And if Virginia fell to British occupation, all of Greene's splendid efforts further south would mean little, because the British would be able to cut off supplies from the north, then isolate and suffocate Greene's army.[38]

By the early summer of 1781, then, before the Yorktown opportunity materialized, the prospects for an American victory appeared remote in the extreme. Washington believed, as did several other American statesmen, that the resources of the country were exhausted and the Continental army was on the verge of extinction. The current campaign had to be the last. In the absence of a decisive outcome, the most likely development was a negotiated settlement the following year. We cannot know in detail the particular features of this alternative American future, but two aspects of the likely outcome seem clear: first, that the settlement would have reflected the military situation on the ground at war's end, so that considerable British diplomatic leverage would follow from its control of New York, Charleston, Savannah, and substantial segments of all the states south of the Potomac; second, that complete American independence would not be possible.[39]

Years later, when Washington was asked when he first envisioned leading a southern campaign against Cornwallis, he claimed that the idea was broached at a meeting with Rochambeau in September 1780. Strictly speaking, this was true, but the larger truth was that Washington remained obsessed with New York and resisted pressure from the governors of South Carolina and Virginia to take his army south well into the summer of 1781. He claimed that their understandable sense of desperation needed to be assessed in the broader context of the war, that he was "acting on the great scale." What he meant was that the American cause needed a decisive victory, and he believed that only New York could provide it. A Chesapeake campaign was in fact Rochambeau's preference, which Washington was willing to include as a secondary option only in deference to his French ally. His subsequent distortion of the historical record was designed to make the Yorktown victory a possibility he saw early on, whereas his correspondence reveals that New York had dominated his mind's eye for so long that he only gave it up grudgingly and gradually. Paradoxically, Clinton's interception of letters in which Washington identified New York as his abiding target—this was in June 1781—convinced the British that any Franco-American movement to the south was a mere diversion, thereby delaying their efforts to rescue Cornwallis until it was too late.[40]

Among the multiple reasons why Washington's New York dream had no chance of becoming a reality, one was paramount; namely, the French fleet was not going to New York because Rochambeau did not want it there. In May, without informing Washington, Rochambeau had instructed his colleague, Count de Grasse, to sail his fleet no further north than the Chesapeake. It is difficult to fathom what was in Rochambeau's mind as he and Washington reconnoitered the British defenses around New York in July, since Rochambeau knew full well that New York was never going to be the target. Perhaps he realized that he was dealing with a stubborn man who needed to abandon a long-standing obsession in his own time. That, at any rate, is what happened. In his diary entry for July 30, Washington confessed his concern about "my obstinacy in urging a measure to which his [Rochambeau's] own judgment was oppos'd." Three days later he wrote Robert Morris to request delivery of thirty transport ships in Philadelphia as soon as possible, observing that New York had been "laid aside" and that "Virginia seems to be the next object."[41]

Once Washington shifted his focus from New York to the south, he never looked back. If it was characteristic of him to cling tenaciously to his deepest convictions, it was also characteristic of him to let go when those convictions kept running afoul of what providence obviously intended. And by early September there appeared on the southern horizon an unexpected convergence of forces that could only be described as providential. In August, Cornwallis had moved his entire army of more than seven thousand troops onto the Tidewater peninsula at Yorktown. On September 2, as Washington prepared to board ships at Head of Elk in the northern reaches of the Chesapeake, de Grasse and the main French fleet appeared off Yorktown at Cape Henry. Washington could hardly believe the news or contain his excitement: "You See, how critically important the present Moment is," he wrote Lafayette. "If you get any thing New from any quarter, send it I pray you **on the Spur** of **Speed,** for I am all impatience and anxiety."[42]

Most military operations begin with a detailed plan that unravels and requires improvised adjustments as the details collide with messy realities.

The Yorktown operation followed precisely the opposite course. Initially, Washington was unsure of his destination; he mentioned Virginia, but also Charleston and the Carolinas as prospective targets, all contingent on the location of the French fleet. But then, as he and Rochambeau moved south, the ingredients for a spectacular triumph aligned themselves as if players in a drama written by the gods. Washington gave providence a helpful push by sending forward a vanguard of two thousand troops to join with Lafayette's force and block Cornwallis's escape route off the peninsula. Once the French fleet appeared and Cornwallis realized his predicament, he had only a few days to attempt a breakout. But in a monumental case of miscommunication that rivaled the earlier Howe-Burgoyne fiasco at Saratoga, Cornwallis apparently believed that Clinton had ordered him to stay put. By the time Washington and the main Franco-American army arrived on September 15, the Yorktown trap was sealed shut. "What may be in the Womb of Fate is very uncertain," Washington wrote the following week, "but we anticipate the reduction of Ld. Cornwallis with his Army, with much Satisfaction." The climactic battle that Washington had been envisioning for six years was at last at hand, though later than he expected and not at New York; indeed less than thirty miles from the dower plantation he inherited from Martha, close enough to allow his young stepson, Jackie, to join him as an impromptu aide.[43]

The Yorktown siege was essentially an exercise in engineering, which happened to be one of the Continental army's major weaknesses. Fortunately, the French army included the best military engineers in the world. As a result, though Washington was officially in command, the Yorktown siege was primarily a French operation. Ever meticulous, Washington issued a fifty-five-point memorandum to his officers clarifying their respective duties. He was also given the ceremonial honor of firing the first cannon shot against the British defenses, which according to lore scored a direct hit on a group of British officers gathered at the dinner meal. Most of the time, however, Washington only watched and tried to keep himself busy as the noose tightened around Cornwallis's army.[44]

Sighting: October 5, 1781

It is a moonless and rainy night as a squad of American sappers and miners attempt to extend the trench-line to within five hundred yards of the British perimeter. Sergeant Joseph Plumb Martin is in charge of the digging, only twenty-one but a six-year veteran of the Continental army, one of those poor New England farm boys who had signed up "for the duration" because it seemed like the right thing to do at the time. While digging away in the mud, a stranger appears alongside Martin's squad in the trench and urges the troops to work quietly because British sentries were nearby, and if discovered and captured to avoid divulging valuable information. Martin thinks this is well-intentioned but useless advice, since, as he later puts it, "we knew as well as he did that Sappers and Miners were allowed no quarter," meaning that they would be shot if discovered. Then a group of officers crawl into the trench and Martin hears them address the stranger as "His Excellency." This prompts Martin to wonder why the commander in chief is so needlessly and casually exposing himself to danger. Washington apparently never gives the matter any thought. The next night he joins the squad again, this time carrying a pickaxe, so that it can be recorded, somewhat inaccurately, that General Washington with his own hands first broke ground at the siege of Yorktown.[45]

Cornwallis acknowledged the inevitable on October 17, requesting a meeting to settle terms of surrender. Washington had only negotiated a surrender once before in his life, and that was his own at Fort Necessity twenty-seven years earlier. He insisted on the capitulation of the entire British garrison, though he did permit one British ship carrying Loyalist troops to sail off to New York. His diary entries during the forty-eight-hour truce focus on the logistical details of the surrender rather than the historical significance of the American victory or what he thought about it. His letters to de Grasse, urging an immediate continuation of the campaign, probably against Charleston, reveal that he did not realize that Yorktown was the final battle of the war.[46]

On October 19, as he sat astride Nelson, his favorite mount, while the defeated British troops marched out between the French and American armies, one witness reported that several redcoats ridiculed the American troops for their disheveled appearance and joked about shoeless victors. Cornwallis, pleading illness, excused himself from the surrender ceremony, and his surrogate, apparently confusing Rochambeau for Washington, attempted to present his sword to the French general. Several hundred black slaves, previously under Cornwallis's protection, many dying of smallpox, attempted to flee into the woods. Washington ordered them rounded up and advertisements published to return them to their rightful owners. (It is possible that some of Washington's former slaves at Mount Vernon were in the group.) The most consequential battle in American history, the decisive battle Washington had been questing after for six years, had just been won, but Washington did not understand that the war was over, and the surreal surrender scene itself added to the muddle. On a personal level, a family tragedy soon contributed to the confusion of the crowded moment, when Washington learned that Jackie had come down with camp fever, probably meningitis. He arrived at his stepson's bedside on November 5, just in time to watch him die.[47]

EXTENDED EPILOGUE

RATHER THAN CELEBRATE his victory, Washington spent several months warning everyone who would listen that the British ministry would respond to Yorktown the same way it had responded to Saratoga. "The king will push the War as long as the Nation would find Men or Money," because the leading figures in the British government were convinced that "the Sun of Great Britain will set the moment American Independency is acknowledged." He refused to believe reports from London and Paris that British negotiators tacitly recognized that they had lost their

American empire. Even with the capture of Cornwallis's army, he pointed out, the British still possessed a formidable force on the American continent, considerably larger than the Continental army. During an extended visit to Philadelphia, he urged the Congress to order him to resume the offensive, perhaps against Charleston, or, even better—the old dream again—against the British garrison at New York.[48]

The great revolutionary polemicist and gadfly Thomas Paine tried to calm Washington down, claiming that the number seven had magical powers over British thinking; it was the length of Parliament's terms, apprentice contracts, and property leases, so it stood to reason that this primal number would mark the end of the war, begun in 1775, in 1782. But Washington not only refused to submit America's fate to mere superstition, he insisted on maintaining his army in a state of readiness until the peace treaty in which the British officially acknowledged that America was wholly independent was signed. He admitted that there was a powerfully personal dimension to his feelings on this score. "From the former infatuation, duplicity, and perverse system of British policy," he told Greene, "I confess I am induced to doubt everything, to suspect everything." Never a man to place his fate in trust, he had learned to mistrust everything emanating from London. Even the term "negotiations" troubled him. What was there to negotiate? The British had tried to destroy him and his army, but he had destroyed them. He wanted the personal satisfaction that came with an unqualified, unconditional surrender. He wanted them to say that they had lost and he had won. He wanted his vaunted superiors to admit that they were his inferiors.[49]

Even while the war was still raging there had been critics in the Congress and the state governments who conjured up troubling comparisons between the Continental army and the Roman legions of Julius Caesar or the New Model Army of Oliver Cromwell. Everyone knew that these earlier experiments with republicanism had ended in military dictatorship. And despite glorious tributes to the victories of the Continental army, the very term "standing army" remained an epithet, seared into American memory with woodcut replicas of the Boston Massacre and inscribed in the Declaration of Independence as one of George III's criminal acts against the citizens of Massachusetts. During his Fabian phase Washington was even accused of deliberately prolonging the war in order to extend his quasi-monarchical power as commander in chief. And his well-known contempt for the fighting prowess of militia also made him vulnerable to critics who argued

that militias were safe and republican, while standing armies were dangerous and monarchical.[50]

After Yorktown, moreover, new life was
breathed into these old fears, since Washington's
insistence on maintaining the Continental army
at full strength during a time when the majority of
the citizenry believed, correctly it turned out, that
the war was over only intensified fears that he
intended to become the American Cromwell. It
did not help matters when reports circulated that
Alexander Hamilton, probably in his cups, had let
it be known that the new nation would be infinitely better off if Washington marched the army
to Philadelphia and ordered the Continental
Congress to disperse. Such loose talk triggered the
fear that the infant American republic was about
to be murdered in its infancy by the same kind of
military dictatorship that had destroyed the
Roman and English republics in their formative
phases. And since these were the only two significant efforts to establish republican governments
in recorded history, the pattern did not bode
well.[51]

Washington was fully aware of this pattern, and
therefore recognized the need to make explicit
statements of his intention to defy it. In May
1782 a young officer at the Newburgh encampment, Lewis Nicola, put in writing what many
officers were whispering behind the scenes: that

the Continental Congress's erratic conduct of the war had exposed the weakness of all republics and the certain disaster that would befall postwar America unless Washington declared himself king. (If the title itself caused problems, Nicola wrote, perhaps a less offensive name could be invented to appease public opinion.) Washington responded with a stern lecture to "banish these thoughts from your Mind," and denounced the scheme as "big with the greatest mischiefs that can befall my Country." When word of Washington's response leaked out to the world, no less an expert on the subject than George III was heard to say that, if Washington resisted the monarchical mantle and retired, as he always said he would, he would be "the greatest man in the world."[52]

While George III's judgment as a student of history has never met the highest standards, his opinion on this matter merits our attention, for it underlines the truly exceptional character of Washington's refusal to regard himself as the indispensable steward of the American Revolution. Oliver Cromwell had not surrendered power after the English Revolution. Napoleon, Lenin, Mao, and Castro did not step aside to leave their respective revolutionary settlements to others in subsequent centuries. We need to linger over this moment to ask what was different about Washington, or what was different about the political conditions created by the American Revolution, that allowed him to resist temptations that other revolutionary leaders before and since found irresistible.

It was certainly not a lack of revolutionary stature. He had been the centerpiece around which the army and the cause itself had formed in 1775. And he remained the human face and majestic figure that embodied dedication to American independence throughout the long and tortured path toward Yorktown.

Nor was it a matter of Washington's confidence that the new government, now called the Confederation Congress, could manage the postwar conditions any more competently than it had managed the war itself. He made his skepticism about the discrepancy between the political and economic problems facing the American republic and the wholly inadequate national government abundantly clear: "I am decided in my opinion," he wrote the governor of New York, "that if the powers of Congress are not enlarged, and made competent to all **general purposes,** that the Blood which has been spilt, the expence that has been incurred, and the distresses which have been felt, will avail in nothing; and that the band, already too weak, which holds us together, will soon be broken; when anarchy and confusion must prevail."[53]

Nor did Washington share the deep aversion to executive power, or for that matter centralized political power of any kind, that Virginia's leading political thinkers—including George Mason and Thomas Jefferson—regarded as the seminal impulse of republican government and the true "spirit of '76." The chief political lesson he took from his experience during the war was that the federal and state governments lacked sufficient energy, and that in rejecting the authority of the British Parliament and king, American statesmen had overgeneralized about the need to place tight limits on political authority per se. In his correspondence with the state governments, he often recommended a strengthening of the executive branch, and his constant refrain throughout the war was that the failure of the Continental Congress to behave as a sovereign national government with coercive authority over the states placed him at a distinct disadvantage in the competition with the British leviathan.[54]

Finally, Washington harbored no illusions that the Confederation Congress would keep the promises it had made to the army. In 1780 the Congress had enacted a resolution to give veteran officers half pay for life. But by the winter of 1782–83 it had become clear that the revenue to fund this pension would never be raised. Hamilton, now serving as a delegate in the Congress, reported that even a less expensive proposal of full pay for five years would fall victim to the same fate, an empty promise that would be completely forgotten once the peace treaty was signed and the army disbanded. By January 1783, Washington had concluded that the Congress's fear of a standing army had rendered treatment of the army itself into a standing joke. "The Army, as usual, are without pay; and a great part of the Soldiery without Shirts," he noted caustically, "and if one was to hazard for them [Congress] an opinion, it would be that the Army had contracted such a habit of encountering distresses and difficulties, and of living without money, that it would be impolitic and injurious to introduce other customs into it." He confessed to Hamilton that "the predicament in which I stand as a Citizen and Soldier is as critical and delicate as can well be conceived." His loyalty to the officers and veterans of the Continental army had a powerful emotional edge, for he believed, with some justice, that they had made the personal sacrifices that produced American independence. But he also believed, with equivalent certainty, that virtue would be its own and only reward, that "the prospect for compensation for past Services will terminate with the War."[55]

All of these considerations—Washington's transcendent stature, the weakness of the new federal government, and the grievances of the army—came together in March 1783 to create the Newburgh Conspiracy, which might also be called "the Last Temptation of Washington." In this culminating moment of his military career, Washington demonstrated that he was as immune to the seductions of dictatorial power as he was to smallpox. And, as was so often the case with his most dramatic decisions, the reasons for his behavior were so deeply buried in his character that they functioned like a biological condition requiring no further explanation.

Scholars who have studied the Newburgh Conspiracy agree that it probably originated in Philadelphia within a group of congressmen, led by Robert Morris, who decided to use the threat of a military coup as a political weapon to gain passage of a revenue bill (the impost) and perhaps to expand the powers of the Confederation Congress over the states. Washington got wind of the mischief when he learned of petitions circulating among officers at Newburgh that contained veiled threats of action against the Congress if their pensions were not assured. By early March 1783, as the plot thickened, a split had emerged within the officers' corps between moderates, led by Henry Knox, who were allied with congressional schemers to threaten a coup, and radicals, led by Horatio Gates, who were prepared to act on the threat and attempt a military takeover of the government. For obvious reasons, the secret conversations within the officers' corps never found their way into the historical record, making all efforts to recover the shifting factions in the plot educated guesses at best. We can be sure that the crisis came to a head on March 11, when the dissident officers scheduled a meeting to coordinate their strategy. Washington countermanded the order for a meeting, saying only he could issue such an order, then scheduled a session for all officers on March 16.[56]

He spent the preceding day drafting, in his own hand, the most impressive speech he ever wrote. Beyond the verbal felicities and classic cadences, the speech established a direct link between his own honor and reputation and the abiding goals of the American Revolution. His central message was that any attempted coup by the army was simultaneously a repudiation of the principles for which they had all been fighting and an assault on **his** own integrity. Whereas Cromwell and later Napoleon made themselves synonymous with the revolution in order to justify the assumption of dictatorial power, Washington made himself synonymous with the American Revolution in order to declare that it was incompatible with dictatorial power. It was the father lecturing the children on the meaning of this new American family. Here is the most eloquent and salient passage:

But as I was among the first who embarked in the Cause of our common Country. As I have never left your side one moment, but when called from you on public duty. As I have been the constant companion and witness of your Distress, and not among the last to feel, and acknowledge your Merits. As I have ever considered my own Military reputation as inseparably connected with that of the army. As my Heart has ever expanded with Joy, when I have heard its praises, and my indignation has arisen, when the mouth of detraction has been opened against it; it can **scarcely be supposed** at this late stage of the War, that I am indifferent to its interests. . . . And let me conjure you, in the name of our Common Country, as you value your own sacred honor, as you respect the rights of humanity, and as you regard the Military and National Character of America, to express Your utmost horror and detestation of the Man who wishes, under any specious pretences, to overturn the liberties of our Country, and who wickedly attempts to open the flood Gates of Civil discord, and deluge our rising Empire in Blood.[57]

There it was, simple but profound. At the personal level, Washington was declaring that he had sufficient control over his ambitions to recognize that his place in history would be enhanced, not by enlarging his power, but by surrendering it. He was sufficiently self-confident, assured about who he was and what he had achieved, to ignore all whisperings of his indispensability. At the ideological level, Washington was declaring that he instinctively understood the core principle of republicanism, that all legitimate power derived from the consent of the public. (Interestingly, Washington seldom used the term "republic" to describe the emerging nation that he, more than anyone else, had helped to create. His preferred term was "empire," which had imperial and monarchical implications that **were,** in fact, compatible with Napoleonic aspirations.) He did not agree with the versions of republicanism that emphasized the elimination of executive power altogether, and that opposed energetic government as a violation of all that the American Revolution meant. But he was a republican in the elemental sense that he saw himself as a mere steward for a historical experiment in representative government larger than any single person, larger than himself; an experiment in which all leaders, no matter how indispensable, were disposable, which was what a government of laws and not of men ultimately meant.[58]

Sighting: March 16, 1783

Washington has just entered the New Building at Newburgh, a large auditorium recently built by the troops and also called The Temple. About 500 officers are present in the audience. Horatio Gates is chairing the meeting, a rich irony since Gates is most probably complicitous in the plot to stage a military coup that Washington has come to quash. Everything has been scripted and orchestrated beforehand. Washington's aides fan out into the audience to prompt applause for the general's most crucial lines. Washington walks slowly to the podium and reaches inside his jacket to pull out his prepared remarks. Then he pauses—the gesture is almost certainly planned—and pulls from his waistcoat a pair of spectacles recently sent to him by David Rittenhouse, the Philadelphia scientist. No one has ever seen Washington wear spectacles before on public occasions. He looks out to his assembled officers while adjusting the new glasses and says: "Gentlemen, you will permit me to put on my spectacles, for I have not

**only grown gray, but almost blind in the serv-
ice of my country." Several officers began to
sob. The speech itself is anti-climactic. All
thoughts of a military coup die at that
moment.[59]**

In the summer and fall of 1783, as provisional
versions of the peace treaty were publicized and it
became clear that American independence was
assured, Washington kept drilling the Continental
army to new levels of military discipline just in case
the diplomatic effort collapsed and war resumed.
He was determined to leave nothing to chance.
(Ironically, the Continental army was probably
best prepared to fight when fighting was no longer
necessary.) He barraged the Congress with letters,
pleading for justice to the army in the form of
guaranteed pensions, even though in his heart he
knew that, no matter what the Congress enacted,
there was no money to fund the government's
promises. The army, in truth, had always been an
embarrassing contradiction to federal and state
lawmakers, a source of power and coercion that
simultaneously won the war and defied the revolutionary conviction that power and coercion were
violations of the natural order. The sooner it was
disbanded, its sufferings and achievements forgotten, the better.

As the fullness of the American victory became more evident, Washington summoned his final thoughts on what the triumph meant. If the Newburgh Address was his most eloquent oration, his last Circular Letter to the States, in June 1783, was the most poignant piece of writing he ever composed, a lyrical contrast to the flat and numbing official correspondence—tens of thousands of pages—that a team of secretaries was already transcribing for posterity. It was obviously an inspiring moment that called forth Washington's most visionary energies: "The Citizens of America, placed in the most enviable condition, as the Sole Lords and Proprietors of a vast tract of Continent, comprehending all the various soils and climates of the World, and abounding with all the necessaries and conveniences of life, are now by the late satisfactory pacification, acknowledged to be possessed of absolute freedom and Independency; They are, from this period, to be considered as Actors on a most conspicuous Theatre, which seems to be peculiarly designed by Providence for the display of human greatness and felicity."[60]

The great prize that the war had won, in short, was a continental empire, starting with those lands west of the Alleghenies he had explored as a young man. Washington believed that America's future as an independent nation faced west to the vast interior rather than east toward Europe. When Lafayette proposed a grand tour of the European capitals as a kind of victory parade, Washington countered with a proposal for an American tour of the "New Empire," starting in Detroit, going down the Mississippi River, then heading back through Florida and the Carolinas.[61]

His last Circular Letter also reviewed the recent success of American arms, which he continued to describe as "little short of a standing miracle," and developed the familiar theme of "a concatenation of causes," though this time from a higher elevation: "The foundation of our Empire was not laid in the gloomy age of Ignorance and Suspicion, but at an Epoch when the rights of mankind were better understood and more clearly defined, then at any former period." He then proceeded to identify the treasure trove of human knowledge about society and government that had accumulated over the past century—what was soon to be called the Enlightenment—and its providential arrival on the scene just as Americans launched their experiment with independence. "At this auspicious period," he observed, "the United States came into existence as a Nation, and if their Citizens should not be completely free and happy, the fault will be intirely their own."[62]

There were two dramatic farewell scenes with the army. The first occurred at Newburgh in early

November 1783, soon after word arrived from Paris that the definitive version of the peace treaty had been signed. Washington said goodbye to the ordinary soldiers of the Continental army in an emotional ceremony in which he addressed them as "one patriotic band of Brothers." He expressed his hope that the states would honor their obligation to fund the promised pensions, and he urged all the soldiery to return to their homes as citizens of the United States rather than as Virginians or New Englanders. He later bid teary-eyed personal farewells, at Fraunces Tavern in New York, to the officers who had served with him for more than seven years, the culmination of an experience they all recognized as the shaping event in their lives as well as the shaping event in American history.[63]

A final farewell scene occurred in Annapolis, where the Confederation Congress was sitting temporarily. On December 22 a formal dinner and dance was staged to honor "His Excellency." Washington's toast at the dinner disturbed some of the delegates—"competent powers to Congress for general purposes"—because of its apparent criticism of the limited powers provided by the Articles of Confederation. At the ball afterward Washington danced every dance, as the ladies lined up in rows, as one witness put it, "to get a touch of him." At the official ceremony the following day Thomas Mifflin was in the chair, a final irony since Mifflin had orchestrated the earlier campaign to force Washington's resignation. Now it was coming voluntarily as the culmination of American victory: "Having now finished the work assigned me," Washington solemnly said, "I retire from the great theatre of Action. . . . I here offer my Commission, and take my leave of all the enjoyments of public life." The man who had known how to stay the course now showed that he also understood how to leave it. Horses were waiting at the door immediately after Washington read his statement. The crowd gathered at the doorway to wave him off. It was the greatest exit in American history.[64]

CHAPTER FIVE

Introspective Interlude

NOTHING WOULD EVER be the same again. Before the American Revolution, Washington's reputation was regional rather than national, and it rested—rather precariously, it turned out— on his landed wealth, part of which came with Martha's dowry and part of which came as a consequence of his military service during the French and Indian War. After Yorktown his preeminence was national, indeed international, and it rested on the purity of his revolutionary credentials, a nearly inexhaustible reservoir of conferred grace akin to canonization. He had made himself the center of gravity around which all the revolutionary energies formed, had sustained the Continental army for nearly eight years of desperate fighting, and then had surrendered his unprecedented power in a symbolic scene that struck most observers as the last act in a historical drama written by the gods. He was, as one lyrical tribute put, "the man who unites all hearts," the American Zeus, Moses, and Cincinnatus all rolled into one. The poet Francis Hopkinson described him as "the best and greatest man the world ever knew," adding that "had he lived in the lap of idolatry, he had been worshipped as a god."[1]

No American had ever before enjoyed such a transcendent status. And over the next two hundred years of American history, no public figure would ever reach the same historic heights. (Being present at the creation confers unique opportunities for immortality.) It took a while for Washington to adapt to this new role as America's secular saint. At first he took refuge in silence, noting that the slower cadences of rustic life required a period of adjustment after the crowded routine of wartime, when he was constantly, as he put it, "upon the stretch." After a few months he developed a standard response to the avalanche of accolades: he was not a god, but merely the beneficiary of providential forces which had somehow guided him through what he called "the quicksands and Mines which lay in his way."[2]

Though he began to refer to himself in the third person, Washington could also make jokes about the ludicrousness of it all. When the Confederation Congress sent him a gold box containing his

surrendered commission—his souvenir as Cincinnatus—he observed that a century later it might
become a religious relic worshipped by his descendants. When the King of Spain transported a prize
jackass to Mount Vernon as a gift designed to
establish an improved line of American mules,
Washington observed that the jackass was so defi-
cient as a breeding stud that it must have obtained
its sexual appetite from the dwindling male line of
the Spanish monarchy. As the endless stream of
visitors determined to make a pilgrimage to
Mount Vernon occupied more of his time, he
periodically attempted to offset his reputation for
aloofness with a human touch, as when one perfect stranger who was coughing through the night
found Washington standing by his bedside with a
cup of tea for relief. Another early visitor, a French
dentist who specialized in implants, also com-
mented on Washington's courtesy, though not
even Washington could have predicted that, two
centuries later, his false teeth and bridgework
would become a major tourist attraction at
Mount Vernon.[3]

Of course, being a legend in his own time was
not a novel experience for Washington. He had,
in effect, been posing for posterity ever since his
designation as "His Excellency" during the earliest
weeks of the war. Even earlier, his near-miraculous
talent for surviving the disaster at Fort Necessity

and the massacre at the Monongahela instilled a keen sense that he was blessed, a sense that only deepened during the Revolutionary War when soldiers died in bloody heaps all around him and he emerged unscratched. But after 1783 his legendary status was inscribed in the first page of the new nation's history as a permanent presence to be enshrined and embellished forever. The sculptors, painters, chroniclers, and sheer gawkers descending upon Mount Vernon signaled an installation at the very pinnacle of America's version of Mount Olympus.

There was also one new ingredient in the heroic chemistry: Washington's growing recognition that, just as his place in the heavens was assured, his time on earth was running out. During the war he was too preoccupied with the daily duties of command to notice that he had moved past the allotted time—fifty years—that male members in the Washington line seldom reached and that he referred to as "the meridian of life." As he observed to the officers at Newburgh, his hair had in fact grown gray in service to his country. Those huge eye sockets were now permanently creased. The impressive muscularity of his torso had begun to soften and sag. The massive bone structure that had carried him with such grace on horseback or on the dance floor was now afflicted with rheumatism. (The man who had once led the pack in foxhunts now often declined the invitation to join the hunt rather than bring up the rear.) A somber note of resignation began to appear in his correspondence, the poignant tone of a once-great athlete past his prime who felt, literally in his bones, that he was "gliding down the stream of life." When Lafayette departed Mount Vernon after an extended visit in 1784, the parting prompted nostalgic reminiscences of bygone days and a stoic forecast of encroaching darkness: "I called to mind," he later wrote Lafayette, "the days of my youth, & found they had long since fled to return no more; that I was now descending the hill, I had 52 years been climbing—& that tho' I was blessed with a good constitution, I was of a short lived family—and might soon expect to be entombed in the dreary mansions of my father's—These things darkened the shades & gave a gloom to the picture . . . but I will not repine—I have had my day."[4]

The deaths of several younger protégés and former comrades-in-arms only intensified his fatalistic mood. John Laurens went down in a meaningless skirmish after Yorktown, one of the last casualties of the war. Tench Tilghman, another trusted aide-de-camp, succumbed to a viral infection in 1786. Nathanael Greene, his most loyal and valued subordinate, died of sun-stroke that same year. They all joined Charles Lee, the former colleague and rival, who had gone to his grave in 1782 amidst his beloved hounds and irreverencies. (Lee's will stipulated that he must be buried more than a mile from any Presbyterian or Baptist church, explaining that "I have kept such bad company when living, that I do not choose to continue it when dead.") Though Washington was accustomed to seeing death all around him throughout his life, these departures became morose reminders of his own aging, the narrowing time of his time.[5]

Hindsight permits us to regard Washington's postwar years at Mount Vernon as a mere interlude between two major chapters of active service; if you will, the pastoral interruption separating the general who was "first in war" from the president who was "first in peace." But Washington himself experienced these years as an epilogue rather than an interlude. A decade later, when two other prominent Virginians, Thomas Jefferson and James Madison, retired to their respective versions of rural solitude, John Adams predicted that their political ambitions were merely hibernating, observing that "political plants grow in the shade." Neither Washington nor anyone else believed that his ambitions were growing beneath his vines and fig trees at Mount Vernon. His public career, he firmly believed, was over, his life nearly so.[6]

Though he considered his own contribution complete, he did not feel that the American Revolution was over. The next step, "as plain as any problem in Euclid," and "as clear to me as the A., B., C.," was an enlargement of federal power sufficient to consolidate the energies of an exploding population and the resources of half a continent. Only a more powerful central government, he believed, could secure the gains made by the American Revolution, but it would probably require a crisis to make it happen. "I believe all things will come out right at last," he observed philosophically, "but like a young heir, come a little prematurely to a large inheritance, we shall . . . run riot until we have brought our reputation to the brink of ruin." In effect, things had to get worse before they could get better; or, as he put it, "the people must **feel** before they will **see**." But that would take time, more than he was allotted. He expected to use what remained to him arranging his private papers for the scrutiny of future historians, posing for painters and sculptors, entertaining the steady flow of admiring guests, making the final renovations on his mansion in order to render it as complete as his career. The great man of action was in a contemplative mood.[7]

POSTERITY, THE POTOMAC, AND
THE CINCINNATI

HIS OWN INTIMATIONS of mortality prompted a growing concern about his prospects for immortality. Never a deeply religious man, at least in the traditional Christian sense of the term, Washington thought of God as a distant, impersonal force, the presumed wellspring for what he called destiny or providence. Whether or not there was a hereafter, or a heaven where one's soul lived on, struck him as one of those unfathomable mysteries that Christian theologians wasted much ink and energy trying to resolve. The only certain form of persistence was in the memory of succeeding generations, a secular rather than sacred version of immortality, which Washington was determined to influence and, if possible, control as completely as he had controlled the Continental army. Most of the prominent leaders of the revolutionary generation recognized that they were making history, and took care to preserve their correspondence and edit their memoirs with an eye on posterity's judgment. But none of them, including such assiduous memorialists as Franklin, Jefferson, and John Adams, were as earnest in courting posterity as Washington.[8]

His posterity project had started toward the end of the war. In 1781, Washington persuaded Robert

Morris and the Continental Congress to fund a team of secretaries led by a young officer named Richard Varick and charged with the task of transcribing Washington's entire wartime correspondence. (At a time when the officers and soldiers of the Continental army were not being properly fed, clothed, or paid, Morris's willingness to subsidize this project is truly stunning.) Washington provided meticulous instructions to Varick, warning him that the task would prove more demanding than he could possibly imagine. Varick and his team worked eight hours a day for two years in Poughkeepsie, New York, before producing twenty-eight volumes. When they were completed and about to be shipped to Mount Vernon, Washington assured Varick that "neither the present age or posterity will consider the time and labour which have been employed in accomplishing it, unprofitably spent."[9]

Washington was convinced that his chief claim to fame would be the defeat of Great Britain in the War of Independence. The Varick manuscripts became the treasure trove on which all histories of the war would depend and, so he believed, the primary prism through which biographers and historians would view his life. "Any memoirs of my life," Washington explained, "distinct and unconnected with the general history of the war, would rather hurt my feelings than tickle

my pride whilst I lived." He hoped to avoid interviews about his personal life by referring the
countless chroniclers to the official wartime correspondence, thereby protecting his privacy and
avoiding even the appearance of self-promotion.
Personal interviews also struck him as vain,
adding somewhat imperiously that "I do not
think vanity is a trait of my character."[10]

The first historian granted access to the Varick
manuscripts was William Gordon, a Boston minister who had cultivated a correspondence with
Washington during the war. Gordon visited
Mount Vernon in August 1784 and published a
four-volume history of the War of Independence
four years later. (For several reasons, chiefly its
turgid style, Gordon's pioneering effort never fulfilled its author's soaring expectations.) Washington agreed to amplify Gordon's research with
personal reminiscences of fellow officers, saluting
the passionate patriotism of the recently deceased
Laurens and the abiding fortitude of Knox and
Greene. He offered little commentary on rivals
like Gates and Lee, presumably preferring to let
Lee and his sleeping dogs lie. He did respond to
Gordon's request about the fiasco at Fort Washington in 1776, which remained the major source
of criticism he received about his conduct of the
war. The final decision to defend that indefensible
position, he correctly noted, rested with the offi-

cer on the scene, who was Greene, "not that I want to exculpate myself from any censure which may have fallen on me, by charging another." Greene's untimely death the following year probably caused Washington some silent anguish, since he had shifted the Fort Washington stain to someone whom he deeply respected and who died ingloriously, hounded by creditors.[11]

After a year of retirement Washington concluded that he too was being hounded to an early grave, not by creditors but correspondents. "Many, mistakenly, think that I am retired to ease," he complained, "but in no period of my life—not in the eight years I served the public, have I been obliged to write so much **myself** as I have done since retirement." (Congress had inadvertently exacerbated the problem by making all letters to and from Washington immune to the postage requirement.) When he was commander in chief, Washington had enjoyed the assistance of bright, young aides at headquarters. Now he decided to reinstitute the same system, making Mount Vernon the headquarters for another kind of protracted campaign to protect and preserve the image of a private citizen who now happened to be a national institution.[12]

Tobias Lear, Harvard educated and fluent in French, joined the Washington entourage in May 1786, soon accompanied by David Humphreys,

an aspiring poet and somewhat overpolished styl-
ist educated at Yale. Though Washington never
doubted his own intelligence, he was sensitive
about his lack of formal education, especially his
prose, which tended to be muscular but awkward. Lear and Humphreys could contribute the
requisite felicity to letters that were being sent to
subsequent generations as much as to current correspondents. Which is to say that he recognized
that every letter he signed was likely to be preserved, copied, and catalogued like the Varick
manuscripts, and eventually contribute to that
corpus called the Washington legacy. He was not
just writing to his contemporaries; he was writing
to posterity.[13]

Despite his earlier refusal to cooperate with
any biographical venture that did not confine
itself to the wartime years, Washington felt sufficiently comfortable with Humphreys to cooperate in sketching a memoir of his youthful
exploits during that earlier war in the Ohio
Country. In what might be called revisionist history, he edited out his early ambition to become
a British officer and inserted slight distortions or
evasions designed to conceal the controversies
surrounding his surrender at Fort Necessity and
his partisan behavior during the Forbes campaign,
thereby sanding down the rough edges of his pre-
hero phase of development.[14]

And despite his congenital impatience with the time-consuming demands of visiting artists, he welcomed Robert Edge Pine for a three-week occupation filled with marathon sittings: "I am now so hackneyed to the touches of the Painter's pencil," he confessed, "that I am altogether at their beck, and sit like patience on a Monument whilst they are delineating the lines of my face. . . . No dray moves more readily to the Thill than I do to the Painter's Chair." In the fall of 1785 he welcomed Jean-Antoine Houdon, France's most distinguished sculptor, who had traveled all the way from Paris at Jefferson's request to make a life mask for his classic bust and statue. As Washington explained to Lafayette, these tedious sessions had become like mandatory military formations; artists like Houdon were "the doorkeepers of the temple of fame" who held "the keys of the gate by which Patriots, Sages and Heroes are admitted to immortality." It was the unavoidable price of being an icon.[15]

If posterity was heaven on earth in the future, Washington was certain that the American future was a heavenly location in the West. "If I was a young man, just preparing to begin the world," he told one friend, "I know of no country where I would rather find my habitation than in some part of that region." And he was nearly certain that the river that flowed past Mount Vernon was divinely ordained as the avenue over the Alleghenies into the bounty of the American interior. The massive piazza Washington added to the eastern side of Mount Vernon in the 1780s afforded a magnificent location from which to visualize the Potomac dream, which also carried his imagination upstream and backward in time to his youthful explorations in the Ohio Country, as well as to the continental empire that was the palpable prize of his wartime triumph. For all these reasons, Washington devoted considerable attention and energy during his retirement years trying to transform his Potomac dream into a reality. Like his posterity project, it was an aging man's effort to extend his control over the shape and size of his legacy.[16]

There was both a romantic and a realistic dimension to his thinking. On the romantic side, Washington continued to harbor his long-standing belief that navigation improvements on the upper reaches of the Potomac would provide the best access to the river networks of the Ohio Valley, eventually linking the Chesapeake Bay with the Mississippi and making Alexandria the commercial capital of the nation. As president of the Potomac River Company, he encouraged publications like **Potomac Magazine,** which described the confluence of the Potomac and the Anacostia as the world's greatest natural harbor "where 10,000 ships the size of Noah's arc" could comfortably dock. He urged Robert Morris to invest in the company, claiming that "I would hazard all the money I could raise" on the Potomac's prospects. (Morris declined, though other misguided land speculations eventually landed him in bankruptcy.) Given the subsequent location of the national capital on the Potomac, it is ironic that the western drift of Washington's Potomac thinking led him to oppose proposals in the Confederation Congress—this was in 1785— for a capital on the Atlantic Coast, arguing that "the Seat of Empire . . . will not remain so far to the Eastward long." His embrace of the Potomac mythology also inspired some of his most vision- ary renditions of America as "the Land of prom- ise . . . for the poor, the needy, & oppressed of the Earth." Waves of immigrants would flow over the Atlantic and through "the front door" that was the Potomac, on to "the fertile plains of the Western Country," in one rendition reaching all the way to California.[17]

The Potomac dream was an illusion, but we should be able to overlook one minor misstep by someone so otherwise prescient about where his- tory was headed. And, on the realistic side, Wash- ington's Potomac obsession may have got the "front door" wrong, but it correctly grasped that westward migration would be the central theme of American history for at least the next century. In the 1780s he worried that the Confederation Congress was too distracted and divided by local interests to manage western expansion coherently. He favored what he called "Progressive Seating," meaning the gradual but steady occupation of successive border regions, coupled with federal support for roads and inland navigation. (The Potomac River Company, in short, was a private model for what the federal government should be doing publicly.) If internal improvements were neglected, Washington feared that the swelling population west of the Alleghenies would drift into alien orbits and "would in a few short years be as unconnected to us, indeed more so, than we are with South America." Already, he warned, the western settlements "stand as it were upon a pivot—the touch of a feather would turn them any way."[18]

The most menacing western culprit in the Washington nightmare scenario—no surprise here—was Great Britain, whose troops remained stationed on the frontier in violation of the Treaty of Paris, surely hoping to recover some portion of the empire lost at Yorktown. Spain, the other European power with a presence in the American West, did not trouble him, because he regarded Spanish economic and military weakness as a chronic condition. In 1785 he counseled against diplomatic negotiations with Spain about navigation rights on the Mississippi. "Why should we, prematurely, urge a matter," he asked, "if it is our interest to let it sleep?" In effect, he regarded Spain as a convenient holding company destined to be overwhelmed by the tidal wave of American settlers.[19]

Finally, there was a sharply personal edge to his thinking about the fate of those western lands. To be sure, all of Washington's western concerns flowed directly out of his personal desire to assure that the national domain acquired by the victory over Britain—**his** victory—not be squandered away. In addition to that national legacy, however, Washington himself owned nearly sixty thousand acres of western land, including parcels in the Shenandoah Valley, western Pennsylvania, and— the mother lode—two huge tracts on the Ohio and Great Kanawha. Given the declining fortune of his Mount Vernon farms, his western properties had become his chief source of revenue, in the form of rental fees, as well as the foundation of his net worth. And the value of those lands depended heavily on the settling of western territories by the confederation government in a prompt and prudent fashion.[20]

In all other areas of his public life, Washington was acutely sensitive to any appearance of impropriety when his own financial interest was involved. His refusal to accept a salary as commander in chief, for example, reflected the rock-ribbed conviction that the purity of his motives must match the purity of the cause he served. In 1785, when his fellow trustees of the Potomac River Company offered him fifty shares of company stock as payment for his services, he tortured himself and his friends with questions about the proper way to decline the offer without appearing ungrateful. But in the Washington psyche land was different from stock or money. It triggered a set of alarm bells that rang in that portion of his memory predating his ascendance as a Virginia squire, before the Mount Vernon or Custis inheritances, all the way back to that youthful adventurer-on-the-make with only his physical prowess and military reputation to carry him forward. His appetite for acreage, then, was the single fault line that ran through his otherwise impregnable interior defenses and control points, because land represented the only tangible and abiding measure of his hard-won status, the only form of financial security truly worthy of the name.[21]

His avaricious attitude toward land was put on dramatic display in September 1784, when he decided to tour his western holdings and came upon several families who had settled on plots he owned in western Pennsylvania. One can only imagine the disappointment the settlers felt in learning that the land they had been cultivating as their own for many years actually belonged to an absentee owner, and that the owner was none other than George Washington. When they questioned the legality of his title, Washington hired a lawyer to have them evicted if they refused to leave or pay him rent as tenants. "I viewed the defendants as willful and obstinate Sinners," he explained, "persevering after timely & repeated admonition, in a design to injure me." He seemed to regard his land as an extension of himself, and therefore its occupation as a personal violation. The court case dragged on for two years, pitting the most powerful figure in the nation against a feisty delegation of impoverished farmers. Though he won the case, his victory did nothing to embellish his reputation for soaring majestically above his own private interests. The episode also exposed another anomaly produced by his insatiable hunger for land. Instead of the Jeffersonian model of independent yeoman farmers, Washington had opted for the Fairfax model of tenants and proprietary control, a choice almost calculated to slow westward migration, since no settler in his right mind would willingly opt to rent rather than own. If part of Washington's mind was haunted by memories of his landless Virginia youth, it was also stuck in the hierarchical presumptions of that same earlier era.[22]

Both his memories and presumptions were called into question in the early months of his retirement, when a political firestorm broke out over his membership in the Society of the Cincinnati. Prior to their disbandment, the officers of the Continental army had formed a fraternal order of that name and quite naturally selected Washington as the first president. While its name announced the intention to avoid meddling in politics, and its constitution emphasized fraternal and philanthropic goals, the Society of the Cincinnati was an avowedly elitist enterprise designed to sustain the aristocratic ethos of superior virtue that officers in the Continental army had been harboring since Valley Forge. Most ominously, membership was defined in hereditary terms, passing exclusively to the eldest male descendant in the next generation. (Ironically, this provision meant that Washington's line would die with him, since he had no direct heirs, male or female.) The society immediately became the focus of public ridicule, especially in New England, where the Massachusetts legislature condemned it as a vestige of European aristocratic decadence and a conspicuous threat to the republican values the American Revolution had supposedly established forever. Over in Paris, Franklin lampooned the hereditary requirement by calculating that the amount of patriotic blood passed on would be infinitesimally small after two centuries of primogeniture, so why not reverse the hereditary principle by designating ancestors rather than descendants, preferably mothers rather than fathers, who probably were more responsible for instilling patriotism in their sons than anyone else?[23]

Washington was initially tone-deaf to these criticisms, in part because he shared the fraternal ethos of its members, whom he believed to be the virtuous few who, more than anyone else, had won American independence, in part because his own version of independence also retained an elitist edge of its own. Which is to say that he believed the American Revolution had destroyed monarchy and British imperial rule, and in that sense was a significant political revolution, but he did not believe that it was also a social revolution that destroyed the world of privilege, rank, and deference in which he had risen to prominence before the war. For him, the Society of the Cincinnati did not defy the best ideals of the American Revolution; it embodied them.

Washington never changed his thinking about the society, which he described as an "innocent institution" with "immaculate intentions," but he did change his mind about lending his own prestige to its purposes. Jefferson was apparently the first confidant to warn him that members of the society were widely regarded as an aspiring American nobility, its hereditary requirement "a violation of the natural equality of man," and that Washington's continued association with its agenda would do serious harm to his own reputation. In March 1784, he traveled to the first national meeting of the society in Philadelphia, convinced that he needed to resign the presidency, eliminate the hereditary principle, and, if Jefferson's recollection of a conversation in Annapolis can be believed, call for the abolition of the entire enterprise if halfway measures proved inadequate. "If we cannot convince the people that their fears are ill-founded," he explained, "we should . . . yield to them and not suffer that which was intended for the best of purposes to produce a bad one."[24]

Accustomed to getting his way, Washington presumed that his warnings would be heeded and the society would die a speedy death. But the younger members, plus a delegation of French applicants, forced another meeting in May in which a few minor modifications of the bylaws, which did not include eliminating the hereditary principle, were approved as sufficient to answer the public criticism. Washington attended the May meeting and released a statement designed to put the best face on the proceedings, though in private he confessed that "we have been most amazingly embarrassed in the business that brought us here." The Society of the Cincinnati not only remained alive, the members also continued to elect Washington as president, despite his best efforts to maintain a discreet distance from their meetings. Writing from France in 1786, Jefferson reported that the society posed even greater dangers than he had previously recognized, that it was like a cancer growing in the heart of the American republic, and that "a single fibre left of this institution will provide an hereditary aristocracy which will change the form of our governments from the best to the worst in the world."[25]

The Society of the Cincinnati thus became a kind of lovable albatross tied permanently around Washington's neck. It was lovable because he felt deep emotional attachments to most of the society's prominent members, who were the "band of brothers" with whom he had shared the most intense experience of his life, and theirs. It was an albatross because the society became a convenient symbol of aristocratic attitudes and values, and therefore a lightning rod for the kind of conspiratorial fears that Jefferson, among others, harbored toward any institutionalized expression of social inequality. As his new aide, David Humphreys, put it in 1786: "I am sensible the subject is a very delicate one, that it will be discussed by posterity as well as by the present age, and that you have much to lose and nothing to gain by it."[26]

Looking ahead, the accusations leveled at the society provided a preview of the ideological battles destined to engulf Washington during his second term as president. Looking backward, the charges echoed the arguments directed at the Continental army as a menacing threat to the very values the American Revolution claimed to stand for. Washington was on record as believing the latter charges were at best naive and at worst traitorous. And he confided to friends that he found the accusations against the society to be hyperbolic prejudices, "conjured up by designing men, to work their own purposes upon terrified imaginations." That said, his association with the Society of the Cincinnati clashed with his chief preoccupation, which was the courting of posterity's judgment, so throughout the 1780s he chose to keep his criticism of its enemies private and his connections with its public functions limited. Most tellingly, the outcry over the society forced him to realize, probably for the first time, that the American Revolution had released egalitarian ideas that he was at pains to understand, much less find compatible with his own version of an American republic, which was elitist, deferential, virtuous, and honorable—in short, pretty much like him.[27]

THIS SPECIES OF PROPERTY

IN DECEMBER 1785, Washington received a letter calculated to focus his mind on another worrisome association even more damaging to his abiding public image than the Society of the Cincinnati. It came from Robert Pleasants, a Virginia Quaker who had recently emancipated all eighty of his own slaves and minced no words in instructing Washington to do the same: "How strange then it must appear to impartial thinking men, to be informed, that many who were warm advocates for that noble cause during the War, are now sitting down in a state of ease, dissipation and extravigence on the labour of slaves? And most especially that thou . . . should now withold that inestimable blessing from any who are absolutely in thy power, & after the Right of freedom, is acknowledged to be the natural & unalienable Right of all mankind." Pleasants somewhat gratuitously suggested that Washington had probably been too preoccupied with the inevitable details of his retirement routine to think about "a subject so Noble and interesting," because once he did think about it, his response must be as self-evident as those truths that Jefferson had enshrined in the Declaration of Independence.

Pleasants did not stop there. He concluded with a little lecture designed to strike Washington, otherwise invulnerable, in his most vulnerable spot. If he acted decisively at this propitious moment by freeing his slaves, it would crown his career and assure his place in the history books. But if he faltered and lost this opportunity, the failure would haunt his reputation forever: "For not withstanding thou art now receiving the tribute of praise from a grateful people, the time is coming when all actions shall be weighed in an equal balance, and undergo an impartial explanation." How sad it would then be to read that the great hero of American independence, "the destroyer of tyranny and oppression," had failed the final test by holding "a number of People in absolute slavery, who were by nature equally entitled to freedom as himself."[28]

Washington did not answer Pleasants's letter. He was not accustomed to being the butt of lectures, especially from strangers dripping with moral superiority, and most especially from Quakers, whose pristine consciences had obliged them to sit out the war as spectators. Nevertheless, the letter could not be summarily dismissed as a mere irritation. It linked the subject Washington cared about most, posterity's judgment, with the subject he had come to recognize as the central contradiction of the revolutionary era. Which is to say that Pleasants was incorrect in assuming that Washington had given little thought to the question of slavery. To be sure, the subject remained the proverbial ghost at the banquet, so obviously and ominously a violation of all the Revolution stood for that no one felt free to talk about it openly, lest the guests at the table transform the polite conversation into a shouting match. Despite the code of silence and circumspection, there is considerable evidence that slavery was very much on Washington's mind during his retirement. And the ideas swirling through his head, to the extent that we can draw them out into the open for scrutiny, followed two separate lines of thought.[29]

One line of thought was initially prompted by the exigencies of war. Washington had grudgingly accepted free blacks into the Continental army in 1775, then had commanded a racially integrated force for nearly eight years. Characteristically, he made no comment on this development, though it exposed him to a range of racial relationships that he had never encountered as the master of Mount Vernon. The first indication that Washington recognized the disjunction between the purported goals of the War of Independence and the continuation of slavery occurred in 1779, when John Laurens proposed arming three thousand slaves in South Carolina and offering emancipation in return for service to the end of the war. Though clearly a wartime scheme driven by manpower needs, the Laurens proposal broached the possibility of making military service the opening wedge for a more general, if gradual, emancipation. Perhaps Washington was only humoring Laurens, telling a bright young favorite what he wanted to hear, but he endorsed the idea, adding the cautionary note that a partial emancipation could backfire by "rendering Slavery more irksome to those who remain in it" and acknowledging that "this is a subject that has never before employed much of my thoughts." When the South Carolina legislature rejected the Laurens proposal, as Washington had predicted it would, he described the rejection as a sign that the revolutionary fires, which had burned so brightly early in the conflict, had now subsided, "and every selfish Passion has taken its place."[30]

Lafayette, even more than Laurens, also prompted Washington to acknowledge that ending slavery was a logical outcome of the American Revolution. Just before the end of the war, in 1783, Lafayette urged an experiment in emancipation whereby a group of Virginia slaves would be freed and resettled as tenant farmers in some unspecified western region of the state. Washington embraced the plan without reservation: "The scheme, my dear Marquis, which you propose as a precedent to encourage the emancipation of the black people of this Country from that state of

Bondage in which they are held, is a striking evidence of the benevolence of your Heart. I shall be happy to join you in so laudable a work."[31]

Nothing came of Lafayette's proposal. And perhaps, as with Laurens, Washington was indulging a dear friend whose visionary scheme, so symptomatic of Lafayette's romantic temperament, could be safely endorsed precisely because Washington knew that it would never happen. At any rate, Washington's public behavior at the end of the war cut in the opposite direction. In the aftermath of Yorktown, then again during the British evacuation of New York, he insisted on the return of all escaped slaves in British custody to their respective owners. (Four of his own slaves were included in the contingent of about three thousand carried from New York to freedom by the British navy.) By the start of his retirement, then, any picture of Washington's mind on the slavery question would be blurry; but there **would** be a picture, because he now recognized that slavery was a massive American anomaly. Before the war the picture would have been completely blank.[32]

The picture became more focused three years into his retirement. Lafayette made two extended visits to Mount Vernon in 1784–85, and subsequent correspondence between them as well as the commentary of other visitors confirm that Lafayette prodded Washington to take a more outspoken position on slavery. The Virginia legislature was then debating the right of freed slaves to remain in the state, so the question of emancipation was in the political air. In April 1786, Washington wrote Robert Morris: "I can only say that there is not a man living who wishes more sincerely than I do, to see a plan adopted for the abolition of it [slavery]—but there is only one proper and effectual mode by which it can be accomplished, & that is by Legislative authority: and this, as far as my suffrage will go, shall never be wanting." He wrote a similar letter to Lafayette the following month, also endorsing gradual emancipation. Then in September he wrote John Francis Mercer, who owed him money, saying that he could not accept slaves as payment: "I never mean (unless some particular circumstances should compel me to it) to possess another slave by purchase; it being among my first wishes to see some plan adopted, by the legislature by which slavery in this Country may be abolished by slow, sure, & imperceptible degrees." Whether Lafayette's affectionate prodding, Pleasants's lecturish warning, or the natural drift of his own thinking was most influential cannot be known. Whether his motives were purely moral, or mainly a fixation on his future reputation, or some seamless mixture of the two, is equally unknowable. But he was now on record, at least in private, endorsing slavery's eventual end.[33]

A second line of thought focused, not on slavery as a national institution, but on slavery at Mount Vernon. During the early months of the war Washington had presumed that his estate would become a target of British or Loyalist recriminations. By 1779, when Mount Vernon still remained miraculously intact, he began to think anew about his labor force. He told his manager, Lund Washington, that he had decided to abandon slave labor if and when the war ended favorably. (If the war ended badly, all plans were meaningless.) The question was not whether he should sell his slaves, he told Lund, but "where, and in what manner it will be best to sell." The currency inflation mitigated against an immediate sale, and his own convictions precluded any sale that split up families. But he had decided to replace slaves at Mount Vernon with hired workers.[34]

The correspondence about slavery at Mount Vernon and that with Laurens about emancipating South Carolina slaves in return for service occurred at the same time, the winter of 1779, so it is possible that the two lines of thought crossed. But the language Washington used about slavery at Mount Vernon made no mention of moral or ideological motives. It was a hardheaded business decision rooted in his conviction that slave labor was more inefficient and costly than free labor. And he was thinking about **selling** his slaves into bondage to others, not freeing them. His train of thought about slavery at Mount Vernon was apparently not driven by idealistic considerations but by realistic calculations about profit and loss.

His voluminous correspondence about the management of Mount Vernon during his wartime absence is filled with detailed instructions about which hogs to slaughter, which fields to manure and cultivate with specific kinds of wheat, where to dig irrigation ditches and plant locust trees, but says precious little about the larger contours of his thinking about the operation as a whole. In the absence of conclusive evidence, the most plausible speculation is that the decision to abandon slaves as a labor force followed logically from his earlier decision to abandon tobacco as a cash crop in favor of wheat. Once he made that decision, his Mount Vernon farms resembled the diversified farms of Pennsylvania more than the plantations of the Tidewater or Carolinas. In that altered agrarian scheme, he gradually concluded that the cost of maintaining a slave labor force became prohibitively expensive. In fact, he owned more slaves than he could productively employ. And the surplus was costing him dearly.

Despite his assiduous attention to the most minute details of management, Mount Vernon made only a marginal profit in the best years before the war, and during the war it began to resemble those many Virginia plantations declining toward bankruptcy. Washington's decision to abandon slave labor, then, fit sensibly into a larger pattern of decisions driven by his acute appreciation of the bottom line and his personal obsession with economic independence. He had recognized that tobacco would not work, and moved to wheat. He had recognized that the consignment system locked him into mounting debts with Cary & Company, and had broken that connection, indeed had eventually seen fit to break with the British Empire itself. Now he recognized that slavery was as much the source of the problem as tobacco or imperial regulations, so he needed to free himself, though not his slaves, from the costs of bondage.[35]

There was a simple but sweeping quality to Washington's grasp of the elemental realities underlying the plantation economy of Virginia, which conjured up a vision of slavery as an economic anachronism that went hand in hand with his still developing picture of slavery as a moral anachronism. Carried to its logical and imaginative limits, it was a vision of the Old Dominion as the southern outpost of a Middle Atlantic economy based on crop diversification and free labor, rather than the northern outpost of a Deep South economy based on a single cash crop and slavery. (If this vision had ever been implemented, the political chemistry of the subsequent national debate over slavery would have been dramatically different, as would the inevitability of the Civil War, which is difficult to imagine with Virginia on the Union side.) By the time he began his retirement, Washington's mind had not changed on this score, at least in terms of what he preferred for sensible economic reasons. But neither had the swollen size of the slave population at Mount Vernon, which now numbered slightly more than two hundred men, women, and children.[36]

Given Washington's justifiable reputation for carrying through on his convictions, the question becomes: Why did he not carry through on his decision to sell his slaves? The desire to do so apparently remained alive in August 1784, when William Gordon, visiting Mount Vernon to do research for his history of the war, reported a conversation between Washington and Lafayette: "You wish to get rid of all your Negroes," Gordon recalled, "& the Marquis wisht that an end might be put to the slavery of all of them," a complementary set of goals that would "give the finishing stroke & polish to your political characters."

About this time, however, it was gradually dawning on Washington that any wholesale scheme for selling his slaves encountered three overlapping difficulties that, taken together, posed an intractable dilemma: first, the dower slaves inherited through the Custis estate did not legally belong to him, and were therefore not his to sell; second, the eldest slaves, who had been acquired when he was developing his Mount Vernon properties in the 1760s, were now beyond their prime work years and therefore nearly impossible to sell; third, and most importantly, the multiple and many-layered connections by blood and marriage within the slave population at Mount Vernon virtually precluded any general sale once Washington had resolved not to break up families. By the middle of the 1780s, then, he faced what we might call a truly Faulknerian situation; both he and his black workforce were trapped together in a network of mutual dependency that was spiraling slowly downward toward economic ruin.[37]

Hindsight permits us the clairvoyance to see that the only escape from this trap, the solution that Robert Pleasants urged then and modern-day moralists have echoed in our own time, was to free his slaves outright. If he gave that possibility any serious consideration in the 1780s, the idea did not make it into the historical record. (It does seem plausible, though there is no evidence for it, that this was the moment when he first considered freeing his slaves in his will.) The evidence that does exist suggests a more muddled position: he vowed never again to purchase another slave, a somewhat hollow promise since, as he himself acknowledged, he was already overstocked with "this species of property"; he accepted, grudgingly, the fact that Mount Vernon would never show a profit, because it had become a retirement home and child-care center for many of his slave residents, whom he was morally obliged to care for.[38]

In 1787 he admitted that Mount Vernon had run a deficit for the past eleven years, and there was every reason to expect that trend to continue. The following year he reported that his annual losses caused him "to feel **more sensibly** the want of money, than I have ever done at any period of my life." An English farmer, James Bloxam, whom he hired in 1786 to improve techniques of cultivation, claimed that the soil around Mount Vernon was one obstacle, but the lackadaisical workforce was the major liability: "The General have some very (**illegible**) But badly manedge and he will never have them no Better for he have a Sett About him which I nor you would be trobled with. But the General is goot them and he must keep them. But they are a verey Disagreable People." (Some of the slaves, finding Bloxam equally disagreeable, threatened to poison him if he stayed at Mount Vernon.) Washington himself noted that the youngest slaves were seldom assigned chores, "for at present to skulk from house to house under some frivolous pretence or another seems to be the principal employment of most of them." The prewar master of Mount Vernon would never have allowed such behavior. The postwar master was mellower, more willing to accept the fact that much of what he grew on his farms would never reach the marketplace, but would be consumed on the grounds by his black laborers and their families. In sum, if he could not sell them, Washington chose to make the maintenance of slave families at Mount Vernon a higher priority than profit. At some unspoken level, he saw this as a moral posture, and a small price for a troubled conscience to pay for a measure of solace.[39]

INFANT EMPIRE

IN JULY 1784, Washington received a long letter from an anonymous admirer which took the form of a sermon in the jeremiad mode. It described the early days of the American Revolution as a magic moment when virtuous values flourished, patriots rallied to the cause, private interests were surrendered to public ideals, and Washington himself stepped forward to embody the self-sacrificing "spirit of '76." But since those heady times, the writer lamented, the Revolution had followed a precipitous downhill course much like the corruption of the Garden of Eden after the Fall. "Extortioners, speculators, Hucksters & Practising Lawyers" had transformed the glorious cause into a degenerate exercise in profiteering and fraud. The money changers, in effect, had taken over the temple, and only the second coming of the messiah could redeem the Revolution by recovering its original character and course. There was no doubt in the writer's mind who the American messiah was: "I am therefore, from a Conviction that the Present is a Critical moment for America, irresistibly impeled to address you Great Sir, not only as the fittest, but I fear the only Person on Earth, that together with the inclination, possesses the Probity and Abilities sufficient to avert the impending ruin."[40]

Just as he required no instruction from Robert Pleasants about the evil of slavery, Washington did not need to hear a sermon on the decline of American virtue from some anonymous stranger. He had, in fact, lived that story as commander in chief of the chronically undermanned, underfed, undersupplied Continental army. But the lamentation about virtue, or the lack thereof, presumed that the answer to the problem was moral reformation (or perhaps an extensive series of frontal lobotomies). During the war Washington had learned, the hard way, that depending upon a virtuous citizenry was futile, for it asked more than human nature was capable of delivering. Rather than pray for moral reform, he preferred to lobby for political reform. "No Man in the United States," he told Hamilton at the end of the war, "is, or can be more deeply impressed with the necessity of reform in our present Confederation than myself." Making voluntary sacrifice the operative principle of republican government had proved to be a romantic delusion. Both individual citizens and sovereign states often required coercion to behave responsibly, which meant that the federal government required expanded powers of taxation and ultimate control over fiscal policy. Lacking those powers, Washington believed that "the Confederation appears to me to be little more than an empty sound, and Congress a nugatory body which, in their current weak condition could only give the vital stab to public credit, and must sink into contempt in the eyes of Europe." During the initial years of his retirement, Washington made no secret of his contempt for the Confederation Congress, which he described as "wretchedly managed," or his conviction that the Articles of Confederation were "fatally flawed."[41]

However unexceptional these opinions might appear to us today, at the time they were distinctive. For a central impulse of the American Revolution, and the core meaning of "the spirit of '76" in most minds, was an instinctive aversion to coercive political power of any sort, most especially centralized power emanating from any distant location beyond the surveillance of the citizens it affected. These fears haunted all conversations about the proper shape of republican government in the revolutionary era, making the very weakness of the federal government under the Articles of Confederation the ideal expression of revolutionary intentions. In a sense, these same fears have haunted all scholarly conversations about "the critical decade" of the 1780s ever since, as historians have argued endlessly about the motives, whether sinister or sensible, of those demanding radical reforms of the Articles of Confederation. The terms historians have imposed on the two sides of the debate—liberals vs. conservatives, democrats vs. aristocrats—have all proved anachronistic and misleading. And efforts to align the different constituencies according to wealth or discernible patterns of economic interest have also proved futile. In Washington's case, however, the reasons for regarding the confederation government as wholly inadequate were elemental and clear, and they cast a shaft of light onto a piece of historical terrain that has sometimes been rendered darker (and bloodier) than necessary.[42]

Washington regarded the American Revolution as a movement to establish both American independence **and** American nationhood; indeed, he did not believe you could have one without the other. Most of the officers in the Continental army shared this view, because they had also experienced the frustrations of trying to fight and win a war without a federal government empowered to provide resources in the reliable fashion of the British ministry. The fear that haunted Washington was not one of excessive federal power reminiscent of Parliament's arbitrary and imperial policies, but rather that of a weak confederation reminiscent of the Continental Congress's woefully inadequate performance during the war. He expressed his convictions on this score to an up-and-coming Virginia statesman, James Madison, in 1785: "We are either a United people, or we are not. If the former, let us, in all matters of general concern act as a nation; which have national objects to promote, and a National character to support—If we are not, let us no longer act a farce by pretending to it." In effect, Washington believed that America's hard-won independence would be short-lived unless the "United States" became a singular rather than a plural term, because a mere confederation of states would become, as he put it, "the dupes of some [foreign] powers and, most assuredly, the contempt of all."[43]

There was one additional, and quite distinctive, ingredient in his thinking, which had its roots in the earlier war he also knew so well. The French and Indian War was a competition among three imperial powers—Great Britain, France, and the Six Nations—for domination of North America east of the Mississippi. Washington saw the American Revolution as a continuation of that contest, in which the newly independent America displaced Britain as the dominant imperial power on the continent. "However unimportant America may be considered at present," he predicted to Lafayette, "there will assuredly come a day when this country will have some weight in the scale of Empires," adding that it was already "an infant-empire." The strategic stakes were huge, stretching geographically across a continent and chronologically across the next century, and they could only be achieved by a federal government fully empowered to harness and manage the enormous energies and resources entailed in such a large-scale imperial project. From this perspective, to dither about the danger of consolidated political power was like arguing about a few pieces of cordwood when a boundless forest lay visibly on the horizon.[44]

While he was sure what the American future required, he was equally sure that any movement to reform the Articles of Confederation was not imminent, and if and when it occurred he would not be around to see it, much less be the messiah to lead it. The first indication that he might need to rethink those assurances arrived at Mount Vernon in March 1786 in the form of a letter from John Jay, who was overseeing foreign policy for the confederation government. Jay informed him of behind-the-scenes conversations in which "an opinion begins to prevail that a general convention for revising the articles of Confederation would be expedient." Jay acknowledged that "we are in a delicate Situation," and a premature effort at reform that failed would be worse than no effort at all. But if events did move in that direction, Jay observed, "I am persuaded you cannot view them with the Eye of an unconcerned Spectator." Washington concurred that the situation was indeed delicate, but doubted that the time was ripe for a convention. The fiscal problems needed to fester and deepen, some unforeseeable crisis needed to galvanize public opinion in favor of reform. As for his own role, "having happily assisted in bringing the ship into port & having been fairly discharged; it is not my business to embark again on a sea of troubles."[45]

And so on this dismissive note began a yearlong negotiation that eventually ended with Washington attending, and of course chairing, the Constitutional Convention, then becoming the inevitable and unanimous selection as the first president of the United States. But what has the look, at least in retrospect, of a foregone conclusion happened in a genuinely grudging and truly tortured fashion. A cynic might be tempted to argue that Washington played the role of an elusive coquette, rejecting all suitors while knowing full well that she is headed for the altar. The cynic would be wrong, however, because Washington's personal correspondence reveals a thoroughly retired hero who felt less like a young coquette than an old soldier past his prime. He was also the American Cincinnatus, who relished his retirement as the final testament to his heroic status, the immortal whose fame derived more from his surrender than his exercise of power. What we see clearly as a glorious capstone to his career appeared initially to Washington more like a highly problematic sequel.

Almost on cue, the galvanizing crisis that he had half hoped for occurred in western Massachusetts. In the fall of 1786, Daniel Shays, a veteran of Bunker Hill and Saratoga, mobilized two thousand indebted farmers to protest mortgage foreclosures and higher taxes by threatening to capture the federal armory at Springfield in western Massachusetts. Initial reports to Washington of what was called Shays's Rebellion were hyperbolic and alarmist, describing "a body of 12 or

15000 desperate and unprincipled men" about to transform all New England into a bloodbath. Actually, the most alarming feature of the "little rebellion," as Jefferson called it, was the set of principles the rebels declared, which were eerily similar to the revolutionary principles of 1776, thereby suggesting that the grievances hurled at British rulers could also be used to undermine elected officials in Massachusetts and beyond. Eventually Washington received more detached assessments of the uprising from Benjamin Lincoln, a former colleague in the Continental army who led the Massachusetts militia units that suppressed the rebellion. Nevertheless, Washington insisted on seeing the crisis as a harbinger of prospective anarchy, which seemed to confirm what British and other European observers had been predicting all along: that the infant American republic was destined to die in the cradle:

The picture which you have drawn, & the accounts which are published, of the commotions . . . in the Eastern States, are equally to be lamented and deprecated. They exhibit a melancholy proof of what our trans Atlantic foes have predicted; and of another thing perhaps, which is still more to be regretted, and is yet more unaccountable; that mankind left to themselves are unfit for their own government. I am mortified beyond expression whenever I view the clouds which have spread over the brightest morn that ever dawned upon my Country. . . . For it is hardly to be imagined that the great body of the people . . . can be so enveloped in darkness, or short sighted as not to see the rays of distant sun through all this mist of intoxication & folly.[46]

Shays's Rebellion was less a cause for calling the Constitutional Convention than a trigger, the justification to implement those behind-the-scenes conversations that Jay had described to Washington the previous spring. As those conversations developed in the form of plans to gather state delegations in Philadelphia in May 1787, arguments formed in his mind that allowed him to resist the mounting pressure to lead the Virginia delegation. Up until the last possible minute, Washington performed a political minuet that let him dance away from all invitations and overtures to resume his public career.

The first line of defense was the Society of the Cincinnati. In keeping with his decision to maintain a discreet distance from the aristocratic aura surrounding the society, Washington had declined the invitation to attend the annual meeting, which just happened to be scheduled for Philadelphia in May. He could not possibly attend a political convention at the same time and place without giving offense to the former officers of the Continental army, he explained, though the Virginia delegation had his heartfelt support.[47]

The second line of defense was that very Virginia delegation, for he had noted that the list of delegates did not include his name. This was a rather lame and hollow excuse, since Washington had not been elected to the delegation only because the Virginia legislature had presumed that he would decline to serve. Once he tried this line of defense, Edmund Randolph used his power as governor to breach it by requesting and receiving a unanimous vote from the legislature on behalf of the one man "who began, carried on & consummated the revolution." Though tactically outmaneuvered on this front, Washington insisted that the endorsement by the Virginia legislature, while edifying, made no difference, since rheumatism and a host of other ailments made a trip to Philadelphia impossible.[48]

One senses that these official excuses were convenient covers for deeper reasons that could not be aired so publicly and that lay within him in two overlapping pools of reticence. The first was the conviction that, once he had assumed the role of American Cincinnatus, he could not change the script. In 1783 he had promised to leave public life forever, so attending the Constitutional Convention would, as he put it to a friend, "be

considered as inconsistent with my public declaration, delivered in a solemn manner at an interesting Aera of my life, never more to meddle in
public matters"; this was a declaration that "not
only stands in the files of Congress, but is I believe
registered in almost all the Gazettes and magazines that are published." Cincinnatus, in effect,
could never come back.[49]

A second private reservation flowed directly out
of the first, though in a slightly more strategic
direction; namely, he could not risk his reputation
in a venture that might not succeed. Henry Knox,
his old wartime colleague, warned him that the
different state delegations were likely to be
divided into three factions: moderates, who
wished only modest changes in the Articles; conservatives, who wished no change at all; and radicals, who wished a major transformation and an
energetic national government. Only if one could
be assured that the latter group would triumph
was the gamble of Washington's prestige worth
the risk. Knox preferred military metaphors, com-
paring the decision to attend the convention to
the decision to engage the enemy in battle, which
should only occur when the outcome was likely
and conclusive. Washington observed that the
current government was more "like a house on
fire." If one could be assured the delegates
intended to extinguish the blaze, he could join the

effort. But if not, perhaps the best course was to let the house burn down and hope that others would build a new one later. Why risk his reputation, especially when "gliding down the stream of life in tranquil retirement is so much the wish of my Soul, that nothing on this side of Elysium can be placed in competition with it?"[50]

But the reputation argument, the more Washington thought about it, was double-edged. On the one hand, his singular status—what he referred to as "the peculiar circumstances of my case"—cut toward caution, since his legacy as America's greatest revolutionary hero was already secure, so investing this priceless asset in an uncertain cause appeared imprudent. On the other hand, suppose the convention succeeded in producing a viable political framework that secured the Revolution? Knox acknowledged that such an outcome would also secure the Washington legacy, which would be diminished if, in his terms, the house was permitted to burn down: "But were an energetic, and judicious system to be proposed with your Signature, it would be a circumstance highly honorable to your fame, in the judgment of the present and future ages; and doubly entitle you to the glorious republican epithet—The Father of Your Country." Washington had already begun to gauge the consequences for his reputation if he stayed away from Philadelphia, wondering "whether my non-attendance in this Convention will not be considered as a dereliction to republicanism—nay more—whether other motives may not (however injuriously) be ascribed to me for not exerting myself on this occasion in support of it."[51]

These crisscrossing thoughts began to move in a discernibly positive direction in mid-March 1787, largely as a result of Madison's influence. No one was more adept than the precocious Madison at assessing the nettlesome details that spelled the difference between success and failure in a political contest. He informed Washington that his canvas of the roster of state delegations revealed an impressive array of talent heavily weighted in favor of much more than tinkering, indeed disposed to a thorough transformation of the existent political system. This piece of intelligence tipped the balance. Though he retained his reservations about "again appearing on a public theatre after a public declaration to the contrary," and though he cringed at the realization that his participation in the convention "will have a tendency to sweep me back into the tide of public affairs," Madison's report altered his sense of the odds. Once convinced that the convention would address the fundamental problem, that it would "adopt no temporizing expedient, but probe the defects of the Constitution to the bottom, and provide radical cures, whether they are agreed to or not," Washington decided to cast his lot, and his reputation, with Madison and the Virginia delegation.[52]

Once on board, an informal council of advisors quickly formed around him that included some of the sharpest political minds in the country. For his part, Washington knew what he knew, essentially that the Articles must be replaced rather than revised, and that the new government needed to possess expanded powers sufficient to make laws for the nation as a whole. Beyond that—more specifically, what the shape of the political architecture constructed on the new foundation might look like—he acknowledged his need for education. Since it was a foregone conclusion that he would be chosen to preside over the convention, Jay and Madison volunteered their services to give him a tutorial in republican theory.

Washington was accustomed to leading by listening. During the Revolution he had chaired countless councils of war in which junior officers presented options to the commander in chief. Before the war George Mason had helped him understand the constitutional arguments against parliamentary taxation. In 1787, as in these previous instances, he already possessed a firm grasp of the elemental forces at work and a clear set of convictions about the strategic direction in which to lead those forces. Where he needed assistance—

and he was completely comfortable requesting and receiving it—was in mastering the theoretical vocabulary that more formally educated colleagues possessed, learning the intellectual road map to reach the destination he had already decided upon.[53]

In a remarkably prescient letter, Jay described the preferred conclusion in Philadelphia as a federal government comprised of three separate branches: executive, legislative, and judicial. The executive branch should stop short of monarchy, but only slightly. The national government should have a veto over all state laws, much like the British king's veto over colonial legislation. The knotty question of sovereignty—did it reside in the states or the federal government?—might be ingeniously resolved by locating it in the fountainhead of all authority, "**The People.**"[54]

Madison was equally thoughtful in anticipating the major controversies likely to dominate the debates in Philadelphia. He predicted that the big fight would center on the question of representation in the legislative, whether by state or population. If the former option prevailed, it meant that the new constitution would fail, since only a congress that accurately reflected the population as a whole could claim to be a national institution. Like Jay, Madison also wanted a federal veto over state laws. And on the sovereignty problem, he had begun to entertain an unprecedented solution, which was to dispense with the assumption that sovereignty must be clear and indivisible: "I have sought for some middle ground, which may at once support a due supremacy of the national authority, and not exclude the local authorities whenever they can be subordinately useful." Here was the core principle of what became "federalism," mutual and shared sovereignty between the state and federal governments.[55]

No one could have received a better briefing on the arguments that would shape the political agenda of the Constitutional Convention. It was, to be sure, a briefing from the nationalist side of the argument. But Washington, who as the presiding presence at the convention would have to project otherworldly detachment—one of his best and favorite roles—was in fact a charter member of the nationalist camp. Soon after arriving in Philadelphia he conveyed his personal convictions to Jefferson, who was watching from Paris: "Much is expected by some—but little by others—and nothing by a few. That something is necessary, all will agree; for the situation of the General Government (if it can be called a government) is shaken to its foundation. . . . In a word, it is at an end, and unless a remedy is soon applied, anarchy & confusion will inevitably ensue." Whether the situation in the spring of 1787 was as desperate as the situation in the spring of 1775 was a debatable question. They were, however, linked together in Washington's mind as two critical chapters in the same ongoing story called the American Revolution. His very presence in Philadelphia certified the connection between the two founding moments, the first to win independence and the second to secure it. He was stepping forward again to play his accustomed and indispensable role. The first time his life had been at stake. This time it was his legacy.[56]

VOTES AND VOICES

WASHINGTON WAS simultaneously the most important person at the Constitutional Convention and the least involved in the debate that shaped the document that emerged. His importance was a function of his presence, which lent an air of legitimacy to the proceedings that otherwise might have been criticized as extralegal, if not a coup d'état. (The convention was legally empowered to revise the Articles of Confederation, not replace them.) His silence during the debates was partially a function of his congenital reticence, but mostly the result of his role as president, whose job was to gavel the sessions to order, then listen as others spoke. The role suited him, for it allowed him to remain above the fray in the transcendent location that he preferred and that almost everyone accorded him. He entered the debate on only one occasion, the last day of the convention, when he endorsed a revision of the final draft that reduced the number of representatives constituting a congressional district from forty thousand to thirty thousand, a gesture probably designed to assure that he was on record as a participant as well as a signer. Otherwise, he enjoyed the best seat from which to hear the most consequential political debate in American history.[57]

What was he thinking? To the extent that his diary entries and correspondence during the summer of 1787 are guides, his mind was elsewhere: on the oppressive heat and humidity; on the renovations of his prized chariot; on the opportunity Philadelphia accorded to purchase rare items like a gold watch chain and two velvet jockey caps; and on Mount Vernon, where his nephew and new manager, George Augustine Washington, needed instruction about where to plant the pumpkins and peas, when to harvest the potatoes, and how to manage the mating of his reluctant jackass. On one occasion, June 4, a witness described the crowds that gathered around him on Market Street when he was going to dinner, but Washington himself made no mention of his thoughts or feelings about experiencing public adulation after four years off the stage. Of course his mind was not really as blank or distracted as the written record suggests, for the record reflects the vow of confidentiality all delegates were under to avoid any disclosure of the deliberations while the convention was in session.[58]

There were two breaks in the code of silence which provide clues to his state of mind on the substantive issues before the delegates. On July 10, he wrote Hamilton, who had recently left the convention, pleading with him to return. Washington seemed to believe a crisis was at hand that required Hamilton's presence. "In a word," he confessed, "I **almost** despair of seeing a favourable issue to the proceedings of the Convention, and do therefore repent having had any agency in the business." Ironically, this remark occurred just after what most scholars have come to regard as the major breakthrough of the convention, the Great Compromise, which resolved the impasse over representation by making it proportional to population in the lower house and by state in the senate. Washington initially interpreted the compromise as a defeat instead of a great victory, because it diluted the principle of federal supremacy over the states.[59]

Then, on August 19, when the delegates were engaged in a protracted debate about the powers of the executive and the mode of selecting him,

Washington expressed his frustration with the timidity of some delegates and the somewhat diluted character of the document likely to result. "I am fully persuaded it is the best that can be obtained at the present moment," he told Knox, "under such diversity of ideas that prevail." A letter he wrote to Lafayette the day after the convention adjourned repeated the same equivocal endorsement: "It is now a child of fortune, to be fostered by some and buffeted by others. What will be the General opinion on, or reception of it, is not for me to decide, nor shall I say anything for or against it—if it be good I suppose it will work its way good—if bad it will recoil on the Framers."[60]

Over the subsequent decades, and now centuries, the Constitution has been most admired for its artful ambiguities, in effect for refusing to resolve the question of state versus federal sovereignty, for sketching rather faintly the powers of the executive and judicial branches, for establishing a framework in which constitutional arrangements could evolve over the years, rather than providing clear answers at that time. If this has proved to be the genius of the document, Washington thought it was its major weakness. He wanted the ambiguities clarified and the sketches filled out, at least sufficiently so to assure the creation of a national government empowered to force the states and citizenry into a budding American empire.[61]

Chairing the convention provided him with an extended education in political realities that exposed his preference for coercive clarity as an impossibility. For he witnessed a bewildering variety of regional interests and accents that could only be bundled together by compromises designed to leave the lines of authority blurred. In truth, there was as yet no such thing as an American nation that the Constitution could consolidate. No matter what Washington thought about America's providential future, it remained a latent prospect still haunted by potent fears of centralized power that even the most thoughtful observers—though not Washington himself—considered the core political legacy of the American Revolution. The debates in Philadelphia demonstrated, then, that a unified nation was still a work-in-progress. And in that sense the ambiguous document that emerged accurately reflected both the limitations and the implications of that unsettled condition.

On the return trip to Mount Vernon there was a mishap at Head of Elk in which the bridge collapsed, seriously injuring Washington's horse. Luckily, or perhaps providentially, Washington had just dismounted before the accident, which led some observers to speculate that the old sol-

dier was still destiny's child, obviously being preserved for one last chapter of public service. At
some unspoken level Washington realized that his
reentry into public life at Philadelphia had forced
a rewriting of the Cincinnatus script from which
he could never turn back. Though he had purchased a four-volume translation of **Don Quixote**
before departing Philadelphia, Washington was
temperamentally incapable of tilting at windmills
or living by illusion, which meant that he knew
full well that the ratification of the Constitution
would carry him inexorably into the presidency. If
he harbored any doubts on that score, his former
aide disabused him in the inimitably assertive
Hamiltonian style: "I take it for granted, Sir, that
you have concluded to comply with what will no
doubt be the general call of your country in relation to the new government. You will permit me
to say that it is indispensable you should lend
yourself to the first operation—it is of little use to
have **introduced** a system, if the weightiest influence is not given to its firm establishment, at the
outset."[62]

If history and the American electorate were
determined to hustle him down the path to power
again, Washington was determined to take it one
step at a time. The ratification of the Constitution, after all, was hardly a foregone conclusion.
Indeed, the debates in the state conventions were

likely to provide a more robust picture of the ideological disagreements than those at the Constitutional Convention, because the most outspoken enemies of reform had stayed away from Philadelphia. Washington had vowed to play no public role in the ratification process, but he had not promised to remain a disinterested observer. As he told Hamilton, "I have read every performance which has been printed on one side and the other of the great question lately agitated." He was most impressed with the series of essays by Publius, later entitled **The Federalist Papers**, which he correctly predicted would outlive the current crisis to become a classic: "When the transient circumstances and fugitive performances which attend the crisis shall have disappeared," he apprised Hamilton, "that work will merit the notice of Posterity." He was fully aware that Hamilton, Madison, and Jay were the authors of the Publius series, for they also formed the entourage of talented advisors that again surrounded him, making Mount Vernon into the electoral headquarters for plotting strategy and tracking the state-by-state results as they rolled in throughout the spring of 1788.[63]

Washington's ongoing assessment of the ratification process benefited from the peerless advice of Madison, who was proving himself the shrewdest political thinker in Virginia, perhaps in the nation. It also drew upon his own experience at winning a contest that, on the face of it, looked dubious at best. Like the War of Independence, he explained, the ratification struggle mobilized latent talents—he mentioned Publius—that would otherwise have remained dormant. And such desperate occasions as Shays's Rebellion, much like the winter encampment at Valley Forge, actually created the conditions for ultimate victory. He expressed confidence that, despite formidable opposition in such key states as Virginia and New York, ratification enjoyed certain strategic advantages. Because only nine states were necessary for ratification, and because the most problematic debates in Virginia and New York occurred late in the convention cycle, enormous pressure to join the winning coalition would be exerted on opponents there. Washington paid particular attention to the debates in Virginia, where two old friends and former colleagues, Patrick Henry and George Mason, were leading the opposition. In an oblique reference to the burden of slavery being carried by Virginia's planter class, he noted that it was "a little strange that the men of large property in the South, should be more afraid that the Constitution should produce an Aristocracy or Monarchy, than the genuine democratical people of the East." He also expressed the opinion that Virginia's most prominent Tidewater planters, many on the verge of bankruptcy, retained an unrealistic and inflated sense of their current prowess: "I am sorry to add in this place that Virginians entertain **too** high an opinion of the importance of their own country." Instead of regarding itself as **primus inter pares** among the states, Virginia should recognize that "in point of strength, it is, comparatively weak" and in fact had more to gain than lose by joining the union.[64]

When ratification became official in the late summer of 1788, even though he had been plotting and cheerleading from the sidelines for nearly a year, Washington was still dancing his private minuet about what ratification meant for him. His correspondence is littered with tortured declarations of uncertainty and platitudinous statements about entering "a vale of tears" or "a field enveloped on every side with clouds & darkness." By this time, however, he was dancing only with himself, since ratification had closed off any escape. Upon hearing that his former chief continued to mutter threats about rejecting the presidency, Hamilton sent a bracing rebuke, reminding Washington that by chairing the Constitutional Convention he had "pledged to take a part in the execution of the government." All his personal anguishing implied that he had some choice in the matter, which was a delusion. Washington thanked Hamilton for the forthright message with its "manly tone" and stopped leaking threats about barricading himself at Mount Vernon. But he never completely ended his litany of lamentations, telling Knox on the very eve of his inauguration that "My movement to the Chair of Government will be accompanied by feelings not unlike those of a culprit who is going to the place of his execution."[65]

Though he unquestionably meant what he said, his thinking was multilayered, like his earlier expressions of reticence about becoming commander in chief of the Continental army. Modern sensibilities make it difficult to comprehend Washington's psychological chemistry on this score and dispose us to interpret his routinized reticence as either a disingenuous ploy or a massive case of denial. But in Washington's world no prominent statesman regarded the forthright expression of political ambition as legitimate; and anyone who actively campaigned for national office was thereby confessing he was unworthy of election. What makes then so different from now was the aristocratic assumption that any explicit projection of self-interest in the political arena betrayed a lack of control over one's own passions, which did not bode well for the public interest. Washington carried this ethos to an extreme, insisting that any mention of his willingness to serve as president prior to the election violated the code.

Of course he knew that he was a candidate; he also knew that Madison was counting the electoral votes for president as the different states tallied up the results in January 1789. But when a correspondent mentioned his foreordained presidency, he expressed outrage that the subject was raised or "even obliquely forced upon my mind." This was both a sincere statement and a scripted role. Indeed, at the time he wrote it, Washington was outlining his domestic and foreign policy priorities as president to Lafayette and consulting with David Humphreys about the contents of a seventy-three-page draft of his inaugural address. In effect, by denying his interest in the office, he demonstrated that he was in control of his ambitions; by privately preparing to serve, he began to assume control of his forthcoming responsibilities. Part of him did feel old, and longed to live out whatever years remained beneath his vines and fig trees. Another part realized that Hamilton was right, and that part was beginning to gird up for the next appointment with destiny. The public posture melded the two feelings: he did not seek this assignment, indeed had hoped to avoid it; but when called he would be ready, once again, to serve.[66]

As in 1775, when he was made commander in

chief, the vote was unanimous. All sixty-nine elec-
tors voted for Washington, and enough of them,
thirty-four, also voted for John Adams to make
him vice president. On April 7 the Confederation
Congress dispatched its secretary, Charles Thomson, to Mount Vernon in order to apprise Washington officially of the results. (Just as Washington
had sustained the fiction that he was unaware of
his candidacy, Congress sustained the fiction that,
until informed, Washington did not know he had
won.) Humphreys had already drafted an acceptance speech containing the customary platitudes
about being called to an arduous task for which he
was woefully unprepared. On April 14, surrounded by a small entourage of secretaries and
servants, Washington at last ended his evasive
dance, declaring officially to Thomson that the
unanimous vote "scarcely leaves me the alternative
for an option."[67]

The first presidential election had in fact been a
plebiscite on who most embodied the values of
the American Revolution. Although the debates
in the Constitutional Convention and then in the
state ratifying conventions had demonstrated that
these values were bitterly contested, the unanimous vote for Washington demonstrated that one
man provided a symbolic solution acceptable to
all sides. There had been no campaign platform
providing voters with his position on the con-

tested issues, because there had been no campaign. He was not chosen for what he thought, but for who he was. In the political vocabulary of the day, there was no word fit to describe his unique status, but the word that came closest was stigmatized by the very values he had been chosen to embody. "You are now a king, under a different name," wrote one thrilled supporter, James McHenry from Maryland, "and, I am well satisfied that sovereign prerogatives have in no age or country been more honorably obtained; or that, at any time they will be more prudently and wisely exercised."[68]

This was dangerous talk, and Washington knew it. The ill-defined powers of the American presidency left considerable room for honest disagreement, but one point on which all sides could agree was that it was not an electoral version of monarchy and George Washington was not the second coming of George III. (Writing from Paris, Gouverneur Morris reported the delectable piece of gossip that George III's mounting insanity had produced a delusional fit in which he imagined himself to be the second coming of Washington.) In the lengthy first draft of his inaugural address—blessedly never delivered—Washington had seen fit to insert a defensive comment, observing that he had no direct heirs or "immediate offspring" and therefore "no family to build in greatness upon my Country's ruin." There could be no Washington monarchy because there could be no Washington dynasty. His decision to order several yards of superfine broadcloth from a Hartford manufacturer for his inaugural suit also suggested that he wanted to make a sartorial statement of republican simplicity that countered the royal image.[69]

But no matter what he said or what he wore at his inauguration—eventually he discarded the broadcloth outfit for a suit of black velvet—Washington was revered by the bulk of the American citizenry as a quasi-king whose special status had been earned rather than inherited. The public reverence accorded to royalty was put on display during Washington's weeklong trip from Mount Vernon to New York, which became one prolonged coronation ceremony. It began with crowds of more than ten thousand celebrants cheering him amidst cannon salutes and poetic tributes at Baltimore and Wilmington. Outside Philadelphia he was obliged to mount a white horse so that the twenty thousand spectators could see him as he crossed the Schuylkill. Charles Willson Peale had designed an arch of triumph over the bridge, and his daughter Angelica lowered a laurel crown upon Washington's head as he passed under the arch. At Trenton a chorus of white-robed girls tossed flowers from their baskets in his path while singing a tribute to "The Defender of the Mothers, The Protector of the Daughters." A congressional committee greeted him at Elizabethtown, where a fifty-foot barge manned by thirteen white-smocked sailors rowed him across the Hudson. A flotilla of decorated ships and sloops pulled alongside the barge as he approached New York Harbor and a chorus aboard one of the sloops sang an ode composed for the occasion to the tune of "God Save the King":

> Thrice welcome to this shore,
> Our Leader now no more,
> But Ruler thou;
> Oh, truly good and great!
> Long live to glad our State,
> Where countless Honors Wait
> To deck thy brow.[70]

And so the retirement which had begun in the expectation of solitude and the presumption of finality now ended with a plebiscite of unprecedented approval and the adoring voices of ordinary American citizens ringing in his ears. What was he thinking at this dramatic moment of transition back into the public arena? Reading Washington's famously (and often purposely) enigmatic mind is always a tricky business, never more so than on emotionally complicated occasions like his acceptance of the presidency. When he delivered his brief and willfully innocuous inaugural address in the Senate chamber of Federal Hall on April 30, one witness found his performance appropriately solemn and sure-handed. Another thought the speech uninspired and Washington's demeanor awkward, as if he wished to be somewhere else, and more nervous before the audience than he had ever been when facing British cannon and muskets.[71]

The inaugural address itself was deliberately elliptical, offering little indication of his political agenda for the new government. His fullest statement on that score had been made in a private letter to Lafayette the previous summer. It seemed to suggest that his twin priorities were the restoration of fiscal responsibility and the creation of political credibility for the nascent national government:

> When the people shall find themselves secure under an energetic government, when foreign Nations shall be disposed to give us equal advantages in commerce from dread of retaliation, when the burdens of the war shall be in a manner done away by the sale of western lands, when the seeds of happiness which are sown here shall begin to expand themselves, and when every one (under his own vine and fig-tree) shall

begin to taste the fruits of freedom—then all these blessings (for all these blessings will come) will be referred to the fostering influence of the new government. . . . Indeed, I do not believe that Providence has done so much for nothing.[72]

In effect, he hoped to lend his prestige to the fledgling federal government, thereby helping it survive its most formative and fragile phase, providing the necessary credibility until this nation-in-the-making began to feel comfortable behaving as a single people instead of a confederation of states.

The contradictory reactions to his inaugural address probably reflected his own conflicting emotions. His reservations were real, we know, because the Cincinnatus pose had always been more than a pose. Physically, we know, he felt past his prime, no longer oblivious to the fatigue and demanding regimen that accompanied life at center stage in the public arena. Also on the negative side, his most intimate confidante, Martha, was not with him. She had elected to stay behind at Mount Vernon until the celebratory fireworks died down and accommodations in New York had been arranged. His personal servant, Billy Lee, who had accompanied him on all his previous campaigns, was also missing. He had tried to make the trip, but two crippling knee injuries had forced him to drop out of the procession in Philadelphia. Someone else would have to comb and tie Washington's hair and anticipate his daily needs.

But alongside his personal doubts about risking his hard-won reputation, alongside reservations about his advancing age, and the absence of his accustomed support system, there were those crowds of cheering well-wishers stretching from Virginia to New York, expressing their bottomless confidence that he **was** the indispensable man. If he were truly superhuman, as many of his admirers believed, he would have felt no surge of fresh energy listening to their cheers. But, of course, he was not. The protracted coronation procession served as the palpable companion of the unanimous electoral vote and probably combined to buoy him above his personal doubts—his silence and code of control precludes certainty here—propelling him forward toward the presidency. If this were not enough, the applause reinforced his lifelong experience of winning every wager against the odds, whether it was at the Monongahela, Princeton, or Yorktown. It seems likely that his remarks to Lafayette about American national destiny, namely that it was foreordained, also described his sense of his own fate. In any event, his inauguration now joined at the hip the two destinies, which boded well for both. If the doubts were real, the providential forces were more potent. When the mix of moods coalesced, he entered the presidency with a bittersweet sense that he had done everything humanly possible to avoid this outcome, but that he was, once again, the chosen instrument of history.

CHAPTER SIX

First in Peace

Looking back over two hundred years of the American presidency, it seems safe to say that no one entered the office with more personal prestige than Washington, and only two presidents— Abraham Lincoln and Franklin Roosevelt—faced comparable crises. The Civil War and the Great Depression, though distant in time, remain more recent and raw in our collective memory than the American founding, so we find it easier to appreciate the impressive achievements of Lincoln and Roosevelt in negotiating the nation through these latter-day challenges. Washington's achievement must be recovered before it can be appreciated, which means that we must recognize that there was no such thing as a viable American nation when he took office as president, that the opening words of the Constitution ("We the people of the United States") expressed a fervent but fragile hope rather

than a social reality. The roughly four million settlers spread along the coastline and streaming over
the Alleghenies felt their primary allegiance, to the
extent they felt any allegiance at all, to local, state,
and regional authorities. No republican government had ever before exercised control over a population this diffuse or a land mass this large, and the
prevailing assumption among the most informed
European observers was that, to paraphrase Lincoln's later formulation, a nation so conceived and
so dedicated could not endure.

Washington's core achievement as president,
much as it had been as commander in chief of the
Continental army, was to transform the improbable into the inevitable. The point was put nicely
by a French nobleman visiting Mount Vernon in
1791 before setting out on a quest for the elusive
(in fact, nonexistent) water route across the North
American continent: "But it is less difficult to
discover the North-West Passage," he explained,
"than to create a people, as you have done."[1]

Assessments of Washington's presidency tend to
be forward-looking, understandably concerned
with the constitutional precedents he set for the
executive branch in such specific areas as the cabinet system, control over foreign policy, the veto,
executive appointments, and setting the legislative agenda. But, once again, any comprehensive
appraisal of Washington's legacy must also be

backward-looking, which means recovering the highly problematical attitude toward executive power that pervaded the political culture when he assumed office.[2]

When he observed that "I walk on untrodden ground," Washington obviously meant that, as the first American president, everything he did set a precedent. Less obviously, his privileged perch at the Constitutional Convention allowed him to recognize that the ground surrounding the American presidency was not just untrodden; the air around it was filled with menacing memories of George III. There was an unspoken reason why the final draft of the Constitution devoted more space to the rules for electing or removing the president than to delineating the powers of the office itself. Much like the reluctance to mention slavery explicitly, the reticence about the scope of presidential authority reflected a widespread apprehension that any direct discussion of the subject subverted the core principles of republicanism itself.

If slavery was the proverbial "ghost at the banquet" at the Constitutional Convention, monarchy was its spectral accomplice. When Patrick Henry claimed that the Constitution "squints toward monarchy," he spoke for a potent collection of skeptics who regarded any projection of executive power as a betrayal of the "spirit of

'76." Although Washington did not share Henry's conspiratorial suspicions, he did understand that accepting the presidency meant living the central paradox of the early American republic: that is, what was politically essential for a viable American nation was ideologically at odds with what it claimed to stand for.[3]

The specter of monarchy haunted Washington's entire presidency, especially during his second term, when the monarchical murmurs became full-fledged attacks on both his policies and character; they wounded him more deeply than any criticism he received as commander in chief during the war. The personal criticism also stunned him because he was both intellectually and emotionally ill-equipped to comprehend the shrill partisanship that came to define the political culture of the 1790s and that shredded any and all efforts to stand above the fray. He found himself in the ironic position of being the indispensable man in a political world that regarded all leaders as disposable. Without him to center it, the political experiment in republicanism might very well have failed. With him, and in great part because of him, it succeeded; but in so doing it rendered the nonpartisan values he embodied anachronistic.

Another specter that hovered over the Washington presidency was age. From the time that Governor Dinwiddie had dispatched him into the western wilderness as a youthful emissary, Washington's physical prowess had been his most elemental asset. At the Monongahela, then in the battles at Trenton, Princeton, and Yorktown during the War of Independence, bullets and shrapnel seemed to veer away from his body as if he were surrounded by an electromagnetic field of invulnerability. Like a natural athlete who takes his superb body for granted, Washington was accustomed to commanding any room or scene visually and physically. As we have seen, chinks in his armor began to appear in the 1780s, when the inevitable ravages of age started to soften him. And these symptoms of physical deterioration gave palpable shape to his increasingly fatalistic recognition that Washington men were genetically programmed to wear out early and die relatively young.

Two events early in his presidency reinforced these intimations of mortality. In June 1789 a large tumor appeared on his left thigh which eventually required surgery to remove. For a few days his condition was critical, and the street in front of the presidential mansion was roped off to prevent passing carriages from disturbing his recovery. Then in May 1790 he collapsed with influenza and lingered near death for three days with pulmonary complications. During his lengthy recuperation visitors reported that his eyes were permanently teary, his hearing was almost completely blocked, and his famously robust constitution seemed to have aged overnight. Washington himself acknowledged that recovery from the two illnesses had drained all his recuperative resources, so that another serious sickness, as he put it, would "put me to sleep with my fathers." Jefferson's gloss on Washington's physical decline, as we shall see, is not to be fully trusted, but he suggested the assaults on the president's body also had mental consequences: "The firm tone of his mind, for which he had been remarkable, was beginning to relax; a listlessness of labor, a desire for tranquility had crept on him, and a willingness to let others act, or even think, for him."[4]

Washington was not creeping toward senility, as Jefferson implied, nor was he too dazed to manage the duties of his presidency, as Jefferson claimed. But he was no longer the same vigorous man who had spent nearly eight years in the field leading the Continental army. Throughout his presidency he felt the sand in his personal hourglass running out, the relentless burdens of the office squeezing out the last remaining months, weeks, days, and hours of private serenity allotted him. Martha spoke for both of them when, soon after joining him in New York in May 1789, she exclaimed that she "felt more like a prisoner than anything else." Washington's constant refrain about retiring to bucolic splendor beneath his vines and fig trees was, true enough, a formulaic refrain within the leadership class of the revolutionary generation, especially the Virginia dynasty. And his previous declarations of reticence when called to command the Continental army or chair the Constitutional Convention were classical lines in a Ciceronian motif designed to conceal his ambitions from the world, and even, perhaps, from himself. But now the role of Cincinnatus had become his truly preferred destination. No president in American history wished to avoid the office more than Washington.[5]

All of which helps explain one of the chief curiosities of his presidential correspondence. The longest letters, and more of them than he devoted to any official topic, deal with the management of his farms at Mount Vernon. Even when immersed in crucial diplomatic negotiations with France or controversial deliberations about Hamilton's fiscal policy, Washington found time to compose meticulous instructions to his managers about plowing, weeding, worming, or grubbing schedules, about when to stock the ice house, about the personalities and work habits of different overseers or slave laborers, about proper food and rum rations at harvest time. One can read these letters as a continuance of his obsessive urge to remain the strenuous squire, the honest inclinations of a man who felt more genuine excitement discussing the merits of a new threshing machine than the intricacies of the Jay Treaty. Or one could, more speculatively, argue that the Mount Vernon correspondence allowed him to retain a zone of personal control amidst an increasingly discordant political world that seemed to defy control altogether. But, in the end, the most compelling explanation is that Washington's soul, or at least the last sliver of his private personality, never made the trip to New York (and then Philadelphia) but remained ensconced at Mount Vernon.[6]

One of the shrewdest of Washington's biographers has suggested his private self had been effectively obliterated by the time he reached the presidency; that the man, if you will, had become the monument. While this was probably true for the way most of Washington's contemporaries viewed him, it was not the way Washington viewed himself. And this personal perspective must stand as the final context for understanding his presidency. If the constitutional context looks forward to the landmark precedents for the executive branch, and if the historical context looks backward to the specter of monarchy haunting all energetic projections of executive power, the personal context looks southward toward Mount Vernon, the only place where he could shed his public role and be himself.[7]

PRESIDING PRESIDENCY

NOT MUCH HAPPENED at the executive level during the first year of Washington's presidency, which was exactly the way he wanted it. His official correspondence was dominated by job applications from veterans of the war, former friends, and total strangers, most of whom pleaded for patronage in the highly deferential style that Washington himself had employed toward his British betters during the French and Indian War. They all received the same republican response: merit rather than favoritism must determine all federal appointments. As for the president himself, it was not clear whether he was taking the helm or merely occupying the bridge. Rumors began to circulate that he regarded his role as primarily ceremonial and symbolic, that after two years he intended to step down, having launched the American ship of state and contributed his personal prestige as ballast on its maiden voyage. There was talk of a brief and wholly presiding presidency.[8]

As it turned out, even ceremonial occasions raised troubling questions, because no one knew how the symbolic centerpiece of a republic should behave, or even what to call him. Vice President Adams, trying to be helpful, ignited a fiery debate in the Senate by suggesting such regal titles as "His Elective Majesty" or "His Mightiness," which provoked a lethal combination of shock and laughter, as well as the observation that Adams himself should be called "His Rotundity." Eventually the Senate resolved on the most innocuous option available: the president of the United States should be called exactly that, no more and no less. Matters of social etiquette— how should the president interact with the public? Where should he be accessible and where insulated?—prompted multiple memoranda on the importance of what Hamilton called "a pretty high tone" that stopped short of secluding the president "like an Eastern Lama." The solution was a weekly open house called the levee, part imperial court ceremony replete with choreographed bows and curtsies, part drop-in parlor social. The levees struck the proper middle note between courtly formality and republican simplicity, though at the expense of becoming notoriously boring and wholly scripted occasions only periodically enlivened by impromptu acts of spontaneity, as when Washington once bent over to kiss the widow of Nathanael Greene on the cheek.[9]

The very awkwardness of the levees fit Washington's temperament nicely, since he possessed a nearly preternatural ability to remain silent while everyone around him was squirming under the social pressure to fill the silence with chatty conversation. (Adams later claimed that this "gift of silence" was Washington's greatest political asset, which Adams himself so envied because he lacked the gift altogether.) Washington also possessed distancing mechanisms that deflected intrusions into the space around his body much as they had deflected bullets on the battlefield. The formal etiquette of the levees combined with Washington's natural dignity (or was it aloofness?) to create a political atmosphere unimaginable in any modern-day national capital. Namely, in a year when the French Revolution broke out in violent spasms destined to reshape the entire political landscape of Europe, and the Congress, under Madison's deft guidance, ratified a Bill of Rights that codified the most sweeping guarantee of individual rights ever enacted, no one at the levees discussed these major events or expected Washington to comment on them.

Washington's urge to keep himself and his presidency hovering above the political fray received assistance from the only other unequivocal occupant of America's pantheon. In April 1790 his sole rival as the premier American hero, Benjamin Franklin, finally went to his maker. In his will Franklin bequeathed his crabtree walking stick to Washington, explaining that "if it were a sceptre, he has merited it, and would become it." (The notion of a crabtree scepter had the perfect

Franklin touch, a seamless blend of the ordinary and the elevated.) A month earlier the first medal minted in the United States bearing Washington's image on one side and his accomplishments on the other appeared in Philadelphia. And a month before then, in February 1790, the practice of celebrating Washington's birthday as a national holiday became a tradition. It all contributed to the impression that Washington was not directing the government so much as floating above the infant republic as a sagacious and beloved guardian.[10]

Even the matters of etiquette and symbolism, however, could have constitutional consequences, as Washington learned in August 1789. The treaty-making power of the president required that he seek "the Advice and Consent of the Senate." He initially interpreted the phrase to require his personal appearance in the Senate and the solicitation of senatorial opinion on specific treaty provisions in the mode of a large advisory council. But when he brought his proposals for treaties with several southern Indian tribes to the Senate, the debate became a prolonged shouting match over questions of procedure. The longer the debate went on the more irritated Washington became, eventually declaring, "This defeats every purpose of my coming here." He abruptly stalked out of the session, as one witness reported, "with a discontented Air . . . of sullen dignity." From that time onward, the phrase "advise and consent" meant something less than direct executive solicitation of senatorial opinion, and the role of the Senate as an equal partner in the crafting of treaties came to be regarded as a violation of the separation of powers principle.[11]

Though he never revisited the Senate, he did honor his pledge to visit all the states in the union. In the fall of 1789 he launched a month-long tour of New England that carried him through sixty towns and hamlets. Everywhere he went the residents turned out in droves to glimpse America's greatest hero parading past. And everywhere he went New Englanders became Americans, at least for the duration of his visit. The only sour note was a patch of bad weather at the end, which produced an epidemic of respiratory infections among the throngs of well-wishers who had waited for hours in the cold rain to see him in the flesh. (In an ironic tribute, newspapers named the epidemic after him.) Since Rhode Island had not yet ratified the Constitution, he skipped it, then made a separate trip the following summer to welcome the proudly independent latecomer into the new nation. During a visit to the Jewish synagogue in Newport he published an address on religious freedom that turned out to be the most uncompromising endorsement of the principle he ever made. (One must say "made" rather than "wrote," because there is considerable evidence that Jefferson wrote it.) Whatever sectional suspicions New Englanders might harbor toward that faraway thing called the federal government, when it appeared in their local neighborhoods in the majestic form of George Washington, they saluted, cheered, toasted, and embraced it as their own.[12]

The southern tour was a more grueling affair, covering nearly two thousand miles during the spring of 1791. Instead of regarding it as a threat to his health, however, Washington described it as a tonic; the real risk, he believed, was the sedentary life of a desk-bound president. The entourage of eleven horses included his white parade steed, Prescott, whom he mounted at the edge of each town in order to make an entrance that accorded with the heroic mythology surrounding his military career. Prescott's hooves were painted and polished before each appearance, and Washington usually brought along his favorite greyhound, mischievously named Cornwallis, to add to the dramatic effect. Much like a modern political candidate on the campaign trail, Washington's speeches at each stop repeated the same platitudinous themes, linking the glory of the War of Independence with the latent glory of the newly established United States. (The linkage came naturally at places like Charleston, Camden, and Guilford Court House, former battlefields in the southern campaign that Washington was seeing for the first time.) The ladies of Charleston fluttered alongside their fans when Washington took the dance floor; Prescott and the four carriage horses held up despite the nearly impassable and often nonexistent roads; Cornwallis, however, wore out and was buried on the banks of the Savannah River in a brick vault with a marble tombstone that local residents maintained for decades as a memorial to his master's historic visit. In the end all the states south of the Potomac could say they had seen the palpable version of the flag, which was Washington himself.[13]

During the southern tour, one of the earliest editorial critiques of Washington's rather conspicuous embodiment of authority appeared in the press. He was being treated at each stop like a canonized American saint, the editorial lamented, or perhaps like a demigod "perfumed by the incense of addresses." But the chief complaint harked back to the primordial fear haunting all republics: "However highly we may consider the character of the Chief Magistrate of the Union, yet we cannot but think the fashionable mode of expressing our attachment . . . favors too much of Monarchy to be used by Republicans, or to be received with pleasure by the President of a Commonwealth."[14]

Such criticisms were rarely uttered publicly during the initial years of Washington's presidency.

But they lurked in the background, exposing how double-edged the political imperatives of the American Revolution had become. To secure the revolutionary legacy on the national level required a "singular character" who embodied national authority more visibly than any collective body like Congress could convey. Washington had committed himself to playing that role by accepting the presidency; indeed, he regarded his symbolic role as the core function of his presidency. But at the center of the revolutionary legacy lay a virulent suspicion of any potent projection of political power by a "singular figure." And since the very idea of a republican chief executive was a novelty, there was no available vocabulary to characterize such a creature except the verbal traditions surrounding European courts and kings. By playing the role that he believed history required, Washington made himself vulnerable to the most potent set of apprehensions about monarchical power that recent American history could muster.

He could justifiably claim to be the one and only "singular character" who could credibly insist that he had earned the right to be trusted with power. He could also argue, as he did to several friends throughout his first term, that no man was more poised for retirement, that he sincerely resented the obligations of his office as a lengthening shadow of public responsibility that kept spreading over his dwindling days on earth. If critics wished to whisper behind his back that he looked too regal riding a white stallion with a leopard-skin cloth and gold-rimmed saddle, so be it. He himself knew that he longed for a crabtree walking stick more than a scepter. In the meantime he would play his assigned role as America's presiding presence; or, as the multiple toasts in his honor put it, "the man who unites all hearts."

THE GREAT DELEGATOR

EXERCISING EXECUTIVE authority called for a completely different set of leadership skills than symbolizing it. Washington's administrative style had evolved through decades of experience as master of Mount Vernon and commander of the Continental army. (In fact, he had fewer subordinates to supervise as president than he did in those earlier incarnations.) The cabinet system he installed represented a civilian adaptation of his military staff, with executive sessions of the cabinet resembling councils of war designed to provide collective wisdom in a crisis. As Jefferson later described the arrangement, Washington made himself "the hub of the wheel" with routine business delegated to the department heads at the rim. It was a system that maximized executive control while also creating the essential distance from details. Its successful operation depended upon two acquired skills Washington had developed over his lengthy career: first, identifying and recruiting talented and ambitious young men, usually possessing superior formal education to his own, then trusting them with considerable responsibility and treating them as surrogate sons in his official family; second, knowing when to remain the hedgehog who keeps his distance and when to become the fox who dives into the details.

On the first score, as a judge of talent, Washington surrounded himself with the most intellectually sophisticated collection of statesmen in American presidential history. His first recruit, James Madison, became his most trusted consultant on judicial and executive appointments and his unofficial liaison with Congress. The Virginian was then at the peak of his powers, having just completed a remarkable string of triumphs as the dominant force behind the nationalist agenda at the Constitutional Convention and the Virginia ratifying convention, as well as coauthor of **The Federalist Papers.** From his position in the House of Representatives he drafted the address welcoming Washington to the presidency, then drafted Washington's response to it, making him a one-man shadow government. Madison's unique combination of abilities as a profound student of politics and a brilliant

political tactician had captured Washington's attention even before the debates in Philadelphia, when
he had helped to prepare Washington for his chairman's role in the convention. Soon after the inaugural ceremony Madison showed Washington his
draft of twelve amendments to the Constitution,
subsequently reduced to ten and immortalized as
the Bill of Rights. Washington approved the historic proposal without changing a word, and
trusted Madison to usher it through Congress with
his customary proficiency.[15]

One of Madison's early assignments was to persuade his reluctant friend from Monticello to
serve as secretary of state. Thomas Jefferson combined nearly spotless revolutionary credentials
with five years of diplomatic experience in Paris,
all buoyed by a lyrical way with words and ideas
most famously displayed in his draft of the Declaration of Independence. Though ironic in retrospect, Jefferson's acceptance letter set a deferential
tone and expressed a willingness to harness his
vaunted powers to Washington's foreign policy
agenda: "My chief comfort," he promised, "will
be to work under your eye, & the wisdom of
measures to be dictated by you, & implicitly executed by me."[16]

Alexander Hamilton was the third member of
this talented trinity, in terms of sheer brainpower
probably the brightest of the lot. While Madison

and Jefferson had come up through the Virginia school of politics, which put a premium on an understated style that emphasized indirection and stealth, Hamilton had come out of nowhere (actually impoverished origins in the Caribbean), which produced a dashing, out-of-my-way style that imposed itself ostentatiously, much in the manner of the bayonet charge he had led at York-town. As Washington's aide-de-camp during the war, Hamilton had occasionally shown himself to be a somewhat feisty and headstrong surrogate son, always searching for an independent com-mand beyond Washington's shadow. But his loy-alty to his mentor was unquestioned, and his affinity for the way Washington thought was unequaled. Moreover, throughout the 1780s Hamilton had made himself the chief advocate for fiscal reform as the essential prerequisite for an energetic national government, making him the obvious choice as secretary of treasury once Robert Morris declined.

The inner circle was rounded out with three appointments of lesser luster. Henry Knox had served alongside Washington from the Boston siege to Yorktown and had long ago learned to subsume his own personality so thoroughly within his chief's that disagreements became virtually impossible. More than a cipher, as some critics of Washington's policies later claimed, Knox joined Vice President

Adams as a seasoned New England voice within the councils of power. Indeed, his role as secretary of war continued the duties he had performed in the old confederation government. John Jay added New York's most distinguished legal and political mind to the mix, and also brought extensive foreign policy experience to the ongoing conversation. As the first attorney general, Edmund Randolph lacked the gravitas of Jay and the experience of Knox, but his reputation for endless vacillations was offset by solid political connections within the Tidewater elite, reinforced by impeccable bloodlines. Washington's judgment of the assembled team was unequivocal: "I feel myself supported by able co-adjutors," he observed in June 1790, "who harmonize extremely well together."[17]

In three significant areas of domestic policy, each loaded with explosive political and constitutional implications, Washington chose to delegate nearly complete control to his "co-adjutors." His reasons for maintaining a discreet distance differed in each case, but taken together, they reflected his recognition that executive power still lived under a monarchical cloud of suspicion and could only be exercised selectively. Much like his Fabian role during the war, choosing when to avoid conflict struck him as the essence of effective executive leadership, especially when he enjoyed capable surrogates brimming over with energy and ambition.

The first battle he evaded focused on the shape and powers of the federal courts. The Constitution offered even less guidance on the judiciary than it did on the executive branch. And once again the studied ambiguity reflected the widespread apprehension toward any menacing projection of federal power that upset the compromise between state and federal sovereignty. Washington personally preferred a unified body of national law, regarding it as a crucial step in the creation of what the Constitution had described as "a more perfect union." When nominating Jay to head the Supreme Court he argued that the federal judiciary "must be considered as the Key-Stone of our political fabric," since a coherent court system that tied the states and regions together with the ligaments of law would achieve more in the way of national unity than any other possible reform.[18]

But that, of course, was also the reason why it proved so controversial. The debate over the Judiciary Act of 1789 exposed the latent hostility toward any consolidated court system. The act created a six-member Supreme Court, three circuit courts, and thirteen district courts, but left questions of original or appellate jurisdiction intentionally blurred so as to conciliate the advocates of state sovereignty. Despite his private preferences, Washington deferred to the trade-offs worked out in congressional committees, chiefly a committee chaired by Oliver Ellsworth of Connecticut, which designed a framework of overlapping authorities that was neither rational nor wholly national in scope. In subsequent decades John Marshall, Washington's most loyal and influential disciple, would move this ambiguous arrangement toward a more coherent version of national law. But throughout Washington's presidency the one thing the Supreme Court could not be, or appear to be, was supreme, a political reality that Washington chose not to contest.[19]

A second occasion for calculated executive reticence occurred in February 1790 when the forbidden subject of slavery came before Congress. Two Quaker petitions, one arguing for the immediate end of the slave trade, the other advocating the gradual abolition of slavery itself, provoked a bitter debate in the House. The petitions would almost surely have been consigned to legislative oblivion except for the signature of Benjamin Franklin on the second, which transformed a beyond-the-pale protest into an unavoidable challenge to debate the moral compatibility of slavery with America's avowed revolutionary principles. In what turned out to be his last public act, Franklin was investing his great prestige to force the first public discussion of the sectional differences over slavery at the national level. (The debates at the Constitutional Convention had occurred behind closed doors, and even the sanitized record of those debates remained sealed in the vaults of the State Department.) If only in retrospect, the debates in the House during the spring of 1790 represented the final opportunity on the part of the revolutionary generation to place slavery on the road to ultimate extinction.[20]

Washington shared Franklin's views on slavery as a moral and political anachronism. On three occasions during the 1780s he had let it be known that he favored the adoption of some kind of gradual emancipation scheme, and would give his personal support to such a scheme whenever it materialized. Warner Mifflin, one of the Quaker petitioners who knew of Washington's previous statements, obtained a private interview in order to plead that this was now the ideal occasion for Washington to step forward in the manner of Franklin. And since he was the only American with more prestige than Franklin, Washington's intervention at this propitious moment could make the decisive difference in removing this stain on the revolutionary legacy, as well as his own.[21]

We can never know what might have happened if Washington had taken this advice. He listened politely to Mifflin's request, but refused to commit himself on the grounds that the matter was properly the province of Congress and "might come before me for official decision." He struck a more cynical tone in letters to friends back in Virginia: "the introduction of the Quaker Memorial, rejecting slavery, was to be sure, not only an ill-judged piece of business, but occasioned a great waste of time." He endorsed Madison's deft management of the debate and his behind-the-scenes maneuvering in the House, which voted to prohibit any further consideration of ending the slave trade until 1808, as the Constitution specified; more significantly, Madison managed to take slavery off the national agenda by making any legislation seeking to end it a state rather than federal prerogative. Washington expressed his satisfaction that the threatening subject "has at last been put to sleep, and will scarcely awake before the year 1808."[22]

What strikes us as a poignant failure of moral leadership appeared to Washington as a prudent exercise in political judgment. There is no evidence that he struggled over the decision. Whatever his personal views on slavery may have been, his highest public priority was the creation of a unified American nation. The debates in the House only dramatized the intractable sectional differences he had witnessed from the chair at the Constitutional Convention. They reinforced his conviction that slavery was the one issue with the political potential to destroy the republican experiment in its infancy. With one important difference, he embraced Madison's resolution of the crisis, which established a moratorium on the subject at the federal level for the foreseeable future. In Washington's view, the moratorium should last until 1808, when the larger subject of slavery could be taken up with the ending of the slave trade. But until then, and surely for the remainder of his presidency, the issue was too controversial to risk executive involvement and too combustible to talk about publicly at all.

Despite the vows of public silence, the taboo topic came up in an awkwardly personal way the following year, soon after the federal government made its scheduled move from New York to Philadelphia. Attorney General Randolph alerted Washington to the awkward fact that Pennsylvania law allowed any slave who was resident for six months within the state to demand emancipation. Washington asked Tobias Lear to look into the law in order to determine if the six-month rule could be skirted by removing his household slaves to Mount Vernon before the time expired, then returning them to Philadelphia to start the clock again. Part of his concern was financial, since the loss of any dower slaves would require him to reimburse the Custis estate. He was especially concerned with losing two of his most trusted slaves, Hercules and Paris. He instructed Lear to have Martha take them back with her to Mount

Vernon, but without letting anyone except Martha know the motive for the trip. "I wish to both have it accomplished under pretext that may deceive both them and the public," he confided to Lear. When Hercules got wind of the scheme, he expressed a sense of personal insult that his loyalty to Washington was not taken for granted. Eventually Hercules was allowed to stay in Philadelphia, where he remained Washington's highly valued cook until the end of the second presidential term, at which point he absconded, much to Washington's surprise and chagrin. The incident served to expose the widening gap on the slavery question north and south of the Potomac, as well as the gap between Washington's professed convictions about slavery and his dependence on enslaved servants.[23]

Finally, the most dramatic delegation of all, Washington gave total responsibility for rescuing the debt-burdened American economy to his charismatic secretary of treasury. Before Hamilton was appointed in September 1789, Washington had requested financial records from the old confederation government and quickly discovered that he had inherited a messy mass of state, domestic, and foreign debt. The records were filled with floating bond rates, complicated currency conversion tables, and guesswork revenue projections that, taken together, resembled an accountant's worst nightmare. The world in which fortunes were made and lost against a background of shuffling papers and shifting numbers felt to him like a foreign country. (This was one reason he always suspected that Cary & Company was cheating him in the pre-revolutionary days.) After making a heroic effort of his own that only confirmed his sense of futility, Washington handed the records and fiscal policy of the new nation to his former aide-de-camp, who turned out to be, among other things, a financial genius.[24]

Hamilton buried himself in the numbers for three months, then emerged with a forty-thousand-word document entitled **Report on Public Credit.** His calculations revealed that the total debt of the United States had reached the daunting (for then) size of $77.1 million, which was divided into three separate ledgers: foreign debt ($11.7 million); federal debt ($40.4 million); and state debt ($25 million). Several generations of historians and economists have analyzed the intricacies of Hamilton's **Report** and created a formidable body of scholarship on its technical complexities. For our purposes, however, it is sufficient to know that Hamilton's calculations were accurate and his strategy simple: namely, consolidate the messy columns of foreign and domestic debt into one central pile. He proposed funding the federal debt at par, assuming all the state debts, then creating a National Bank to manage all the investments and payments at the federal level.[25]

This made excellent economic sense, as the improved credit rating of the United States in foreign banks and the surging productivity of the commercial sector demonstrated after Hamilton's financial plan was adopted. But it also proved to be a political bombshell that shook Congress for over a year with its reverberations. For Hamilton had managed to create, almost single-handedly, an unambiguously national economic policy that presumed the sovereign power of the federal government. He had pursued a bolder course than the more cautious framers of the Judiciary Act had followed in designing the court system, leaving no doubt that control over fiscal policy would not be brokered to accommodate the states. All three ingredients in his plan—funding, assumption, and the bank—were vigorously contested in Congress, with Madison (an ominous sign) leading the opposition on each front. The watchword of the critics was "consolidation," an ideological cousin to "monarchy," both terms suggesting a threatening aggregation of political power reminiscent of the tyrannical British government that the American colonies had defied and then overthrown. There was also a sectional edge to the criticism, especially the Virginia version, which described Hamilton's financial plan as a hostile takeover of the American Revolution by northern bankers and speculators. "In an Agricultural Country like this," Virginia's governor wrote to Washington, "to erect and concentrate and perpetuate a large insured interest . . . must in the course of human events, produce one or other of two evils—the Prostration of Agriculture at the feet of Commerce, or a change in the present form of Federal Government, fatal to the existence of American liberty."[26]

Washington did not respond. Indeed, he played no public role at all in defending Hamilton's program during the fierce congressional debates. For his part, Hamilton never requested presidential advice or assistance, regarding control over his own bailiwick as a commander's responsibility. A reader of the correspondence between them might plausibly conclude that the important topics of business were the location and staffing of lighthouses and the proper design of coast guard cutters to enforce customs collections. Privately, Washington confided to friends that he deeply regretted the accusations emanating from his home state, which were "poisoning the minds of the Southern people." Virginia's veiled threats at secession struck him as desperate gestures on the part of a state that needed to reassess its own

inflated sense of importance. But no public statements were necessary, in part because Hamilton
was a one-man army in defending his program, "a
host unto himself," as Jefferson later called him;
and by February 1791 the last piece of the Hamiltonian scheme, the bank, had been passed by
Congress and now only required the presidential
signature.[27]

But the bank proved to be the one controversial
issue that Washington could not completely delegate to Hamilton. As a symbol it was every bit as
threatening, as palpable an embodiment of federal
power, as a sovereign Supreme Court. As part of a
last-ditch campaign to scuttle the bank, the three
Virginians within Washington's official family
mobilized to attack it on constitutional grounds.
Jefferson, Madison, and Randolph submitted separate briefs, all arguing that the power to create a
corporation was nowhere specified by the Constitution; and that the Tenth Amendment clearly
specified that powers not granted to the federal
government were retained by the states. Before rendering his own verdict, Washington sent the three
negative opinions to Hamilton for rebuttal. His
response, which exceeded thirteen thousand words,
became a landmark in American legal history, arguing that the "necessary and proper" clause of the
Constitution (Article 1, Section 8) granted implied
powers to the federal government beyond the

explicit powers specified in the document. (Madison, ironically, had made the same argument three years earlier in **The Federalist Papers.**) Though there is some evidence that Washington was wavering before Hamilton delivered his opinion, it was not the brilliance of the opinion that persuaded him. Rather, it provided the legal rationale he needed to do what he always wanted to do. For the truth was that Washington was just as much an economic nationalist as Hamilton, a fact that Hamilton's virtuoso leadership throughout the year-long debate had conveniently obscured.[28]

THE IMPERIAL PRESIDENCY

As BOTH a symbolic political centerpiece and a deft delegator of responsibility, Washington managed to levitate above the political landscape. That was his preferred position, personally because it made his natural aloofness into an asset, politically because it removed the presidency from the edgy partisan battles on the ground. In three policy areas, however, the location of the national capital, foreign policy, and Indian affairs, he abandoned levitation or delegation for meticulous personal management in the mode of his Mount Vernon leadership style.

What was called "the residence question" had its

origins in a provision of the Constitution calling for Congress to establish a "seat of government" without specifying the location. By the spring of 1790 the debates in Congress had deteriorated into a comic parody on the gridlock theme. Sixteen different sites had been proposed, then rejected, as the state and regional voting blocs mobilized against each alternative in order to preserve their own respective preferences. One frustrated congressman suggested sarcastically that perhaps they should put the new capital on wheels and roll it from place to place. An equally frustrated newspaper editor observed that, "since the usual custom is for the capital of new empires to be selected by the whim or caprice of a despot," and since Washington "had never given bad advice to his country," why not "let him point to a map and say 'here'?"[29]

That is not quite how the Potomac site emerged victorious. Madison had been leading the fight in the House for a Potomac location, earning the nickname "Big Knife" for cutting deals to block the other alternatives. (One of Madison's most inspired arguments was that the geographic midpoint of the nation on a north-south axis was not just the mouth of the Potomac, but Mount Vernon itself, a revelation of providential proportions.) Eventually a private bargain was struck over dinner at Jefferson's apartment, subsequently enshrined in lore as the most consequential dinner party in American history, where Hamilton agreed to deliver sufficient votes from several northern states to clinch the Potomac location in return for Madison's pledge to permit passage of Hamilton's Assumption Bill. Actually, there were multiple behind-the-scenes bargaining sessions going on at the same time, but the notion that an apparently intractable political controversy could be resolved by a friendly conversation over port and cigars has always possessed an irresistible narrative charm. The story also conjured up the attractive picture of brotherly cooperation within his official family that Washington liked to encourage.

Soon after the Residency Act designating a Potomac location passed in July 1790, the previous suggestion of the newspaper editor (i.e., give the messy question to Washington) became fully operative. Jefferson feared that the Potomac site would be sabotaged if the endless management details for developing a city **de novo** were left to Congress. So he proposed a thoroughly imperial solution: bypass Congress altogether by making all subsequent decisions about architects, managers, and construction schedules an executive responsibility "subject to the President's direction in every point."[30]

And so they were. What became Washington,

D.C., was aptly named, for while the project had many troops involved in its design and construction, it had only one supreme commander. He selected the specific site on the Potomac between Rock Creek and Goose Creek, rather deceptively pretending to prefer a more upstream location in order to hold down the purchase price for lots in the ultimate site. He appointed the commissioners, who reported directly to him rather than Congress. He chose Pierre L'Enfant as chief architect, personally endorsing L'Enfant's plan for a huge tract encompassing nine and a half square miles, thereby rejecting Jefferson's preference for a small village that would gradually expand in favor of a massive area that would gradually fill up. When L'Enfant's grandiose vision led to equivalently grandiose demands—he refused to take orders from the commissioners and responded to one stubborn owner of a key lot by blowing up his house—Washington fired him. He approved the sites for the presidential mansion and the Capitol as well as the architects who designed them. All in all, he treated the nascent national capital as a public version of his Mount Vernon plantation, right down to the supervision of the slave labor force that did much of the work.[31]

It helped that the construction site was located near Mount Vernon, so he could make regular visits to monitor progress on his way home. It also helped that Jefferson and Madison could confer with him at the site on their trips back to Monticello and Montpelier. At a time when both Virginians were leading the opposition to Hamilton's financial program, their cooperation on this ongoing project served to bridge the widening chasm within the official family over the Hamiltonian vision of federal power. However therapeutic the cooperation, it belied a fundamental disagreement over the political implications of their mutual interests in the Federal City, as it was then called. For Jefferson and Madison regarded the Potomac location of the permanent capital as a guarantee of Virginia's abiding hegemony within the union; as a form of geographic assurance that the federal government would always speak with a southern accent. Washington thought more expansively, envisioning the capital as a focusing device for national energies that overcame regional jealousies; in effect a place that would perform the same unifying function geographically that he performed symbolically. His personal hobbyhorse became a national university within the capital, where the brightest young men from all regions could congregate and share a common experience as Americans that helped to "rub off" their sectional habits and accents.

His hands-on approach toward foreign policy was only slightly less direct than his control of the

Potomac project. The major foreign policy crisis of the Washington presidency did not occur until his second term, but the basic principles underlying his view of the national interest were present from the start, and he showed no reluctance in imposing them as the elemental convictions he had acquired from long experience in two wars for control of the North American continent.

Most elementally, he was a thoroughgoing realist. Though he embraced republican ideals, he believed that the behavior of nations was not driven by ideals but by interests. This put him at odds ideologically and temperamentally with his secretary of state, since Jefferson was one of the most eloquent spokesmen for the belief that American ideals **were** American interests. Jefferson's recent experience in Paris as a witness to the onset of the French Revolution had only confirmed his conviction that a global struggle on behalf of those ideals had just begun, and that it had a moral claim on American support. Washington was pleased to receive the key to the Bastille from Lafayette; he also knew as well or better than anyone else that the victory over Great Britain would have been impossible without French economic and military assistance. But he was determined to prevent his personal affection for Lafayette or his warm memories of Rochambeau's soldiers and de Grasse's ships at Yorktown from influencing his judgment about the long-term interests of the United States.

Those interests, he was convinced, did not lie across the Atlantic but across the Alleghenies, in those forests and fields he had explored as a young man. To be sure, Europe was the cockpit of international affairs and the central theater in the ongoing Anglo-French struggle for global supremacy. But Washington regarded Europe as only a sideshow that must not divert attention from the enduring strategic interests of the United States. The chief task, as he saw it, was to consolidate control of the continent east of the Mississippi. Although Jefferson had never been west of the Blue Ridge Mountains, he shared Washington's preference for western vistas. (During his own presidency, Jefferson would do more than anyone to expand those vistas beyond the Mississippi to the Pacific.) Both men regarded the Spanish presence in Florida and the Mississippi Valley as a temporary occupation by a declining European power that was destined to be overwhelmed by waves of American settlers within two or three generations.

Tight presidential control over foreign policy was unavoidable at the start, because Jefferson did not come on board until March 1790. Washington immediately delegated all routine business to him, but preserved his own private lines of communication on French developments, describing reports of escalating bloodshed he received from Paris "as if they were the events of another planet." He kept up a joke with Rochambeau about hot soup: the French were inclined to swallow it in huge gulps, they agreed, thereby burning their throats; the Americans preferred to sip it slowly, after it had cooled.[32]

This cautionary posture toward revolutionary France received reinforcement from Gouverneur Morris, the willfully eccentric and thoroughly irreverent American in Paris whom Washington cultivated as a correspondent. Morris minced no words, or perhaps designed them to maximize their political impact. He described France's revolutionary leaders as "a Fleet at Anchor in the fog," and he dismissed Jefferson's view that a Gallic version of 1776 was under way as a hopelessly romantic illusion: the American Revolution, Morris observed, had been guided by experience and light, while the French were obsessed with experiment and lightning. Morris's reports on the unfolding chaos eventually became invaluable documents in the historical record, famous for their combination of detachment and wit. Washington relied on them for accurate intelligence and eventually appointed Morris the American minister to France, over Senate opposition to his iconoclastic style. For his part, Morris returned the favor. Despite having a peg leg, he was a robust physical specimen who posed for Houdon as Washington's stand-in when the sculptor needed a model to complete the statue of his more famous subject.[33]

In addition to his personal monitoring of the explosive events in France, Washington's supervisory style as well as his realistic foreign policy convictions were put on display when a potential crisis surfaced in the summer of 1790. A minor incident involving Great Britain and Spain in Nootka Sound (near modern-day Vancouver) prompted a major appraisal of American national interests. The British appeared poised to use the incident to launch an invasion from Canada down the Mississippi designed to displace Spain as the dominant European power in the American West. This threatened to change the entire strategic chemistry on the continent and raised the daunting prospect of another major war with Great Britain.

Washington convened his cabinet in executive session, thereby making clear for the first time that the cabinet and not the more cumbersome Senate would be his advisory council on foreign policy. Written opinions were solicited from all the major players, including Adams, Hamilton, Jay, Jefferson, and Knox. The crisis fizzled away when the British decided to back off, but during the deliberations two revealing facts became clear: first, that Washington was resolved to avoid war at almost any cost, convinced that the fragile American republic was neither militarily nor economically capable of confronting the British leviathan at this time; second, that Hamilton's strategic assessment, not Jefferson's, was more closely aligned with his own, which turned out to be a preview of coming attractions.[34]

Strictly speaking, the federal government's relations with the Native American tribes were also a foreign policy matter. From the start, however, Indian affairs came under the authority of the secretary of war. As ominous as this might appear in retrospect, Jefferson's late arrival on the scene effectively forced Knox to assume responsibility for negotiating the disputed terms of several treaties approved by the Confederation Congress. More significantly, for both personal and policy reasons, Washington wanted his own hand firmly on this particular tiller, and his intimate relationship with Knox assured a seamless coordination guided by his own judgment. He had been present at the start of the struggle for control of the American interior, and regarded the final fate of the Indian inhabitants as an important piece of unfinished business that must not be allowed to end on a tragic note.

At the policy level, if America's future lay to the

west, as Washington believed, it followed that the region between the Alleghenies and the Mississippi merited executive attention more than the diplomatic doings in Europe. Knox estimated that about 76,000 Native Americans lived in the region, about 20,000 of them warriors, which meant that venerable tribal chiefs like Cornplanter and Joseph Brant deserved more cultivation as valuable allies than heads of state across the Atlantic. At the personal level, as commander of the Virginia Regiment and then alongside Braddock at the Monongahela, Washington had experienced Indian power firsthand. He did not view Native Americans as exotic savages, but as familiar and formidable adversaries fighting for their own independence: in effect, behaving pretty much as he would do in their place. Moreover, the letters the new president received from several tribal chiefs provided poignant testimony that they now regarded him as their personal protector: "Brother," wrote one Cherokee chief, "we give up to our white brothers all the land we could any how spare, and have but little left . . . and we hope you wont let any people take any more from us without our consent. We are neither Birds nor Fish; we can neither fly in the air nor live under water. . . . We are made by the same hand and in the same shape as yourselves."[35]

Such pleas did not fall on deaf ears. Working

closely with Knox, Washington devised a policy
designed to create several sovereign Indian
"homelands." He concurred when Knox insisted
that "the independent tribes of indians ought to
be considered as foreign nations, not as the subjects of any particular State." Treaties with these
tribes ought to be regarded as binding contracts
sanctioned by the federal government, whose
jurisdiction could not be compromised: "Indians
being the prior occupants possess the right of the
Soil . . . To dispossess them . . . would be a gross
violation of the fundamental Laws of Nature and
of that distributive Justice which is the glory of a
nation." A more coercive policy of outright confiscation, Washington believed, would constitute
a moral failure that "would stain the character of
the nation." He sought to avoid the outcome—
Indian removal—that occurred more than forty
years later under Andrew Jackson. Instead, he
envisioned multiple sanctuaries under tribal control that would be bypassed by the surging wave of
white settlers and whose occupants would gradually, over the course of the next century, become
assimilated as full-fledged American citizens.[36]

Attempting to make this vision a reality occupied more of Washington's time and energy than
any foreign or domestic issue during his first
term. Success depended on identifying key tribal
leaders willing to negotiate and capable of

imposing the settlement on other tribes in the region. Knox and Washington identified one charismatic Creek chief named Alexander McGillivray, a literate half-breed with diplomatic skills and survival instincts that made him the Indian version of France's Talleyrand on the southern frontier. In the summer of 1790, Washington hosted McGillivray and twenty-six chiefs for several weeks of official dinners, parades, and diplomatic ceremonies more lavish than any European delegation experienced. (McGillivray expected and received a personal bribe of $1,200 a year to offset the sum the Spanish were already paying him not to negotiate with the Americans.) Washington and the chiefs locked arms in Indian style and invoked the Great Spirit, then the chiefs made their marks on the Treaty of New York, redrawing the borders for a sovereign Creek Nation. Washington reinforced the terms of the treaty by issuing the Proclamation of 1790, an executive order forbidding private or state encroachments on all Indian lands guaranteed by treaty with the United States. Ironically, it was a presidential version of George III's Proclamation of 1763, which a younger Washington had found so offensive.[37]

But much like George III, Washington soon found that it was one thing to proclaim, and quite another to sustain. The Georgia legislature defied the proclamation by making a thoroughly corrupt bargain to sell more than fifteen million acres on its western border to speculators calling themselves the Yazoo Companies, thereby rendering the Treaty of New York a worthless piece of paper. In the northern district above the Ohio, no equivalent to McGillivray could be found, mostly because the Six Nations, which Washington could remember as a potent force in the region, had been virtually destroyed in the War of Independence and could no longer exercise hegemony over the Ohio Valley tribes.[38]

Washington was forced to approve a series of military expeditions into the Ohio Valley to put down uprisings by the Miami, Wyandot, and Shawnee, even though he believed that the chief culprits were white vigilante groups determined to provoke hostilities. The Indian side of the story, Washington complained, would never make it into the history books: "They, poor wretches, have no press thro' which their grievances are related; and it is well known, that when one side only of a Story is heard, and often repeated, the human mind becomes impressed with it, insensibly." Worse still, the expedition commanded by Arthur St. Clair was virtually annihilated in the fall of 1791—reading St. Clair's battle orders is like watching Custer prepare for the Little Big Horn—thereby creating white martyrs and provoking congressional cries for reprisals in what had become an escalating cycle of violence that defied Washington's efforts at conciliation.[39]

Eventually Washington was forced to acknowledge that his vision of secure Indian sanctuaries could not be enforced. "I believe scarcely any thing short of a Chinese wall," he lamented, "will restrain Land jobbers and the encroachment of settlers upon the Indian country." Knox concurred, estimating that federal control on the frontier would require an arc of forts stretching from Lake Erie to the Gulf of Mexico and garrisoned by no fewer than fifty thousand troops. This was a logistical, economic, and political impossibility. Washington's vision of peaceful coexistence also required that federal jurisdiction over the states as the ultimate guarantor of all treaties be recognized as supreme, which helps to explain why he was so passionate about the issue, but also why it could never happen. If a just accommodation with the Native American populations was the major preoccupation of his first term, it was also the singular failure.[40]

PARTIES AND PARTISANS

WHAT WASHINGTON had once imagined as a brief caretaker presidency lasting a year or two had, by

1792, grown into a judicious projection of executive power that was nearing the end of its designated term. He had performed his central mission flawlessly, providing invaluable legitimacy to the "more perfect union" that was still, in truth, a work in progress. He had demonstrated many of the same leadership skills in the political arena that he had previously displayed as commander in chief during the war. If victory then had meant preserving the Continental army by avoiding battles that risked its survival, he had fashioned a kind of Fabian presidency that sustained the credibility of the federal government by avoiding political battles (the court system and slavery, for instance) that threatened to push federal sovereignty further and faster than public opinion allowed. And just as he had once delegated control over the crucial military campaign in the south to Nathanael Greene, he had also delegated control over the crucial question of fiscal reform to Alexander Hamilton, who had performed just as brilliantly as Greene, while willingly absorbing the political criticism that would otherwise have been directed at Washington himself. The only major battle in which he had chosen to lead the charge personally, and lost, was the fight for federal jurisdiction over Indian affairs. But he did not regret that effort, which he continued to hope, perhaps like Brandywine or Germantown, would come to be regarded as a temporary setback on the longer road to ultimate victory. It was now time to resume his preferred role as Cincinnatus by declaring his heartfelt intention to retire at the end of his term.

In conversations with several members of his official family during the spring of 1792, he described his declining energy and appetite for the demanding work schedule, his advancing years, his resolute sense that now was the time to go. In May he called in Madison, reiterated his resolve, then asked Madison to draft "a Valedictory address" telling the American citizenry that he would not allow his name to be put forward as a candidate in the fall election. Madison protested the decision, as did all the members of the cabinet, but complied by preparing a three-page statement in the format of an open letter to the American people that was aimed for release to the newspapers the following September.[41]

That letter, of course, never appeared, and Washington went on to serve a second term. The immediate reason for his decision, reached with great reluctance, became obvious in several spirited conversations with Jefferson and Hamilton during succeeding months which exposed the widening chasm within his official family. Washington tried to treat the conflict as a fraternal spat between two of his surrogate sons. But the core of the disagreement, as Washington surely knew, went much deeper than that. Indeed, the only issue on which Jefferson and Hamilton could apparently agree was Washington's indispensability. Beyond that, Jefferson accused Hamilton of plotting to commandeer the government after Washington's departure, establishing his banker friends as a new American aristocracy and himself as king, emperor, or dictator, depending on Hamilton's whim. For his part, Hamilton charged Jefferson with working behind the scenes to undermine the Hamiltonian fiscal program and subvert Washington's policy of neutrality by aligning the United States with France, all part of a well-orchestrated Virginia conspiracy to capture the federal government for its slave-owning supporters.

The hatred between the two men had become palpable, mutual, and personal. It had, in fact, been simmering for over a year, and only the patriarchal dominance of Washington's personality had prevented it from exploding earlier. While Hamilton managed to restrain his anger in consultations with Washington, the customarily serene Jefferson eventually lost his composure. He told Washington he could no longer allow his reputation "to be clouded by the slanders of a man whose history, from the moment at which history can stoop to notice him, is a tissue of machinations against the liberty of the country which has not only received and given him bread, but heaped its honors upon his head."[42]

Although no one knew it at the time—indeed no one yet possessed the vocabulary to talk or think about it sensibly—political parties were in the process of being born. The split between Jefferson and Hamilton was destined to foster the creation of the two-party system as a central feature in the American political universe. Though full-fledged parties, with national platforms, campaigns, and conventions, would not emerge until the 1830s, their embryonic origins first became visible during Washington's presidency. Over time it would eventually become clear that a two-party system was a major contribution to modern political science; for by forcing the wide spectrum of political opinion into two camps, it institutionalized the ongoing dialogue into an organized format that routinized dissent. In retrospect, the two-party system has come to be regarded as one of the most significant and enduring legacies of the founding generation. But what is now seen as a great contribution was regarded by its creators as a great curse. And the man who did more to invent political parties expressed most memorably the loathing felt by all: "If I could not go to heaven but with a party," declared Jefferson, "I would not go at all."[43]

The seminal impulse for what was to become

the Republican Party began in Virginia during the spring and summer of 1790. First, the lengthy debate in the House over slavery startled most Virginia planters, whose livelihood was switching from tobacco and wheat to the sale of their own excess slaves to the burgeoning cotton plantations of the Carolinas. The mere suggestion that the federal government could legislate slavery out of existence generated panic within the Tidewater elite who dominated Virginia politics. Second, Hamilton's financial program, especially the Assumption Bill and National Bank, signaled the triumph of northern commerce—what Jefferson called "that speculating phalanx"—over southern agriculture and Virginia's economic stature as the dominant state in the union. Accustomed to regarding themselves as the leading citizens of the new American republic—as Adams so nicely put it, in Virginia "all geese are swans"—Virginians began to have second thoughts about the constitutional settlement of 1787–88, as they witnessed the emergence of a federal government moving in a direction hostile to their economic interest and beyond their political control.

The key player in this unfolding drama, and the leader whose conversion to a Virginia-writ-large version of the nation best illustrated how the political templates were moving, was Madison. He led the fight in Congress against both federal jurisdiction over slavery and the entire Hamiltonian fiscal program. Jefferson soon joined him in mobilizing the opposition, claiming that he had been "duped by Hamilton" to support the Assumption Bill, "and of all the errors of my political life this has occasioned me the deepest regret." What historians have dubbed "the great collaboration" began in earnest during the summer of 1791, when Jefferson and Madison made a so-called botanical tour up the Connecticut River to seek support in New England and New York for their agenda of opposition. Though both men were trusted members of Washington's official family, and Jefferson a key officer of the cabinet, they launched an orchestrated attack on the administration they were officially serving. Jefferson hired Philip Freneau, a prominent poet and essayist, who wrote articles in the **National Gazette** castigating Washington's policy of neutrality as a vile repudiation of America's obligations to France. Madison wrote several anonymous essays for the same paper which gave a distinctive shape to the core arguments of what was beginning to be called the Republican Party.[44]

The resonant term was "consolidation." Madison described the aggregation of power by the federal government as an ominous second coming on American soil of the British monster that the American Revolution had supposedly banished forever. All the familiar chords in the old revolutionary melody then played themselves out accordingly: the executive branch had become a royal court; northern bankers were "monocrats" and "stockjobbers" who enjoyed privileged access to power at court; Hamilton's program was a homemade version of the Stamp Act; the federal government was an imperial power that treated the states as mere colonies. In effect, the money changers had taken over the American temple, and the original promise of the Revolution had fallen into enemy hands.[45]

The genius of this formulation was that it transformed a regional or sectional grievance rooted in economic interest into a patriotic rallying cry rooted in a rhetoric with all the hallowed echoes of 1776. Despite its rhetorical genius, Washington found it both flawed and fanciful: flawed because, unlike George III and Parliament, he had been duly elected, as had all the members of Congress; and fanciful because it confused a strong executive with monarchy, almost willfully so. When Jefferson expressed his personal conviction that Hamilton had monarchical intentions, Washington countered that "he did not believe that there were ten men in the United States whose opinions were worth attention who entertained such a thought"; and

Hamilton, despite his impolitic remarks on that score at the Constitutional Convention, was not one of them.[46]

More basically, Washington was immune to the virulent antigovernment strain of revolutionary ideology that Jefferson and Madison were deploying because he had witnessed its consequences as commander in chief. The Continental army had nearly starved to death, and the war itself had been prolonged and nearly lost, all for lack of a viable central government empowered to raise money and troops. In Washington's version of "the spirit of '76" the key lesson was that independence required a fully empowered federal government, thus making his own election the proper culmination of America's revolutionary experience. Indeed, as Washington saw it, if one wished to talk about a hostile takeover of the American Revolution, the chief culprits were those Virginians, most of whom had never fired a shot in anger during the war, who were now trying to rewrite history in order to preserve their fading status and provincial privileges.

Arguments about history aside, the fact remained that two of the most trusted and talented members of his inner circle were being described in the press as "the General and the Generalissimo" of the emerging opposition party. Jefferson's continued presence in the cabinet struck several observers as the most glaring anomaly: "Beware," wrote one anonymous Washington supporter. "Be upon your guard. You have cherished in your Bosom a Serpent, and he is now endeavoring to sting you to death. . . . His vanity makes him believe that he will certainly be your Successor. . . . Believe him not. He is a Hypocrite and is deceiving you." But instead of regarding Jefferson as the serpent in the garden, Washington preferred to see him as the prodigal son who would eventually recognize the error of his ways and return to the bosom of the family. Washington's confidence in both the correctness of his political vision and the strength of his dominating personal presence made him impervious to gossip about Jefferson's duplicity. He continued to meet with Jefferson over breakfast to discuss recent dispatches from Paris or London. He continued to rely on advice from Madison and Jefferson about nettlesome details related to the construction of the city going up on the Potomac. The criticism of his policies that they were drafting or sponsoring in other quarters never came up, by mutual consent.[47]

The psychological minuet had its corollary on the other side. Whenever Washington unburdened himself in private conversations with Jefferson or Madison about his physical fatigue, his declining energy, his insatiable urge for retirement to Mount Vernon, they recorded their recollections of the conversation as evidence of his growing mental detachment from the duties of the office. In effect, they apparently convinced themselves, and left a written record of their conviction, that the aging patriarch was not really in charge or fully responsible for the policies going forward under the protection of his own name. The satanic presence and true power behind the scene was, they believed, Hamilton. This somewhat strained interpretation of Washington's genuine fatigue had two huge advantages: at the personal level, it allowed Jefferson and Madison to argue that they were not betraying their venerable father figure, who simply did not know what was going on; at a public level, it allowed for a distinction between their criticism of the Washington administration and of Washington himself, thereby avoiding the politically insurmountable task of taking on the most beloved and respected hero of the age.[48]

Washington danced his own minuet throughout the summer of 1792, hoping against hope that it would carry him southward toward Mount Vernon. Ironically, it was Jefferson who most candidly informed him that the sectional tensions created by Virginia's reaction to the Hamiltonian program rendered all such hopes superfluous. "North & South will hang together," Jefferson warned, only "if they have you to hang on." Though he himself planned to retire soon, Jefferson explained that Washington was not permitted the same luxury: "There is sometimes an eminence of character in which society have such peculiar claims as to control the predilection of the individual. . . . This seems to be your condition." When Washington asked Tobias Lear to inquire discreetly about alternative candidates, Lear reported that "No other person is contemplated."[49]

Even as late as November, with the election imminent, Washington apparently clung to the illusion that he still had a choice in the matter. At least he told the prominent Philadelphia socialite Elizabeth Willing Powel that a second term remained inconceivable to both him and Martha. Powel reiterated Jefferson's warning about sectional tensions, noting that Washington's departure would be used "as an Argument for dissolving the Union." She then went on to offer perhaps the most psychologically astute diagnosis of Washington's unique status by any of his contemporaries: "Be assured that a great Deal of the well earned Popularity you are now in Possession of will be torn from you by the Envious and Malignant should you follow the bent of your Inclinations. You know human Nature too well not to believe that you have Enemies. Merit & Virtue, when placed on an Eminence, will as certainly attract Envy as the Magnet does the Needle." In short, his host of admirers included ambitious men whose admiration barely concealed their latent hatred of his greater greatness. As long as he retained power they would be afraid to show themselves. But they were lurking in the background, poised to ravage his reputation and render his retirement less serene than he envisioned.[50]

Washington took it all in and remained silent. Once again, he did not need to declare his candidacy. By keeping Madison's draft of his "Valedictory address" in his drawer, his candidacy was presumed. Once again, the electoral vote was unanimous. His second inaugural address accurately expressed his mood. It was the briefest in presidential history, only two short paragraphs long, wholly devoid of content, respectful but regretful in tone.[51]

UP AS A MARK

IF WASHINGTON originally approached his presidency as a mandatory sentence ironically imposed on him for good behavior, the second term began as pure purgatory. And before the year was out events seemed to be tumbling toward hell: on the southern frontier McGillivray's stabilizing influence eroded under Spanish prodding and bribes, producing violent clashes with white settlers from Kentucky to Florida; the Six Nations tried but failed to exercise control over the Ohio tribes, whose leaders declared war on "any person of a white skin" entering what they called "our Island"; the French Revolution moved from "liberty, equality, and fraternity" to the guillotine, and Lafayette, fleeing the chaos, was captured and placed in an Austrian dungeon; farmers in western Pennsylvania staged mass protests against an excise tax on whiskey, claiming it was an updated version of the Stamp Act; a yellow fever epidemic broke out in Philadelphia, forcing the government to take up makeshift quarters in Germantown; and the battle within the cabinet between Jefferson and Hamilton escalated, ending only at the end of the year when Jefferson took his wounds and principles back home to Monticello and retirement.[52]

More personally, Washington's favorite nephew, who was responsible for managing Mount Vernon, died of tuberculosis; a cancer-like growth appeared on Washington's right cheek, requiring another debilitating surgery; finally, while Hamilton remained the chief villain in Republican editorials, the moratorium on Washington himself ended as both Freneau's **National Gazette** and Benjamin Franklin Bache's **Aurora** began targeting him as either a senile accomplice or a willing

co-conspirator in the Hamiltonian plot to establish an American monarchy. Washington found the
personal attacks "outrages on common decency,"
but resolved to suffer in silence. "The arrows of
malevolence," he observed, "however barbed and
well pointed, never can reach the most vulnerable
part of me; though, while I am up as a mark, they
will be continually aimed." He would in fact be "up
as a mark" for the remainder of his presidency.[53]

He would also be enveloped by foreign policy
challenges and their domestic ramifications. The
cataclysmic event that shaped his political agenda
occurred in April 1793, when war broke out
between Great Britain and revolutionary France.
Washington immediately recognized the threatening implications of this resumption of a century-
old conflict between the two contending powers
of Europe, this time with France brandishing its
revolutionary obligation to extend an "empire of
liberty" around the globe. As soon as the news
arrived, he convened the cabinet—Jefferson had
yet to depart—and extracted their unanimous
support for a policy of strict American neutrality,
which was released to the world as an executive
proclamation the following week. But what was
intended to sound a clear and conclusive note
turned out to be just the start of a cacophonous
story.[54]

In a remarkably convenient sense, the interlacing

strands of the story assumed a palpable shape in the recently arrived minister from France, Edmond Genet. Citizen Genet—the title a measure of France's current intoxication with egalitarianism—arrived in America brimming over with assurance that there could be no such thing as neutrality when the cause of liberty was on the march. Several conversations with Jefferson confirmed his conviction that the spiritual bonds uniting the American with the French Revolution were more powerful than any presidential proclamation. A series of essays in the **National Gazette** reinforced this impression, arguing that the historic link between America and France, codified in the Franco-American Treaty of 1778, could not be repudiated by any executive decision. Genet then unburdened himself in a flurry of pronouncements that effectively doomed his mission: outfitting American privateers to oppose British control of the seas; scheming to send an expedition to seize control of New Orleans from Spain in the name of the Franco-American alliance; and most preposterously, announcing that he, Citizen Genet, spoke for the true interests of the American people, and urging Congress to override Washington's proclamation at its next session.[55]

By then even Jefferson acknowledged privately that Genet, originally seen as an invaluable ally, had become an albatross for the Republican opposition. For his part, Washington confided to friends that no official rejection of Genet was necessary, since the man's own suicidal instincts would suffice. But the Genet affair exposed for the first time that foreign policy had become inextricably entangled with partisan politics. Genet's behavior was wildly irresponsible, but the cause of France was also wildly popular in 1793, producing mass demonstrations demanding war with Great Britain and activist organizations called Democratic Societies that modeled themselves on the old Sons of Liberty. These were powerful sentiments with resonant echoes of '76 that the Republicans were determined to exploit, in part because it was good politics, in part because many Republicans, Jefferson for one, believed in them passionately.

Washington was absolutely certain—and history eventually proved him right—that America's long-term interest was best served by steering a neutral course that avoided war with any of the European powers. He was also convinced that his Republican opponents were manipulating popular opinion toward France as a political weapon. "It is not the cause of France (nor, I believe, Liberty) which they regard," he observed, "for, could they involve the Country in war (no matter with whom) and disgrace, they would be among the first and loudest of the clamourers against the expense and impolicy of the measure." And yet, while determined to have his own realistic assessment of America's interest prevail, the reigning romance of all things French gave the Republican press new ammunition to depict him as an arbitrary monarch rather than a farsighted leader. Perhaps to offset the charges, he made a point at the height of the Genet affair of questioning his own authority to convene Congress in Germantown because of the yellow fever epidemic. Such modest gestures went unnoticed in the **National Gazette** and **Aurora,** where Washington himself now replaced Hamilton as the central target.[56]

Another event had nostalgic implications, for it played out in the western counties of Pennsylvania where Washington's military career had begun forty years earlier. The story had its origins in 1791, when Congress passed an excise tax on whiskey to help pay the debt created by Hamilton's funding and assumption program. Protests against the tax by western grain farmers followed immediately, claiming that it fell disproportionately on distilleries making the whiskey that allowed them to transport their product to eastern markets. Despite Washington's efforts to work through the courts to punish offenders, resistance to the tax was so widespread that collectors were forced to flee for their lives. The protest movement culminated in August 1794, when more than six thousand men gathered in Braddock's Field outside Pittsburgh, very near the scene of the Monongahela massacre. They set up mock guillotines to register their solidarity with French revolutionaries, imbibed freely of their favorite liquid, then defied the federal government to come after them. "Should an attempt be made to suppress these people," warned one witness, "I am afraid the question will not be, whether you will march to Pittsburgh, but whether they will march to Philadelphia." The rebels saw themselves, as had the Shays's rebels in Massachusetts nearly a decade earlier, as actors in a dramatic sequel to the resistance movement against arbitrary taxation.[57]

"I consider this insurrection as the first formidable fruit of the Democratic Societies," Washington insisted, meaning that it was inspired more by the French than the American Revolution and was encouraged by Republican operatives in Pennsylvania. He had earlier described military action against the rebels as "a dernier resort," but by September 1794 concluded that rebel intransigence left him no alternative, claiming that these "self-created societies"—he nearly spit out the words—represented a tyranny of the minority against the will of the majority, and that their only revolutionary principle was that "every man can cut and carve for himself." Moreover, he decided to take personal command of the thirteen thousand troops raised by militia enlistments to crush the insurrection.[58]

This decision produced a scene that provides the most graphic and dramatic illustration of the two competing versions of what the American Revolution had come to mean in the 1790s. On one side stood the rebels, a defiant collection of aggrieved farmers emboldened by their conviction that the excise tax levied by Congress was every bit as illegitimate as the taxes levied by the British ministry. On the other side stood Washington and his federalized troops, an updated version of the Continental army, marching west to enforce the authority of the constitutionally elected government that claimed to represent all the American people. It was "the spirit of '76" against "the spirit of '87," one historic embodiment of "the people" against another. And there was Washington, back in the saddle again as commander in chief, with former aide-de-camp Hamilton at his side, traveling on the old Forbes Road he had objected to so strenuously as a route in his earlier incarnation as a soldier. It also turned out to be the first and only time a sitting American president led troops in the field.

In truth, Washington only accompanied the army as far as Carlisle. By then it was clear that the bravado of the rebels had evaporated at the approach of such a formidable force. Hamilton led the army in what became a triumphant parade to Pittsburgh, obeying Washington's orders to offer amnesty to all rebels who signed an oath to obey the laws of the federal government. Back in Philadelphia, Washington addressed Congress, justifying his military response on the grounds that "certain self-created societies" were in fact subversive organizations that threatened the survival of the national union. He was not disputing the right of aggrieved citizens to dissent, but he was insisting that dissent could not take the form of flagrant violation of federal authority. Congress overwhelmingly agreed, congratulating him on defending the Constitution. Only Madison struck a sour note in an uncharacteristically rambling speech that worried about the precedent this set. Down at Monticello, the recently retired Jefferson confided to Madison that the Republican cause had suffered a massive blow, but that Washington on horseback trumped anything they could muster in response. A close reading of Washington's speech to Congress somewhat consoled him, wrote Jefferson, since the language resembled "shreds of stuff from Aesop's fables and Tom Thumb," which he interpreted as evidence that Hamilton composed it, so that the grand old man probably did not know what he was doing or saying.[59]

Finally, the greatest crisis of the Washington presidency was the debate over the Jay Treaty. It seems safe to say no treaty in American history generated so many diplomatic, constitutional, and political reverberations; and no treaty so unpopular in its own day proved so beneficial over the stretch of time. What Hamilton's financial program was to the first term, the Jay Treaty was to the second, a projection of executive power that most infuriated Washington's enemies. Unlike the Hamilton program, which bore only his signature, Washington's distinctive mark on the Jay Treaty was conspicuously registered at every step of the lengthy and anguishing process. It was his most besieged and finest hour.[60]

Here is the essential background. By 1794 the prospects of war with Great Britain were approaching a crisis. In defiance of the Treaty of Paris, British troops had remained stationed on the northwestern frontier, justified as a strategic response to America's refusal to compensate British creditors for pre-revolutionary debts. (Virginia's planter class owed the bulk of the money.) Merely as a symbol, the British military presence suggested a hovering reminder that American victory in the War of Independence was still incomplete. More substantively, British troops were encouraging the Ohio tribes to defy Washington's efforts at accommodation. The outbreak of war between Britain and France had escalated the tensions, in part because the sentiments of the American citizenry were decidedly pro-French, and in part because British cruisers were scooping up American merchant vessels in the Caribbean with impunity in an effort to block all trade with France.

In April 1794, Washington dispatched Chief Justice John Jay to London to negotiate a realistic bargain that would remove the British troops and redefine commercial relations with Britain in terms that avoided war. This last item was most crucial in Washington's mind. Whatever unfinished business remained between the two former adversaries, Washington believed that America could not afford to risk war with the British army or navy for at least a generation, or, as he put it, "for about twenty years." A war before then would be economically and militarily disastrous. It also had the potential to kill the infant nation in the cradle.[61]

These were sensible and farsighted goals (indeed, the War of 1812 arrived right on Washington's schedule), but at the time the very thought of negotiating with the British was wildly unpopular. The selection of Jay also created a furor within the Virginia camp, because he was known to favor payment of the long-standing debts to British creditors that Virginians preferred to finesse. Madison denounced Jay's selection as a diabolical choice, though he confidentially noticed a silver lining in this dark cloud; namely, Jay's unpopularity was likely to rub off on Washington and render the impregnable hero suddenly vulnerable. Bache's **Aurora** joined the chorus of criticism, going so far as to suggest that Jay had been chosen because sending the chief justice to London would make impeachment proceedings against Washington impossible. This was preposterous, to be sure, but also an accurate barometer of the fanatical atmosphere surrounding the issues at stake.[62]

The terms Jay was able to negotiate only made matters worse. On the positive side, the treaty required the removal of British troops from the frontier; and it committed the British to arbitrate American claims of compensation for cargoes confiscated by their navy. But otherwise the terms were decidedly unfavorable, accepting British economic and naval supremacy in language that gave American neutrality a British tilt. Critics could plausibly argue, and Jefferson did, that the treaty created a neocolonial status for the United States within the British Empire. Advocates might have responded that American merchants would be the chief beneficiaries of this arrangement, which only codified diplomatically what was already a fact commercially: trade with Great Britain was the lifeblood of the American economy. But this would only become clear later.

In any event, the Republican press had a field day as soon as the terms of the treaty were leaked to the **Aurora** and made public. Jay claimed he could have walked the entire eastern seaboard at night and had his way illuminated by protesters burning him in effigy. Adams later recalled that the presidential mansion in Philadelphia was "surrounded by innumerable multitudes, from day to day buzzing, demanding war against England, cursing Washington, and crying success to the French patriots and virtuous Republicans." Washington believed that Jay had probably gotten the best terms possible; and while not all that he had hoped for, the treaty averted a popular but misguided war and preserved economic relations with America's major trading partner. But he also conceded that "at present the cry against the Treaty is like that against a mad dog; and everyone, in a manner, seems engaged in running it down."[63]

Should he sign it? Strategically, he thought the treaty was a sensible compromise with British power that bought precious time for America to mature toward its own destiny as a player on the world stage. Politically, his cabinet was divided, and letters were pouring in from around the country describing the treaty as a pact with the British satan. Though he was probably leaning toward a positive decision, what pushed him over the edge was a dramatic crisis in his cabinet that graphically exposed the conspiratorial mentality of the treaty's opponents.

Edmund Randolph, who succeeded Jefferson as secretary of state, had opposed the treaty. In August 1795, Washington was shown confidential documents exposing Randolph's off-the-record conversations with the outgoing French minister, Joseph Fauchet. Although it is unlikely that Randolph requested a bribe to assist the French cause, as some documents seemed to imply, the whole tenor of his remarks conveyed the impression that Washington was a dazed, over-the-hill patriarch, the dupe of scheming northern bankers and closet monarchists, who were plotting to capture the republic for their own sinister purposes. As Randolph described the executive branch, only his own patriotic influence within the cabinet offered any prospect of rescuing the presidency from ruin. This, in effect, was Jefferson-talk, the kind of over-heated and melodramatic depiction of the purported evil lurking in Washington's administration that passed for self-evident truths within Republican headquarters in Virginia. The conspiratorial mentality was so widespread within the Virginia camp that Randolph had lost all perspective on how conspiratorial it sounded to those denied the vision. Washington accepted Randolph's resignation on the spot and signed the Jay Treaty the next day.[64]

But the story did not end there. Jefferson could not believe that a treaty so unpopular could ever become law, since it was, as he said, "really nothing more than a treaty of alliance between England and the Anglomen of this country against the legislature and people of the United States." Though the Constitution nowhere specifically mentioned it, Jefferson persuaded himself that the "true meaning of the constitution" gave the House of Representatives sovereign power over all legislation, including treaties. Madison's more oblique but cunning formulation was that the House, which had authority over all money bills, could sabotage the Jay Treaty by denying the funds necessary for its implementation.

The drama played out in the House in the spring of 1796. During the debate, Robert Livingston of New York requested that Washington hand over all documents related to the treaty, implying that full disclosure would reveal mischief behind the scenes. Washington rejected the request as "a dangerous precedent" that violated the separation of powers doctrine by extending congressional scrutiny into the executive branch. (He also inquired on what grounds the House claimed any role in approving treaties.) Undeterred, Madison pressed on as the floor leader in the debate, confident that he had the votes to carry the day regardless of constitutional niceties. As the votes began to melt away, Madison experienced firsthand the humiliation that befell anyone who went up against Washington in a political battle he was determined to win. The treaty passed by a slim majority (51–48) on the last day of April.[65]

As he surveyed the wreckage from Monticello, Jefferson tried to console Madison with the observation that Washington's stature alone caused the defeat, for he was "the one man who outweighs them all in influence over all the people." He quoted a famous line from Joseph Addison's **Cato,** Washington's favorite play, and applied it to Washington himself: "a curse on his virtues, they have undone his country." In the Jeffersonian formulation, Washington remained a marvelously well intentioned but quasi-senile front man for a Federalist conspiracy, inadvertently lending his enormous credibility to the treacheries being hatched all around him.

For his part, Washington described the Republican campaign against the Jay Treaty as a blatantly partisan effort masquerading as a noble cause, one that somehow the Virginians had convinced themselves was in the national and not just their regional interest: "With respect to the motives wch. Have led to these measures, and wch. Have not only brought the Constitution to the brink of precipice, put the happiness and prosperity of the Country into imminent danger, I shall say nothing. Charity tells us they ought to be good; but suspicions say they must be bad. At present my tongue shall be quiet." He confessed to Jay that the vicious personal attacks and willful misrepresentations that dominated the debate were ominous signs of a new kind of party politics for which he had no stomach: "These things, as you have supposed, fill my mind with much concern, and with serious anxiety. Indeed, the trouble and perplexities which they occasion, added to the weight of years which have passed over me, have worn away my mind more than my body; and renders ease and retirement indisputably necessary to both during the short time I have to stay here."[66]

THE FAREWELL

THE DEBATE over the Jay Treaty exposed the major fault line running through the entire revolutionary era. On one side stood those who wished America's revolutionary energies to be harnessed to the larger purposes of nation building; on the other side stood those who interpreted that very process as a betrayal of the Revolution itself. Washington did not try to straddle that divide in the Jay Treaty debate, or delegate the front-line position in the battle to surrogates. Just as he had at Trenton and Princeton during the war, he took the lead. But what no British musket or cannon had been able to do on the military battlefield, the Republican press had managed to accomplish on the political one. Washington was wounded, struck in the spot he cared about most passionately, his reputation as the "singular figure" who embodied the meaning of the American Revolution in its most elevated and transcendent form. The partisan character of the debate over the Jay Treaty rendered all claims to transcendence obsolete. Washington could neither accept that fact nor ignore the wounds that this new form of politics had inflicted on him and on his legacy.

The personal attacks became even more savage in the summer of 1796. In response to the Jay Treaty, the French Directory had declared commercial war on American shipping, and one of the first prizes captured was an American cruiser coincidentally named the **Mount Vernon.** Editorials in the **Aurora,** taking a line that would have been regarded as treasonable in any later international conflict, saluted the French campaign on the high seas and chortled over the capture of a ship associated with Washington's reputation. Bache subsequently launched a direct assault on Washington's character by printing documents purporting to show that the president had accepted a bribe from the British early in the Revolutionary War, so that all along he had really been a British spy in the Benedict Arnold mode. This bizarre charge was based on British forgeries during the war, which had long ago been exposed as part of a British scheme to have Washington removed as commander in chief. Washington tried to laugh off the smear campaign, observing that Bache "has a celebrity in a certain way, for his calumnies are to be exceeded only by his impudence, and both stand unrivaled." But in the supercharged atmosphere of the time, all political attacks, no matter how preposterous, enjoyed some claim on credibility. Washington spent several days assuring that the official record of the British forgeries was put on file in the archives of the State Department.[67]

Another painful wound that he felt personally was Jefferson's betrayal. Even though Jefferson had been describing him in private correspondence as quasi-senile, Washington learned of these charges from secondhand sources whom he chose not to believe. And Jefferson had taken care to assure that his own fingerprints were never left on any public documents. Indeed, when he retired from the cabinet late in 1793, Washington made a point of saluting Jefferson's integrity and the personal trust that remained intact despite the policy differences between them. At some level Washington knew full well that Jefferson was orchestrating the Republican campaign against his presidency. But at another level Jefferson remained one of his cherished surrogate sons, perhaps prodigal, surely misguided in his romantic attachments to France and to a Virginia-writ-large vision of the American republic, but cherished nonetheless. Both men desperately wished to preserve the semblance of mutual trust and friendship.

The break came in July 1796. Perhaps out of a sense of guilt, perhaps because he realized how thoroughly his duplicity had been exposed, Jefferson wrote to offer assurances that he had played no direct role in the recent press attacks on Washington's character. Washington's response was a masterful example of how one Virginia gentleman tells another that he has violated the unspoken code: "As you have mentioned the subject yourself, it would not be frank, candid, or friendly to conceal, that your conduct has been represented as derogatory from that opinion I had conceived you entertained to me." He then proceeded to list the litany of libels in the **Aurora,** accusations that "could scarcely be applied to a Nero, a notorious defaulter; or even to a common pick-pocket." Then came the devastating clincher. Though everyone had been warning him about Jefferson, "my answer invariably has been that I had never discovered anything in the conduct of Mr. Jefferson to raise suspicions, in my mind, of his sincerity." From that moment, Jefferson knew that Washington no longer trusted him. The two men exchanged a few more letters the following year, all safely focused on agrarian topics like their respective vetch crops. Then, when one of Jefferson's more offensive private letters condemning Washington's leadership was reprinted in the newspapers—Jefferson claimed it was not quite what he had said—all correspondence between Monticello and Mount Vernon ceased. Historians have always had a difficult time trying to pinpoint the moment when the party system displaced a government founded on trust and bipartisan assumptions. For Washington, this was it.[68]

By then Washington had already asked his other surrogate son to draft what came to be called the Farewell Address. Hamilton had left the cabinet more than a year earlier, but had remained Washington's chief advisor throughout the Jay Treaty imbroglio. He also had more experience than anyone else at crafting language for Washington's signature. In this instance, Washington let it be known from the start that more than his signature would be required on this final statement of his public career. He sent Hamilton a first draft comprised of his own words, plus Madison's "Valedictory Address" of 1792, along with extensive instructions about content and style. On the latter score, he insisted on a conspicuously "plain style" that could "be handed to the public in an honest; unaffected; simple garb." No amount of special pleading could change his mind this time about retirement, and Hamilton did not even try. But the announcement must in its very tone and language be discernibly republican. While the very act of stepping down voluntarily put the lie to the incessant charges that he harbored monarchical ambitions, the style itself must make the same antimonarchical point.[69]

The inclusion of Madison's draft from four years earlier was both ironic and essential: ironic because Madison had long since gone over to the other side and become Jefferson's most invaluable acolyte; and essential because Washington wanted to remind all concerned that he had attempted to retire after his first term. By including the Madison draft, he undermined the claim currently circulating in the Republican press that he was now being forced out against his will and would be defeated if he ran again. This was a ludicrous claim, since Washington would have won another election handily, though not unanimously. But he was in a vulnerable frame of mind and wanted to leave nothing to chance. It was imperative that his decision to step down be perceived as a **voluntary** act, another dramatic surrender of power in the Cincinnatus mode, his last and greatest exit.

The draft Washington sent to Hamilton contained the following passage, which never made it into the final version of the Farewell Address— Hamilton saw to that—but provides a revealing glimpse into his battered, thoroughly exhausted emotional condition at the time:

> I did not seek the office with which you have honored me . . . [and now can show] only the grey hairs of a man who has . . . either in a civil or military character, spent five and forty years—All the prime of his life—in serving his country . . . [who only wanted to] be suffered to pass quietly to the grave, and that his errors, however numerous; if they are not criminal, may be consigned to the Tomb of oblivion, as he himself will soon be to the Mansion of Retirement.

This was all wrong: plaintive, self-pitying, verging on pathetic. It conveyed the impression of an aging patriarch beyond his prime, just the kind of image Jefferson had been whispering behind the scenes for years. One of Hamilton's major responsibilities was to assure that the grand old man of the revolutionary era appear more grand than old. In this final performance on the public stage Washington did not need to be coached—he knew what he wanted to say—but Hamilton needed to ensure that the script moved forward in stately and dignified cadences.[70]

Hamilton also realized that he was being asked to write for posterity. "It has been my object to render this act importantly and lastingly useful," he confided to Washington, "and . . . to embrace such reflections and sentiments as will wear well, progress in approbation with time & redound to future reputation." (This was precocious on Hamilton's part, though not even he could have predicted the impact his words would have over the ages.) Several drafts were exchanged between the two men in late summer of 1796, with Washington deleting several passages, making marginal additions in pencil, and warning Hamilton to mark all revisions so that no last-minute changes could be smuggled in without his approval. When the final draft was ready for the printer in September, Washington sat with the text as the presses were being set and made changes in 174 out of the 1,086 lines in his own hand, a final scan, so the printer reported, "in which he was very minute." It seems fair to resolve the perennial question about authorship of the Farewell Address by concluding that it was a collaborative effort in which Hamilton was the draftsman who wrote most of the words, while Washington was the author whose ideas prevailed throughout. It should also be noticed in passing that the document is somewhat misleadingly titled, since it was never delivered as an address or speech. Better to think of it as an open letter to the American people, published in newspapers throughout the country in the fall of 1796, offering Washington's distilled wisdom on what he regarded as the true meaning of the American Revolution.[71]

Sifting through the mound of scholarship that has built up around the Farewell Address over the past two centuries is a bit like joining an archeological dig. Each generation has discovered meanings that speak to its own problems; all generations have labeled it an American classic, though for different reasons. The central interpretive strain, however, has been to read the Farewell Address as the seminal statement of American isolationism. Ironically, the phrase most associated with this interpretive tradition, "entangling alliances with none," is not present in the Farewell Address. (Double irony, it appears in Jefferson's first inaugural, of all places.) Here are the salient words, which isolationists hurled against Woodrow Wilson in 1917 and Franklin Roosevelt in 1941: "Europe has a set of primary interests, which to us have none, or a very remote relation. Hence she must be engaged in frequent controversies, the causes of which are foreign to our concerns. . . . 'Tis our true policy to steer clear of permanent Alliances, with any portion of the foreign world."[72]

In truth, Washington's isolationist prescription rests atop a deeper message about American foreign policy, which deserves more recognition than it has received as the seminal statement in the realistic tradition. Here are the key words: "There can be no greater error to expect, or calculate upon real favours from Nation to Nation. 'Tis an illusion which experience must cure, which a just pride ought to discard." Washington was saying that the relationship between nations was not like the relationship between individuals, which could periodically be conducted on the basis of mutual trust. Nations always had and always would behave solely on the basis of interest.[73]

It followed that all treaties were merely temporary arrangements destined to be discarded once those interests shifted. In the context of his own time, this was a defense of the Jay Treaty, which repudiated the Franco-American alliance and aligned America's commercial interests with British markets as well as the protection of the all-powerful British fleet. It was also a rejection of Jefferson's love affair with the French Revolution as a sentimental attachment, temporarily buoyed by popular opinion but blissfully oblivious to the long-term interests of the American public.

In the larger historical context, the isolationist message was intended to have a limited life span that would last through the gestative phase of domestic expansion in the nineteenth century. The realistic message, on the other hand, was Washington's eternal principle, intended to endure forever. Looking backward, it links Washington with the classical values advocated by Thucydides in the Melian Dialogue. Looking forward, it connects the Farewell Address with the foreign policy perspective of the likes of Hans Morgenthau, George Kennan, and Henry Kissinger. It was a vision of international relations formed from experience rather than reading, confirmed by early encounters with hardship and imminent death, rooted in a relentlessly realistic view of human nature.[74]

The foreign policy sections of the Farewell Address were only a part, in fact the lesser part, of what he intended to say. His major point is difficult for us to hear, because the vision he projects has long since arrived, making it hard to appreciate the time when the vision remained visionary. Our eyes run quickly over those paragraphs urging New Englanders and Virginians to think of themselves as Americans, to understand their regional differences as complementary strengths in a flourishing national mosaic. The one brief section that Hamilton kept deleting and Washington kept restoring called for a national university in the new capital, Washington's old request, designed to congregate the rising generation of future leaders on common ground. These national exhortations were not affirmations of what we were, but rather pleadings for what we must become. In this sense, the Farewell Address was primarily a great prophecy that the first word in the term "United States" was destined to trump the second.

As a historical argument this was a frontal assault on the Republican interpretation of all that the American Revolution meant. The following passage was designed to make Jefferson and his colleagues squirm:

> This government, the offspring of our own choice uninfluenced and unawed, adopted upon full investigation and mature deliberation, completely free in its principles, in the distribution of its owners, uniting security with energy, and containing within itself a provision for its own amendment, has first claim to your confidence and support. . . . The very idea of the power and right of the People to establish Government presupposes the duty of every Individual to obey the established government.

Here was the lesson Washington had learned commanding the Continental army: American independence, if it were to endure, required a federal government capable of coercing the states to behave responsibly. This put him squarely at odds with the Republican argument that a sovereign national government violated the "spirit of '76." In the Farewell Address, Washington reiterated his conviction that the centralizing impulses of the

411

American Revolution were not violations but ful-
fillments of its original ethos. As one who could
claim considerable credibility on the question, he
was planting his standard squarely in the national
camp and urging his fellow American citizens to
rally around him.[75]

Apart from its core message—independence
abroad and unity at home—the Farewell Address
was a personal assertion of competence. All those
rumors of creeping senility and fading mental
powers would be forced to encounter the old
commander in chief, still very much in charge. He
was going out as he came in: dignified, defiant,
and decisive; clear about what was primary, what
peripheral; confident about where history was
headed.

Two huge subjects, slavery and Indian policy,
are conspicuously missing from the Farewell
Address, primarily because Washington wanted to
sound a unifying note, and these topics had
proved resistant to compromise or even conversation. By insisting that the federal government was
the legitimate expression of America's revolutionary intentions, he implicitly recognized that both
forbidden subjects should be addressed at the federal rather than state level. This was precisely the
point the Republicans contested so fiercely, at
least in part because it threatened to place slavery
on the national agenda beyond the control of the

planter class living south of the Potomac. But Washington himself had conceded that slavery was the one issue that could not be pushed forward without placing the entire national experiment at risk. His silence on the subject in the Farewell Address accurately reflected his judgment that debate over slavery must be postponed for at least a generation.

He did not feel the same way about the Indian question. In August 1796, while making final revisions in the Farewell Address, Washington decided to publish an open letter to the Cherokee Nation. No tribe had done as much as the Cherokees to accommodate itself to white encroachments on its tribal land and to adapt its own customs and mores to permit peaceful coexistence with the advancing wave of white settlements. "I have thought much on this subject," Washington explained, "and anxiously wished that these various Indian tribes, as well as their neighbours, the White People, might enjoy in abundance all the good things which make life comfortable and happy." He saw the Cherokees as perhaps the best hope for making his vision of sovereign Indian enclaves within the United States a reality. If the Cherokees would continue to do their part, Washington promised them that the federal government would enforce the treaties honorably so as to assure Cherokee survival as a people and a nation.

Washington described his commitment as a matter of law as well as a personal promise. He meant every word, and the Cherokees responded by accepting it as the sacred vow of the retiring White Father. But despite his sincerity and personal commitment, this was one promise that even Washington could not keep.[76]

In his final address to Congress he sounded an upbeat note: British troops were evacuating their western posts; border disputes in Maine and Florida were being sensibly adjudicated; the economy was humming along nicely; a new treaty with the Creeks offered hope for an end to frontier violence in the Southwest. The only dark cloud, French raids on American shipping in the Caribbean, was regretful, but surely the French would come to their senses. The tone was patriarchal, as if a father granted custody of an infant child was reporting proudly that the child was doing well and was now safely past its infancy.

Then Washington made several specific recommendations. The nation desperately needed a small navy to police its coastline and protect American commerce from predatory Islamic pirates in the Mediterranean. It also needed a national military academy to provide a professional officer class for the army and, the old plea, a national university on the Potomac. Congress should also consider legislation to encourage the country's nascent but latent manufacturing sector. Federal subsidies to encourage improved agricultural techniques were also a shrewd investment, as were increased salaries for federal employees in order to assure recruitment of the most able citizens. All in all, it was a call for an expanded federal mandate, so robust that nothing like it would be proposed again until John Quincy Adams assumed the presidency in 1824. The Republicans had always described such federal initiatives as Hamiltonian. The outgoing president wished to leave no doubt that they had always been Washingtonian as well. Though he liked to think of himself and his presidency as above the fray, he was going out as an avowed Federalist. Indeed, he suggested that his departure from the national scene would require even greater enlargements of federal power to compensate for his absence, that his retirement necessitated the creation of centering forces institutionalized at the federal level to sustain the focusing functions he had performed personally.[77]

His correspondence during his last months in office makes no mention of the ongoing election to choose his successor. (Jefferson carried the same studied detachment to an extreme, claiming that he did not even realize that he was a candidate.) Washington was surely pleased when Adams won a narrow electoral victory, since it meant a continuation of Federalist policies, but his expression of congratulation was deliberately restrained and official. His one piece of advice to Adams was to retain John Quincy, his son, in the foreign service, despite the inevitable accusations of nepotism. Showing that his eye for young talent remained sharp, Washington described the younger Adams as a precocious lad who would "prove himself to be the ablest of all in the Diplomatic Corps." Otherwise, he busied himself in packing for the move back to Mount Vernon, drafting final commands to the commissioners at Federal City to focus all their energies on the completion of the Capitol, complaining that the French Directory was misnamed because it lacked any sense of direction, and ordering new dentures to replace the temporary set, which did not fit and caused his lips to protrude discernibly in a way he found embarrassing.[78]

The last days were spent hosting dinners and dances in his honor. The ceremonials culminated with the Adams inauguration, where, somewhat to Adams's irritation, more attention was paid to the outgoing than incoming president. Adams reported to Abigail that he thought he heard Washington murmuring under his breath at the end of the ceremony: "Ay! I am fairly out and you fairly in! See which of us will be the happiest." But the story is probably apocryphal. Washington's diary entry for the day was typically flat and unrevealing: "Much such a day as yesterday in all respects. Mercury at 41." The public man was already receding into the proverbial mists. The private man could not wait to get those new dentures and place himself beneath those vines and fig trees.[79]

CHAPTER SEVEN

Testament

THE VINE and fig tree motif suggested bucolic
splendor, afternoon naps in the shade, relaxed
routines aligned with the undulating contours of
rolling hills. Nothing could have been more alien
to Washington's temperament. "We are all on lit-
ter and dirt," he explained less than a month after
his retirement, "occasioned by Joiners, Masons &
Painters working in the house, all part of which,
as well as the out buildings, I find, upon examina-
tion, to be exceedingly out of Repair." While he
had been tending to the business of the nation, no
one had tended to the business of Mount Vernon,
at least according to his own exacting standards.
The required renovations meant hiring a small
army of carpenters and painters, then adjusting to
the chaos created by what he called "the Music of
hammers, or the odiferous smell of Paint."[1]
   A day in the life of George Washington in

retirement began at five o'clock with the rising of the sun: "If my hirelings are not in their places at that time, I send them messages of my sorrow for their indisposition." In other words, he woke them up, then provided meticulous instructions about their respective assignments for the day. At seven o'clock he ate a light breakfast, often corn cakes lathered with butter and honey, cut in thin slices in order to limit the work required of his ill-fitting dentures and swollen gums. Then he was on horseback, riding around his farms for six hours, ordering drainage ditches to be widened, inspecting the operation of a new distillery he had recently constructed on the premises, warning poachers that the deer on his property had become domesticated and must not be hunted, inquiring after a favored house slave who had recently been bitten by a mad dog.

He arrived back at the mansion at two o'clock. No one needed to take the reins of his horse. Washington simply slapped him on the backside and he trotted over to the barn on his own. (Horses, like men, seemed disposed to acknowledge his authority.) He then dressed for dinner, at three o'clock sharp, which usually featured multiple courses and multiple guests, some of whom were perfect strangers who had made the pilgrimage to Mount Vernon to witness the great man in the flesh and could not be turned away without violating the open-ended Virginia code of hospitality. As a living legend Washington recognized that he remained public property, though even he observed that it was somewhat disconcerting to realize that he and Martha had not sat down for a meal by themselves in over twenty years. Even the sheer gawkers, he acknowledged, "came out of respect to me," then added, "would not the word curiosity answer as well?"

After dinner he liked to show guests his collection of medals, the key to the Bastille sent by Lafayette, and prints done by John Trumbull depicting famous battles in the War of Independence, all this done with becoming modesty about his own contribution to the cause. He then led his guests to the piazza facing the Potomac, where he paced back and forth and liked to talk about farming (plow designs, the dreaded Hessian fly, crop rotation schemes). He often enjoyed an after-dinner glass of Madeira, which he held casually with his arm draped over a chair while listening impassively to any political talk that he preferred to avoid. Awkward silences did not disturb him, and one guest, expecting a more engaged conversationalist, expressed disappointment that "he did not, at anytime, speak with any remarkable fluency." On the other hand, several visitors reported that he went on at considerable length about the obvious advantage of placing a national university in the still-unfinished Federal City. A visiting Polish nobleman also described him delivering an impassioned soliloquy on the destructive consequences of the French Revolution and the tragic fate of his beloved Lafayette, who was still imprisoned in Austria.

It was his custom to leave his guests at about five o'clock in order to spend two hours in his study, writing letters and reading one or more of the ten newspapers to which he subscribed. At seven he reappeared for tea, bowed to the ladies, then resumed pacing and chatting with the men. He and Martha retired at nine for the night, leaving first-time visitors with the distinct impression that they had been privileged to witness the most commanding physical presence on the planet in its most natural habitat.[2]

At least on the physical side, appearances were not wholly deceptive. Throughout his final retirement Washington experienced no debilitating injury or discernible deterioration of his mental or physical powers. The long midday ride provided more exercise than he could manage during the presidency, making him more trim and fit than he had been in eight years. (In 1798 he estimated his weight at 210 pounds.) To be sure, the creases around his eyes continued to deepen; his hair, though still full, was now completely gray; and he turned down an invitation to the annual ball in

Alexandria by claiming that neither he nor Martha could move on the dance floor with their previous elegance. But he was, in fact, aging gracefully, putting the lie to all those Jeffersonian rumors of his imminent descent into decrepitude and senility. Friends who recommended special diets or health potions received a polite rebuttal that suggested a man at peace with his mortality. "Against the effect of time, and age, no remedy has yet been discovered; and like the rest of my fellow mortals, I must (if life is prolonged) submit." His stoicism on this score was real, not a brave pose. When the grim reaper eventually came to claim him, he was vulnerable only because he had insisted on making his daily rounds with utter disdain for a raging sleet storm that drove everyone else to cover.[3]

Two shadows loomed over his serenity during his final retirement. The first came from those fields and farms he inspected every day. For visitors, Mount Vernon was a mansion, a national shrine with a majestic view of the Potomac that visually embodied the majesty of their host and hero. For Washington, Mount Vernon was the land and all its occupants beyond the mansion, which posed problems that no amount of carpentry or fresh coats of paint could cure. An inventory done in April 1797 by James Anderson, the new and forever beset manager at Mount Vernon, revealed a collection of farms containing 123 horses, mules, and asses, 680 cattle and sheep, and approximately 300 slaves, of which only 100 were fully employed, the rest being too old, too young, or too sick to do a day's work. Economically, Mount Vernon had long ceased to be a plantation in the Tidewater mode with tobacco or wheat as its chief cash crop. It had become a highly diversified collection of farms dedicated to multiple crops and livestock, much of which were consumed on the premises. Two overlapping and interacting questions preoccupied Washington on his daily rides: what could be done with the land to transform the lethal chemistry of high expenses and negligible or nonexistent profits, and what should be done with those three hundred black residents of Mount Vernon, whom he could not in good conscience sell without breaking up families, could not afford to keep without enlarging his annual costs, and whose very presence constituted a massive contradiction of the principles on which his heroic reputation rested.[4]

The other shadow came from the direction of Philadelphia, where the prospects of war with France and the increasingly partisan political battles between Federalists and Republicans formed ominous clouds that soon drifted over Mount Vernon. Being an ex-president proved just as unprecedented as being president. (Kings and emperors did not have the problem, since they always died in office or exile, whereas Washington remained alive and lurking in the middle distance.) He had come out of retirement twice before: in 1787 to chair the Constitutional Convention; and in 1789 to head the national government. The pressure to extend this pattern, or else witness the dissolution of all that he had worked for as commander in chief and then president, mounted throughout 1797. His response to that pressure proved to be the poorest judgment of his political career, for he allowed himself to become a pawn in a dangerous scheme that threatened the republican experiment and eventually killed the Federalist Party.

A USEFUL AEGIS

EVEN BEFORE Washington settled into his retirement routine, Jefferson made a shrewd prediction about the post-Washington political world: "The President is fortunate to get off as the bubble is bursting, leaving others to hold the bag. Yet, as his departure will mark the moment when the difficulties begin to work, you will see that they will be ascribed to the new administration." Jefferson even claimed that he felt relieved to have lost the presidential election to Adams, who now faced the "shadow of Washington" problem, as well as the legacy of a looming war with France, all amidst an increasingly shrill press. Before the **Aurora** shifted its guns toward Adams, it fired one final salvo at Washington himself that accurately previewed the escalating character of the verbal warfare that would rage for the next four years.[5]

Tom Paine wrote an open letter to Washington in which he actually prayed for his imminent death, then wondered out loud "whether the world will be puzzled to decide whether you are an apostate or an impostor, whether you have abandoned good principles, or whether you ever had any." Other editorials described Washington as "a tyrannical monster" and his Farewell Address as "the loathings of a sick mind." Washington, for his part, pretended not to notice. Letters going out from Mount Vernon repeated the major themes of the Farewell Address—neutrality abroad and unity at home—and urged that "instead of being Frenchmen, or Englishmen in Politics" all citizens come together as Americans. He regretted the partisan bickering and personal invective, which now, he claimed, had the faint sound of cannon shots in the distance. "Having taken my seat in the shade of my Vine & Fig tree," he postured, "I shall endeavor to view things in the Calm Lights of mild Philosophy."[6]

This was not what he truly felt or thought. A visitor who accompanied him on a tour of the construction sites in Federal City reported that

Washington could joke about the unfinished buildings, suggesting the congressmen and senators might have to camp out for a few years. But when the subject of French attacks on American shipping came up, he went into a tirade about the destructive consequences of the French Revolution. "I never heard him speak with so much candor," observed the witness, "nor with such heat." A more private outburst occurred in March 1798, when James Monroe published a lengthy defense of his conduct as American minister to France. (He described his insubordination as a higher form of patriotism and Washington's decision to remove him as a treasonable act.) Washington went into his study, venting his anger in a line-by-line critique of Monroe's pamphlet that was more sarcastic and scathing than anything he had ever written. Finally, in the same month, he denounced Jefferson more directly than he had ever done before. The specific occasion was a strange incident involving Jefferson's nephew, Peter Carr, who hatched a misguided plan to write Washington under a pseudonym in the hope of eliciting a response that might generate incriminating evidence of Washington's anti-French sentiments the Republican press could then circulate. Nothing came of this, though Washington endorsed his informant's characterization of Jefferson as "one of the most artful, intriguing, industrious and double-faced politicians in America." Whether Jefferson was directly involved in this plot to stigmatize Washington is unclear, but Washington's willingness to believe so put yet another nail in the coffin of their relationship and unleashed a diatribe against Jefferson's integrity more explicit than anything he had permitted himself during his presidency.[7]

His letters began to describe "the French Party" or "the Bachites" as a well-organized conspiracy determined to destroy what he had painstakingly achieved over eight years of nation building, and to smear anyone, himself included, who stood in its way. He told Lafayette that "a party exists in the United States, formed by a combination of causes, who oppose the government in all its measures, and are determined (as all their conduct evinces) by clogging its wheels, indirectly to change the nature of it, and to subvert the Constitution." Some of the conspirators, he claimed, wanted to turn the clock back to 1787, thereby repudiating the hard-won constitutional settlement. Others hoped to return to 1776, an urge that Washington regarded as a death wish for any national union. Moreover, at least as he saw it, those orchestrating this conspiracy were devoid of honor or any principle except the acquisition of power. They had seized upon the pro-French sentiment of the American populace during the debate over the Jay Treaty, but they would have grabbed at anything, he claimed, that served "as an instrument to facilitate the destruction of their own Government." Their purported affection for France was a disingenuous ploy, "for they had no more regard for that Nation than for the Grand Turk, farther than their own views were promoted by it." And they had seen fit to release their running dogs in the **Aurora** to libel him, even though the two chief conspirators—Jefferson's and Madison's names were too painful to mention—knew that Bache and his minions were practicing character assassination against a man the Virginians purported to admire.[8]

What could Jefferson and Madison have said in response to this indictment? Surely they would have not recognized themselves as the political villains Washington described. Probably they would have explained the accusations as clinching evidence that the aging patriarch had completely lost his mind. But, in truth, Jefferson and Madison were so caught up in their conspiratorial indictment of the Federalists that they lacked any perspective on how their own conduct appeared when seen from the enemy's camp. Though there was a discernibly personal edge to Washington's charges—the political wounds inflicted on him during his second term by the Republican press still festered—Jefferson and Madison **had** in fact been orchestrating a concerted and often covert campaign against the Federalists since 1791. They **had** played politics with foreign policy during the debate over the Jay Treaty. They **had** paid scandal-mongers to libel Hamilton and Washington. And they **had** on several occasions (as in the Genet affair, endorsing Monroe's conduct in Paris) engaged in skullduggery that would have been regarded as treasonable in any modern court of law. Doubtless Jefferson would have been able to pass a lie-detector test disavowing any knowledge of behind-the-scenes mischief, and would have then mounted an eloquent defense of the elevated principles governing his conduct and the Republican agenda. But Washington's rebuttal would have enjoyed the benefit of a substantial body of historical evidence, documenting what Jefferson, in another context, had described as "a long train of abuses."

All of which helps to explain what is otherwise inexplicable, and a major deviation from Washington's usual pattern of behavior: namely, his decision to lend his name and prestige to a Federalist plot—whether it was a full-fledged conspiracy remains shrouded in mystery—designed to establish a standing army that could, among other uses, intimidate and eventually crush the Republican opposition. In the spring of 1798, President Adams released decoded dispatches revealing that the French Directory had demanded a £50,000 bribe as a precondition for negotiating with three envoys Adams had sent to Paris in order to seek a diplomatic solution to the ongoing crisis. Labeled the XYZ Affair—a reference to the initials used by the French operatives demanding the bribe—the revelations produced a dramatic reversal in public opinion toward France and a surge of hostility toward French supporters in America. Abigail Adams reported one Fourth of July toast: "John Adams. May he, like **Samson**, slay thousands of Frenchmen with the **jawbone** of Jefferson." Anti-Jefferson editorials described him as the covert leader of "the frenchified faction in this country" and the secret head of "the American Directory." War hysteria mounted as newspapers reported the existence of a 50,000-man French army, purportedly poised to cross the Atlantic and invade the United States.[9]

Washington's initial response to the hysteria was characteristically measured. He thought the prospects of a French invasion were remote in the extreme, concurring with Adams's more colorful assessment that seeing a French army in America was like imagining a snowball in Philadelphia at the height of summer. He did take some delight at the plight of Bache and his fellow scandalmongers at the **Aurora,** who were surrounded by a hostile mob after suggesting that the United States pay the bribe demanded by the French in order to avert war. And, more tellingly, he tacitly endorsed four pieces of legislation rushed through Congress by Federalist extremists and known collectively as the Alien and Sedition Acts, which were designed to deport foreign-born residents suspected of French sympathies and shut down newspapers publishing "any false, scandalous, and malicious writing or writings against the Government of the United States."

Adams subsequently, if grudgingly, acknowledged that signing the Alien and Sedition Acts was the biggest blunder of his presidency. And historians have almost unanimously concluded that these statutes deserve to live in infamy as blatant examples of flagrant government repression. But they did not appear flagrant to Washington at the time, convinced as he was—and not without reason—that the Republicans had been waging a subversive campaign for many years against the very legitimacy of the elected government. In retrospect, the Federalists were exploiting the anti-French hysteria in the same partisan fashion that the Republicans had exploited the pro-French hysteria during the debate over the Jay Treaty. But the Federalists were also crossing a line they had never crossed as long as they enjoyed Washington's leadership; namely, they were aiming to silence their political opponents. It is intriguing, though in the end futile, to speculate whether they would have overreached so fatally if Washington had remained in office, or if Washington himself would have thought differently if located in Philadelphia at the center of the deliberations. What can be said with certainty is that Washington cheered the ill-starred Federalist campaign from the sidelines.[10]

The plot had already begun to thicken even before passage of the Alien and Sedition Acts. In May 1798, Congress had approved the creation of ten new regiments, more than ten thousand men, for what was described as the Provisional army. The name conveyed the conditional character of the military commitment, which was contingent upon the threat of a French invasion. Additional legislation permitted the recruitment of an additional twenty regiments if and when a French fleet actually materialized off the American coast. Soon thereafter, Washington received a letter from Hamilton, warning him that duty was about to call him out of retirement again: "You ought to be aware, my Dear Sir, that in the event of an open rupture with France, the public voice will again call you to command the armies of your Country." Washington's initial response was dismissive. The prospect of a French army crossing the Atlantic still struck him as highly unlikely, especially since the French were fully engaged with the

British in Europe. And even if war should occur, the American commander should be someone younger, "a man more in his prime." Indeed, Washington concluded, he would regard another call to service "much as I would go to the tombs of my Ancestors." But he left the door slightly ajar.[11]

Throughout the summer of 1798, Washington came under increasing pressure from Hamilton and two members of Adams's cabinet, Secretary of State Timothy Pickering and Secretary of War James McHenry, to take the French threat seriously. They urged him to make two commitments: first, to agree to serve, if only provisionally, as commander of the Provisional army, meaning he would not need to take the field unless and until hostilities commenced; second, to appoint Hamilton as his next in command and, as Pickering put it, "the **Chief in your absence.**" Washington should have sensed that something was awry at this moment, since the urgency of the political pressure he was receiving was at odds with the urgency of the strategic threat it was designed to meet. But he did not.[12]

On July 11, McHenry appeared at Mount Vernon to make a personal appeal, which produced reluctant consent from Washington, again on the condition that he need not budge from Mount Vernon "until the Army is in a Situation to require my presence, or it becomes indispensable by the urgency of circumstances." As for Hamilton's rank, Washington thought it made eminent sense, but he needed to apprise Henry Knox of the decision, since Knox had outranked Hamilton in the previous war and might be offended at serving under him in any subsequent conflict. Knox responded immediately, deeply wounded at the suggestion of deferring to what he caustically described as "the transcendent military talents of Colonel Hamilton." Then Knox expressed bewilderment at this rush to judgment, both to create an army and to elevate Hamilton to its head, and confided that he smelled something foul lurking in the background, speculating that "there has been a species of management in this affair of which you are not apprised." Washington wrote back plaintively to Knox, disappointed that he had taken the rank matter so personally, and assuring him that "if there was any management in this business, it has been concealed from me."[13]

There was, and it had. In collusion with disaffected and disloyal members of Adams's cabinet, Hamilton had hatched a scheme to transform the Provisional army into a permanent military establishment and an instrument for his expanded power within the Federalist Party. To be fair, Hamilton had convinced himself that Napoleon's imperial ambitions **did** include North America, not an implausible conviction, and that he alone possessed the vision and energy not only to thwart such threats, but also to out-Napoleon Napoleon himself. In typical Hamiltonian fashion, his plans were quite grandiose; if his letters to fellow Federalists are to be believed, he envisioned marching his army through Virginia, thereby intimidating the Republican leadership in its major sanctuary, then launching a preemptive invasion of Florida and the Louisiana Territory, where French and Spanish residents would be offered citizenship in a vastly expanded American empire, then marching his force southward through Mexico and Central America. Washington was unwittingly providing the imprimatur of his name to this wild scheme. And by insisting on Hamilton's appointment as his second in command, then refusing to take the field while the army was being raised, Washington was inadvertently playing directly into Hamilton's hands. Two years later, after Washington's death, Hamilton made the remarkable comment: "He was a useful **Aegis** to me." This was perhaps the moment he had in mind. At any rate, the moment exposed the dangerous tendencies of Hamilton's genius once released from Washington's control.[14]

There is little question that Washington would have condemned the more bizarre features of Hamilton's plan if he had known what was afoot. True enough, he believed in the creation of national institutions that would focus the energies of a far-flung population: a capital city, a national university, the National Bank, a conspicuous chief executive. He also favored a modest expansion of the regular army, along with a military academy to educate a new corps of professional officers. But a permanent standing army marching across the countryside conjured up the kind of menacing and thoroughly coercive embodiment of government power that epitomized the dreaded "consolidation" the Republicans had always been warning against. Washington's entire presidency had been spent assuring the citizenry that such fears were unfounded, hyperbolic, and politically motivated. Now, with one bold stroke, Hamilton was inadvertently undoing all of Washington's painstaking work. Almost as bad, Washington's complicity in the plot lent credibility to the Republican claim that the old patriarch was a rather dazed front man for the conspiratorial manipulations of an evil genius behind the curtain.

Hamilton's scheme hit a snag in the fall of 1798, when Adams insisted on ranking Knox as second in command. Pickering explained to Washington that "the President has an extreme aversion to Colo. Hamilton—a personal resentment—and if allowed his own wishes and feelings alone, would scarcely have given him the rank of brigadier." Again, Washington was called to the rescue; again, he played his appointed role; and again, he should have known better. Pickering and McHenry explained that Adams would be forced to reverse his decision once Washington made it abundantly clear that Hamilton was his own unequivocal choice. Washington complied, providing Adams with a description of Hamilton that probably prompted one of Adams's Vesuvial eruptions. It was also a characterization that an elder statesman might have made of a younger Washington: "By some he is considered as an ambitious man, and therefore a dangerous one. That he is ambitious I shall readily grant, but it is of that laudable kind which prompts a man to excel in whatever he takes in hand. He is enterprising, quick in his perceptions, and his judgment intuitively great; qualities essential in a great military character, and therefore I repeat, that his loss will be irreparable."[15]

Adams was just beginning to suspect that members of his own cabinet were engaged in behind-the-scenes plotting with Hamilton, but he could not afford to alienate America's preeminent hero. By forcing Hamilton on him, Washington violated the cardinal rule for all ex-presidents: Never interfere with the decisions of your successor. (And Adams, who believed that holding grudges was a measure of personal integrity, never forgave him for this.) It finally began to dawn on Washington that he was engaged in clandestine conversations with a hostile faction of Adams's cabinet. "You will readily perceive," he wrote McHenry, "that even the rumor of a misunderstanding between the President & me . . . would be attended with unpleasant consequences." He asked McHenry to destroy all copies of their recent correspondence that mentioned Adams, warning that their publication "may induce him to believe in good earnest, that intrigues are carrying on, in which I am an Actor—than which, nothing is more foreign from my heart." However sincere, this was a naive sentiment, which we know about only because McHenry ignored the request and saved all the letters.[16]

Knowing as we do that the French invasion was a mirage, and that Hamilton was fully prepared to exploit it for personal and political purposes, Washington's blinkered response to the ongoing intrigue becomes difficult to explain, except perhaps as a serious lapse in judgment occasioned by his dwindling powers of concentration, his distance from political headquarters in Philadelphia, and his excessive trust in Hamilton's motives. Such an explanation, in fact, captures a lion's share of the truth, and therefore must serve as a somewhat sad, near-the-end exception to an impressive list of extraordinarily prescient judgments made when a misstep of equivalent magnitude would have possibly put the survival of the republic at risk.

What the explanation misses—and the irony

here runs deep—is how Washington's previous experience helped lead him astray in this instance. Both sides, Federalists and Republicans, believed that the fate of the republic was very much at risk in 1798. Both sides viewed the crisis through the prism of the American Revolution. The Republicans saw the Provisional army, now being referred to as the New army—an ominous acknowledgment that it was intended to remain intact forevermore—as a domestic version of the standing army the British had imposed on the colonies in the 1770s. The Federalists saw it as the second coming of the Continental army, which had not only won an improbable victory over Great Britain, but also had provided the only reliable source of national unity when all else was collapsing in huge heaps of political and economic chaos. Washington was uniquely vulnerable to the Federalist interpretation, since it touched all the patriotic chords that reverberated in his memory and aligned itself with the story line that had defined the shaping experience of his public life. The fact that it recast the elder statesman in his more youthful role as savior of the embattled republic only added to its psychological appeal. Part of its appeal to Hamilton was that it allowed the surrogate son to assume the patriarchal role as commander in chief.

The potency of the old revolutionary memories was put on graphic display in November 1798, when Washington traveled to Philadelphia, the only time he ranged very far from Mount Vernon during his retirement. He had agreed to confer with Hamilton and Charles Cotesworth Pinckney, South Carolina's contribution to the triumvirate of the New army, all Revolutionary War veterans who spent ten hours a day for six weeks huddled over lists of candidates for the new officers' corps. It quickly became clear that the Continental army would be the model for the New army and that previous service in the old army would be the chief criterion for inclusion in the new one. Although several battle-scarred veterans were judged to be over the hill, younger men who lacked the revolutionary credentials were deemed untrustworthy. Washington's memory of old comrades-in-arms was prodigious, reflected in the detailed notes he made on more than sixty candidates based on their conduct under his eye during the War of Independence: "unquestioned bravery & great popularity," read one entry, "but a great Gambler & weighs 4 or 500 lbs. Good for nothing."[17]

Washington also placed an order with a Philadelphia tailor for an exact replica of his old "buff and blue" uniform, complete with precise specifications about the cuffs, buttons, sashes, and embroidery to assure an authentic match. The tailor was able to come up with all the items, except the gold thread for the embroidery. Then, when a special shipment of the proper thread arrived from New York, the tailor was forced to tell Washington that he could not find an embroiderer capable of duplicating the design perfectly, so the uniform was never completed. This little episode served as a nice metaphor for the larger project of re-creating the Continental army. Memories of the old "band of brothers" were palpable for Washington, but the world had moved on, and the ghosts from a glorious past could never return except in memory. The New army, in fact, was destined to remain just as incomplete and fanciful as Washington's new uniform.[18]

Adams was determined to see to that. He never believed the French intended to invade America; and if they ever did he preferred a naval buildup, what he called "wooden walls," to an enlarged army, which he associated with the much-feared standing armies of English and European history. Though he was slow to realize the full extent of the plotting between Hamilton and members of his cabinet, his antennae perked up as the enormous scale of planning for the New army took shape. Moreover, his personal loathing for Hamilton made him suspicious in all the ways that Washington was gullible. In February 1799, he stunned Federalists and Republicans alike by announcing his decision to send another peace commission to France. With this simple stroke Adams eliminated the prospect of war and thereby destroyed the rationale for the New army. Though it would take several months before the peace commission was dispatched to Paris, all of Hamilton's hopes for military glory died with Adams's decision. (So, for that matter, did Adams's hopes for reelection, since he immediately became a pariah within the Federalist Party. But Adams never regretted the decision, indeed always described it as the crowning moment of his presidency.) For over a year Hamilton continued to work feverishly on the logistical and organizational details for a phantom army that chiefly existed only in his own imagination.[19]

Washington, for his part, began to back away from the floundering project. He questioned the impulsiveness of the Adams decision, never fully understanding how Adams had in fact rescued him from an embarrassing blunder and the nation itself from a dangerous brush with martial law. He remained oblivious to the political machinations that had gone on behind the scenes to manipulate his cooperation until McHenry inadvertently provided him with a candid account of the rampant subversion within the Adams cabinet. "I have been stricken dumb," he confessed upon receiving the news, "and I believe it better that I should remain mute than to express any sentiment on the important matters which are related therein." He vowed never again to allow himself to be drawn into any decisions facing the executive branch: "I shall trust to the Mariners whose duty is to Watch—to steer it into a safe Port." His remaining energies, he also realized, had plenty of problems to focus on within the expansive confines of Mount Vernon.[20]

ENTANGLING ALLIANCES

THE PROBLEMS came at him from multiple angles and in various sizes and shapes: the steady procession of houseguests that made Mount Vernon a hotel and Washington himself a perpetual host; the endless negotiations about building lots and construction schedules at Federal City; the ominously familiar conduct of George Washington Parke Custis, his step-grandson (son of Jackie), who dropped out of the College of New Jersey (Princeton), then idled away his days in a sullen stupor, all despite Washington's best efforts at mentoring, and who seemed committed to the same downward trajectory as his father; the routine requests for financial assistance from indigent relatives and utter strangers pleading their plight. Washington's correspondence during his final retirement conjures up the picture of a beleaguered patriarch, juggling his duties with due diligence, parceling out the pieces of his time and energy like an overscheduled chief executive no longer protected by a small army of secretaries, the ultimate embodiment of self-control who now found himself, near the end, completely controlled by the agenda of others.[21]

But appearances, in this instance, are somewhat misleading, because the demand-driven character of Washington's correspondence is not a reliable guide to what was on his mind; nor, for that matter, is it an accurate measure of his silent determination to exercise control over the one problem he cared about most. That problem could be summed up in one word, and Washington's preference for a euphemism—"that species of property"—only confirms, albeit in a backhanded way, how much the unmentionable subject haunted him in those last years. "I shall frankly declare," he confessed to one friend, "that I do not like to think, much less talk about it." But it was an inescapable presence that enveloped his day-by-day experience from the moment he walked out the front door of his mansion until he returned from his midday ride around his farms.[22]

The last time Washington had given slavery his full attention was during his first retirement in the 1780s. Three salient points are worth noticing about his thinking at this earlier stage: first, it represented a dramatic advance over his previous moral numbness on the issue, an advance that had been fostered by his experience commanding black troops during the war and his exposure to antislavery opinions never before encountered in pre-revolutionary Virginia; second, he was interested in liberating himself from slavery, in "getting quit of negroes," but not in liberating his slaves, whom he still regarded as his property and therefore as valuable parts of his personal estate not to be surrendered without compensation; third, he had found his efforts to sell his slaves blocked, rather ironically, by a moral consideration—his refusal to break up families, which were intermarried with the dower slaves owned by Martha. Hovering over this complex tangle of moral and economic considerations was a personal calculus about his legacy. He knew that his place in posterity's judgment depended on getting this right as much as any decision he had made as commander in chief.

The first indication of a significant shift in his thinking occurred in May 1794, three years before his retirement. He was already beginning to plan for his return to private life and described to Tobias Lear the first glimmerings of a scheme to sell off all or most of his western land so that he and Martha could live comfortably in retirement on the interest from those sales. Then he added: "I have another motive which makes me earnestly wish for an accomplishment of these things, it is indeed more powerful than all the rest, namely to liberate a certain species of property which I possess, very repugnantly to my own feelings." Here is the first clear statement of his intention to free, not sell, his slaves; in effect, to liberate his bondsmen as well as his own conscience.[23]

The full outline of his plan materialized two years later, when he took out advertisements for the sale of his huge tracts on the Ohio and Great Kanawha alongside his offer to lease all the farms at Mount Vernon save for Mansion Farm, on which he and Martha would reside. He confided to David Stuart, who was married to Jackie's widow, "that I am making an essay to accomplish what I communicated to you in confidence when last in Virginia." The public part of the plan was a consolidation of his landed assets into cash in order to permit what he described as "tranquillity with a **certain** income." The private, indeed secret, part of the plan was the emancipation of all his slaves once his new source of revenue made it possible. He asked Stuart to keep the secret part of the plan to himself, since it might take several years for full implementation and, once implemented, would generate considerable anguish within the slave quarters because of "how much the Dower Negros and my own are intermarried, and the former with the neighbouring Negros."[24]

The trouble with Washington's plan was that its ultimate goal, the emancipation of his slaves, was the final step in a lengthy series of economic transactions, which effectively meant that the moral principle was held hostage to the caprice of the marketplace. The key variable was the sale of his western land. He did sell a few small parcels. And he received several tentative offers for his larger tracts, including one for his land on the Great Kanawha that would have yielded the handsome sum of $200,000. But all the major deals fell through, as did the multiple efforts to lease all the outlying farms at Mount Vernon. As a result, two years into his retirement he found himself in much the same predicament he faced at the start: an expanding slave population—he counted 216 in 1786 and 317 in 1799—only a minority of whom could be gainfully employed; ownership of tracts in the west that he valued at over $500,000, but that no one wished to purchase at a price he deemed fair; annual costs at Mount Vernon that were regularly outrunning his income; and the moral shadow of slavery still hanging over his head and his legacy. Economic rather than moral considerations seemed to weigh more heavily on his mind. In fact, his major moral concern—breaking up families— was in fact a deterrent to action: "It is demonstrably clear," he lamented, "that on this Estate (Mount Vernon) I have more working Negros by a full moiety, than can be employed to any advantage in the farming system; and I shall never turn to Planter thereon. . . . To sell the surplus I cannot, because I am principled against this kind of traffic in the human species. . . . What then is to be done? Something must, or I shall be ruined, for all the money . . . that have been received for Lands, sold within the last four years, to the amount of Fifty thousand dollars, has scarce been able to keep me afloat."[25]

Looking back from the present, the moral issue at stake seems all important. And Washington himself claimed on at least one occasion that it was his highest priority. Why, then, delay the big decision? Why make emancipation of his slaves contingent upon an overly elaborate financial scheme, which resembled one of his excessively intricate battle plans during the war that prevented his troops from reaching the objective in a timely fashion? Why, given his own diagnosis of the costs created by the oversupply of slaves, did he not free some of them, a moral statement that would also cut his losses?

First of all, we need to recognize that Washington did not think about slavery in exclusively moral terms. Just as his own slaves and the dower slaves were entangled on his farms, his conscience and more self-interested calculations were entangled in his own mind. Granted, there was a clear long-term evolution in his thinking toward the recognition that human bondage was a moral travesty. But when Quaker critics pleaded with him to act on this principle, he never took their advice. Quakers, of course, had been pacifists during the war, and if he had allowed himself to be guided by their uncorrupted idealism on that occasion, he and they would still be subjects of the British Empire.

The second long-term pattern in his thinking about slavery was a relentlessly realistic insistence that ideals per se must never define his agenda; indeed, he associated an idealistic agenda with sentimental illusions, like the belief that American virtue was sufficient to defeat Great Britain in the war, or that the French Revolution would succeed because it was a noble cause. His earliest apprehensions about slavery, after all, were more economic than moral; namely, that it was an inefficient labor system ill-suited for the kind of diversified farming he had begun to practice at Mount Vernon in the 1760s. During the war he had entertained suggestions of arming slaves and promising them freedom in return for service for the duration, but moral considerations took a back seat to a higher priority, the manpower needs of the Continental army. Similarly, during his presidency he had opposed federal action on a gradual emancipation scheme, despite a personal acknowledgment of its moral rightness, because the issue threatened to split the nation at the moment of its birth. Ideals were not irrelevant to Washington, but he was deeply suspicious of any idealistic agenda that floated above the realities of power on the ground. And much as we might regret his moral reticence on this occasion, it was an integral part of the same rock-ribbed realism that had proved invaluable, indeed his trademark quality, as commander in chief and president.

Two other factors cut against the kind of clear moral statement about slavery that we might wish. The first was Washington's obsession with control, which in this case meant deferring emancipation until he was assured that his own financial independence was secure. He had spent a lifetime acquiring an impressive estate, and he was extremely reluctant to give it up except on his terms. The sale of his western land, for example, must meet **his** expectations of a fair price. The decision to emancipate his slaves must be **his** decision, made when **he** ordered it done. It was not easy for him to surrender what he had spent a lifetime accumulating, for it meant shedding assumptions that had served him well in his remarkable ascent to the pinnacle of power in Virginia and the nation at large.

He spared no expense, for example, in seeking to recover two of his most valued slaves: the cook, Hercules; and Martha's body servant, Ona Judge, both of whom escaped just before his retirement. He told the slave hunter he sent after Hercules to be stealthful, "for if Hercules was to get the least hint of the design he would elude all your vigilance," a warning that proved prescient, since Hercules escaped detection and remained a free man, probably in Philadelphia. Washington also spent three years trying to repossess Ona Judge, who had fled to New Hampshire. Once he located her there, he tried to persuade Judge to return voluntarily, but she insisted she would do so only on the condition that Washington promise to free her upon his death. Washington refused: "To enter into such a compromise with her . . . is totally inadmissible," he protested, "for reasons that must strike at first view. For however well disposed I might be to a gradual emancipation, or even to an entire emancipation of that description of People (if the latter was in itself practicable at this moment) it would neither be politic or just to reward unfaithfulness with a premature preference." Ona Judge eluded capture and remained free in New Hampshire.[26]

Another mitigating factor, admittedly more speculative, was Martha. There is no direct evidence—and if there ever was, it disappeared with the letters she burned after Washington's death—but there is reason to believe that Martha did not share her husband's principled aversion to slavery or agree with his emancipation plan. As noted earlier, that scheme created problems for her dower slaves, which she fully intended to pass on to her surviving heirs in the Custis and Dandridge lines as part of her estate. (Indeed, in a strictly legal sense Martha did not own the dower slaves. They were part of the Custis estate which **had to be** passed on to her descendants.) One of the possible reasons why Washington did not like to talk more openly about his decision to free his slaves is that it was a sore subject within the household, for it raised doubts about Martha's status after her husband was gone and about her own control over her financial legacy.

THE WILL AND THE DREAM

THERE IS a seductive story about Washington's decision to write his will that has become a mainstay of the lore about his latter days. According to the story, which is based on a letter from Martha to an anonymous recipient, Washington woke her up in the middle of the night in September 1799 to describe a disturbing dream. In it he foresaw Martha's death, which he interpreted as a premonition of his own imminent departure, and therefore as an auspicious sign that he needed to put his affairs in order. Since Washington's will is one of the most historically significant and personally revealing documents he ever wrote—a more intimate version, if you will, of his Farewell Address—the notion that it was prompted by a dream has always had an irresistibly dramatic appeal. The more prosaic fact is that the letter on which the story is based is almost certainly a forgery. Even if authentic—and Martha **was** quite ill in the fall of 1799—it cannot explain Washington's decision to draft a will, for the simple reason that he had already done so earlier that summer.[27]

This time there was no Hamilton or Lear to serve as draftsman. Washington secluded himself in his study in June and July and wrote every word with his own hand, taking care to sign each of the twenty-three pages of the document—he did miss one page by mistake—in order to preclude subsequent doubts about its accuracy as a statement of his intentions. Though he knew his days were numbered, he was not ailing at the time, so there is no plausible reason to explain his motivation in terms of some grim glimpse of the final curtain, dream-driven or not. Given the contents of the will, it makes more sense to understand his decision in terms of the estate planning he had been doing for the past five years. It was becoming obvious to Washington that his complex scheme for property consolidation to be followed by human emancipation was not progressing according to schedule. The drafting of his will was his way of assuring that, if he was not able to implement the plan while alive, he could do so from beyond the grave.

In preparation, Washington compiled a comprehensive assessment of all his property. It revealed a personal empire that included acreage in Kentucky, Maryland, New York, and Pennsylvania, housing lots in Alexandria and Federal City— which he identified for the first time as "City of Washington"—and multiple plots in Virginia beyond the borders of Mount Vernon. The mother lode, however, were his tracts on the Ohio and Great Kanawha, which accounted for more than half his landed wealth. In total, he estimated his net worth at $530,000, which did not include the land and slaves at Mount Vernon.[28]

Two facts leap out from these numbers. First, Washington was hardly the impoverished farmer he often claimed to be, especially when friends or family asked him for financial assistance. He did have what we might call a cash flow problem, meaning that his assets were tied up in land rather than more liquid forms of wealth, so he could honestly refuse a request for money on the grounds that he did not have any to spare. But the belief that Washington was living out his retirement on the edge of bankruptcy, a view that has seeped into some of the history books, is dead wrong. In fact, Washington was one of the richest men in America.

Second, the core of his wealth had been acquired early in his life as a result of his prominent role in the French and Indian War. To be sure, he had assiduously protected and amplified his holdings throughout his later years. And one could interpret his victory in the War of Independence, at least at the personal level, as a successful effort to secure his control over holdings in the Ohio Valley that would otherwise have been lost if the American Revolution had failed. But nothing that he did as America's preeminent soldier and statesman paid the same economic dividends as his youthful service on behalf of the British crown. Ironically, his lasting fame depended upon defeating an enemy that had, in the person of Virginia's royal governor, given him his lasting fortune. The old man was rich primarily because of what the young man had done.

What Washington called his "Schedule of Property" included a farm-by-farm, name-by-name listing of slaves. It showed that there were 317 at Mount Vernon, of which Washington owned 124 outright, plus another 40 he had leased from a neighbor. This meant that, although he had been managing all the Mount Vernon slaves for forty years, Washington had legal control over less than half those on the premises. They were the focal point of the most dramatic words in Washington's will, which deserve to be quoted in full:

Upon the decease of my wife, it is my Will & desire that all the slaves which I hold in my **own** right, shall receive their freedom. . . . I do hereby expressly forbid the Sale, or transportation out of the said Commonwealth of any slave I may die possessed of, under any pretence whatsoever. And I do most pointedly and solemnly enjoin it upon my Executors hereafter named . . . to see that this clause respecting Slaves, and every part thereof be religiously fulfilled at the Epoch at which it is directed to take place without evasion, neglect or delay.[29]

He also stipulated that, once freed, his slaves must not be simply abandoned to their fate. All the old and infirm slaves "shall be comfortably cloathed and fed by my heirs while they live." The very young slaves should be supported until they reached adulthood, which he defined as twenty-five years, and taught to read and as well as "brought up to some useful occupation." His final instruction concerned Billy Lee, who had been hobbling around Mount Vernon for over a decade on two badly damaged knees. He should be freed outright upon Washington's death and provided with a small annuity along with room and board, "as a testimony to my sense of his attachment to me, and for his faithful services during the Revolutionary War."[30]

456

There it was, a clear statement of his personal rejection of slavery. As we have seen, he had been groping toward this position for many reasons and for more than thirty years, more gradually than we might prefer, more steadily than most of his fellow slave owners in Virginia. He was, in fact, the only politically prominent member of the Virginia dynasty to act on Jefferson's famous words in the Declaration of Independence by freeing his slaves. He had been brooding about how to do it for over five years, procrastinating within a tangle of financial factors, and the drafting of his will represented his ultimate recognition that the only way to do it was, well, to do it. Though conscience, his deep moral revulsion at the blatant wrongness of human bondage, surely played an important role in his decision, his motives were not purely or merely moral, as they seldom were. For he knew that posterity was watching, and that his statement on this score would help to clear his legacy of the major impediment to his secular immortality. Sifting through the different layers of Washington's thinking on this tortured topic is an inherently tricky business, but doing the right thing for his slaves became imperative because it also meant doing the right thing for his historic reputation. Finally, the quite imperious language he used in ordering his executors to carry out his commands suggests that he anticipated resistance from Martha's side of the family, perhaps an attempt to defy his will by selling off his slaves after he died, but while Martha was still alive and legally controlled them. He wanted to make sure he closed that loophole.

The remainder of Washington's will dealt with the apportionment of his other property. His papers, for example, went to Bushrod Washington, a nephew recently appointed to the Supreme Court; the crabtree walking stick bequeathed to him by Franklin went to his sole surviving brother, Charles, who unfortunately did not live long enough to inherit it; his stock in the Potomac Company went toward that long-standing hope of his heart, a national university in the capital. Apart from the specific provisions, however, the principle he chose to apply in distributing the fortune he had accumulated represented a personal statement almost as dramatic as his decision to free his slaves: there would be an equal division among twenty-three heirs.[31]

The customary practice within wealthy families was an unequal distribution, which preserved the core of the estate intact in order to sustain family wealth and status over several generations. Washington's decision to give equal shares to his many descendants effectively precluded the possibility of a dynasty that would live on under the patriarch's name well into the future. His decision to divide Mount Vernon into five separate plots with different heirs embodied the same distributive principle, though Bushrod received the largest plot. Washington clearly wanted to live on in the memory of succeeding generations as the founding father of an emerging American empire, but the terms of his will assured that he would not live on as the founding father of a prominent American family. As a remembered national hero, he wished to live forever. As an ancestral presence, he wished to disappear. Moreover, the equal distribution meant that none of his heirs received more than a modest nest egg; none would be guaranteed a head start in life; or, to put it differently, none would be burdened by unearned wealth as Jackie and Jackie's son had been. All would have to fend for themselves, just as he had done. If the provisions in the will concerning slavery constituted a statement about freedom, those allocating his assets constituted a statement about equality of opportunity. While it was Jefferson who wrote lyrical tributes to the idea that "the earth belongs to the living," it was Washington who put the principle into practice.[32]

All in all, then, when Washington signed his will on July 9, 1799, he was doing more than putting his financial affairs in order. The will was also intended as a final testament to the human values he cherished most. He had time and again shown himself to be an aficionado of exits, whether it was the theatrical performance before the officers of the Continental army at Newburgh, surrendering his sword at Annapolis, or the stately cadences of the Farewell Address. These earlier exits, of course, had been orchestrated affairs, dramatic departures from the public stage designed as conspicuous demonstrations of self-mastery, the triumph of virtue over power. His will was his ultimate exit statement, a wholly personal expression of his willingness to surrender power in a truly final fashion as he prepared to depart the stage of life itself.

LAST THINGS

AT THE START of his retirement he had joked with Elizabeth Powel that reading the libelous essays by Bache in the **Aurora** provided him with a preview of what would be said about him after he was gone. He promised Powel that he fully intended to outlast Bache and make it into the next century, a vow he would violate only under "dire necessity." Bache obliged him by dying in the yellow fever epidemic of 1798. And as the end of the century approached in the fall of 1799, Washington's excellent health continued to hold. Martha came down with a life-threatening fever in September, at the same time that Washington's younger brother, Charles, passed away, events that prompted premonitions of his own mortality: "I was the first, and am now the last of my father's children by the second marriage who remain. When I shall be called upon to follow them, is known only to the giver of life. When the summons comes I shall endeavor to obey it with good grace." But he had been making fatalistic statements of this sort ever since he had cracked the half-century mark. There seemed no reason to doubt that his promise to Powel was a safe bet.[33]

There is some evidence that he was going back in his memory to the formative years of his life. He made another scan of his papers from the French and Indian War, once again noting that providence had seemed to preserve him for subsequent service, that by all rights he should have gone down with Braddock at the Monongahela. In November he broke out his old surveying instruments to locate the boundaries of a small parcel of land once belonging to the Fairfax estate at Belvoir, which he had decided to purchase, probably for sentimental reasons. Over a year earlier he had written to Sally Fairfax, the forbidden love of his youth, who was now an aging widow living out her time in England. A letter from Martha was included with his, a clear sign that Washington's words of affection were not intended as an expression of regret about the romantic choices he had made. The letter to Sally ended with a description of the physical changes in the local landscape since she had last seen it, most dramatically the new city going up on the Potomac: "A Century hence," he predicted, "if this Country keeps united (and it is surely its policy and interest to do so) will produce a City—though not as large as London—yet of a magnitude inferior to few others in Europe, on the Banks of the Potomac." He did not mention that it was sure to be named after him.[34]

Meanwhile the old routines buoyed his days. The guests kept coming in small waves, most of them referring to their host as "The General" rather than "The President," a few harking back to the old honorific "His Excellency." Hamilton kept writing to ask for advice about the proper deployment of the never-to-be New army, letters which Washington answered in his old commander-in-chief mode, warning that deployments on the western frontier risked war with Spain, which was probably just what Hamilton wanted to provoke. A few Federalists, noting recent Republican gains in state elections, urged him to remain open to a draft if it seemed likely that Jefferson would oust Adams in the next election. He dismissed these urgings with a backhanded slap at the partisan atmosphere, then unburdened himself one final time on the dishonorable tactics of Jefferson's supporters, who would surely, and now with greater plausibility, accuse him of being senile: "Let That party set up a broomstick," he shouted, "and call it a true son of liberty, a Democrat, or give it any other epithet that will suit their purpose, and it will command their votes in toto!" At some level he recognized that political parties were transforming the shape of national politics, making character as he understood it irrelevant, even a liability. The new ground rules, soon to triumph in the new century, struck him as both alien and awful, a world in which he had no place.[35]

He made one intriguing gesture on the political front, a letter requesting Patrick Henry to reenter the political arena in Virginia in order to stem the Republican tide that was swelling around Jefferson's prospective presidency. It was an odd request, since Henry shared Jefferson's political principles, most especially his hatred of a fully empowered federal government that threatened Virginia's domestic agenda. But Washington had fond memories of Henry's political support during the darkest days of the war. He believed that Henry, unlike Jefferson, was a man of character who would not allow his Republican convictions to take precedence over the national interest. (He probably also knew that Henry and Jefferson utterly detested one another.) But it all came to nothing when Henry's chronic illness proved fatal.[36]

Mount Vernon remained the bittersweet object

of his affections and frustrations. He continued to search out ways to consolidate his holdings by leasing outlying farms. His updated plan, another meticulously crafted blueprint more detailed than any of his military campaigns during the war, called for reducing the size of his operation, releasing James Anderson, his dutiful but overmatched manager, then taking personal control over the surviving remnant of land and laborers. If he could not lease them locally, he was apparently considering moving his surplus slaves to his western lands in order to make more productive use of their labor on virgin soil. Though his will made a clear moral statement about slavery after he was gone, he continued to juggle moral and economic priorities with mutual regard for both considerations. Morality, in Washington's mind, needed constantly to negotiate its way against the harsh realities of the world as it is, rather than as it ought to be.[37]

These same harsh realities came to claim him on December 12, 1799. Despite a storm that deposited a blanket of snow, sleet, and hail on the region, Washington maintained his regular routine, riding his rounds for five hours in the storm, then choosing not to change his wet clothes, because dinner was ready upon his return and he did not wish to inconvenience his guests with a delay. The following day he was hoarse, but insisted on going out in the still inclement weather to mark some trees for cutting. He presumed he had caught a cold, and felt the best treatment was to ignore it: "Let it go as it came," as he explained. During the night, however, he awakened Martha to report severe shortness of breath and pain in his throat. Word went out at dawn to fetch Lear and Dr. James Craik, Washington's personal physician and friend for over forty years. Craik immediately diagnosed Washington's condition as serious, possibly terminal, and he dispatched riders to bring two local physicians to Mount Vernon to assist him in prescribing treatment.[38]

Washington enjoyed the best care that medical science of that time could provide. Unfortunately, everything the doctors did made matters worse. They bled him four times, extracting more than five pints of his blood. They blistered him around the neck. They administered several strong laxatives— all misguided attempts to purge his body of infection. If antibiotics had been available then, Washington would almost surely have survived to keep his promise to Mrs. Powel. As it was, the infection that had invaded his throat was untreatable and fatal.

Subsequent studies by modern medical experts have concluded that Washington most probably suffered from a virulent bacterial infection of the epiglottis, a plum-sized flexible cartilage at the entry of the larynx. Epiglottitis is an extremely painful and horrific way to die, especially for a man as compulsively committed to self-control as Washington. As it swells, the epiglottis closes off the windpipe, making breathing and swallowing extremely difficult, eventually impossible. The fully conscious patient has the sensation of being slowly strangled to death by involuntary muscles inside his own body. In Washington's case the last hours must have been even more excruciating, since he was essentially being tortured to death by his doctors at the same time.[39]

Eventually Washington ordered his doctors to cease their barbarisms and let him go in peace. "Doctor, I die hard," he muttered, "but I am not afraid to go." Then he gave an intriguing final instruction to Lear: "I am just going. Have me decently buried, and do not let my body be put into the Vault in less than two days after I am dead. . . . Do you understand me?" Washington believed that several apparently dead people, perhaps including Jesus, had really been buried alive, a fate he wished to avoid. His statement also calls attention to a missing presence at the deathbed scene: there were no ministers in the room, no prayers uttered, no Christian rituals offering the solace of everlasting life. The inevitable renderings of Washington's death by nineteenth-century artists often added religious symbols to the scene, frequently depicting his body ascending into heaven surrounded by a chorus of angels. The historical evidence suggests that Washington did not think much about heaven or angels; the only place he knew his body was going was into the ground, and as for his soul, its ultimate location was unknowable. He died as a Roman stoic rather than a Christian saint.

The end came between ten and eleven o'clock on the evening of December 14. Besides the doctors, Lear, and Martha, the bedside entourage included three women slaves serving as nurses and Washington's body servant, Christopher Sheels, who had replaced the crippled Billy Lee a few years earlier. (Christopher had recently tried to escape slavery with his new wife, but Washington chose not to punish him for making the effort and Christopher remained at his side until the end.) As that end approached, Washington noticed that Christopher, who had been standing for many hours, was visibly fatigued, so he invited him to sit down. His last words were, "'Tis well." His last act, taking charge for the final time, was to feel his own pulse as he expired.[40]

He was buried in the family vault four days later. The culminating piece of evidence in the long debate about his height materialized at this time, when his corpse was measured in order to provide specifications for his lead-lined mahogany coffin. It showed that he was 6′ 3½″ tall, though some scholars have questioned its accuracy. As far as his contemporaries were concerned, there was no question about his stature in American history. In the extravaganza of mourning that occurred in more than four hundred towns and hamlets throughout the land, he was described as the only indisputable hero of the age, the one and only "His Excellency."

EULOGIES

MOST OF THE EULOGIES provided only platitudinous lamentations on his passing, often observing that his departure coincided with the end of the century, obviously a sign that the first chapter of American history was ending. Two of the eulogists, however, managed to sound more resonant notes that afford an opportunity to take his measure as a man in that last moment before the legendary renderings, already being composed, gathered around him like ivy on a statue to obscure his human features.

In the eulogy that has echoed through the ages, Henry Lee proclaimed that Washington was "First in war, first in peace, and first in the hearts of his countrymen." This formulation offered an elegantly concise summation of the three historical achievements on which his reputation rested: leading the Continental army to victory against the odds and thereby winning American independence; securing the Revolution by overseeing the establishment of a new nation-state during its most fragile and formative phase of development; and embodying that elusive and still latent thing called "the American people," thereby providing the illusion of coherence to what was in fact a messy collage of regional and state allegiances. There was a consensus at the time, since confirmed for all time, that no one else could have performed these elemental tasks as well, and perhaps that no one could have performed them at all.

In effect, there were two distinct creative moments in the American founding, the winning of independence and the invention of nationhood, and Washington was the central figure in both creations. No one else in the founding generation could match these revolutionary credentials, so no one else could plausibly challenge his place atop the American version of Mount Olympus. Whatever minor missteps he had made along the way, his judgment on all the major political and military questions had invariably proved prescient, as if he had known where history was headed; or, perhaps, as if the future had felt compelled to align itself with his choices. He was that rarest of men: a supremely realistic visionary, a prudent prophet whose final position on slavery

served as the capstone to a career devoted to getting the big things right. His genius was his judgment.

But where did that come from? Clearly, it did
not emanate from books or formal education,
places where it is customary and often correct to
look for the wellspring that filled the minds of
such eminent colleagues as Adams, Jefferson, and
Madison with their guiding ideas. Though it
might seem sacrilegious to suggest, Washington's
powers of judgment derived in part from the fact
that his mind was uncluttered with sophisticated
intellectual preconceptions. As much a self-made
man as Franklin, the self he made was less protean
and more primal because his education was more
elemental. From his youthful experience on the
Virginia frontier as an adventurer and soldier he
had internalized a visceral understanding of the
arbitrary and capricious ways of the world. Without ever reading Thucydides, Hobbes, or Calvin,
he had concluded that men and nations were
driven by interests rather than ideals, and that surrendering control to another was invariably harm-
ful, often fatal.

Armed with these basic convictions, he was
capable of a remarkably unblinkered and unburdened response to the increasingly consequential
decisions that history placed before him. He no
more expected George III and his ministers to

respond to conciliatory pleas from the American colonists than he expected Indians to surrender their tribal lands without a fight. He took it for granted that the slaves at Mount Vernon would not work unless closely supervised. He presumed that the Articles of Confederation would collapse in failure or be replaced by a more energetic and empowered federal government, for the same reasons that militia volunteers could never defeat the British army. It also was quite predictable that the purportedly self-enacting ideals of the French Revolution would lead to tragedy and tyranny. With the exception of his Potomac dream, a huge geographic miscalculation, he was incapable of illusion, fully attuned to the specter of evil in the world. All of which inoculated him against the grand illusion of the age, the presumption that there was a natural order in human affairs that would generate perfect harmony once, in Diderot's phrase, the last king was strangled with the entrails of the last priest. For Washington, the American Revolution was not about destroying political power, as it was for Jefferson, but rather seizing it and using it wisely. Ultimately, his life was all about power: facing it, taming it, channeling it, projecting it. His remarkably reliable judgment derived from his elemental understanding of how power worked in the world.

A second memorable eulogy, this one delivered by Gouverneur Morris, made an intriguing connection between Washington's grasp of the dynamics of power and his grip on himself. Morris observed that Washington's legendary calmness and statue-like stolidity masked truly volcanic energies and emotions. Anyone who knew him well could testify, Morris claimed, that he was a man of "tumultuous passions" and could "bear witness that his wrath was terrible." Intimate acquaintances felt the explosive energy lurking beneath the surface "and have seen boiling in his bosom, passions almost too mighty for man." In Morris's formulations, the potency of Washington's vaunted capacity for self control derived from the virulence of the internal demons he had been required to master.[41]

The image of a volcanic Washington seething with barely contained emotions and ambitions flies in the face of conventional wisdom, which emphasizes the serenity of the man who would not be king. But no less a source than Gilbert Stuart, who brought a trained artist's eye to the subject, confirmed the Morris assessment. "Had he been born in the forests," Stuart observed while painting Washington, "he would have been the fiercest man among the savage tribes."[42]

If we adopt the Morris and Stuart perspective, all kinds of lights go on up and down the line of Washington's life: the frequent harangues against his overseers at Mount Vernon; the tirade against the retreating Charles Lee at Monmouth Court House; the outburst against Philip Freneau's journalistic diatribes during a cabinet meeting; the secluded seething against James Monroe's attacks on the Jay Treaty during his final retirement. These discernible leaks suggest that a massive reservoir of emotional intensity remained pent up inside the mature Washington, and that his interior wrestling match to subdue them never resulted in a conclusive triumph, as Morris suggested, because the ambitions never died. This is a man, after all, who kept coming back to center stage and who, despite his thoroughly sincere protestations in the Ciceronian vein, remained obsessed with imposing his will even after his death.

The clearest evidence that we are talking about a truly monumental ego with a massive personal agenda comes from the early years before and during the French and Indian War. At this youthful stage the internal editing process had yet to develop its later strength, and the record more fully reveals the self-made man feverishly striving to become a self-made hero, which is the chief reason Washington kept returning to his early correspondence to edit out the evidence. Though George III and his ministers did not decide to place their empire in North America at risk in order to provide a Virginia squire with a larger stage on which to display his talents, that is precisely what happened. And it happened, at least in part, because Washington was alert to the opportunity the political crisis presented, much as he had been alert to the availability of Virginia's wealthiest widow. Ambitions this gargantuan were only glorious if harnessed to a cause larger than oneself, which they most assuredly were after 1775. But even in the glorious rendition of "His Excellency" serving "The Cause," a leader driven by such internal propulsion needed to be aware of arrogant appearances. Two of Washington's abiding characteristics—his aloofness and his capacity for remaining silent—were in all likelihood protective tactics developed to prevent detection of the combustible materials simmering inside.[43]

Of course, Morris's main point was that the passions that stirred Washington's soul required the creation of control mechanisms that subsequently served the nation so well when Washington voluntarily stepped away from power, first in 1783, and then again in 1796. Morris was saying that his psychological struggle for self-control prepared Washington to perform the crowning political achievement of his career. What we might call Washington's internal muscularity is, of course, impossible to see, though Morris implied that it was just as impressive as his marvelous physique. We can only describe its visible manifestations.

And on that score there were five self-denying decisions that stand out: the rejection of his love for Sally Fairfax; the adoption of a Fabian strategy against the British army in 1777, despite his own aggressive instincts; the symbolic surrender of his sword at Annapolis; the refusal to serve a third term as president; and the dismemberment of his estate in his will. While Morris's formulation focuses attention on what Washington was prepared to give up in each instance, we should also notice that all the surrenders paved the way to larger acquisitions: a great fortune; victory in the war; and secular immortality. All the disciplined denials were also occasions to catch the next wave forward.

We might nudge Morris's line of thought in a slightly different direction, focusing not on the dramatic displays of self-control themselves but on the ongoing internal struggle as a lifelong educational process in which Washington hammered out, on the anvil of his own ambitions, his elemental convictions about political power. His insistence, for example, on a powerful Continental army and a wholly sovereign federal government become projections onto the national screen of the need for the same kind of controlling authority he had orchestrated within his own personality; a recognition that he could no more trust the people to behave virtuously than he could trust his own instincts to behave altruistically. One of the reasons, to take another example, he eventually found Jefferson dishonorable was that, unlike Hamilton, Jefferson could never acknowledge the depth of his own political ambitions.

A final example, his trademark decision to surrender power as commander in chief and then president, was not, as Morris insisted, a sign that he had conquered his ambitions, but rather that he fully realized that all ambitions were inherently insatiable and unconquerable. He knew himself well enough to resist the illusion that he transcended his human nature. Unlike Julius Caesar and Oliver Cromwell before him, and Napoleon, Lenin, and Mao after him, he understood that the greater glory resided in posterity's judgment. If you aspire to live forever in the memory of future generations, you must demonstrate the ultimate self-confidence to leave the final judgment to them. And he did.

At the very least, the eulogies of Lee and Morris, composed when the great man's body and the memories of him remained warm, allow us to conjure up the outlines of a more potent, less iconic, portrait. Even at that moment of mourning, however, more legendary renderings were being fabricated by Parson Weems and his legion of imitators in the cherry-tree mode. And over the ensuing years the mythology that a new and more democratic nation required of its symbolic hero arose around him to form a smothering blanket of lullabies more impenetrable than Washington's contrived silences and more wooden than his alleged teeth. But that, as they say, is another story.

ACKNOWLEDGMENTS
NOTES
INDEX

ACKNOWLEDGMENTS

My goal at the start was to read **The Papers of George Washington** in their entirety with my own eyes. Though I achieved my goal, it quickly became apparent that other eyes would be necessary to challenge my interpretive instincts and correct my inevitable gaffes. I sent those sections of the manuscript dealing with slavery to Philip Morgan, those on Washington's early career to Douglas Wilson, those on the presidency to Susan Dunn and James MacGregor Burns, those on the politics of the 1790s to Stanley Elkins. My peerless guide to the art on Washington was Paul Staiti.

Three scholarly friends, each of whom knows a great deal more about Washington's career than I did when I began, agreed to read all the chapters as they dribbled out. Robert Dalzell, Don Higginbotham, and Peter Henriques cheered and chastised me in the margins of multiple drafts. They were my version of Washington's councils of war, or perhaps his star-studded cabinet. Mary Thompson, who oversees the archives at Mount Vernon, gave the penultimate draft a careful scan, and sent me a twelve-page list of suggested corrections. As with my last two books, I asked Stephen Smith, now at the Brookings Institution, to read the final draft for style and flow, and he solidified his reputation as the sharpest editorial eye inside the beltway. James Rees, who heads up Mount Vernon, weighed in graciously with his thoughts at the very end.

Taken together, it is no exaggeration to observe that I enjoyed the advice of a stellar crew. Because I was sufficiently stubborn to reject their advice on occasion, responsibility for the book itself must remain my own.

Three of my students at Mount Holyoke—Carin Peller, Gretchen Snoeyenbos, and Brittany Suttell—read early drafts of certain chapters and let me know whether I was on the right track. Dara Cohen, then at Brown and now at Stanford, was never properly acknowledged for her assistance with my previous book, and echoes of her advice also helped me with this one.

My technological incompetence has now achieved legendary status. The original manuscript was handwritten in black ink, then transcribed onto disk by Holly Sharac, who deciphered my scrawl with her customary grace. She also had a major role in deciding the title.

My agent, Ike Williams, negotiated the contract, held my hand, and took me to lunch in Boston, but most important, he read each chapter as it materialized and let me know what he thought. When the research or writing bogged down, we generated energy by talking about the Red Sox and redemption.

At Knopf, Luba Ostashevsky never put me on hold and Gabriele Wilson allowed me to lobby her about the cover. My editor, Ashbel Green, is generally regarded as the wisest man in the publishing business. His running argument with me about adjectives and semicolons never threatened the trust that three books together have created. I can never repay his confidence.

Only my youngest son, Alexander, remains in the nest, but he left many notes on my desk blotter urging me forward as he did his own homework. Peter, the eldest, first heard of the project as a Peace Corps volunteer in the jungles of Africa, then learned of its completion in the forests of northern Vermont, where he read the page proofs. Scott, my middle son, called in from rest spots on the Appalachian Trail, which he hiked more swiftly than I wrote. My wife, Ellen, endured nightly readings of the day's work and the vacant stares of a husband more attuned to events two hundred years ago than to pressing household logistics. When times were truly tough, she never wavered.

The book is dedicated to a man who diplomatically declined to read my draft chapters because he wanted his former student to work it out on his own. Bill Abbot introduced me to early American history at the College of William and Mary years ago. He subsequently served as the founding editor of the modern edition of **The Papers of George Washington,** the meticulously constructed documentary edifice on which this book is based. Like Washington, he too is a patriarchal figure deserving a personal and professional salute.

NOTES

The notes that follow represent my attempt to adopt a policy toward citation that is both scholarly and sensible. All direct quotations are cited, most of which come from primary sources. All secondary sources that directly influenced my thinking or shaped my interpretation have also been identified. And my assessments of the secondary literature are littered throughout the notes, giving them the occasional flavor of a bibliographic essay. On the other hand, I have not attempted to provide an exhaustive account of all the scholarly books and articles related to Washington that I consulted, believing that such an accounting would burden the book with scaffolding that most readers would find excessive. If I have thereby slighted the contributions of my many predecessors, let me offer a blanket apology here. Let me also acknowledge that, when it comes to Washington, no one can claim to have read everything, and anyone who tried to do so would make another contribution to that venerable library of unwritten books. I have done all the research myself—with no research assistants—and made the modern edition of the **Washington Papers** the central focus of my inquiry and the home base from which all other explorations were launched. My dedication of this book to the founding editor of that massive project is both a personal and professional expression of my indebtedness.

ABBREVIATIONS

AFC Lyman Butterfield et al., eds., **Adams Family Correspondence,** 7 vols. (Cambridge, 1963–).

Diaries Donald Jackson and Dorothy Twohig, eds., **The Diaries of George Washington,** 6 vols. (Charlottesville, 1976–79).

Flexner James Thomas Flexner, **George Washington,** 4 vols. (Boston, 1965–72).

Freeman Douglas Southall Freeman, **George Washington: A Biography,** 7 vols. (New York, 1948–57). Volume 7 completed by John A. Carroll and Mary W. Ashworth.

GWR Don Higginbotham, ed., **George Washington Reconsidered** (Charlottesville, 2001).

Hamilton Howard Syrett, ed., **The Papers of Alexander Hamilton,** 26 vols. (New York, 1974–92).

JCC   W. C. Ford et al., eds., **Journals of the Continental Congress,** 24 vols. (Washington, D.C., 1904–37).

Jefferson   Julian Boyd et al., eds., **The Papers of Thomas Jefferson,** 27 vols. (Princeton, 1950–).

Jefferson-Madison   James Morton Smith, ed., **The Republic of Letters: The Correspondence Between Thomas Jefferson and James Madison, 1776–1826,** 3 vols. (New York, 1995).

PWC   W. W. Abbot, Dorothy Twohig, and Philander D. Chase, eds., **The Papers of George Washington: Colonial Series,** 10 vols. (Charlottesville, 1983–95).

PWCF   W. W. Abbot and Dorothy Twohig, eds., **The Papers of George Washington, Confederation Series,** 6 vols. (Charlottesville, 1992–97).

PWP   W. W. Abbot and Dorothy Twohig, eds., **The Papers of George Washington: Presidential Series,** 11 vols. (Charlottesville, 1987–).

PWR   W. W. Abbot, Dorothy Twohig, and Philander D. Chase, eds., **The Papers of George Washington: Revolutionary War Series,** 12 vols. (Charlottesville, 1985–).

PWRT W. W. Abbot, ed., **The Papers of George Washington: Retirement Series,** 4 vols. (Charlottesville, 1998–99).

WMQ **William and Mary Quarterly,** 3rd ser.

WW John C. Fitzpatrick, ed., **Writings of George Washington,** 39 vols. (Washington, DC, 1931–39).

CHAPTER ONE

1. **Diaries** 1:127–28.
2. Ibid., 130–61, for the entire journal.
3. Ibid., 153–57.
4. Ibid., 146–47.
5. Ibid., 144–51.
6. **PWC** 1:56–62; **Diaries** 1:183–84. The spelling of the Half-King's Indian name varies. I have followed the version adopted by the editors of **PWC.** For background on the Indian cultures of the Ohio Country, see the following: Fred Anderson, **Crucible of War: The Seven Years' War and the Fate of Empire in British North America** (New York, 2000), 11–32; Erick Hindesaker, **Elusive Empires: Constructing Colonialism in the Ohio Valley** (New York, 1997); Daniel K. Richter, **The Ordeal of the Longhouse: The Peoples of the Iroquois League in the Era of European Colonization** (Chapel Hill, 1992).
7. **Diaries** 1:136–40.
8. John Marshall, **The Life of George Washington,** 5 vols. (Philadelphia, 1805–07), 2:1; Marcus Cunliffe,

ed., **The Life of George Washington by Mason L. Weems** (Cambridge, MA, 1962). Among the hundreds of books on the Washington legend, three stand out: Marcus Cunliffe, **George Washington: Man and Monument** (Boston, 1958); Richard Brookhiser, **Founding Father: Rediscovering George Washington** (New York, 1996); Barry Schwartz, **George Washington: The Making of an American Symbol** (New York, 1987). The most reliable study of Washington's early years is Bernard Knollenberg, **George Washington: The Virginia Period** (Durham, 1964).

9. Flexner 1:9–17; Martin H. Quitt, "The English Cleric and the Virginia Adventurer: The Washingtons, Father and Son," **GWR**, 15–37.

10. Charles Moore, ed., **George Washington's Rules of Civility and Decent Behavior** (Boston, 1926). Among the single-volume biographies, the fullest assessment of Washington's adolescent influences is Paul Longmore, **The Invention of George Washington** (Berkeley, 1988), 1–16. Also excellent on these early years is Guthrie Sayen, **"A Compleat Gentleman": The Making of George Washington** (University of Virginia Press, forthcoming), which I read as a doctoral dissertation.

11. Joseph Ball to Mary Washington, 19 May 1747, quoted in Freeman 1:198–99; **PWC** 1:54.

12. **Diaries** 1:24–117, for the Barbados trip; **PWC**, 232–35, for Lawrence's will.

13. Edward D. Neill, **The Fairfaxes of England and America** (Albany, 1868); Flexner 1:26–33.

14. **Diaries** 1:10, 13, 18.

15. **PWC** 1:8–37, for the surveys. For the Ohio Company, see Kenneth P. Bailey, **The Ohio Company of Virginia and the Westward Movement, 1748–92** (Glendale, CA, 1939).

16. **PWC** 1:40–41, 46–59.

17. The physical description of young Washington is based on George Mercer's famous description in 1759, in **PWC** 6:192. Washington's height is a matter of disagreement. Mercer's account says six feet two inches, but this will be a running debate throughout Washington's life, and even after his death. Flexner 1:80 and Longmore, **Invention of Washington,** 181–82, offer convenient synthesis of the lore about his physical prowess.

18. Washington to Robert Dinwiddie, 10 June 1752, **PWC** 1:50–51.

19. Dinwiddie's Instructions, January 1754, **PWC** 1:65–67; **Diaries** 1:189–90.

20. See the correspondence with Dinwiddie in May 1754, **PWC** 1:93–95, 99; **Diaries** 1:192–96; Washington to Dinwiddie, 29 May 1754, **PWC** 1:107–13, and **Diaries** 1:195–96, for the quotations.

21. Anderson, **Crucible of War,** 5–7, 51–59, for the best scholarly version of the massacre. For an excellent summary of the several eyewitness accounts, see **PWC** 1:114–15, notes 12–14.

22. **Diaries** 1:198; Washington to John Augustine Washington, 31 May 1754, **PWC** 1:118–19; for the quote from George II, see the editorial note, **Diaries** 1:197.

23. Washington to Robert Dinwiddie, 3 June 1754, **PWC** 1:124, and the extensive editorial notes on Fort

Necessity on 125–26. Dinwiddie's endorsement of Washington's decision to make a stand is provided in their correspondence during early June, **PWC** 1:192–202.

24. **Diaries**, 1:164–65, 203–8.

25. **PWC** 1:155–57, 162–64; Anderson, **Crucible of War,** 50–65, which sustains the kind of magisterial tone and narrative verve for this incident that makes his book one of the seminal sources for this phase of Washington's career.

26. The Capitulation of Fort Necessity, **PWC** 1:157–64.

27. Ibid., 162–66.

28. Duquesne's remarks of 8 September 1754 are available in the editorial notes, **Diaries** 1:172.

29. John Robinson to Washington, 15 September 1754, Washington to John Robinson, 23 October 1754, **PWC** 1:209–10, 219–20.

30. Washington to John Augustine Washington, 2 August 1755, Robert Dinwiddie to Washington, 11 September 1754, Washington to William Fitzhugh, 15 November 1754, **PWC** 1:206–8, 225–26, 351–52.

31. Franklin T. Nichols, "The Organization of Braddock's Army," **WMQ** 4 (1947), 130–33; Peter E. Russell, "Redcoats in the Wilderness: British Officers and Irregular Warfare in Europe and America, 1740–1760," **WMQ** 34 (1978), 629–52. The best full-length study is Paul E. Kopperman, **Braddock at the Monongahela** (Pittsburgh, 1977).

32. See the editorial note on the revisions of his letterbook in **PWC** 1:236–40; Robert Orme to Washing-

ton, 2 March 1755, Washington to Robert Orme, 15 March 1755, Washington to John Augustine Washington, 14 May 1755, ibid. 240–45, 277–78.

33. **PWC** 1:259, where the size of Braddock's train is assessed by the editors. The Braddock quotation is in Stanley Pargellis, ed., **Military Affairs in North America, 1748–1765** (New York, 1936), 81–84.

34. Washington to John Carlyle, 14 May 1755, Washington to Augustine Washington, 28 June–2 July 1755, Memorandum, 8–9 July 1755, **PWC** 1:274–75, 319–24, 331–33. See also Lee McCardell, **Ill-Starred General: Braddock of the Coldstream Guards** (Pittsburgh, 1958).

35. Washington to Robert Dinwiddie, 18 July 1755, **PWC** 1:339–40; see also ibid., 341, for an editorial note on the surgeon's report showing that most members of the Virginia Regiment were shot in the back by British regulars.

36. Washington to John Augustine Washington, 18 July 1755, **PWC** 1:343. On Boone's role in the battle, see John Mack Faragher, **Daniel Boone: The Life and Legend of an American Pioneer** (New York, 1992), 37–39.

37. Washington to Mary Ball Washington, 18 July 1755, Washington to John Augustine Washington, 18 July 1755, **PWC** 1:336–37, 343. See also the editorial note on casualties on both sides in **PWC** 2:10–11.

38. Washington to Robert Jackson, 2 August 1755, **PWC** 1:349–50. The Dinwiddie quotation is on 351, note 2. Washington to Warner Lewis, 14 August 1755, ibid., 360–63.

39. The Davies quotation can be found in Longmore, **Invention of Washington,** 30.

40. For the larger strategic picture of British policy during this phase of the French and Indian War, see Anderson, **Crucible of War,** 108–32. The quotation is from Cunliffe, **Man and Monument,** 51. For an assessment of Washington as commander of the Virginia Regiment, see Don Higginbotham, "Washington and the Colonial Military Tradition," **GWR,** 38–66.

41. Washington to Richard Washington, 15 April 1757, **PWC** 4:132–33; Washington to John Robinson, 25 October 1757, **PWC** 5:33.

42. Washington to Robert Dinwiddie, 7 April 1756, **PWC** 2:333; Washington to Robert Dinwiddie, 24 April 1756, **PWC** 3:45; Orders, 27 October 1756, ibid., 445.

43. Orders, 6 October 1755, **PWC** 2:76.

44. Washington to Robert Dinwiddie, 10 March 1757, **PWC** 4:112–15. The correspondence with Dinwiddie throughout 1756–57 is full of complaints that he and the regiment are not sufficiently supported or recognized for their accomplishments.

45. The examples come from correspondence in the summer and fall of 1755, **PWC** 2:213–248; Washington to John Ashby, 28 December 1755, ibid., 241.

46. Role of George Washington's Company, 28 August 1757, **PWC** 4:389–91.

47. General Court Martial, 25–26 July 1757, ibid., 329–35; Washington to John Stanwix, 15 July 1757, ibid., 306–7. Washington had preferred to execute deserters a year earlier, but was prevented from doing so because his authority on this score was unclear.

48. Washington to Robert Dinwiddie, 10 October 1756, **PWC** 3:430–35; Washington to Robert Dinwiddie, 9 November 1756, **PWC** 4:1–6; Washington to John Robinson, 9 November 1756, ibid., 11–18.

49. Washington to John Robinson, 19 December 1756, ibid., 67–69.

50. Jack P. Greene, **The Quest for Power: The Lower Houses of Assembly in the Southern Royal Colonies, 1689–1776** (Chapel Hill, 1963). See also John R. Alden, **Robert Dinwiddie: Servant of the Crown** (Charlottesville, 1973), 90–110.

51. See, for example, Washington to Robert Dinwiddie and Washington to John Robinson, 5 December 1755, **PWC** 2:200–5; Washington to Robert Dinwiddie, 17 September 1757, **PWC** 4:411–12.

52. Stanley Pargellis, **Lord Loudoun in North America** (1933; reprint, Hamden, CT, 1968); Anderson, **Crucible of War,** 135–49; Washington to John Campbell, Earl of Loudoun, 25 July 1756, **PWC** 3:293–94.

53. Washington to John Campbell, Earl of Loudoun, 10 January 1757, **PWC** 4:79–83. Longmore, **Invention of Washington,** 46–47, is particularly good on this theme.

54. Washington to John Stanwix, 4 March 1758, **PWC** 5:100–01.

55. Washington to Thomas Gage, 12 April 1756, **PWC** 5:126. See also the editorial notes on Forbes and Bouquet on 118–19.

56. Washington to John Forbes, 19 June 1758, and the editorial note on Forbes's decision to use "Indian dress," **PWC** 5:224–27, 259; Washington to John

Forbes, 8 October 1758, **PWC** 6:66–70; Washington to Henry Bouquet, 21 July 1758, **PWC** 5:311.

57. Editorial notes on the road controversy in **PWC** 5:316; Washington to Henry Bouquet, 24 July 1758 and 2 August 1758, ibid., 318–19, 353–60.

58. Henry Bouquet to Washington, 27 July 1758 and 3 August 1758, ibid., 344–45, 364–65.

59. Washington to John Robinson, 1 September 1758, Washington to Francis Fauquier, 2 September 1758 and 5 August 1758, ibid., 433–34, 439–44, 369–71.

60. Washington to Francis Fauquier, 5 November 1758, Washington to Henry Bouquet, 6 November 1758, **PWC** 6:113–16.

61. Orderly Book, 12 November 1758, Orderly Book, 13–19 November 1758, Washington to Francis Fauquier, 28 November 1758, 2 December 1758, ibid., 120–23, 125–45, 158–60, 161–64. Anderson, **Crucible of War**, 267–85, provides his typically masterful narrative of the Forbes campaign. The fall of Fort Frontenac on the St. Lawrence in late August 1758 had made any effective French reinforcement of Fort Duquesne impossible.

62. See the editorial note on the Custis estate, **PWC** 6:202–9. Invoice from Thomas Knox, 18 August 1578, **PWC** 5:399–402, for the order of furnishings. The alcohol bill from the tavern is available on 332–34. Washington kept a roster of all the voters and how they voted, ibid., 334–43. See also George William Fairfax to Washington, 25 July 1758, on 329.

63. Washington to Sarah Cary Fairfax, 16 May 1798, **PWRT** 2:272–73.

64. Washington to Sarah Cary Fairfax, 12 September 1758, 25 September 1758, **PWC** 6:10–13, 41–43.

65. Address from the Officers of the Virginia Regiment, 31 December 1758, To the Officers of the Virginia Regiment, 10 January 1758, ibid., 178–81, 186–87. Washington to Richard Washington, 7 May 1579, ibid., 319.

CHAPTER TWO

1. Invoice to Robert Cary & Company, 20 September 1759, **PWC** 6:352–58.

2. Andrew Burnaby to Washington, 4 June 1760, ibid., 380–81. The authoritative account of Mount Vernon in all its material and metaphoric meanings is Robert F. Dalzell Jr. and Lee Baldwin Dalzell, **George Washington's Mount Vernon: At Home in Revolutionary America** (New York and Oxford, 1998), which both synthesizes and surpasses all previous scholarship on the subject.

3. **Diaries** 1:240–41, provides a map and key to the growth of Mount Vernon over these years. The number of slaves at Mount Vernon is difficult to calculate with precision because white servants are also listed among the "tithables" and the accounting varies, sometimes providing those slaves above sixteen years, sometimes below. Dalzell and Dalzell, **Mount Vernon**, 47–73, 129–49, gives the fullest discussion of both the acreage and the plantation workers.

4. This is my own distillation of both the evidence

and the informed conjecturing available in the major biographies. See Flexner 1:227–48 and, even more compelling, Bernard Knollenberg, **George Washington: The Virginia Period, 1732–1775** (Durham, 1964), 70–80, along with the extensive endnotes. Knollenberg's conclusions are especially persuasive because his interpretation of Washington is more critical than admiring, so evidence of a negative character would not have been ignored. On the promiscuity matter, see John C. Fitzpatrick, **The George Washington Scandals** (New York, 1929). Dalzell and Dalzell, **Mount Vernon,** 42–43, concur with this line of thought. The exception among recent biographers is John E. Ferling, **The First of Men: A Life of George Washington** (Knoxville, 1988), 34–35, 53–54, which is skeptical of Washington's love for Sally Fairfax to begin with.

5. Washington to Jonathan Boucher, 16 December 1770, Jonathan Boucher to Washington, 18 December 1770, **PWC** 8:411–17. For additional correspondence on Jackie's education, see 89–91, 120–21, 336–41. For the tutoring at Mount Vernon, see **PWC** 7:77.

6. For the correspondence and editorial notes on the sad arc of Jackie's life, see **PWC** 8:550 and 9:154–55, 209–11, 221–24, 264–67, 406–7.

7. Washington to Burwell Bassett, 20 June 1773, **PWC** 9:243–44. **Diaries** 1:168 for the iron ring; ibid., 257, for Washington's account of Patsy's seizures; Washington to Robert Cary, 10 July 1773, **PWC** 9:271–76, for the cloak.

8. **Diaries** 2:37–39, 105, and **PWC** 9:67–69, for the foxhunts and hounds; **PWC** 7:158–59, for the role

of Thomas Bishop; ibid., 407, for the role of Lund Washington; ibid., 458–59, for a typical wine order; **PWC** 10:222–23, for card-playing expenses for two years.

9. Washington to Charles Lawrence, 28 September 1760, **PWC** 6:459–60, for the first complaint about size; Washington to Charles Lawrence, 20 July 1767, **PWC** 8:8, for the quotation; Washington to Jonathan Boucher, 21 May 1772, **PWC** 9:49, for his description of the Peale sitting: "Inclination having yielded to Importunity, I am now contrary to all expectation under the hands of Mr. Peale, but in so grave—so sullen a Mood—and now and then under the influence of Morpheus, when some critical strokes are making, that I fancy the skill of the Gentleman's Pencil will be put to it, in describing to the World what manner of Man I am." See also **Diaries** 3:108–9.

10. **PWC** 7:143–51, for typically meticulous instructions to his overseers; 296–97, for his Truro Parish duties. **Diaries** 1:230, 266, 293–94, and 2:102–3, for representative examples of his busy routines.

11. Dorothy Twohig, " 'That Species of Property': Washington's Role in the Controversy Over Slavery," **GWR** 114–38, was the best scholarly study of the subject until the more recent book by Henry Wiencek, **An Imperfect God: George Washington, His Slaves and the Creation of America** (New York, 2003). Though my interpretation is somewhat different than Wiencek's, I benefited greatly from reading his book while making final revisions in mine. See Advertisement for Runaway Slaves, 11 August 1761, **PWC** 7:65–68, and the editorial note, **PWC** 8:520–21, for an escaped slave from one

of the Custis plantations. For the quotation on Tom, see Washington to Joseph Thompson, 2 July 1766, **PWC** 7:453.

12. Washington to Daniel Jenifer Adams, 20 July 1772, **PWC** 9:70. See Washington to Gilbert Simpson, 23 February 1773, ibid., 185–87, for his recognition of the need to avoid breaking up families when selling slaves. Dalzell and Dalzell, **Mount Vernon,** 129–49, offers the best account of the slave community at Mount Vernon. The two outstanding studies of slavery in the Chesapeake during the revolutionary era are Edmund S. Morgan, **American Slavery, American Freedom: The Ordeal of Colonial Virginia** (New York, 1975), and Philip D. Morgan, **Slave Counterpoint: Black Culture in the Eighteenth-Century Chesapeake and Low Country** (Chapel Hill, 1998).

13. The record of Washington's behavior in this mode defies a full accounting. See the correspondence and editorial notes in the following for the most salient examples: **PWC** 6:383, 407–16, 422–25, 478; **PWC** 7:61, 157, 459, 482–91; **PWC** 8:68–69; **PWC** 10:55–58. The quotation is from Washington to Valentine Crawford, 30 March 1774, ibid., 12–18.

14. For background on attitudes within Virginia's planter aristocracy, see Louis B. Wright, **First Gentlemen of Virginia: Intellectual Qualities of the Early Colonial Ruling Class** (San Marino, 1940), and T. H. Breen, **Tobacco Culture: The Mentality of the Great Tidewater Planters on the Eve of the Revolution** (Princeton, 1985).

15. Washington to Robert Cary & Company, 12 June

1759, **PWC** 6:326–27. For the litany of complaints during these early years of the relationship with Cary & Company, see the following correspondence with Cary, whose responses have not survived: **PWC** 6:348–52, 448–51; 7:76–77, 135–37, 153–55, 202–05, 251–53, 444–47; 8:9–12.

16. For the terms of the Custis will with regard to the "dower plantations," see **PWC** 7:81–93. For the dominant role of tobacco on these plantations, see **PWC** 8:421–24. For the size of the slave population in 1771, see 587–92.

17. Washington to Robert Cary & Company, 13 February 1764, **PWC** 8:286–87. For background on the evolution of the tobacco economy in the Chesapeake, the following books convey the complicated story: Jacob Price, **Capital and Credit in the British Overseas Trade: The View from the Chesapeake** (Cambridge, 1980); Alan Kulikoff, **Tobacco and Slaves: The Development of Southern Culture in the Chesapeake, 1680–1800** (Chapel Hill, 1986); Bruce A. Ragsdale, **A Planters' Republic: The Search for Economic Independence in Revolutionary Virginia** (Madison, 1996). On the consumer revolution sweeping England and Virginia, see T. H. Breen, **The Marketplace of Revolution: How Consumer Politics Shaped American Independence** (New York, 2004).

18. The invoices for this cornucopia of goods are reproduced in **PWC** 6:317–18, 327–36, 392–402, 461–66; 7:22–31, 124–31, 198–99, 253–57, 287–95, 353–57, 418–23, 432–33, 470–76; 8:44–50, 130–36, 295–99, 397–400, 558–66; 9:103–9. The best brief

treatment of Washington's economic relationship with Cary & Company is Bruce A. Ragsdale, "George Washington, the British Tobacco Trade, and Economic Opportunity in Pre-Revolutionary Virginia," **GWR**, 67–93.

19. Washington to Robert Stewart, 27 April 1763, **PWC** 7:205–8; Washington to Robert Cary, 1 May 1764, ibid., 305–6; Thomas Jefferson to Maria Jefferson Eppes, 7 January 1798, Sarah N. Randolph, **The Domestic Life of Thomas Jefferson** (Charlottesville, 1978), 247; Thomas Jefferson, Answers to Demeunier's Additional Queries, January–February 1786, **Jefferson** 10:27.

20. Washington to Robert Cary & Company, 10 August 1764, 20 September 1765, **PWC** 7:323–26, 398–402.

21. See the abovementioned essay by Bruce A. Ragsdale in **GWR** 67–93, for the best distillation of the scholarly literature. The old standard by Avery O. Craven, **Soil Exhaustion as a Factor in the Agricultural History of Virginia and Maryland, 1660–1860** (Urbana, 1926), is still excellent. My summary of the scholarship is most indebted to Morgan, **American Slavery, American Freedom;** Kulikoff, **Tobacco and Slaves;** and Breen, **Tobacco Culture.**

22. Washington to Francis Dandridge, 20 September 1765, Washington to Robert Cary, 20 September 1765, **PWC** 7:395–96, 401. The classic study of the colonial response to the Stamp Act is Edmund S. and Helen S. Morgan, **The Stamp Act Crisis: Prologue to Revolution** (Chapel Hill, 1953).

23. For correspondence with various merchants about his wheat crop, with ship captains about his flour, and for spinning and weaving records at Mount Vernon, see **PWC** 7:359–61, 509; 8:85–86, 154–55; 10:210, note 6.

24. Washington to John Posey, 24 June 1767, **PWC** 8:3; Dalzell and Dalzell, **Mount Vernon**, 52–53, for the symbolic significance of the westward entrance.

25. The earliest correspondence on the improvement of the Potomac, destined to occupy Washington until the very end, is in **PWC** 7:175–78; 8:284–90, 349–54.

26. Dismal Swamp Land Company Articles of Agreement, 3 November 1763, and Appraisment of Dismal Swamp Slaves, 4 July 1764, **PWC** 7:269–74, 315–16. See also Charles Royster, **The Fabulous History of the Dismal Swamp Company: A Story of George Washington's Times** (New York, 1999).

27. The standard study of the subject, old but reliable, is Thomas P. Abernethy, **Western Lands and the American Revolution** (New York, 1939). The issue receives thoughtful and poignant treatment in Anderson, **Crucible of War,** 518–28, 565–71.

28. Washington to William Crawford, 17 September 1767, **PWC** 8:26–30.

29. The intricate, indeed tortured, speculative scheme is capable of being followed in the following correspondence and editorial notes: **PWC** 7:219–25, 242–50, 415–16, 511–13; 8:62–65, 149–53, 307–9, 378–80. The quotation is from Washington to Thomas Lewis, 17 February 1774, **PWC** 9:483.

30. During the entire pre-revolutionary era, no single

concern generated as much correspondence from Washington as this one. See **PWC** 8:257–58, 272–79, 300–04, 366, 428–29, 439–41; 9:477; 10:230–33, for the key letters. For the surveying trip to the Great Kanawha, see **Diaries** 2:277–328. For the total acreage Washington claimed, see Advertisements for Western lands, 15 July 1773, **PWC** 9:278–80.

31. Washington to George Muse, 29 January 1774, **PWC** 9:460–61.

32. Washington to George Mercer, 7 November 1771, **PWC** 8:541–45.

33. Washington to Thomas Lewis, 17 February 1774; Washington to James Wood, 20 February 1774, **PWC** 9:481–83, 490.

34. Washington to Robert Cary & Company, 21 July 1766, **PWC** 7:457.

35. Washington's attendance record at the sessions in Williamsburg was decent but not diligent. He left town before Patrick Henry delivered his famous challenge to George III in 1765 and missed altogether the session in spring 1768. After 1765 he became a delegate from Fairfax County rather than Frederick County. He usually lodged and took his meals at Christiana Campbell's tavern and used the trip to visit the Custis estates nearby.

36. Washington to George Mason, 5 April 1769, **PWC** 8:177–81. On the appeal of austerity offered by the non-importation agreements, see Edmund S. Morgan, "The Puritan Ethic and the American Revolution," **WMQ** 24 (1967), 3–43.

37. For Washington's role in presenting Mason's plan, see the editorial note, **PWC** 8:187–90; Washington to

Robert Cary & Company, 25 July 1769, ibid., 229–31. The best biography of Mason is Robert A. Rutland, **George Mason: Reluctant Statesman** (Williamsburg, 1961).

38. Washington to George William Fairfax, 10–15 June 1774, Washington to Bryan Fairfax, 4 July 1774, **PWC** 10:94–101, 109–11.

39. The scholarly literature on radical Whig ideology is vast, but the two seminal works are Bernard Bailyn, **Ideological Origins of the American Revolution** (Cambridge, 1967), and Gordon Wood, **The Creation of the American Republic, 1776–1787** (New York, 1969).

40. Fairfax County Resolves, 18 July 1774, **PWC** 10:119–28; Donald M. Zweig, "A New-Found Washington Letter of 1774 and the Fairfax Revolves," **WMQ** 40 (1983), 283–91. See also Washington to Bryan Fairfax, 20 July 1774, **PWC** 10:128–31.

41. Washington to Bryan Fairfax, 24 August 1774, **PWC** 10:154–56.

42. William J. Van Schreeven and Robert L. Scribner, eds., **Revolutionary Virginia: The Road to Independence,** 2 vols. (Charlottesville, 1973–75), 1:230–39; **PWC** 10:142–43; Cunliffe, **Man and Monument,** 74.

43. Robert McKenzie to Washington, 13 September 1774, Washington to Robert McKenzie, 9 October 1774, **PWC** 10:151–62, 171–72. For the items purchased in Philadelphia, William Milnor to Washington, 29 November 1774, ibid., 189–98.

44. Washington to John Connolly, 25 February 1774, ibid., 273–74.

45. For the correspondence describing these various

activities, see **PWC** 10:242–44, 288–92, 314–15, 320–22. He had begun to make plans for the renovations of Mount Vernon a year earlier, so the decision described here represents a commitment to persist in his plans.

46. Van Schreeven and Scribner, eds., **Revolutionary Virginia** 2:347–86; **PWC** 10:308–9.

47. **Diaries** 3:320–25; Longmore, **Invention of Washington,** 154–56, for Mason's proposal about officer rotation.

48. **JCC** 2:13–45; Washington to George William Fairfax, 31 May 1775, **PWC** 10:367–68. For the purchases, see 369–70.

49. Lyman Butterfield, ed., **The Diary and Autobiography of John Adams,** 4 vols. (Cambridge, 1961), 3:322–23. Flexner 1:336–40, tends to accept the Adams version. Knollenberg, **Washington: The Virginia Period,** 113–16, and Longmore, **Invention of Washington,** 162–67, do not.

50. Benjamin Rush to Thomas Ruston, 29 October 1775, in Lyman Butterfield, ed., **The Letters of Benjamin Rush,** 2 vols. (Princeton, 1951), 1:92. Cunliffe, **Man and Monument,** 74, also suggests that his silence and reserve in the Continental Congress impressed his talkative colleagues.

51. **JCC** 2:49–66. The Adams quotation is in Butterfield, ed., **Diary and Autobiography** 2:117.

52. Address to the Continental Congress, 16 June 1775, **PWC** 1:1–3; **Diaries** 3:336–37; **JCC** 2:91–94.

53. Washington to Martha Washington, 18 June 1775, Washington to John Augustine Washington, 20

June 1775, Washington to Burwell Bassett, 19 June 1775, **PWR** 1:3–4, 12–14, 19–20.

54. I am making an argument here about the improbability of the American Revolution succeeding that I make more fully in **Founding Brothers: The Revolutionary Generation** (New York, 2000), 3–19.

55. The thoughts about a retreat to the western wilderness is based on Washington's later reminiscence about his distressed state of mind at that moment. See Flexner 1:336. He actually arrived at Cambridge on July 2, but officially assumed command the following day. See **PWR** 1:49–50.

CHAPTER THREE

1. The story of Lund Washington's effort to appease the British naval officer and Washington's hostile reaction to the effort is nicely told in Dalzell and Dalzell, **Mount Vernon**, xv–xvi. The most succinct overview of Washington's military career during the Revolution is Glenn A. Phelps, "The Republican General," **GWR**, 165–97.

2. Washington to Joseph Reed, 10 February 1776, **PWR** 3:288; Washington to John Augustine Washington, 31 May–4 June 1776, **PWR** 4:412–13. See also Washington to Philip Schuyler, 4 October 1775, **PWR** 2:95–96.

3. On the Bunker Hill casualties and lessons, see the letters in **PWR** 1:71, 134–36, 183–84, 289–90. The standard history of the battle itself is Richard Ketchum, **The Battle for Bunker Hill** (Garden City, 1962).

4. For a typical expression of the belief that one deci-

sive blow at Boston could end the war, see Richard Henry Lee to Washington, 29 August 1775, **PWR** 1:209–10. For the belief that volunteers would defeat mercenaries, see General Orders, 3 January 1776, **PWR** 3:14.

5. Washington to John Hancock, 9 February 1776, **PWR** 3:274–75. See also Washington to Joseph Reed, 28 November 1775, **PWR** 2:448–51, for the inadequacy of militia.

6. Address from the New York Provincial Congress, 26 June 1775, Address from the Massachusetts Provincial Congress, 3 July 1775, **PWR** 1:40, 52–53. Longmore, **Invention of Washington,** 184–201, is especially good on the quasi-king theme.

7. Phillis Wheatley to Washington, 26 October 1775, **PWR** 2:252–54; Washington to Phillis Wheatley, 28 February 1776, **PWR** 3:387. Fritz Hirschfeld, **George Washington and Slavery: A Documentary Portrayal** (Columbia, MO, 1997), 93–94. Washington to Thomas Gage, 19 August 1775, **PWR** 1:326–28.

8. Washington to Lund Washington, 20 August 1775, **PWR** 1:335–36; Washington to Joseph Reed, 15 December 1775, **PWR** 2:552; Washington to Joseph Reed, 14 January 1776 and 10 February 1776, **PWR** 3:87–92, 286–91.

9. Washington to Charles Lee, 10 February 1776, **PWR** 3:282–84; Washington to Joseph Reed, 20 November 1775, **PWR** 2:407–9; General Orders, 27 February 1776, **PWR** 3:379–81; Washington to Joseph Reed, 23 January 1776, ibid., 172–75. For the role of Billy Lee, see Hirschfeld, **Washington and Slavery,** 96–111.

10. Hugh Rankin, "Washington's Lieutenants and the American Victory," in John Ferling, ed., **The World Turned Upside Down: The American Victory in the War for Independence** (Westport, 1988), 71–90; John Shy, **A People Numerous and Armed: Reflections on the Military Struggle for American Independence** (New York, 1976), 133–62; George Billias, ed., **George Washington's Generals and Opponents** (New York, 1994).

11. The case for Washington as a fundamentally insecure leader, nervous about the superior credentials of Lee and Gates, is made best by John Ferling, **The First of Men: A Life of George Washington** (Knoxville, 1988). A more succinct version is available in Ferling, ed., **The World Turned Upside Down**, 53–70.

12. For typical examples of Washington's deference to John Hancock as president of the Continental Congress, see his letters in **PWR** 2:444–47, 483–87, 533–35.

13. General Orders, 20 August 1775, **PWR** 1:329–30, for "United Colonies"; Washington to Joseph Reed, 4 January 1776, **PWR** 3:23–27, for the "union flag"; Minutes of the Conference, 18–24 October 1775, **PWR** 2:190–95, for the meeting with the delegation of the Continental Congress.

14. Washington to John Hancock, 4 January 1776, **PWR** 3:18–21. See also, General Orders, 1 January 1776, ibid., 1–5, especially the editorial note, for the transition problem as troops came and went.

15. Council of War, 8 October 1775, **PWR** 2:123–38; General Orders, 12 November 1775, ibid., 353–55; Washington to John Hancock, 31 December 1775, ibid., 623.

16. Circular to the General Officers, 8 September 1775, **PWR** 1:432–34; Council of War, 16 January 1776, **PWR** 3:103–4; Council of War, 16 February 1776, ibid., 319–24; Washington to Joseph Reed, 26 February–9 March 1776, ibid., 369–79.

17. For the correspondence on the Quebec mission, see **PWR** 1:331–33, 431–32, 455–56, 461–62; **PWR** 2:155–56, 160–62, 300–01; **PWR** 3:78–80. The comment to Arnold is in Washington to Benedict Arnold, 27 January 1776, ibid., 197–98.

18. Kenneth Roberts, **March to Quebec** (New York, 1942), 201–6.

19. Elizabeth A. Fenn, **Pox Americana: The Great Smallpox Epidemic of 1775–82** (New York, 2001).

20. John Hancock to Washington, 2 April 1776, **PWR** 4:16–17.

21. For Washington's trip to and arrival at New York, see **PWR** 4:40–43, 58–60. For the size of the British expeditionary force, see Mary B. Wickwire, "Naval Warfare and the American Victory," in Ferling, ed., **The World Turned Upside Down**, 193–96.

22. This entire section represents my own digestion and interpretation of the rather massive scholarly literature on the military history of the War of Independence. The following books and articles have exercised the greatest influence on my thinking: on the Continental army and its essential if threatening role, Charles Royster, **A Revolutionary People at War: The Continental Army and American Character** (Chapel Hill, 1979), and Robert K. Wright, **The Continental Army** (Washington, D.C., 1983); on the decline of popular support

for the war and the Continental army, Ray Raphael, **A People's History of the American Revolution: How Common People Shaped the Fight for Independence** (New York, 2001), and Joseph Plumb Martin, **Private Yankee Doodle: Some of the Adventures, Dangers, and Sufferings of Joseph Plumb Martin** (New York, 2001); on the role of the Continental Congress, Jack N. Rakove, **The Beginnings of National Politics: An Interpretive History of the Continental Congress** (New York, 1979); on the role of the militia, John Shy, **A People Numerous and Armed,** and John Shy, "The American Revolution Considered as a Revolutionary War," in Stephen Kurtz and James Huston, eds., **Essays on the American Revolution** (Chapel Hill, 1973), 121–56; on the British perspective, Ira D. Gruber, **The Howe Brothers and the American Revolution** (New York, 1972), and Paul H. Smith, **Loyalists and Redcoats: A Study in the British Revolutionary Policy** (Chapel Hill, 1964); on the American perspective, Don Higginbotham, **The War of American Independence** (New York, 1971), Robert Middlekauf, **The Glorious Cause: The American Revolution** (New York, 1982), and Dave R. Palmer, **The Way of the Fox: American Strategy in the War for America** (Westport, 1975). Excellent collections of essays that shed light on multiple dimensions of the conflict are: Ferling, ed., **The World Turned Upside Down;** Jack P. Greene, ed., **The American Revolution: Its Character and Limits** (New York, 1987); Don Higginbotham, ed., **Reconsiderations on the Revolutionary War: Selected Essays** (Westport, 1978); and Ronald

Hoffmann and Peter J. Albert, eds., **Arms and Independence: The Military Character of the American Revolution** (Charlottesville, 1984).

23. John Keegan, **Fields of Battle: The War for North America** (New York, 1996), 152–54, which includes the quotation from Lord Camden.

24. For the modern parallel, see Don Higginbotham, "Reflections on the War for Independence, Modern Guerrilla Warfare, and the War in Vietnam," in Hoffman and Albert, eds., **Arms and Independence**, 1–24.

25. The best brief review of this huge subject is Piers Mackesy, "What the British Army Learned," ibid., 191–215.

26. See Russell Weigley, "American Strategy: A Call for a Critical Strategic History," in Higginbotham, **Reconsiderations on the Revolutionary War,** 32–53. See also Don Higginbotham, **George Washington and the American Military Tradition** (Athens, 1985).

27. Washington to the New York Provincial Congress, 9 June 1776, **PWR** 4:473, for the first statement of his intentions to defend New York at all costs.

28. For the visit to Philadelphia, see the correspondence in **PWR** 4:346–53, 363–68; **JCC** 4:389–91, for the conference with the Continental Congress; **PWR** 4:526, for the creation of the Board of War and Ordnance; Washington to John Hancock, 10 July 1776, **PWR** 5:260; General Orders, 23 August 1776, **PWR** 6:109–10; Washington to John Hancock, ibid., 627.

29. Lord Richard Howe to Washington, 13 July 1776, **PWR** 5:296–97; Memorandum of an Interview

with Lieutenant Colonel James Patterson, 20 July 1776, ibid., 398–403, which includes invaluable editorial notes on the details of the meeting.

30. General Orders, 13 August 1776, **PWR** 6:1; Washington to Charles Lee, 12 August 1776, **PWR** 5:686–87; John Adams to Abigail Adams, 30 August 1776, **AFC** 2:89.

31. John Adams to Abigail Adams, 8 October 1776, **AFC** 2:140; Nathanael Greene to Washington, 5 September 1776, **PWR** 6:222–24; Abigail Adams to John Adams, 20 September 1776, **AFC** 2:129.

32. Council of War, 12 September 1776, **PWR** 6:288–89; Washington to John Hancock, 8 September 1776, ibid., 248–54. One of the best, certainly most readable accounts of the maneuverings on Manhattan, is Bruce Bliven Jr., **Battle for Manhattan** (New York, 1956).

33. Keegan, **Fields of Battle,** 162–65, for a convenient summary of scholarly judgments; Washington to Lund Washington, 30 September 1776, **PWR** 6:440–43; Washington to John Hancock, 16 November 1776, **PWR** 7:162–69, for the account of the Fort Washington disaster. See also Washington to John Augustine Washington, 6–19 November 1776, ibid., 102–6, for his sense of desperation and mortification at the capture of Fort Washington.

34. Washington to John Hancock, 4 October 1776, **PWR** 6:463–66; Washington to John Hancock, 25 September 1776, ibid., 304; Washington to Samuel Ward, 18 December 1776, **PWR** 7:370–71.

35. For two different but compatible assessments of

Howe's failure to pursue the remnants of the Continental army, see Gruber, **The Howe Brothers and the American Revolution,** 127–57, and Kevin Phillips, **The Cousins' War: Religion, Politics and the Triumph of Anglo-America** (New York, 1999), 291–99; Washington to John Hancock, 5 December 1776, **PWR** 7:262–63; Joseph Reed to Washington, 22 December 1776, ibid., 416.

36. For Washington's account of the crossing of the Delaware and subsequent victory at Trenton, along with editorial notes that synthesize the scholarship, see Washington to John Hancock, 27 December 1776, ibid., 454–61. An excellent secondary account is in Richard Ketchum, **The Winter Soldiers** (Garden City, 1973), now superseded by David Hackett Fischer's splendid account, **Washington's Crossing** (New York, 2004).

37. Washington to John Hancock, 5 January 1777, **PWR** 7:519–30, for his report on the action at Princeton. Old but invaluable for its detail is William Stryker, **The Battles of Trenton and Princeton** (1858; reprint, Spartansburg, SC, 1967). Flexner, 2:185, is especially vivid on Washington's heroic demeanor under fire.

38. Washington to John Hancock, 20 December 1776, **OWR** 7:382; Bartholomew Dandridge to Washington, 16 January 1777, **PWR** 8:79; on the depleted state of his army, see Washington to George Clinton, 19 January 1777, and Washington to John Hancock, 19 January 1777, ibid., 102–3. He made a special plea for soldiers whose enlistments expired with the new year to remain on duty for an extra six weeks in order to assure the preservation of a fighting force.

39. Washington to John Hancock, 14 February 1777, **PWR** 8:334; for the policy making inoculation mandatory, see Washington to William Shippen, 6 February 1777, and the Circular to the Continental Regiments, 12 March 1777, ibid., 556.

40. Washington to John Hancock, 26 March 1777, ibid., 635; Washington to Richard Henry Lee, 1 June 1777, **PWR** 9:581; on the disappointing lack of new recruits, see Washington to John Hancock, 12–13 April 1777, ibid., 129; the defensive strategy is officially endorsed in Council of War, 2 May 1777, ibid., 324. The remark about French enthusiasm for the cause is quoted in Shy, **A People Numerous and Armed,** 13.

41. Nathanael Greene to Washington, 24 March 1777, **PWR** 8:627; John Adams to Abigail Adams, 18 June 1777, **AFC** 2:268; Richard Henry Lee to Washington, 10 April 1777, **PWR** 9:118.

42. John Adams to Abigail Adams, 30 July 1777, **AFC** 2:297. The correspondence tracking Howe's fleet and trying to predict its destination throughout the summer of 1777 is voluminous. The most salient items are **PWR** 9:201–4; **PWR** 10:58, 84–86, 157, 171, 289; **PWR** 11:147–48.

43. General Orders, 5 September 1777, **PWR** 11:147–48; Washington to Thomas Wharton Jr., 13 September 1777, ibid., 222; Council of War, 23 September 1777, ibid., 294–98.

44. The Battle of Brandywine, 11 September 1777, ibid., 187–95, which includes editorial notes containing views of the battle from both sides. See also Samuel E. Smith, **The Battle of Brandywine** (Monmouth, NJ,

1976). See Washington to John Hancock, 11 September 1777, **PWR** 11:200–1, for the first of several falsifications of the casualties.

45. This scene is based on the after-action reports and subsequent memoirs, all reproduced in editorial notes in ibid., 398–400.

46. General Order for Attacking Germantown, 3 October 1777, ibid., 375–81, where the editorial notes, once again, do a marvelous job of synthesizing the scholarly evidence on the battle; Washington to Israel Putnam, 8 October 1777, ibid., 447, for the quotation; Washington to John Trumbull Sr., 7 October 1777, and Washington to John Page, 11 October 1777, ibid., 426–27, 487, for the distorted casualty lists; Washington to William Howe, 6 October 1777, ibid., 410, for the return of Howe's dog; Thomas McKean to Washington, 8 October 1777, ibid., 442–45.

47. Washington to Benjamin Lincoln, 12 August 1777, **PWR** 10:592–93, where Washington predicts that Burgoyne's army "must be ruined" if Howe failed to rendezvous; Washington to John Hancock, 3 August 1777, ibid., 492–93, approving Gates as commander in place of Philip Schuyler; Washington to Daniel Morgan, 16 August 1777, ibid., 641, sending Morgan and Arnold to join Gates; Washington to Landon Carter, 27 October 1777, **PWR** 12:27, where he contrasts the militia spirit in New England with the lack of same in Pennsylvania and New Jersey. On the battle, see Richard Ketcham, **Saratoga** (New York, 1997), and Phillips, **Cousins' War**, 269–314.

48. Washington to Horatio Gates, 30 October 1777,

PWR 12:59–60; Washington to Alexander Hamilton, 30 October 1777, ibid., 60–62. Gates resisted Washington's order and Hamilton found himself caught in a quandary as Gates claimed that he reported to the Continental Congress and not to Washington.

49. The best brief narratives of the whispering campaign, and what subsequently became known as the Conway Cabal, are in Higginbotham, **War of American Independence,** 216–22, and Royster, **A Revolutionary People at War,** 179–89. John Adams to Abigail Adams, 26 October 1777, **AFC** 2:361.

50. Du Condray's dramatic demise is described in the editorial note in **PWR** 11:254–55; Washington to Benjamin Franklin, 17 August 1777, **PWR** 10:647–49, for the political problem posed by the extravagant expectations of French volunteers; Washington to Richard Henry Lee, 16 October 1777, **PWR** 11:529–30, on Conway's self-importance.

51. Washington to Thomas Conway, 5 November 1777, **PWR** 12:129–30; Conway to Washington, 5 November 1777, ibid., 130–31; Horatio Gates to Washington, 8 December 1777, ibid., 576–77. Conway has few scholarly defenders, but Gates does. See Samuel W. Patterson, **Horatio Gates: Defender of American Liberties** (New York, 1941).

52. Nathanael Greene to Washington, 24 November 1777, **PWR** 12:377–78; Henry Knox to Washington, 26 November 1777, ibid., 414–17. See also, Council of War, 8 November 1777, ibid., 163.

53. Nathanael Greene to Washington, 24 November 1777, ibid., 379–80.

54. Nathanael Greene to Washington, 3 December 1777, ibid., 518–21.

55. General Orders, 17 December 1777, ibid., 620–21.

CHAPTER FOUR

1. On Great Britain's development of the capacity to wage war, see John Brewer, **The Sinews of Power: War, Money, and the British State, 1688–1783** (New York, 1988). See also Stephen Conway, **The British Isles and the War of American Independence** (New York, 2000), which argues that popular support for the war within the middle levels of British society was both voluntary and stronger than previously realized. My own sense is that the eighteenth-century British state was more coercive.

2. Washington to Henry Laurens, 23 December 1777, 12:683.

3. Washington to Nathanael Greene, 6 February 1783, **WW** 26:104; Washington to Robert Howe, **WW** 10:301–2.

4. Washington to William Gordon, 8 July 1783, **WW** 27:51–52.

5. Washington to John Bannister, 21 April 1778, **WW** 11:291–92. The reference to Lincoln was first suggested by Charles Royster in "Founding a Nation in Blood: Military Conflict and American Nationality," Hoffman and Albert, **Arms and Independence**, 26–49. On Valley Forge more generally, see Royster, **A Revolutionary People**, 190–254; E. Wayne Carp, **To Starve the Army at Pleasure: Continental Army Administration and American Political Culture, 1775–1783** (Chapel

Hill, 1984), 56–72, 116–24; Wayne K. Bodle and Jacqueline Thibault, **Valley Forge Historical Research Report,** 3 vols. (Valley Forge, 1980); and Wayne K. Bodle, **The Valley Forge Winter: Civilians and Soldiers in War** (University Park, PA, 2002), which contests the influence of Steuben.

6. Washington to Committee of Congress, 29 January 1778, **WW** 10:363–64. On the altered composition of the Continental army, see Robert K. Wright, " 'Nor Is Their Standing Army to Be Despised': The Emergence of the Continental Army as a Military Institution," Hoffman and Albert, **Arms and Independence,** 50–74.

7. Royster, **A Revolutionary People,** 200–4; Wright, **Continental Army,** 91–120.

8. Joseph Plumb Martin, **A Narrative of a Revolutionary Soldier: Some of the Adventures, Dangers, and Sufferings of Joseph Plumb Martin** (New York, 2001), 121, previously published as **Private Yankee Doodle.** For the Pennsylvania almanac and other celebrations of Washington in 1778–79, see Don Higginbotham, **George Washington: Uniting a Nation** (Lanham, MD, 2002), 7–14.

9. Royster, **A Revolutionary People,** 197–210. For the regulation against dueling, see General Orders, 26 January 1778, **WW** 10:351. I would argue that Valley Forge became the honor-driven place where dueling first became a fixture in national politics. See Joanne B. Freeman, **Affairs of Honor: National Politics in the New Republic** (New Haven, 2001).

10. Jean Edward Smith, **John Marshall: Definer of a Nation** (New York, 1996), 61–65.

11. See the correspondence in **PWR** 11:4–5, 12:409, for Washington's initial impression of Lafayette. See also Louis R. Gottschalk, **Lafayette Joins the American Army** (Chicago, 1937).

12. Washington to Lafayette, 25 September 1778, **WW** 12:500–4; 30 September 1779, **WW** 16:368–76, for typical expressions of affection and playful banter.

13. Royster, **A Revolutionary People,** 213–54; Wright, **Continental Army,** 121–52; Washington to Baron Steuben, 26 February 1779, **WW** 14:151–53.

14. The quotation is in Washington to William Gordon, 23 January 1778, **WW** 10:338. For Washington's growing awareness of Mifflin's mischievous role, see his letters in **WW** 10:410–11, 462–63, 528–29; **WW** 11:275–76. The standard biography is Kenneth R. Rossman, **Thomas Mifflin and the Politics of the American Revolution** (Chapel Hill, 1952).

15. Washington to Henry Laurens, 3 October 1778, **WW** 13:15–16; for the forgeries, Washington to Richard Henry Lee, 25 May 1778, **WW** 11:450.

16. Thoughts Upon a Plan of Operation for Campaign 1778, 31 March 1778, **WW** 11:185–94; Council of War, 24 June 1778, and Charles Lee to Washington, 25 June 1778, **WW** 12:115–19. On Lafayette's blunder, see Alexander Hamilton to Washington, 26 June 1778, and Washington to Lafayette, 26 June 1778, ibid., 120–23.

17. George W. P. Custis, **Recollections and Private Memories of Washington** (New York, 1860), 224.

18. Martin, **Narrative of a Revolutionary Soldier,** 115.

19. For critical assessments of Lee's behavior, see John Laurens to Henry Laurens, 30 June and 2 July 1778, John Rhodehamel, ed., **The American Revolution: Writings from the War of Independence** (New York, 2001), 470–75, and Washington to Charles Lee, 30 June 1778, **WW** 12:132–33. For a soldier's recollection of Washington's anger upon reaching Lee in retreat, see Martin, **Narrative of a Revolutionary Soldier,** 110–11. The fullest defense of Lee is Theodore Thayer, **The Making of a Scapegoat: Washington and Lee at Monmouth** (Point Washington, NY, 1976). Ferling, **The First of Men,** 247–48, also tends to exonerate Lee.

20. Washington to Thomas Nelson, 20 August 1778, **WW** 12:343.

21. Washington to d'Estaing, 29 September 1778, **WW** 12:516–18, Washington to d'Estaing, 2 October 1778, **WW** 13:9–13. On the futile effort at Rhode Island, see Washington to John Sullivan, 28 August 1778, **WW** 12:369.

22. Washington to d'Estaing, 4 October 1779 and 7 October 1779, **WW** 16:408–14, 428–29. See also Washington to Nathanael Greene, 14 July 1780, **WW** 19:169.

23. For the deployment of the army and the fixation on New York, see the correspondence in **WW** 13:178–80, 346–47; **WW** 19:104–5, 174–76, 235, 391–94, 403–4, 481–83; **WW** 20:76–81.

24. Washington to Henry Laurens, 14 November 1778, **WW** 13:254–57. For his strenuous opposition to a Canadian campaign, see Washington to the President of Congress, 11 November 1778, ibid., 223–44.

25. Washington to John Sullivan, 31 May 1779, **WW** 15:189–93. The extensive planning for the western campaign can be followed in **WW** 13:501–2; **WW** 14:199–201, 278–81, 314–18. The success of the campaign is assessed in **WW** 16:242, 293, 347–48.

26. Washington to the President of Congress, 15 March 1779, **WW** 14:243–44. For Washington's effort to comprehend the British strategy in 1778, see the correspondence in **WW** 13:35–37, 85–87, 463; **WW** 16:240–41.

27. Washington to Benjamin Harrison, 5–7 May 1779, **WW** 15:5–11; Washington to Joseph Reed, 28 May 1780, **WW** 18:434–35; Washington to William Livingston, 4 May 1779, **WW** 14:489–92. The authoritative work on the creation of the British war machine over the course of the eighteenth century is Brewer, **Sinews of Power.** The final quotation is from Washington to James Duane, 1 October 1780, **WW** 20:117.

28. Washington to Benjamin Harrison, 18–30 December 1778, **WW** 13:466–68; Washington to Joseph Reed, 12 December 1778, ibid., 382–85; Washington to Gouverneur Morris, 4 October 1778, ibid., 21–22, Washington to William Fitzhugh, 10 April 1779, **WW** 14:363–65. This litany continues in **WW** 13:79–81, 334–37; **WW** 14:26–32, 246, 298–302; **WW** 15:23–26, 57–62, 293; **WW** 16:15–19, 51–53; **WW** 17:72–73.

29. Washington to Joseph Jones, 31 May 1780, **WW** 18:453; Washington to Fielding Lewis, 6 July 1780, **WW** 19:131. See also, along the same theme, **WW** 17:425–28; **WW** 18:207–11; **WW** 21:13–16, 318–21.

30. Circular to the States, 27 August 1780, **WW** 19:450–51; Washington to George Mason, 22 October 1780, **WW** 20:242; Washington to the President of Congress, 20 June 1780, **WW** 19:35.

31. Washington to James Bowdoin, 14 June 1780, **WW** 19:9; Washington to the President of Congress, 15 September 1780, **WW** 20:49–50; Washington to Nathanael Greene, 13 December 1780, **WW** 20:469–71. For more on his reaction to the fall of Charleston, see also **WW** 18:463–506.

32. Washington to Nathanael Greene, 25 September 1780, **WW** 20:84–85. See also General Orders, 26 September 1780, ibid., 95, and Charles Royster, " 'The Nature of Treason': Revolutionary Virtue and American Reactions to Benedict Arnold," **WMQ** 36 (1979), 163–93. For André's trial and execution, see Washington to Board of General Officers, 29 September 1780, **WW** 20:101; General Orders, 1 October 1780, ibid., 109–10; Washington to the President of Congress, 17 October 1780, ibid., 130–31.

33. Washington to Anthony Wayne, 3–4 January 1781, **WW** 22:55–58; Circular to the States, 5 January 1781, ibid., 51–53; Washington to the Commissioners for Redressing the Grievances of the New Jersey Line, 27 January 1781, ibid., 147–48; General Orders, 30 January 1781, ibid., 158–60. See also correspondence on the mutinies in **WW** 21:71, 123–24, 128, 132, 135. See also James Kirby Martin, " 'A Most Undisciplined, Profligate Crew': Protest and Defiance in the Continental Ranks, 1776–1783," in Hoffman and Albert, **Arms and Independence**, 119–40.

34. Washington to John Laurens, 9 April 1781, **WW** 21:438–40.

35. The quotation is from Piers Mackesy, **The War for America, 1775–1783** (Cambridge, MA, 1964), 434.

36. Conference with Count Rochambeau, 23 May 1781, **WW** 22:105–7; Circular to the States, 24 May 1781, ibid., 9–11. For the naval dilemma, see Jonathan R. Dull, **The French Navy and American Independence: A Study of Arms and Diplomacy, 1774–1787** (Princeton, 1975).

37. Theodore Thayer, **Nathanael Greene: Strategist of the Revolution** (New York, 1960), and John S. Pancake, **This Destructive War: The British Campaign in the Carolinas, 1780–1782** (Tuscaloosa, 1985), are the standard works. On Guilford Court House, see Washington to Rochambeau, 3 April 1781, **WW** 21:402–3.

38. For Washington's response to the British successes in Virginia, see Washington to Rochambeau, 7 June 1781, **WW** 22:171.

39. Washington confided to Lafayette that his greatest fear was an inconclusive campaign in 1781, leading to a negotiated settlement based on the current deployment of both armies. See Washington to Lafayette, 30 July 1781, **WW** 22:431–32.

40. Washington to Joseph Jones, 7 June 1781, **WW** 22:178–79; Washington to Thomas Jefferson, 8 June 1781, ibid., 181–82. Memorandum, 1 May 1781, ibid., 23; Henry Clinton to George Germain, 9 June 1781, in ibid., 132, where Clinton claims to have learned "most perfect knowledge of the designs of the Enemy." For his later claim about a southern campaign, see Washington

to Noah Webster, 31 July 1788, **PWCF** 6:413–15. See also **Diaries** 3:375. Washington resumed making entries in his diary in the spring of 1781 after several years of neglect.

41. See the editorial note in **WW** 22:208 for Rochambeau's letter to de Grasse, urging the French admiral to sail for the Chesapeake rather than New York; **Diaries** 3:403; Washington to Robert Morris, 2 August 1781, **WW** 22:450–51. See also Washington to Lafayette, 30 July 1781, ibid., 432–33.

42. Washington to de Grasse, 17 August 1781, **WW** 23:7–10; Washington to Lafayette, 2 September 1781, ibid., 75. See also Washington to William Greene, 22–24 August 1781, ibid., 46.

43. Washington to Robert Howe, 24 September 1781, ibid., 132. See also Washington to de Grasse, 6 September 1781, ibid., 92–93.

44. General Orders, 5 October 1781, ibid., 179–85; Washington to President of Congress, 12 October 1781, ibid., 212–13. See also Lee Kennett, **The French Forces in America, 1780–83** (Westport, 1977), 48–141.

45. Martin, **Narrative of a Revolutionary Soldier,** 198–99.

46. Washington to Cornwallis, 18 October 1781, **WW** 23:237–38; Washington to President of Congress, ibid., 241–44; **Diaries** 3:429–30; Washington to de Grasse, 20 October 1781, ibid., 248–50.

47. **Diaries** 3:432–33, which contains editorial notes on the surrender ceremony; Martin, **Narrative of a Revolutionary Soldier,** 206–8, which is especially good on the released slaves; Washington to David Ross, 24 Octo-

ber 1781, **WW** 23:262, on the policy toward the slaves; for Jackie's illness and death, see **Diaries** 3:437 and Washington to President of Congress, 6 November 1781, **WW** 23:338.

48. Washington to James McHenry, 12 September 1782, **WW** 25:151; Washington to Jonathan Trumbull, 28 November 1781, **WW** 23:359–60; Circular to the States, 19 December 1781, ibid., 397–99.

49. Washington to Thomas Paine, 18 September 1782, **WW** 25:176–77; Washington to Nathanael Greene, 6 August 1782, **WW** 24:471. For Washington's insistence on remaining prepared to renew the war, see the correspondence in **WW** 24:63, 121–25, 243; **WW** 25:265.

50. Washington addressed the persistent rumors about his Cromwellian intentions in Washington to William Gordon, 2 August 1779 and 23 October 1782, **WW** 16:39; 25:287. See also the editorial note, reproducing John Sullivan's report on a sermon in Boston warning of Washington's dictatorial power, in **WW** 17:266–67.

51. Washington to Alexander Hamilton, 2 May 1780, **WW** 18:320, asking Hamilton to respond to charges about his provocative remarks.

52. Washington to Lewis Nicola, 22 May 1782, **WW** 24:272–73, which also reproduces sections of Nicola's letter to Washington. For the remark by George III, see Garry Wills, **Cincinnatus: George Washington and the Enlightenment** (Garden City, 1984), 13.

53. Washington to Benjamin Harrison, 4 March 1783, **WW** 26:184–85.

54. Washington to James Bowdoin, 26 April 1780, **WW** 18:298, on executive power; Washington to Arthur Lee, 29 March 1783, **WW** 26:265–66; Washington to Alexander Hamilton, 31 March 1783, ibid., 276–77. And these are but a few of the multiple letters on this theme.

55. Washington to John Armstrong, 10 January 1783, **WW** 26:26–27; Washington to Alexander Hamilton, 4 March 1783, ibid., 185–88.

56. The authoritative work on the Newburgh Conspiracy is Richard H. Kohn, **Eagle and Sword: The Beginnings of the Military Establishment in America** (New York, 1975), 17–39. See also the scholarly article by Kohn, "The Inside History of the Newburgh Conspiracy: America and the Coup d'Etat," **WMQ** 27 (1970), 187–220. Washington himself believed that the conspiracy originated in the Congress and apprised Hamilton, who was probably implicated, that "there is something very mysterious in this business." See Washington to Alexander Hamilton, 12 March 1783, **WW** 26:217.

57. To the Officers of the Army, 15 March 1783, **WW** 26:224.

58. The most recent and best assessment of Washington's understanding of republicanism, which was narrow but deep, is Glenn A. Phelps, "The Republican General," **GWR** 165–97.

59. To the Officers of the Army, 15 March 1783, **WW** 26:222–23. See Washington to David Rittenhouse, 16 February 1783, ibid., 136, thanking him for the glasses, and ibid., 76, for a description of the New

disagreement among the wit-
Washington's gesture with the
re, which places it at the start
sense to me.

States, 8 June 1783, **WW**

ayette, 12 October 1783, **WW**

States, 8 June 1783, **WW**
miracle" remark comes from
Armies of the United States,
27:223.

o the Armies of the United
, ibid., 224–27. The army was
November 1783.
ss on Resigning His Commis-
, ibid., 284–86.

CHAPTER FIVE

1. Francis Hopkinson, **Miscellaneous Essays**, 2 vols. (Philadelphia, 1792), 1:120.

2. Washington to Henry Knox, 20 February 1785, **PWCF** 1:136–39; Washington to Tench Tilghman, 24 April 1783, **WW** 26:358; Washington to Lucretia Will-hemenia van Winter, 30 March 1785, **PWCF** 2:473.

3. Washington to Charles Thomson, 22 January 1784, **PWCF** 1:71–72; Jean Le Mayeur to Washington, 20 January 1784, ibid., 63–64; Washington to William Fitzhugh, 15 May 1786, **PWCF** 4:52; editorial note on visit to Mount Vernon by Elkanah Watson, 19–20 January 1785, **PWCF** 2:457. There is some circumstantial

evidence that Washington obtained the teeth for his new implants by purchasing them from his slaves. See Wiencek, **Imperfect God**, 112–13.

4. Washington to Lafayette, 8 December 1784, **PWCF** 2:175–76. On the aging theme and physical deterioration, see also the correspondence in **PWCF** 2:386–90, **PWCF** 3:50, **PWCF** 4:126.

5. Lee's irreverent request is from his will, quoted in the editorial note, **PWCF** 1:401. Washington's response to the deaths of close friends is in **PWCF** 4:39–40, 154, 183–85, 298–99.

6. John Adams to Abigail Adams, 14 January 1797, quoted in Ellis, **American Sphinx: The Character of Thomas Jefferson**, 119.

7. Washington to Benjamin Harrison, 18 January 1784, **PWCF** 1:56–57; on his Ciceronian vision of a rustic retirement, see Washington to Armand, 7 October 1785, **PWCF** 3:296.

8. W. W. Abbot, "An Uncommon Awareness of Self: The Papers of George Washington," **GWR**, 275–86; for the larger theme of fame as a form of immortality in the revolutionary era, see the seminal essay by Douglass Adair, "Fame and the Founding Fathers," Trevor Colbourn, ed., **Fame and the Founding Fathers: Essays by Douglass Adair** (New York, 1974), 3–26.

9. Washington to Richard Varick, 24 May 1781, **WW** 22:112; Washington to Richard Varick, 31 December 1781, **WW** 23:417; Washington to Richard Varick, 1 January 1784, plus the excellent editorial note on the Varick project, **PWCF** 1:2–4.

10. Washington to James Craik, 24 March 1784, **PWCF** 1:234–36.

11. Washington to William Gordon, 8 March 1784 and 8 May 1784, **PWCF** 1:177–78, 326–27; Washington to William Gordon, 8 March 1785, **PWCF** 2:411–13.

12. Washington to Henry Knox, 5 January 1785, **PWCF** 2:253–56.

13. For Lear's qualifications, see Benjamin Lincoln to Washington, 4 January 1786, **PWCF** 3:492–93. For Humphreys, see Rosemarie Zagarri, **David Humphreys' "Life of General Washington" with George Washington's Remarks** (Athens, GA, 1991).

14. Humphreys's historical sketch, along with Washington's comments on specific biographical facts, can be found in **PWCF** 5:514–26.

15. Washington to Francis Hopkinson, 16 May 1785, **PWCF** 2:561–62, Pine's visit to Mount Vernon is described in the editorial note, 508–9; Houdon arrived at Mount Vernon on 20 October 1785; his appointment to do the statue is recorded in Thomas Jefferson to Washington, 10 December 1784, ibid., 176–78; Washington to Lafayette, 28 May 1788, **PWCF** 6:297–98.

16. Washington to Richard Henderson, 19 June 1788, **PWCF** 6:339–42; Washington to Thomas Jefferson, 25 February 1785, **PWCF** 2:379–82.

17. The quotations from **Potomac Magazine** are in Kenneth Bowling, **The Creation of Washington, D.C.: The Idea and Location of the American Capital** (Fairfax, VA, 1991), 164–66. Washington to Robert Morris,

1 February 1785, **PWCF** 2:313; Washington to William Grayson, 22 June 1785, **PWCF** 3:69; Washington to David Humphreys, 25 July 1785, ibid., 150–51. Though the Potomac remained his abiding infatuation, reflected in multiple letters on its prowess and promise, Washington glimpsed the possibility that an alternative route through New York and the Great Lakes might prove more practical. See Washington to William Irvine, 18 February 1788, **PWCF** 6:117.

18. Washington to Richard Henry Lee, 15 March 1785, **PWCF** 2:437–38; Washington to Jacob Read, 3 November 1784, **PWCF** 2:121; Washington to Benjamin Harrison, 10 October 1784, ibid., 92.

19. Washington to Henry Lee Jr., 18 June 1786, **PWCF** 4:117–18.

20. For Washington's various parcels of western land, see the editorial note, **PWCF** 2:338–56.

21. For the resolution of his moral dilemma about accepting stock in the Potomac River Company and James River Company, see Washington to Patrick Henry, 29 October 1785, **PWCF** 3:326–27.

22. The extensive legal haggling concerning his land in western Pennsylvania is nicely summarized in the editorial note, **PWP** 1:53–54. Representative pieces of correspondence on this protracted court case are in **PWCF** 1:500; **PWCF** 2:78–80; **PWCF** 3:38–39, 246, 438–39. See also **Diaries** 4:1–71, for his trip to visit his lands in the fall of 1784.

23. Henry Knox to Washington, 21 February 1784, **PWCF** 1:142–44; Washington to Henry Knox, 28 March 1784, ibid., 229–30. Franklin's satiric remarks on

the society are in Benjamin Franklin to Sarah Bache, 26 January 1785, Albert H. Smyth, **The Writings of Benjamin Franklin,** 10 vols. (New York, 1905–7), 8:202–3.

24. General Meeting of the Society of the Cincinnati, 4–18 March 1784, **PWCF** 1:328–69; see especially the editorial note on Washington's thinking prior to the meeting, ibid., 351–52; Thomas Jefferson to Washington, 16 April 1784, ibid., 287–92; Washington to Jonathan Trumbull, 4 April 1784, ibid., 260–61.

25. Washington to Philip Schuyler, 15 May 1784, ibid., 364; Thomas Jefferson to Washington, 14 November 1786, **PWCF** 4:364–65.

26. David Humphreys to Washington, 24 September 1786, ibid., 264–65.

27. Washington to William Barton, 7 September 1788, **PWCF** 6:501–3; see also Nathanael Greene to Washington, 29 August 1784, **PWCF** 2:59–61, and Washington to Samuel Vaughn, 30 November 1785, **PWCF** 3:426–27.

28. Robert Pleasants to Washington, 11 December 1785, ibid., 449–51.

29. Dorothy Twohig, " 'That Species of Property': Washington's Role in the Controversy Over Slavery," **GWR,** 114–38, which provided the most recent synthesis of scholarship on this crucial subject until the publication of Wiencek, **Imperfect God,** which appeared in time to influence my revisions of this chapter.

30. Washington to Henry Laurens, 20 March 1779, **WW** 14:267; Washington to Henry Laurens, 10 July 1782, **WW** 24:421.

31. Washington to Lafayette, 5 April 1783, **WW**

26:300; see also Lafayette to Washington, 14 July 1785, **PWCF** 3:121.

32. Washington to David Ross, 24 October 1781, **WW** 23:262, for the Yorktown decision; Commissioners of Embarkation at New York to Washington, 18 January 1784, **PWCF** 1:50–56, for the New York decision.

33. Washington to Robert Morris, 12 April 1786, **PWCF** 4:15–16; Washington to Lafayette, 10 May 1786, ibid., 43–44; Washington to John Francis Mercer, 9 September 1786, ibid., 243.

34. Washington to Lund Washington, 24–26 February 1779, **WW** 14:147–49.

35. My own treatment of the economic problems Washington faced at Mount Vernon in the pre-revolutionary years can be found above in chapter two. The best of the recent studies is Bruce A. Ragsdale, "George Washington, the British Tobacco Trade, and Economic Opportunity in Pre-Revolutionary Virginia," **GWR**, 67–93. The argument being offered here is that the marginal status of his farms at Mount Vernon before the war declined further after the war, a condition from which they never recovered despite heroic efforts by Washington to diversify his crops and pursue the latest methods of fertilization and cultivation. His assiduous pursuit of overdue rental fees on his western properties in the 1780s reflected his increasing dependence on those revenues for his annual income. By the end of the decade he was forced to borrow money and consider the sale of several western parcels to meet his annual expenses. On the latter score, see Washington to David Stuart,

2 December 1788, **PWP** 1:149, and Washington to Richard Conway, 8 March 1789, ibid., 361–62.

36. For the size of the slave population at Mount Vernon, see List of Tithables, April 1788, **PWCF** 6:304–5, and Farm Reports, 1785–86, **PWCF** 3:389–410. The latter shows there were 216 slaves on his five Mount Vernon farms in February 1786.

37. William Gordon to Washington, 30 August 1784, **PWCF** 2:65–66. On his commitment to keep slave families intact, see Washington to William Fowler, 2 February 1788, **PWCF** 6:77–78; see also the editorial note, **PWCF** 4:464, and Washington to Burwell Bassett Jr., 9 March 1788, **PWCF** 6:149.

38. Washington to John Francis Mercer, 19 December 1786, **PWCF** 4:464. He broke his vow never to purchase another slave on several special occasions: once to accept slaves as partial payment on a debt; once to purchase slaves from the Dandridge estate whom Martha had known and who would otherwise have been sold without concern for family connections; and once to obtain skilled artisans for work on Mount Vernon's final renovation. See John Francis Mercer, 6 November 1786, **PWCF** 6:386; Washington to Burwell Bassett Jr., 9 March 1788, ibid., 149; Washington to Henry Lee Jr., 6 November 1786, **PWCF** 5:10–11.

39. Washington to Lund Washington, 7 May 1787, ibid., 173; Washington to David Stuart, 2 December 1788, **PWP** 1:149; James Bloxam to William Peacey, 23 July 1786, **PWCF** 4:194; Washington to John Fairfax, 1 January 1789, **PWP** 1:223.

40. Unknown Author to Washington, 15 July 1784, **PWCF** 1:504–26.

41. Washington to Alexander Hamilton, 31 March 1783, **WW** 26:276–77; Washington to James Warren, 7 October 1785, **PWCF** 3:299; Washington to Jacob Read, 11 August 1784, **PWCF** 2:29–30; Washington to Henry Knox, 5 December 1784, ibid., 170–72.

42. The seminal study of republican ideology as a defiant repudiation of consolidated power is Bernard Bailyn, **Ideological Origins of the American Revolution** (Cambridge, 1967); as applied to the 1780s, the authoritative work is Gordon Wood, **The Creation of the American Republic** (Chapel Hill, 1969). The best collection of recent scholarly opinion on the question of "the critical period" is Richard Beeman, Stephen Botein, Edward Carter, eds., **Beyond Confederation: Origins of the Constitution and American National Identity** (Chapel Hill, 1987).

43. Washington to James Madison, 30 November 1785, **PWCF** 3:420.

44. Washington to Lafayette, 15 August 1785, **PWCF** 5:215; see also on the same theme Henry Knox to Washington, 31 January 1785, **PWCF** 2:302, and Washington to William Grayson, 26 July 1786, **PWCF** 4:169.

45. John Jay to Washington, 16 March 1786, **PWCF** 3:601–2; Washington to John Jay, 18 May 1786, **PWCF** 4:55–56; John Jay to Washington, 27 June 1786, ibid., 130–32; Washington to John Jay, 15 August 1786, ibid., 212–13.

46. The lengthy quotation is from Washington to

Henry Lee Jr., 31 October 1786, ibid., 318. Multiple reports on Shays's Rebellion poured into Mount Vernon and can be found in ibid., 240–41, 281–82, 297, 300–1, 417–36, 460–62. Two recent scholarly studies of Shays's Rebellion are Robert A. Feer, **Shays' Rebellion** (New York, 1988), and Leonard R. Richards, **Shays' Rebellion: The American Revolution's Final Battle** (Philadelphia, 2002).

47. Washington to the Society of the Cincinnati, 31 October 1786, **PWCF** 4:316–17; Washington to James Madison, 18 November 1786, ibid., 382–83; Washington to James Madison, 16 December 1786, ibid., 457–59.

48. Edmund Randolph to Washington, 6 December 1786, ibid., 445; see also James Madison to Washington, 7 December 1786, ibid., 445.

49. Washington to Edmund Randolph, 9 April 1787, **PWCF**, 5:135–36.

50. Henry Knox to Washington, 14 January 1787, **PWCF** 4:518–23; David Humphreys to Washington, 20 January 1787, ibid., 526–30; Washington to Henry Knox, 3 February 1787, **PWCF** 5:7–9; Washington to Henry Knox, 25 February 1787, ibid., 52–53.

51. Henry Knox to Washington, 19 March 1787, ibid., 95–98; Washington to Henry Knox, 8 March 1787, ibid., 74–75.

52. James Madison to Washington, 18 March 1787, ibid., 94–95; Washington to Edmund Randolph, 28 March 1787, ibid., 112–14; Washington to James Madison, 31 March 1787, ibid., 114–17.

53. Notes on the Sentiments on the Government of

John Jay, Henry Knox, and James Madison, April 1787, ibid., 163–66.

54. John Jay to Washington, 7 January 1787, **PWCF** 4:502–4.

55. James Madison to Washington, 16 April 1787, **PWCF** 5:144–50.

56. Jefferson, 30 May 1787, ibid., 208.

57. Editorial note on 17 September 1787, ibid., 331–32. Two recent books on the Constitutional Convention effectively synthesize decades of scholarship: Carol Berkin, **A Brilliant Solution: Inventing the American Constitution** (New York, 2002); Jack Rakove, **Original Meanings: Politics and Ideas in the Making of the Constitution** (New York, 1997).

58. On the confidentiality theme, see Washington to David Stuart, 1 July 1787, ibid., 240. For his meticulous recording of temperatures, dinners, purchases, etc., see **Diaries** 5:152–87. For correspondence about planting instructions, see **PWCF** 5:241–43. For an account of expenditures in Philadelphia, see Cash Accounts, 27 May to 18 September 1787, ibid., 173–81, and ibid., 239, for three sittings for Charles Willson Peale in early July. For public response to his appearance on Market Street on 4 June 1787, see ibid., 219.

59. Washington to Alexander Hamilton, 10 July 1787, ibid., 257.

60. Washington to Henry Knox, 19 August 1787, ibid., 297; Washington to Lafayette, 18 September 1787, ibid., 334.

61. On the Constitution as a purposely and necessar-

ily ambiguous document, see John Murrin, "A Roof without Walls: The Dilemma of American National Identity," Beeman, Botein, and Carter, eds., **Beyond Confederation,** 334–38. My own effort to make the same argument is in **Founding Brothers: The Revolutionary Generation** (New York, 2001), 13–17, 91–96.

62. On the incident at Head of Elk, see Robert Morris to Washington, 25 October 1787, **PWCF** 5:370–71; on the purchase of **Don Quixote,** see the editorial note, ibid., 419; Alexander Hamilton to Washington, 13 August 1788, **PWCF** 6:444.

63. Washington to Alexander Hamilton, 28 August 1788, ibid., 480–81.

64. Washington to William Gordon, 1 January 1788, ibid., 1; Washington to Thomas Jefferson, 1 January 1788, ibid., 2–4; Washington to Edmund Randolph, 8 January 1788, ibid., 17–18; Washington to Lafayette, 18 June 1788, ibid., 337; Washington to Bushrod Washington, 9 November 1787, **PWCF** 5:422.

65. Washington to Charles Petit, 16 August 1788, **PWCF** 6:447–48; Washington to Lafayette, 7 February 1788, ibid., 95–97; Washington to Nathaniel Gorman, 21 July 1788, ibid., 373; Washington to Benjamin Lincoln, 26 October 1788, **PWP** 1:72; Washington to Henry Lee Jr., 22 September 1788, **PWCF** 6:531; Washington to Alexander Hamilton, 3 October 1788, **PWP** 1:31–33; Washington to Henry Knox, 1 April 1789, **PWP** 2:2.

66. Washington to William Pierce, 1 January 1789, **PWP** 1:227–28; Washington to Lafayette, 29 January

1789, ibid., 262–64; for consultations with Humphreys about the draft of his inaugural address, see the editorial note, **PWP** 2:152–57.

67. Address to Charles Thomson, 14 April 1789, ibid., 56–57.

68. James McHenry to Washington, 29 March 1789, **PWP** 1:461.

69. Gouverneur Morris to Washington, 23 February 1789, ibid., 339; editorial note on the draft inaugural address, **PWP** 2:162; Washington to Henry Knox, 29 January 1789, **PWP** 1:260–61.

70. For the trip from Mount Vernon to New York, see **PWP** 2:60–158. An excellent scholarly account of the procession, containing the various toasts, odes, poems, and tributes at each location, is in Kenneth Silverman, **A Cultural History of the American Revolution** (New York, 1976), 604–7. Apparently there was at least one sour note during the procession, an article critical of Washington's royal entourage, as well as his status as a slave owner, which depicted him mounted on his beloved jackass in the arms of Billy Lee. See the editorial note in **PWP** 2:115.

71. Editorial note, 30 April 1789, ibid., 155–57.

72. Washington to Lafayette, 18 June 1788, **PWCF** 6:338. The inaugural address emphasized Washington's sense of inadequacy for the task and contained one memorable phrase, the desire to preserve "the sacred fire of liberty." As with his acceptance of the position as commander in chief, Washington offered to decline any salary and receive only compensation for expenses. See **PWP** 2:173–77.

CHAPTER SIX

1. **PWP** 8:493. See David C. Hendrickson, **Peace Pact: The Lost World of the American Founding** (Lawrence, 2003), for the fullest and most recent assessment of the absence of national unity after the Revolution.

2. James MacGregor Burns and Susan Dunn graciously allowed me to read their unpublished manuscript on the Washington presidency, **George Washington,** which is excellent at placing it in the context of "presidential history." The standard single-volume account is Forrest McDonald, **The Presidency of George Washington** (Lawrence, 1974), which I found eccentric. More readable and reliable as a narrative is Richard Norton Smith, **Patriarch: George Washington and the New American Nation** (Boston, 1993). For its combination of analysis and intellectual sweep, the relevant chapters in Stanley Elkins and Eric McKitrick, **The Age of Federalism: The Early American Republic** (New York, 1993), set the standard.

3. David Stuart to Washington, 14 July 1789, **PWP** 3:198–204, which discusses Henry's hostility to the power of the executive under the Constitution and cites the famous remark about monarchy.

4. See the correspondence and editorial notes in **PWP** 3:76–77, 536–37; **PWP** 4:1–2; **PWO** 5:393–400, 515; **PWP** 10:5–10.

5. Editorial note, **PWP** 2:205–6, for Martha's comment.

6. The letters home to Mount Vernon are too copious to cite in their entirety. For illustrative examples, see

PWP 3:472–76; **PWP** 11:273–78, 330–34; **WW** 32:297–308, 463–68.

7. The biographer referred to here is Marcus Cunliffe, whose **George Washington: Man and Monument** (Boston, 1958) makes the case in its title as well as its text that Washington's private personality was overwhelmed by his public role.

8. **PWP** 10:535–37, for Jefferson's conversation with Washington in which retirement after two years is suggested.

9. **PWP** 2:192–95, 211–14, 245–50; **PWP** 3:321–27, 391.

10. **PWP** 5:70–72, 110, 131, 388.

11. **PWP** 3:521–27, where an extensive editorial note synthesizes the several firsthand reports on the Senate imbroglio.

12. **PWP** 4:163, for editorial notes on the tour. See also ibid., 200–1, for a map of the tour; **PWP** 6:284–86, for the address to the Hebrew congregation in Newport.

13. **PWP** 7:472–85, for the itinerary of the southern tour; for Prescott and Cornwallis, see **PWP** 8:23, 201, 260.

14. Ibid., 73–74.

15. On Madison's major role during the early months of Washington's presidency, see **PWP** 2:214–16, 419; **PWP** 3:387; **PWP** 4:3–5, 67–68, 125–27, 307–12. More generally, see Stuart Leibeger, **Founding Friendship: George Washington, James Madison, and the Creation of the American Republic** (Charlottesville, 1999).

16. Thomas Jefferson to Washington, 15 December 1789, **PWP** 4:412–13.

17. Washington to Lafayette, 3 June 1790, **PWP** 5:468.

18. Washington to John Jay, 5 October 1789, **PWP** 4:137.

19. Ibid., 76–80, for the editors' synthesis of the scholarship on the Judiciary Act. See also Elkins and McKitrick, **Age of Federalism,** 62–63.

20. I have written about this episode more fully in **Founding Brothers: The Revolutionary Generation** (New York, 2000), 81–119.

21. Warner Mifflin to Washington, 12 March 1790, **PWP** 5:222–24.

22. Washington to David Stuart, 15 June 1790, ibid., 525.

23. Washington to Tobias Lear, 12 April 1791, **PWP** 8:84–86; Tobias Lear to Washington, 24 April 1791, ibid., 132.

24. **PWP** 3:1–31; 265–89.

25. **Hamilton** 6:51–168, which includes a helpful editorial note on the economic technicalities of the **Report.**

26. Beverley Randolph to Washington, 4 January 1791, **PWP** 7:178.

27. On the routine character of business between Hamilton and Washington, see **PWP** 4:520–26; **PWP** 6:413–15, 477–80. On Washington's view of the Virginia campaign against Hamilton's program, see **PWP** 5:286–88, 523–28.

28. **PWP** 7:331–37, 348–58, 395–97, 422–52.

29. Kenneth R. Bowling, **The Creation of Washington, D.C.: The Idea and Location of the American**

Capital (Fairfax, 1991), x–xi, 148, 196. See my assessment in **Founding Brothers**, 69–80.

30. PWP 6:71–73, 368–70, 370–72, 434–37, 463–65.

31. PWP 7:161–68, 258–59, 547–50, 585–86, 589–90; **PWP** 8:27–38, 506–8; **PWO** 9:209–13, 452–68, 603–4; **PWP** 10:62–67. See the excellent article by C. M. Harris, "Washington's Gamble, L'Enfant's Dream: Politics, Design, and the Founding of the National Capital," **WMQ** 56 (July 1999), 527–64.

32. Rochambeau to Washington, 11 April 1790, **PWP** 5:326; Washington to Rochambeau, 10 August 1790, **PWP** 6:231–32.

33. The highlights of Morris's extensive correspondence with Washington are in **PWP** 5:48–58; **PWP** 7:4–7; **PWP** 9:515–17; **PWP** 10:223–25. On the Franco-American issues Morris described, see Susan Dunn, **Sister Revolutions: French Lightning, American Light** (New York, 1999).

34. PWP 6:58–61, 343–45, 356–58, 359–61, 439–60. The best survey of the affair is Elkins and McKitrick, **Age of Federalism**, 212–23.

35. PWP 2:196–200, 370–74, 325–26, 490–95. Good background accounts include: Reginald Horseman, **Expansion and Indian Policy, 1783–1812** (East Lansing, 1967); Eric Hinderaker, **Elusive Empires: Constructing Colonialism in the Ohio Valley** (Cambridge, 1997); and for the Native American perception of the engulfment, Daniel K. Richter, **Facing East from Indian Country: A Native History of Early America** (Cambridge, 2001).

36. Knox to Washington, 6 July 1789, **PWP** 3:123–

29; Knox to Washington, 17 July 1789, ibid., 134–41; Knox to Washington, 4 January 1790, **PWP** 4:529–36.

37. **PWP** 3:337–38, 551–64; **PWP** 4:468–94; **PWP** 5:140–57; **PWP** 6:102–4, 186–96, 213–14, 237–39.

38. **PWP** 7:145–50, 262–71; **PWP** 9:68–70.

39. **PWP** 4:140–44, 331–32; **PWP** 5:11–15, 76–81; **PWP** 6:362–65, 668–70; **PWP** 8:200–25; **PWP** 9:37–41, 158–68. The Washington quotation is from Washington to Edmund Pendleton, 22 January 1792, **WW** 34:98–101.

40. Washington to Secretary of State, 1 July 1796, **WW** 35:112. See also **PWP** 8:49, 57–58, where Washington reiterates his conviction that culpability for most of the frontier violence rests with the whites.

41. **PWP** 10:349–55, 399–403, 478–84.

42. **PWP** 10:69–73, 588–92, 594–96; **PWP** 11:28–32, 38–40, 91–94, 182–85. See also, **Hamilton** 12:229–58 and **Jefferson** 20:718–53, for editorial notes on the political division from each respective side. The Jefferson quotation is from Thomas Jefferson to Washington, 9 September 1792, **PWP** 11:104.

43. Three accounts of the emergence of political parties inform my interpretation here: Joseph Charles, **The Origins of the American Party System** (Williamsburg, 1950); Richard Hofstadter, **The Idea of the Party System: The Rise of Legitimate Opposition in the United States, 1780–1840** (Berkeley, 1969); Richard Buel, **Securing the Revolution: Ideology in American Politics, 1789–1815** (Ithaca, 1972). The Jefferson quotation is in Thomas Jefferson to Frances Hopkinson, 15 March 1789, **Jefferson** 14:650.

44. See **Jefferson** 17:205–7, for Jefferson's post-mortem on the "dinner bargain" as a disaster for Virginia's interests. For a report on the converging sentiment against Hamilton's program in Virginia, see David Stuart to Washington, 2 June 1790, **PWP** 5:458–64.

45. For Madison's dramatic shift, see his correspondence in **Madison** 13:87–91, 142, 147–48, 151, 184–85, 187. The best secondary account is Elkins and McKitrick, **Age of Federalism,** 133–62.

46. **PWP** 11:182–85, 234–39.

47. Anonymous to Washington, 3 January 1792, **PWP** 9:369–70. See also **PWP** 10:174–75.

48. **PWP** 10:5–10.

49. Thomas Jefferson to Washington, 23 May 1792, **PWP** 10:408–14; Tobias Lear to Washington, 21 July 1792, ibid., 556–59.

50. Elizabeth Willing Powel to Washington, 17 November 1792, **PWP** 11:395–98.

51. Second Inaugural Address, 4 March 1793, **WW** 32:374–75.

52. This is my overly concise synthesis of the situation at the start of Washington's second term based on **PWP** 10 and **PWP** 11. The quotation is from Red Jacket in a speech on 31 March 1792, **PWP** 10:194.

53. Washington to Henry Lee, 21 July 1793, **WW** 33:23–24.

54. **WW** 32:419–20, 430–31, 398–400, 415–16.

55. The best secondary account of Genet's mission is Elkins and McKitrick, **Age of Federalism,** 330–73. See also the editorial note in **WW** 33:114.

56. Washington to Richard Henry Lee, 24 October 1793, **WW** 33:137–38; on the Germantown move, ibid., 107–9, 112–13, 116–18.

57. **PWP** 11:59–62, 75–77, 122–24; **WW** 33:457–61. The most recent scholarly monograph is Thomas P. Slaughter, **The Whiskey Rebellion: Frontier Epilogue to the American Revolution** (New York, 1986). My own interpretation tends to concur with Elkins and McKitrick, **Age of Federalism**, 451–88.

58. Washington to Henry Lee, 26 August 1794, **WW** 33:477; see also ibid., 507–9, 523–24; **WW** 34:3–6.

59. **WW** 34:28–37; Thomas Jefferson to James Madison, 28 December 1794, **Jefferson-Madison** 2:866–68.

60. The two standard accounts are: Samuel Flagg Bemis, **Jay's Treaty: A Study in Commerce and Diplomacy** (New Haven, 1962); Jerald Combs, **The Jay Treaty: Political Background of the Founding Fathers** (Berkeley, 1970).

61. **WW** 33:329, 355, 485; **WW** 34:226–28, 237–40.

62. An elegant summary is available in Elkins and McKitrick, **Age of Federalism**, 406–26.

63. **WW** 34:243–46, 251–56. The Washington quotation is in Washington to Alexander Hamilton, 29 July 1795, ibid., 262–64.

64. Ibid., 244–85, for correspondence on the Randolph affair. Randolph is defended from some of the charges in Irving Brant, "Edmund Randolph. Not Guilty!" **WMQ** 7 (1950): 179–98. Again Elkins and McKitrick, **Age of Federalism**, 424–31, provides the most acute analysis.

65. WW 34:295–97, 397, 477, 505; WW 35:2–5, 13, 36–37.

66. Thomas Jefferson to James Madison, 27 March 1796, **Jefferson-Madison** 2:928. For a fuller account of Jefferson's reaction, see Ellis, **American Sphinx,** 191–94.

67. WW 35:91–92, 101–4, 142–43, 363–65, 421. The Washington quotation is in the last citation.

68. Washington to Thomas Jefferson, 6 July 1796, ibid., 118–22.

69. Washington to Alexander Hamilton, 15 May 1796, ibid., 48–61. My earlier and fuller version of the Farewell Address, its drafting and multiple meanings, is in **Founding Brothers,** 120–61. See also Burton I. Kaufman, **Washington's Farewell Address: The View from the Twentieth Century** (Chicago, 1969), and Matthew Spaulding and Patrick J. Garrity, **A Sacred Union of Citizens: George Washington's Farewell Address and the National Character** (Lantham, MD, 1996).

70. Victor H. Palitsis, ed., **Washington's Farewell Address** (New York, 1935), 172.

71. Alexander Hamilton to Washington, 30 July 1796, Palitsis, ed., **Farewell Address,** 249–50. For Washington's meticulous role at the printer's office, see 288–89.

72. WW 35:234.

73. Ibid., 235–36.

74. Arthur A. Markowitz, "Washington's Farewell Address and the Historians," **Pennsylvania Magazine of History and Biography** 94 (1970), 173–91.

75. WW 35:224.

76. Talk to the Cherokee Nation, 29 August 1796, ibid., 193–98.

77. Ibid., 310–20.

78. Ibid., 357–60, 370–71, 385–86, 388–91, 394. The last citation contains the quotation by John Quincy Adams.

79. John Adams to Abigail Adams, 9 March 1797, quoted in Ellis, **Founding Brothers**, 184; **Diaries** 6:236.

CHAPTER SEVEN

1. Washington to George Washington Parke Custis, 3 April 1797, Washington to James McHenry, 3 April 1797, **PWRT** 1:70–71.

2. Washington to James McHenry, 22 May 1797, ibid., 159–60; Julian Ursyn Niemcewicz, **Under Their Vine and Fig Tree: Travels Through America in 1797–99,** trans. and ed. Metchie Budka (Elizabeth, NJ, 1965), 98–108. This is a telescoped account that draws on several different comments by visitors to re-create a typical day that is, in fact, based on multiple incidents over a much longer stretch of time. See **WW** 35:141–42; **PWRT** 1:281, 404–5; **PWRT** 4:19–20, 402.

3. Washington to Landon Carter, 5 October 1798, **PWRT** 3:79; Washington to William Fitzhugh, 5 August 1798, **PWRT** 2:490.

4. On the livestock at Mount Vernon, see the inventory done in April 1797, **PWRT** 2:102.

5. Thomas Jefferson to James Madison, 8 January 1797, **Jefferson-Madison**, 2:955.

6. **Aurora**, 6 March 1797; William Duane, **A Letter**

to George Washington (Philadelphia, 1796), 13; Washington to Rufus King, 25 June 1797, **PWRT** 1:214–15.

7. Niemcewicz, **Under Their Vine and Fig Tree,** 102; for the marginal comments on Monroe's pamphlet, see **PWRT** 2:169–217; John Langhorne [Peter Carr] to Washington, 25 September 1797, **PWRT** 1:373–75, 475–77, for the intrigue by Jefferson's nephew. See also, Washington to John Nicholas, 8 March 1798, **PWRT** 2:127–29.

8. Washington to Lafayette, 25 December 1798, **PWRT** 3:281–83. See also the correspondence in **PWRT** 1:327–29, 499–502; **PWRT** 2:491, 565–66.

9. Richard H. Kohn, **Eagle and Sword: The Beginnings of the Military Establishment in America** (New York, 1975), 193–255; for the quotations from Abigail Adams on Jefferson, see Ellis, **Founding Brothers,** 189–90.

10. For Washington's support of the Alien and Sedition Acts, see the correspondence in **PWRT** 3:108–10, 216–17, 287. The standard work on the legislation is James Morton Smith, **Freedom's Fetters: The Alien and Sedition Laws and American Civil Liberties** (Ithaca, 1956).

11. Alexander Hamilton to Washington, 19 May 1789; Washington to Alexander Hamilton, 27 May 1798, **PWRT** 2:279–81, 297–300.

12. Timothy Pickering to Washington, 6 July 1798, **PWRT** 2:386–87. See also 392–93, 397–400.

13. Washington to John Adams, 13 July 1798, ibid., 402–04; editorial note on Knox's warning of intrigue, ibid., 409–12; Henry Knox to Washington, 29 July

1798, ibid., 469–72; Henry Knox to Washington, 26 August 1798, ibid., 562–63; Washington to Henry Knox, 9 August 1798, ibid., 502–06.

14. **PWRT** 2:279–81, 297–300, 386–87, 392–93, 397–400, for correspondence between members of Adams's cabinet and Washington that should have alerted him to Hamilton's scheme; see **Hamilton** 22:452–54, on Hamilton's plans for using the Provisional army. The Hamilton quotation is in **Hamilton** 24:155. Two excellent secondary accounts are Kohn, **Eagle and Sword,** 239–55, and Elkins and McKitrick, **Age of Federalism,** 714–16. My interpretation here is more critical of Hamilton than most scholarly accounts of this episode, because the evidence strikes me as conclusive that Hamilton regarded the New army as a weapon to wield against the Republicans. What he might actually have done if the New army materialized must remain an open question. The splendid new biography by Ron Chernow, **Alexander Hamilton** (New York, 2004), 546–79, tells the story in gripping detail.

15. Timothy Pickering to Washington, 13 September 1798, **PWRT** 2:608–10; see also ibid., 573–77, 589–90, **PWRT** 3:14–27, for the clash between Adams and his cabinet over the selection of Hamilton. Washington to John Adams, 25 September 1798, ibid., 42, for the insistence upon Hamilton, and John Adams to Washington, 9 October 1798, ibid., 87–88, for Adams's eventual acquiescence.

16. Washington to James McHenry, 26 September 1798, ibid., 44–45; Washington to James McHenry, 21 October 1798, ibid., 124–25.

17. Ibid., 191–97, for the agenda of the Philadelphia

meeting with Hamilton and Pinckney. The list of candidates for the officers' corps of the New army, including Washington's marginal comments on their qualifications, is on 225–40.

18. James Alpin to Washington, 27 June 1799, **PWRT** 4:63–64.

19. I have told the story of Adams's decision to send the second peace commission in **Passionate Sage: The Character and Legacy of John Adams** (New York, 1993), 29–37. For Washington's response to Adams's decision, see Washington to Alexander Hamilton, 27 October 1799, **PWRT** 4:373.

20. Washington to James McHenry, 17 November 1799, ibid., 409–10.

21. On George Washington Parke Custis, see **PWRT** 1:396, **PWRT** 2:4–6. On requests for money, see **PWRT** 3:111–13.

22. Washington to Alexander Spotswood, 23 November 1794, **WW** 34:47–48. As noted earlier, Henry Wiencek's book on Washington and slavery, **An Imperfect God,** appeared after I had drafted this chapter but in time to influence my revisions. I also benefited from multiple conversations with Philip Morgan, who was preparing an essay for a conference at Mount Vernon in October 2003, " 'To Get Quit of Negroes': George Washington and Slavery." All three of us agree that, rather inexplicably, the subject has not received the scholarly attention it deserves and that it was a chief focus of Washington during his final retirement. Morgan and I tend to disagree with Wiencek about how Washington's mind worked on this tortured subject, concluding that moral considera-

tions were always mixed with economic assessments, and that there were no dramatic epiphanies, but rather a gradual and always contested thought process.

23. Washington to Tobias Lear, 6 May 1794, **WW** 33:358.

24. Advertisement, 1 February 1796, ibid., 433–66; Washington to David Stuart, 7 February 1796, ibid., 452–54.

25. For tentative offers on his various plots of western land, see the correspondence in **PWRT** 1:56–57, 68–69, 483, 493–94, 507–9, 511–14. The quotation is from Washington to Robert Lewis, 17 August 1799, **PWRT** 4:256–58. His list of slaves as of June 1799 is in ibid., 527–42. The staff at Mount Vernon suggest that his concern about cost was probably affected by a Virginia law that made him financially responsible for all emancipated slaves too old or infirm to work.

26. Washington to Frederick Kitt, 10 January 1798, **PWRT** 2:16, for the effort to recover Hercules. For the Ona Judge story, see Washington to Joseph Whipple, 28 November 1796, **WW** 35:297, and Washington to Burwell Bassett, 11 August 1799, **PWRT** 4:237–38. Wiencek devotes an entire chapter to Ona Judge in **Imperfect God,** 312–35.

27. The questionable letter, Martha Washington to Unknown Recipient, 18 September 1799, is in Joseph Fields, ed., **"Worthy Partners": The Papers of Martha Washington** (Westport, 1994), 321. The fullest and most detached appraisal of the letter's authenticity is by Peter R. Henriques, **The Death of George Washington: He Died as He Lived** (Mount Vernon, 2000), 77.

28. Schedule of Property, June 1799, **PWRT** 4:512–27.

29. George Washington's Last Will and Testament, 9 July 1799, ibid., 480. The staff at Mount Vernon notes that Washington made a few calculating errors when making his list of slaves. There were actually 316 slaves, of which 123 were owned by him, 153 by the Custis estate, and 40 rented from his neighbor, Mrs. French.

30. Ibid., 481. In a section of the will that has escaped notice by most scholars, Washington also freed thirty-three slaves that he had acquired in 1795 from his brother-in-law, Bartholomew Dandridge, in payment for back debts. Washington proposed a complex scheme for their gradual emancipation upon the death of the widow, Mary Dandridge.

31. Ibid., 477–511, for the full will.

32. The first scholars to emphasize the distributive implications of Washington's will, and I follow their interpretation here, were Dalzell and Dalzell, **George Washington's Mount Vernon,** 220–22.

33. Washington to Elizabeth Willing Powel, 17 December 1797, **PWRT** 1:519–21; Washington to Burgess Ball, 22 September 1799, **PWRT** 4:318.

34. Ibid., 415–16, for the surveying expedition of the old Fairfax estate at Difficulty Run; Washington to Sarah Cary Fairfax, 16 May 1798, **PWRT** 2:272–73.

35. Washington to Alexander Hamilton, 15 September 1799, **PWRT** 4:297–301; Washington to Jonathan Trumbull Jr., 21 July 1799, ibid., 201–4. A plea from Gouverneur Morris to allow his name to be put forward for the presidency again arrived at Mount Vernon shortly

after Washington's death. See Gouverneur Morris to Washington, 8 December 1799, ibid., 452–54.

36. Washington to Patrick Henry, 15 January 1799, ibid., 317–20.

37. Washington to James Anderson, 13 December 1799, ibid., 455–77, for his final blueprint for reorganizing Mount Vernon.

38. The story of Washington's final illness and hours is based on two versions compiled immediately after the event by Tobias Lear in ibid., 542–55.

39. The fullest secondary account, which provides the modern medical diagnosis of Washington's infection, is Henriques, **The Death of George Washington**. Henriques's account has guided my interpretation in this paragraph and the succeeding paragraphs of the chapter. A more succinct version of Henriques's account is available as "The Final Struggle Between George Washington and the Grim King: Washington's Attitude Towards Death and the Afterlife," **GWR**, 250–71.

40. On Christopher's attempt to escape, see Washington to Roger West, 19 September 1799, **PWRT** 4:310–11.

41. **Eulogies of George Washington** (Boston, 1800), 4.

42. Flexner 2:13.

43. Noemie Emery, **George Washington** (New York, 1976), engages in interpretive speculations in several spots that have helped to prompt my own efforts here at the end. The Emery biography deserves a larger readership than it has apparently received, most especially for its psychological insights.

INDEX

Adams, Abigail, 71, 164, 175, 416, 430

Adams, John, xiv, 71, 108, 129, 260, 262, 335–6, 337, 377, 462, 470; American Revolution, 161, 163, 175, 183; as president, 415–17, 424, 429–31, 436–8, 441–2; Washington presidency, 319, 337, 346–7, 366, 396; Washington's selection as Revolutionary commander, 117, 118–19

Adams, John Quincy, 415

Addison, Joseph, 63, 399

Alien and Sedition Acts, 431–2

American Revolution, 295, 471; American defeat in 1781, danger of, 228–30; American military victory, 190–4, 225–7, 235–9, 251–2; Arnold's treachery, 223; blacks' participation, 144, 236–7, 281; Boston, siege of, 127, 128–30, 138, 143, 145–6, 148–50; Brandywine Creek, Battle of, 177–8; British army's advantages and disadvantages, 155–6; British focus on military solution, 152–5; Bunker Hill, Battle of, 130; Canadian campaign, 146–9, 212;

American Revolution *(continued):* civilian control issue, 142; confederation government and, 226; Continental army, 142–5, 166–8, 170–2, 193–8, 201–2, 204, 208, 221, 250; Delaware crossing and Battle of Trenton, 167–9; dictatorship following victory, Washington's rejection of, 239–50; disciplinary standards for American forces, 201–2; dueling by officers, 198; French involvement, 182, 184, 199–200, 204, 209–10, 212, 225, 227–8, 230–4; Germantown, Battle of, 178–81; Indians' participation, 213–14; inevitability of war, Washington's conclusion regarding, 116–17; military preparations by Americans, 114; militia army, 130–2; Monmouth Court House, Battle at, 206–7; Morristown encampment, 222; mutinies by American forces, 224–5; national government to support American effort, Washington's advocacy of, 218–21, 242–3; New York and Long Island campaign (1776), 159–66; New York campaign (1779–81), 211–13, 214, 227, 230–2; officers, 197–8; Ohio Country fighting, 213–14; peace treaty, 239, 250, 253; Philadelphia campaign, 176–80, 205–8; political leadership failures by Continental Congress, 216–18, 220, 225; political solution, failure to achieve, 152–3; popular perception of Washington during, 132–4; popular support for war, 151, 175; Princeton, Battle of, 170–1; Saratoga, Battle of, 156, 182–3; short war issue, 130–1, 166–7; slavery and, 279–83; smallpox and, 148–9, 173–4; soldiery, 195–7; southern theater, 190, 214–15, 221, 222, 228, 230–4; Valley Forge encampment, 189, 194–204; Washington's correspondence during, 136–7, 263–4; Washington's explanation for American victory, 192–3, 251–2; Washington's "family" of staff and aides, 136–40; Washington's farewell scenes, 252–4; Washington's hold on power, threats to, 182–6, 203; Washington's military strategy, 145–7, 157–9, 163–5, 171, 173–6, 185–9, 210–12; Washington's personal development during, 126–7, 134–6, 188–9; Washington's plans in event of American defeat, 124; Washington's reminiscences about, 264–5; Washington's selection as military commander, 114–15, 117–24; Yorktown, siege of, 226, 230, 232–7

Anderson, James, 422, 464

André, Maj. John, 223
Arnold, Benedict, 146–8, 181, 223–4, 228
Articles of Confederation, 219, 226, 294, 471
Aurora (newspaper), 385, 389, 395–6, 401, 425, 428, 430, 460

Bache, Benjamin Franklin, 385, 401–2, 428, 430, 460
Bassett, Burwell, 121
Bill of Rights, 345
Bishop, Thomas, 75–6
blacks: in American Revolution, 144, 236–7, 281. **see also** slavery
Bloxam, James, 290
Bolingbroke, Viscount, 108
Boone, Daniel, 37
Boston, siege of, 127, 128–9, 138–40, 143, 145–6, 148–50
Boston Tea Party, 106
Boucher, Jonathan, 73
Bouquet, Henry, 53–4, 55–7, 59
Braddock, Gen. Edward, 31–9
Brandywine Creek, Battle of, 177–8

Brant, Joseph, 368
Brookhiser, Richard, xv
Bunker Hill, Battle of, 130
Burgoyne, Gen. John, 176, 181
Burnaby, Andrew, 70

Calvert, Benedict, 73
Camden, Lord, 154
Carr, Peter, 426
Cary, Robert, 82, 84, 85–6, 87–91, 101–2, 105, 110
Catawba Indians, 42
Cato (Addison), 63, 399
Cherokee Indians, 42, 53, 96, 413–14
Clinton, Sir Henry, 205–6, 208, 231, 233
colonial rebellion against British rule, 88–90, 101–12. **see also** American Revolution
Common Sense (Paine), 133
confederation government: American Revolution and, 226; Articles of Confederation, 218–19, 226, 294, 471; crisis of prospective anarchy, 299; military coup against, threat of, 244–50; national capital

issue, 268; reform movement targeting, 293–7 (**see also** Constitutional Convention); veterans, treatment of, 243–4; Washington's lack of confidence in, 242
Constitutional Convention: ambiguous results, 310–14, 329; Great Compromise, 310; initiation of planning for, 298–302; issues to be settled, 306–7, 310–11; ratification process following, 313–17; slavery issue, 350; Washington's decision to participate, 297–8, 300–5; Washington's preparations for, 305–8; Washington's role as president, 308–9; Washington's state of mind on issues, 309–11
Continental army, 142–5, 166–8, 172–3, 193–8, 201–2, 204, 208, 221–2, 250
Continental Congress, 108, 111, 114, 128–9, 135, 142–3, 150–1, 160, 172, 175, 182, 183–4,

191–2, 202, 204, 212, 224–5, 240–1, 263; failure of political leadership, 216–18, 220, 225; Washington's selection as Revolutionary military commander, 117–23

Conway, Thomas, 184–5, 198

Cornplanter, Chief, 368

Cornwallis, Gen. Charles, Lord, 170, 190–1, 228, 230–1, 232, 233, 235–6

Country Party, 107–8

Craik, James, 465

Crawford, Valentine, 80

Crawford, William, 97

Creek Indians, 370

Cunliffe, Marcus, xviii

Custis, Eleanor Calvert, 73

Custis, George Washington Parke, 443–4

Custis, Jackie, 71–3, 88, 234, 237

Custis, Patsy, 71, 74, 88

Custis estate, 82–3

Davies, Samuel, 39

Declaration of Independence, 133, 158, 160, 279, 345, 457

Delaware Indians, 41

Democratic Societies, 388, 390

Diderot, Denis, 471

Dinwiddie, Robert, 3, 19, 21, 24, 29, 37–8, 41, 43, 47–8, 96

Dismal Swamp project, 93

Du Condray, Philippe, 184

Dunmore, Lord, 113

Duquesne, Gen., 28–9

economic policy, 353–5, 373

election of 1789, 318–20

election of 1792, 374, 382–4

Ellsworth, Oliver, 349

Emerson, Ralph Waldo, xvii

Fabius Cunctator, 174

Fairfax, Bryan, 106

Fairfax, George William, 16, 61, 72, 106, 117

Fairfax, Sally, 61–3, 67, 72, 106, 461–2, 475

Fairfax, Lord Thomas, 15

Fairfax, William, 15–16, 19, 29, 50

Fairfax Independent Company, 114

Fairfax Resolves, 108

Farewell Address, 404–15

Fauchet, Joseph, 397
Fauntleroy, Betsy, 18
Fauquier, Francis, 56, 57
federal government, attitudes toward establishment and role of, 218–21, 242–3, 261, 293–51, 411–12, 414–15
Federalist Papers, The, 314, 344, 358
Federalist Party, **see** partisan politics
Fitzgerald, Col. Edward, 171
Flexner, James Thomas, xvii–xviii
Forbes, Gen. John, 52–9
foreign policy, 363–8, 388–9, 392–400, 408–11
Fort Necessity, Battle of, 24–8, 29
France: American Revolution, 182, 184, 199–201, 204, 209–11, 212–13, 225, 227–8, 230–4; Anglo-French war of 1790s, 386–8, 393–4; commercial war on American shipping, 401, 414; invasion of United States, American

concerns about, 430, 431–5, 441–2; Washington's presidential policy toward, 363–4, 365, 386–8; XYZ Affair, 430. **see also** French and Indian War; French Revolution
Franklin, Benjamin, xix, 9, 143, 227, 262, 274, 350, 470; death of, 337–8
Freeman, Douglas Southall, xvii
French and Indian War, 20–23, 40, 96, 296; Braddock campaign, 31–9; British strategy in American Revolution, impact on, 153–4, 156; central achievement of, 91; Forbes campaign, 52–9; Fort Necessity, Battle of, 24–8, 29; Jumonville Glen massacre, 21–4, 28–9; Monongahela massacre, 35–9; responsibility for onset of, 28; Washington's mission to Presque Isle, 3–10; Washington's reminiscences about, 266; Washington's status as hero among

Americans, 29, 38–9; Washington's vilification by French, 28–9

French Revolution, 363, 365, 385, 390, 409, 421, 426, 471

Freneau, Philip, 378, 385, 473

Fry, Joshua, 24

Gage, Thomas, 36–7, 52, 116, 133

Gates, Horatio, 138, 139, 141, 181–2, 185, 222, 245, 249, 264

Genet, Edmond, 387–9

George II, King, 23

George III, King, 95, 129, 133, 152, 241, 320

Germain, Lord George, 152

Germantown, Battle of, 178–80

Gist, Christopher, 5

Gordon, Thomas, 108

Gordon, William, 264, 288

Grasse, Count de, 231, 232, 236

Great Britain: Anglo-French war of 1790s, 386–7, 393; Jay Treaty, 394–400, 409; post-war threats to America, 271, 365–71. **see also** Ameri-can Revolution; French and Indian War

Greene, Nathanael, 138, 139–40, 164, 166, 175, 177, 186, 187–8, 190, 223, 228, 229, 238, 256–60, 264

Hamilton, Alexander, xix, 137, 182–3, 223, 240, 243–4, 293, 310, 314, 316–17, 336, 360, 366, 391, 393, 462; economic policy, 353–8, 373; Jefferson's conflict with, 375–6, 379, 385; New army initiative, 433–42, 462, 312**n**14; personal qualities, 345–6; secretary of treasury, appointment as, 346; Washington's Farewell Address, 404–6, 410

Hancock, John, 142, 144, 150, 161–2, 164, 166, 168, 172, 173

Harrison, Benjamin, 216

Henry, Patrick, 111, 114, 315, 329–30, 463

Hercules (slave), 352–3, 450–1

Hillsborough, Earl, 100–1, 110

Hopkinson, Francis, 256

Houdon, Jean-Antoine, 267, 366

House of Burgesses, 20, 29, 102; Washington's service in, 60–1, 77, 104–5

Howe, Adm. Richard, 159

Howe, Gen. William, 131, 146, 159, 162, 163–4, 166, 167, 171, 176, 177, 180, 182, 205

Humphreys, David, 265–6, 277–8, 318

Indians, 13, 16; American Revolution and, 213–14; conflicts with settlers, 40–2, 44–5, 99–100; Washington's French and Indian War encounters with, 3–4, 5, 7–8, 20, 23, 24–6, 27, 34, 35–7, 53–4; Washington's presidential policy toward, 367–72, 373, 385, 412–14

Intolerable Acts of 1774, 106

Iroquois Confederation (Six Nations), 7–8, 96, 213–14, 371, 385

isolationism, 408–9

Jackson, Andrew, 369

Jay, John, 297, 314, 347, 366, 394–6; Constitutional Convention, 304, 307; Jay Treaty, 394, 395, 400–1

Jay Treaty, 394–400, 409

Jefferson, Thomas, xiii, xix, 64, 78, 93, 108, 123, 133, 158, 160, 243, 260, 262, 267, 279, 299, 307, 340, 343, 357, 366–7, 386, 415, 424, 457, 459, 462–3, 470, 471; break with Washington, 377, 378–83, 402–4, 426–7, 476; debt problem, 81, 85–6; foreign policy views, 363–5, 409; Hamilton's conflict with, 375–6, 379–80, 385; Jay Treaty, 395, 398–9; national capital issue, 359–61; partisan politics, 374–6, 428–9; presidency of, 363–4; secretary of state, appointment as, 345; Society of the Cincinnati, 277; on Washington's physical decline, 332, 381–3; Washington's re-election decision in 1792, 383; whiskey tax rebellion, 392

Journal of Major George Washington, The, 4

Judge, Ona, 450, 451

Judiciary Act of 1789, 348–9

Jumonville Glen massacre, 21–4, 28–9

Kalb, Baron de, 197

Kennan, George, 410

Kissinger, Henry, 410

Knox, Henry, 177, 245, 264, 311, 317; American Revolution, 138, 139–40, 169, 179, 186; Constitutional Convention, 302–3; New army initiative, 434, 436; Washington presidency, 346, 366–7, 369, 370, 372

Lafayette, Marquis de, 252, 259, 267, 296, 311, 318, 323–4, 363, 385, 420–1, 427; American Revolution, 199–201, 206, 229, 232, 233; slavery issue, 282–3, 288; Washington's relationship with, 200

Laurens, Henry, 192

Laurens, John, 137, 198, 225, 259, 264, 281–2

Lear, Tobias, 265–6, 352–3, 383, 445, 465, 466, 467

Lee, Billy, 76, 79, 136, 206, 324–5, 456

Lee, Charles, 138–9, 141, 158, 205–6, 207, 260, 264, 473

Lee, Henry, 468

Lee, Richard Henry, 111, 175–6

Le Gardner, Jacques, 7

L'Enfant, Pierre, 361

Leutze, Emanuel, 168–9

Lincoln, Abraham, xiii, 195, 327

Lincoln, Benjamin, 299

Livingston, Robert, 398

Loudoun, John Campbell, Earl of, 49–51

Madison, James, xix, 260, 295, 314, 318, 392, 470; break with Washington, 377–82; conspiratorial indictment of Federalists, 428–9; Constitutional Convention, 304–5, 306–7;

Madison, James *(continued):*
economic policy, 355,
357, 358; Jay Treaty,
394, 398; national cap-
ital issue, 359–60, 362;
slavery policy, 351–2;
Washington presidency
and, 345, 374; Wash-
ington's Farewell
Address and, 405
Marshall, John, 11, 199,
349
Martin, Sgt. Joseph Plumb,
234–5
Mason, George, 102, 105,
108, 115, 243, 305,
315; influence on Wash-
ington, 108, 110
McDaniel, Mary, 18
McGillivray, Alexander,
370–1, 384–5
McHenry, James, 320, 433,
437–8, 442
McKay, Capt. James, 25
McKean, Thomas, 180
McKenzie, Robert,
111–12
mercantile system, 82–7,
109
Mercer, John Francis, 284
Miami Indians, 371
Mifflin, Thomas, 203, 253
Mifflin, Warner, 350

Military Treatise on the
Appointments of the
Army, A (Webb), 112
Mississippi Land Com-
pany, 94–5
Monmouth Court House,
Battle at, 206–7
Monongahela massacre, 35
Monroe, James, 169, 426,
473
Montgomery, Gen.
Richard, 148
Morgan, Daniel, 181, 228
Morgenthau, Hans, 410
Morris, Gouverneur, 320,
365, 472, 473–4, 475–6
Morris, Robert, 226, 232,
245, 262–3, 269, 283,
346
Morristown encampment,
222
Mount Vernon, xi; agricultural operations, 69–70,
77, 90–2, 285–7,
422–3; British threat to,
127–9; mansion renova-
tions, 59, 68, 69, 91,
114, 418; Washington's
concerns during his
presidency, 323–3;
Washington's inheri-
tance of, 15; Washing-
ton's will and, 458

National Bank, 355, 357, 377

national capital issue (residence question), 269, 358–63

National Gazette, 378, 387, 389

Native Americans, see Indians

New army initiative, 429–42, 462–6, 549n14

Newburgh Conspiracy, 245–50

New York and Long Island campaign (1776), 158–60

New York campaign (1779–81), 211–13, 214, 227–9, 230–1

Nicola, Lewis, 240

North, Lord, 152–4

Ohio Company, 17, 20

Oneida Indians, 214

Orme, Robert, 32

Paine, Thomas, 133, 238, 425

partisan politics: New army initiative, 429–42, 462–6, 549n14; Washington presidency and, 375–83, 388, 394–400, 404; Washington's post-presidency denunciations of, 425–8, 463

Patterson, Lt. Col. James, 162

Peale, Charles Willson, 76, 321, 498n9

Philadelphia campaign, 176–80, 205–7

Pickering, Timothy, 433, 436

Pinckney, Charles Cotesworth, 440

Pine, Robert Edge, 267

Pitcher, Molly (Mary Ludwig Hayes), 207

Pleasants, Robert, 279–80

Posey, John, 91

Potomac River project, 93, 113, 268–70, 471, 529n17

Powel, Elizabeth Willing, 383, 460

Princeton, Battle of, 170–1

Proclamation of 1763, 96, 98, 100, 370

Proclamation of 1790, 370

Randolph, Edmund, 301, 347, 352, 357, 397

Reed, Joseph, 135, 137

religious freedom, 339

Report on the Public Credit (Hamilton), 354

Republican Party, see partisan politics

Revolutionary War, see American Revolution

Rittenhouse, David, 249

Robinson, John, 48, 56

Rochambeau, Count, 227, 228, 231–3, 236, 365

Roosevelt, Franklin, 327, 409

Rules of Civility and Decent Behaviour in **Company and Conversation, The**, 14

Rush, Benjamin, 118, 183

St. Clair, Arthur, 371

Sandwich, Earl of, 154

Saratoga, Battle of, 156, 181–2

Sharpe, Horatio, 28

Shawnee Indians, 41, 371

Shays's Rebellion, 300

Sheels, Christopher, 467

Shirley, William, 44

slavery: American Revolution and, 280–4; Constitutional Convention and, 349; emancipation initiatives, 279, 282–4, 349–51; as metaphor for colonists' fears regarding British domination, 107; moratorium on slavery issue at federal level, 351; national capital's construction with slave labor, 362; Washington presidency and, 349–52, 412; Washington's acquisition of slaves, 70, 79, 533n38; Washington's dilemma regarding slaves of Mount Vernon, 285–91, 423, 444–6; Washington's efforts to recover escaped slaves, 77–8, 452; Washington's endorsement of slavery's eventual end, 278–88; Washington's freeing of his own slaves, 287–90, 446–58, 469, 550n22, 552nn29, 30; Washington's long-term pattern in thinking about, 447–52; Washington's treatment of slaves, 77–9

smallpox, 15, 148–9, 173

Society of the Cincinnati, 274–9, 300

Spain, 271, 364, 366

Stamp Act of 1765, 88, 101

Steuben, Baron von, 201–2

Stirling, Lord, 197
Strachey, Lytton, xvii
Stuart, David, 446
Stuart, Gilbert, 472
Sullivan, John, 213
Supreme Court, 348–9

Tanacharison (Half-King),
    3, 7–8, 21, 22, 25
Thomson, Charles, 319
Thucydides, 410
Tilghman, Tench, 259
tobacco crop, 87
Townshend Act, 102, 105
treaty-making, 338
Treaty of New York, 370
Trenchard, John, 108
Trenton, Battle of, 167–70
Trumbull, John, 420

Valley Forge encampment,
    189, 193–202, 204
Varick, Richard, 263–4
Villiers, Joseph Coulon de,
    22–3, 26
Villiers, Louis Coulon de,
    25
Virginia Association, 105
Virginia Convention, 111,
    114
Virginia Regiment, 24, 30;
    Washington's command
    of, 39–54, 57, 61, 65, 67

Walpole, Robert, 107–8
War of Independence, **see**
    American Revolution
Washington, Augustine
    (father), 11–13
Washington, Bushrod
    (nephew), 458
Washington, Charles
    (brother), 458, 460
Washington, George:
    aging's effect on,
    259–60, 331–2, 422;
    ambition of, 64, 122–3;
    anti-British attitudes,
    89, 91, 96, 98, 100,
    101–12, 218–19; aris-
    tocracy, deference to,
    15, 49–50, 65; aristo-
    cratic lifestyle, 68,
    75–6, 85; as authority
    figure for Americans,
    132–4; Barbados visit,
    14; as beleaguered patri-
    arch in later years,
    443–4; Circular Letter
    to the States (June
    1783), 251–2; circum-
    spection of, 134–7;
    civilian authority,
    respect for, 47, 142–3;
    clothing problems,
    76; criticism, sensitivity
    to, 49, 98, 330, 386;

Washington, George *(continued):* Custis plantations, management of, 83; death, attitude toward, 421; death of, 465–7; dictatorial power, refusal of, 238–49; early years, 10–18; economic concerns, 68, 79–81, 82–91, 104–5, 287, 290, 445–7, 455, 532n35; education, 13; eulogies for, 468–77; Farewell Address, 404–5; federal government, support for, 218–22, 243, 261, 294–6, 411–12, 414–15; final months, 460–4; health problems, 15, 35, 331–2, 385–6; "His Excellency" designation, 132; House of Burgesses service, 60, 77, 104; humor of, 257; initial impression made by, 117–19; **The Journal of Major George Washington,** 4–8; judgment, powers of, 470–2; land, avaricious attitude toward, 271–2; military career, beginning of, 19; military leadership, schooling in, 39, 40; as mysterious abstraction, xii; mythology of, 119, 476; new army initiative, 429–42, 462–4; Newburgh Address, 246–51; partisan politics, post-presidency denunciations of, 425–8, 463; passionate nature, 17, 61–2, 472–6; Patriarchal Problem regarding, xiv–xvi; physical appearance, 18–19, 75–6, 118–19, 423, 468; political machinations, 46, 49, 56–7; political power, elemental convictions about, 475; portraits of, 76, 267, 498n9; posterity project, 262–8, 278, 280, 445, 458–9, 475–6; postured reticence, pattern of, 121–2; religious beliefs, 77, 262, 466; republicanism, views on, 248; retirement's daily routine, 418–23; rules of behavior, 13; security, sharp-edged sense of, 81;

self-control, 64–7,
471–6; smallpox infec-
tion, 15; social standing,
concern about, 30, 274,
278; as stepfather, 72;
sterile condition, 71;
surveying work, 16–17;
transcendent status, 258;
Virginia Regiment,
39–54, 57, 61, 65, 67;
virtue, understanding of,
194, 209, 216; wealth
of, 455; western expan-
sion, support for,
267–71; western land
ventures, 66, 91–100,
112–13, 271, 273,
445–7, 454; will of,
452–60, 552n30. **see
also** American Revolu-
tion; Constitutional
Convention; French and
Indian War; Indians;
Mount Vernon; slavery;
Washington presidency;
specific persons
Washington, George Augus-
tine (nephew), 309, 385
Washington, John (great-
grandfather), 8, 13
Washington, Lawrence
(half brother), 14–15,
17, 19

Washington, Lund, 75,
127, 163, 165, 285
**Washington: Man and
Monument** (Cunliffe),
xviii
Washington, Martha Dan-
dridge Custis (wife),
136, 160, 324, 332,
352, 420, 422, 161;
marriage to Washing-
ton, 60–1, 67, 68; as
mother, 73; Washing-
ton's death, 465, 467;
Washington's plan for
freeing slaves and,
451–2; Washington's
relationship with, 71
Washington, Mary Ball
(mother), 13
Washington birthday holi-
day, 338
Washington Papers,
xiii–xiv
Washington presidency:
cabinet appointees,
343–8; challenges upon
taking office, 327–30;
core achievement of,
328; delegation of
authority, 348–58;
economic policy,
253–8, 374; election
of 1789, 318–19;

Washington presidency
(*continued*): election of
1792, 374, 382; eti-
quette and symbolism
concerns, 335–8;
Farewell Address,
404–14; foreign policy,
362–7, 386–9, 393–8,
408–10; inauguration
of 1789, 351–5,
538nn70, 72; Indian
policy, 367–71, 373,
385, 412–13; Jay
Treaty, 392–401, 409;
judiciary policy, 348;
monarchy issue, 320,
329–30, 341–2, 380,
388, 397, 405; national
capital issue, 358–62;
neutrality regarding
European wars, 386–8;
partisan politics and,
374–82, 388, 399–400,
404; patronage system,
334–5; political
agenda, 323; press
attacks on Washington,
331, 340, 378, 388–9,
394, 401–4; religious
freedom policy, 339;
slavery issue, 349–53,
412; tours of the states,
339–40; treaty making,
approach to, 338–9;
Washington's final acts,
415–16; Washington's
health problems and,
331–2; Washington's
private personality and,
333–4; Washington's
reticence about accept-
ing presidency, 313,
316–18, 324–6, 333;
western expansion pol-
icy, 363–4; whiskey tax
rebellion, 389–93
Webb, Thomas, 112
Weems, Parson, xv, 11, 476
western expansion,
267–71, 364–5
Wheatley, Phillis, 133
Whig ideology, 107–9, 110
whiskey tax rebellion,
389–91
Wilson, Woodrow, 408
Wyandot Indians, 371

XYZ Affair, 430

Yazoo Companies, 371
Yorktown, siege of, 226,
230, 232–6

Washington portrait by Charles Willson Peale, 1772: Courtesy of Washington and Lee University

Washington portrait by Charles Willson Peale, 1787: The Pennsylvania Academy of the Fine Arts. Bequest of Mrs. Joseph Harrison, Jr.

Washington presidential portrait by Rembrandt Peale, 1795: Art Resource

Washington presidential portrait by Gilbert Stuart, 1796: Art Resource

Washington bust by Jean Antoine Houdon: Courtesy of the Mount Vernon Ladies' Association

Sears, Roebuck catalog cover by Norman Rockwell, 1932: Courtesy of the Rockwell family

Washington Crossing the Delaware by Emanuel Leutz, 1851: Metropolitan Museum of Art

Attack on Chew House by Howard Pyle, 1898: Delaware Art Museum

Photograph of case and decanters: Courtesy of the Mount Vernon Ladies' Association

Engraving of Mount Vernon, 1804: Courtesy of the Mount Vernon Ladies' Assocation

Plans for the city of Washington, 1792: Virginia Historical Society

Census of slaves at Mount Vernon, 1799: Courtesy of the Mount Vernon Ladies' Association